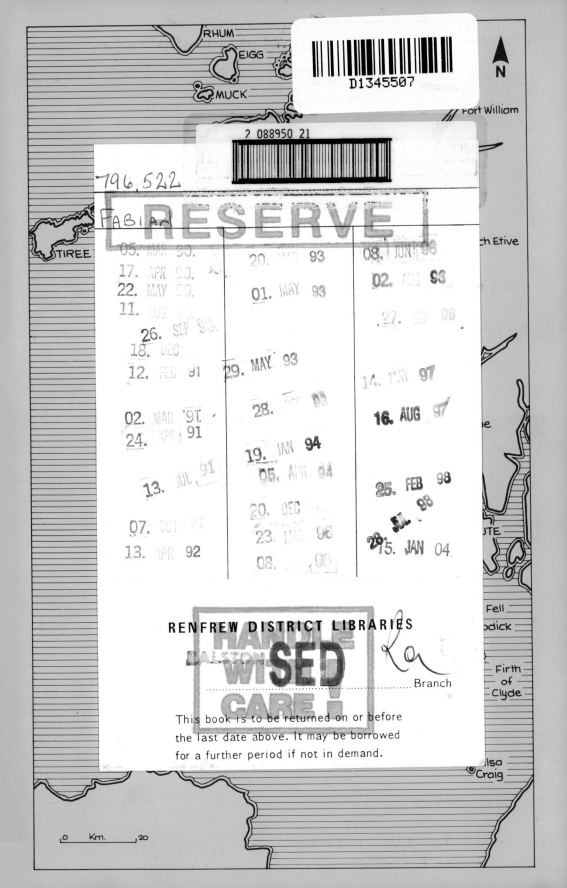

Scottish Mountaineering Club
District Guidebooks

THE ISLANDS OF SCOTLAND
INCLUDING SKYE

Series Editor: D J Bennet

Published by
The Scottish Mountaineering Trust

THE
ISLANDS OF SCOTLAND
INCLUDING
SKYE

Derek J Fabian
Graham E Little
D Noel Williams

Scottish Mountaineering Club District Guidebook

IV

PUBLISHED BY THE SCOTTISH MOUNTAINEERING TRUST: 1989
© THE SCOTTISH MOUNTAINEERING TRUST

British Library Cataloguing in Publication Data
Fabian, Derek J. (Derek John)
  The islands of Scotland including Skye.
  1. Scotland. Islands. Visitors guides
  I. Title II. Little, Graham E. III. Williams, D.
  Noel
  914.11'04858

ISBN 0-907521-23-1

ILLUSTRATIONS:
Front cover. The Cuillin and Bla Bheinn from Sleat. A. Gillespie
Frontispiece. The Cuillin of Skye from Askival. K.Rezin
Back cover. Sunset beyond An Sgurr of Eigg. D.J. Fabian

Book designed by Donald Bennet
Maps drawn by Jim Renny
Production by Peter Hodgkiss
Typeset by Bureau-Graphics, Glasgow
Graphic Origination by Par Graphics, Kirkcaldy
Printed by CWS Printers Ltd, Glasgow
Bound by Hunter & Foulis, Edinburgh

CONTENTS

ILLUSTRATIONS

PREFACE

This is the first District Guidebook in the new series being produced by the Scottish Mountaineering Club at the beginning of its second century. Yet in many ways it maintains the style, content and traditions of the guides which, beginning with articles in the Scottish Mountaineering Club Journal over eighty years ago, have been published continuously since then.

Thus this guidebook owes much to those that have preceded it, and the work of earlier guidebook authors is gladly acknowledged by the authors of this book. William Naismith, E.W. Steeple, Guy Barlow, Harry MacRobert, E.W. Hodge, Norman Tennant and Malcolm Slesser are among those earlier authors whose fund of knowledge of the islands of Scotland has been built upon in the writing of this book.

The authors and editors wish to thank those who have helped in the production of this book. In particular the painstaking work of Jim Renny in drawing a new set of maps is recognised, and those who made their photographs available for selection are thanked. Finally, the patient efforts of Sandra Steele in typing much of the manuscript through many revisions are gratefully acknowledged.

THE CLIMBER AND
THE MOUNTAIN ENVIRONMENT

With increasing numbers of walkers and climbers going to the Scottish hills, it is important that all of us who do so should recognise our responsibilities to those who live and work among the hills and glens, to our fellow climbers and to the mountain environment in which we find our pleasure and recreation.

The Scottish Mountaineering Club and Trust, who jointly produce this and other guidebooks, wish to impress an all who avail themselves of the information in these books that it is essential at all times to consider the sporting and proprietary rights of landowners and farmers. The description of a climbing, walking or skiing route in any of these books does not imply that a right of way exists, and it is the responsibility of all climbers to ascertain the position before setting out. In cases of doubt it is always best to enquire locally.

During the stalking and shooting seasons in particular, much harm can be done in deer forests and on grouse moors by people walking through them. Normally, the deer stalking season is from 1st July to 20th October, when stag shooting ends. Hinds may be culled from then until 15th February. The grouse shooting season is from 12th August until 10th December. These are not merely sporting activities, but essential for the economy of the Highland estates. During these seasons, therefore, especial care should be taken to consult the local landowner, factor or keeper before taking to the hills.

Climbers and hillwalkers are recommended to consult the book *Heading for the Scottish Hills*, published by the Mountaineering Council of Scotland and the Scottish Landowners Federation, which gives the names and addresses of factors and keepers who may be contacted for information regarding access to the hills.

It is also important to avoid disturbance to sheep, particularly during the lambing season between March and May. Dogs should not be taken onto the hills at this season, and at all other times should be kept under close control.

Always try to follow a path or track through cultivated land and forests, and avoid causing damage to fences, dykes and gates by climbing over them carelessly. Do not leave litter anywhere except in your rucksack.

The increasing number of walkers and climbers on the hills is leading to increased, and in some cases very serious and unsightly erosion of footpaths and hillsides. Some of the profits from the sale of this and other SMC guidebooks are used by the Trust to financially assist work being carried out to repair and maintain hill paths in Scotland. However, it is important for all of us to recognise our responsibility to minimise the erosive effect of our passage over the hills so that the enjoyment of future climbers shall not be spoiled by landscape damage caused by ourselves.

As a general rule, where a path exists walkers should follow it and even where it is wet and muddy avoid walking along its edges, thereby extending erosion sideways. Do not take short-cuts at the corners of zig-zag paths. Remember that the worst effects of erosion are likely to be caused during or soon after prolonged wet weather when the ground is soft and waterlogged. A route on a stony or rocky hillside is likely to cause less erosion than on a grassy one at such times.

Finally, the Scottish Mountaineering Trust can accept no liability for damage to property nor for personal injury resulting from use of any route described in its publications.

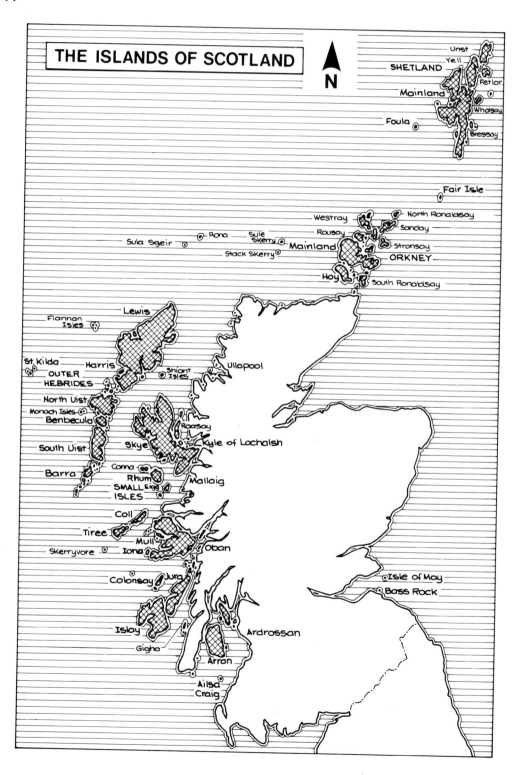

THE ISLANDS OF SCOTLAND

N

INTRODUCTION

The islands of Scotland possess some of the finest mountain and seascape scenery in Europe. They are renowned for their beauty and unique charm. The complexities of their geography, geology and climate, and their natural and social history, all combine to create a distinctive character rarely found on the mainland. The close proximity of mountain and sea largely accounts for this, producing a powerful landscape and a sturdy yet gentle people.

Although this guide is primarily concerned with hillwalking and climbing, all the major islands are included, even those with few significant hills. Apart from Skye and Mull, the islands possess no Munros. However, for the true hillwalker height is of little consequence, quality and situation being the main concerns. We also stray from the hills frequently to describe additional features of interest, including the unrivalled variety of historical relics found on the islands.

Thus the hills are presented in their full island context and likewise this introduction includes not only a general section that covers maps, access, transport, accommodation, weather and rescue information of relevance to the hills, but also dedicated sections on the geology of the islands and their natural and social history.

The islands vary greatly in size, shape and height, yet have in common an essential atmosphere which is easy to appreciate but hard to define. Islands have always held a special fascination for visitors, and this is as true of Scotland as anywhere. However, while the 'bagging' of islands can be as addictive in Scotland as climbing Munros, there are two important differences. Firstly, there is no definitive list of islands, and secondly, we ask the question: What constitutes an island? The dictionary definition is a piece of land surrounded by water. Thus any land mass, no matter how small, could be called an island. A census report in 1861 expanded the definition to "any piece of solid land surrounded by water which affords sufficient vegetation to support one or two sheep, or is inhabited by man". At the other extreme, when the land reaches a certain size it is apparently a country or continent. For example, Tasmania is an island whereas Australia is a continent; while the two islands of New Zealand form a country. Then, in Scotland we have also 'isles' and 'islets', as well as stacks.

The ideal size for an island is also a subject of debate. Undoubtedly one's mode of transport has an important bearing on this. In 1985 Barra was nominated for a European Island award. It was deemed to fulfil the desirable requirements. However, Colonsay could as easily have been selected for its size and character; small enough to be explored on foot and yet large enough never to become totally familiar. Moreover, no island should be 'written off' by the mountaineer. The attractions of Skye and its Cuillin are obvious, but many small and low islands can be as fascinating and rewarding in their own way. The coastal traverse of a remote island is often as demanding as the ascent of a mountain, with the same sense of exploration.

Islands generally possess individual character but usually also several similarities. The more isolated groups tend to uniqueness and vulnerability. Darwin, writing about the Galapagos, noted: "One of the most interesting and engaging characteristics of island species is a lack of sophistication in dealing with the human race, which even the teaching of experience does not quickly alter"...."It is a curious pleasure to have the birds of the wilderness settle upon one's shoulder [fly-catchers that tried to remove hair from the men's heads for nesting material]. The pleasure would be much less rare were man less destructive." We should always remember our obligations as visitors and accept the island culture as we find it.

The trappings of the mainland have now found their way to many inhabited islands, but mostly the pace of life there still follows a time-honoured tradition. As the story goes, a Spanish visitor to the Hebrides was explaining the meaning of the word 'manana' to a crofter. After deliberating a while the crofter commented that no word in Gaelic expressed such urgency.

One of the delights of the islands is the range of outdoor pursuits they offer in addition to hill-walking and climbing: sailing, windsurfing, canoeing, diving, swimming, fishing, bird watching and simply beachcombing. Invariably there is a heightened sense of adventure associated with any of these activities in an island setting. The feeling of remoteness coupled with the environment of sea, sand, cliff, sky and windswept hill, creates a special atmosphere unique to the islands; an atmosphere enhanced in Scotland by the warmth and friendliness of the people.

GENERAL (DJF and GEL)

The majority of Scotland's islands lie in a broad sweep along the west coast, from Ailsa Craig in the Firth of Clyde through the Inner Hebrides to Skye. Further west, across The Minch, is the Long Isle or Outer Hebrides and beyond is the lonely stormlashed St Kilda group. To the north-east of Scotland lie the autonomous and yet complex archipelagos of Orkney and Shetland. Off the east coast there are extraordinarily few islands, although the Bass Rock, in the Firth of Forth, makes an appropriate counterpart to Ailsa Craig in the west. This spread of innumerable islands covers five and a half degrees of latitude, from south of Scotland's border with England to further north than the southern tip of Greenland.

Almost all of the islands have Highland character. Indeed, all but the southeast of Arran and the Cumbraes lie north-west of the Highland Boundary Fault, taken as the geographical demarcation line for the Highlands of Scotland. Some islands, like Colonsay whose highest summit is only 141m, have miniature mountain landscapes that are undeniably Highland in character; while even Benbecula, the lowest sizeable island of the Long Isle and rising nowhere above 123m, is distinctly Highland in its natural and social history.

Maps

By far the best maps for use by climbers or hillwalkers with this guide are the Ordnance Survey 1:50,000 scale, Second Series or Landranger Series. All place and hill names and spellings given in the guide are taken from current 1:50,000 Ordnance Survey maps. Occasionally the splitting of an island or island group among Ordnance Survey sheets is unfortunate, if not to say frustrating. Three sheets are needed to cover Mull, for example, and four for Harris and Lewis.

Readers using the older One Inch to the Mile maps of the islands will find these to be frequently out of date. For example, in the Harris hills the current editions of Ordnance Survey maps adopt the Gaelic *Sron* in place of *Strone*, which was invariably used on the One Inch maps, and current Landranger series maps of Arran use the spelling *Dougarie* as the place name for *Dougrie* given on the older maps. Hill heights also are out of date on older maps (see below).

Recommended map sheets for use with the guide are given separately for each island or island group. Wherever available the Landranger series is to be preferred to First Series 1:50,000 maps, being of current issue with metric contouring every 10 metres as opposed to reprinting metric conversions of previous imperial contours. Ordnance Survey 1:25,000, or Pathfinder Series maps are becoming increasingly popular and are recommended for smaller islands or compact mountain groups.

Where appropriate, the sheet number is also given for the Bartholomew 1:100,000 map covering an island. The contour layer tinting on these maps usually provides a good overall topographical picture of mountain regions, but the scale is too small for extensive hillwalking in some of the complex terrain found on the islands. Significant differences in spelling occur between Ordnance Survey and Bartholomew maps, as well as variations in the use of Gaelic and English names. Without exception we adhere to Ordnance Survey usage. However, occasional differences in spelling occur even between early and later editions of Ordnance Survey Landranger Series maps (see for example Quoyness on Hoy in Orkney).

Island names, as with all names, have evolved over the centuries, although it is surprising just how many are clearly recognisable in their earliest cartographic form. Early maps and charts, being very much concerned with maritime navigation, also depicted the Scottish islands with relative accuracy; though a few island names have changed dramatically, even in the past century or two. In Mackenzie's *Atlas of 1776* Iona appeared as Icolmkil, and the Garvellachs as the Mare Isles. On the other hand both Mull and Jura appeared in their current form.

Hill Heights

Each island or island group is prefaced with a list of its principal hills, giving also the summit height and grid reference. To some degree these lists follow precedents set by previous editions of the guide, although obvious inconsistencies have been rationalised.

In general we have attempted to identify hills that make a significant impression upon the topography of an island. Each island has been viewed subjectively and no common height criterion is used. This has resulted, for example, in the omission of some 500m-plus hills on Mull, whereas hills of less than 200m are listed for Colonsay. However, we see each island as an entity in itself, with its own baseline determining the relative significance of its peaks. Some lesser hills are not given in the introductory list but nonetheless are referred to in the text.

The order of hills listed for a particular island or island group is dictated by topographic convenience. All heights given are in metres (for a useful and nearly precise conversion to feet, divide by three and then multiply by ten). By convention, *metres* is shortened to *m* when referring to height (eg a peak may be 200m above a given bealach) while for lineal distance *metres* is written in full (eg follow a path for 200 metres).

Whereas in previous editions of the SMC District Guides heights have been taken from One Inch to the Mile or 1:50,000 Ordnance Survey maps, heights in this new guide are from current 1:10,000 Ordnance Survey mapping (these values also occur at 1:25,000 scale). The rationale for this is that 1:10,000 scale mapping is a re-survey, based upon aerial photography, with new metric contouring and heighting and its values can therefore be regarded as definitive. Regrettably the Ordnance Survey has not completely incorporated these more accurate heights into its Second Series 1:50,000 maps, inexplicably perpetuating conversions of imperial values from the old One Inch maps (even though metric contouring has been included).

Where no height is depicted on 1:10,000 mapping we have interpolated from contours, taking into account previous published heights and the ground situation. If this has been done, the relevant height is indicated with an asterisk.

A few significant differences will be noted between the 1:50,000 and 1:10,000 values; eg Corra Bheinn (Jura) has gained six metres and Mullach Buidhe (Arran) ten, but perhaps most startling, Suidhe Fhearghas (Arran) is higher by 26 metres! However, it is probably now safe to claim that the accepted heights of the island hills are embarking upon a period of stability.

Access and Transport

Access to the islands varies with their remoteness and their size. It ranges from frequent regular ferries, serving near and popular islands, to private charter (or one's own boat) which is needed for visits to some of the distant outliers. Transport upon individual islands also varies greatly, from regular though infrequent bus services to none at all. There are no train services on any of the islands but several have air services.

In this guide an attempt has been made to give sufficient information on access and transport to help the reader plan a hillwalking or climbing visit to any of the islands. Inevitably the services and timetables change and the reader is urged always to check with one of the various tourist organisations or directly with the appropriate transport company. An invaluable travel guide, entitled *Getting around the Highlands and Islands*, is published in January and May each year by FHG Publications Ltd in association with the Highlands and Islands Development Board. It provides up-to-date and comprehensive information on transport to and on most of the more popular islands for the summer and winter seasons. The handbook is available from many bookstores and station-bookstalls, or can be obtained direct from FHG Publications Ltd in Paisley (telephone 041 887 0428).

In general, all the Western Isles, which includes the Inner and Outer Hebrides, are served by Caledonian MacBrayne vehicle and passenger ferries or by passenger-only ferries; while those in the north, namely the large island groups of Orkney and Shetland, are served by P & O Ferries. Occasionally smaller ferry companies and summer tourist boat services operate and information on these, where appropriate, is given for each island or island group. Such services especially are subject to change.

The principal terminals from which Caledonian MacBrayne vehicle ferries operate are Ardrossan (for Arran), Kennacraig (for Islay and Jura), Oban (for Mull, Colonsay, Coll, Tiree, Barra and South Uist), Kyle of Lochalsh (for Skye), Uig on Skye (for North Uist and Harris) and Ullapool (for Lewis). Passenger ferries are operated from Mallaig to the Small Isles and to Armadale in Skye by Caledonian MacBrayne. The company's office in Gourock (telephone 0475 34531) issues twice annually a brochure, entitled *The Sea-Road to 23 Scottish Islands*, giving comprehensive summer and winter timetables and fares. For those taking a car or other vehicle to the islands, which is to be recommended even when hillwalking or climbing is one's main pursuit, there is a wide variety of island hopscotch tours available, any one of which is usually good value.

The P & O Ferries office in Aberdeen (telephone 0224 572615) provides comprehensive schedules for its vehicle and passenger services to the Northern Isles. Detailed information on these services is also available from the Orkney Tourist Board office in Kirkwall (telephone 0856 2856) and from the Shetland Tourist Organisation in Lerwick (telephone 0595 3434). The main sea-port serving Orkney is Scrabster in Caithness, and those serving Shetland are Aberdeen, and Kirkwall in Orkney.

Air services are available to some of the islands in the west, including Lewis (operated by British Airways), as well as Barra, Benbecula, Tiree and Islay (operated by Loganair). Detailed up-to-date information on scheduled flights from Glasgow and Edinburgh can be obtained from the airline companies. A surprising number of the islands of Orkney and Shetland also have air strips. Frequent flights daily are available (British Airways) from Aberdeen and Inverness to Kirkwall in Orkney and Sumburgh in Shetland, with scheduled connections in Aberdeen from Birmingham, Manchester, London, Bergen and Amsterdam. Loganair operate services from Edinburgh, Inverness and Wick as well as regular scheduled flights between many of the islands. Where air services to the islands exist, information is given in this guide for appropriate islands or island groups, but it is always subject to change.

A brief description of public transport available on individual islands is also given in each chapter or section. Generally this comprises infrequent, though usually regular, local bus services. A scattering of Scottish Royal Mail Postbus services (telephone 0463-234111, Ext. 217) operate on some of the islands, including Islay, Colonsay, Tiree, Skye, Barra, North Uist and Lewis, as well as Mainland Orkney and Mainland Shetland. Detailed bus-service information can be found in the Highland and Islands Development Board's guide, or direct from the appropriate transport company. Timetables tend not to vary much from summer to winter because islanders have often to rely on these bus services for their regular provisions and mail deliveries. By the same token the timetables are not geared to modern tourism; for example, buses seldom connect with air services, but do so almost always with passenger and vehicle ferries.

It is recommended, where possible and appropriate, or economic in relation to the length of a given visit, to take one's own vehicle. When doing so it is worth considering also a canoe or collapsible boat, since transport across narrow sounds to minor interesting islands and over stretches of both inland and tidal waters to reach remoter hill-groups, is sometimes a major problem. Caution though is necessary, especially before embarking in a small craft on any sea crossing, however short; the Hebrides are set in the Atlantic and the islands of Orkney and Shetland in both the Atlantic and the North Sea. These are ocean waters not to be underestimated.

Accommodation

Ample accommodation is available on many of the popular islands, ranging from five-star hotels to bothies, though accommodation - particularly near to the hills - can be a problem on the remoter islands and camping is sometimes the only solution. Information on accommodation is given in each chapter of this guide. It is up-to-date at time of printing but is bound to be subject to change. Detailed information, up-dated annually, is available from appropriate tourist organisations, to which the reader is referred under respective islands or island groups.

Except for the Sligachan Hotel on Skye, located at the northern edge of the Cuillin, there are no climbers' hotels as such on the islands, although hotels on Arran (at Brodick and at Corrie) and in Harris (at Tarbert) are close enough to the hills to be used as bases for hillwalking and climbing. Likewise, there are no established climbing huts on the islands except for those on Skye - in Glen Brittle and near Loch Coruisk - serving the Cuillin.

Throughout the islands there are also few bothies that are well-placed for climbing; though on Rhum there are four which are convenient for the Rhum Cuillin, administered by the Nature Conservancy Council, three of these at Kinloch and one at Dibidil. There is also a bothy at Guirdil useful for the north-west hills. The Dibidil and Guirdil bothies are listed by the Mountain Bothies Association (MBA). On Eigg there are two or three bothies that are privately owned (by the Isle of Eigg Estate) and on Mull there is one (at Tomsleibhe) administered by the MBA. Bothies maintained by the MBA are open for all to use, although for good reasons their locations are not widely publicised. Regrettably vandalism and misuse is a real problem. The Gatliff Trust bothies, often retaining aspects of 19th century island character, are informally managed by a local custodian. A modest charge is made for their use. A visit to one of these cottages, usually in a crofting township, adds to any visit to the islands. It needs no saying that 'open' bothies should be treated with respect and locked ones should not be broken into. Large parties should not plan to use bothies; doing so denies access to others or leads to overcrowding.

Hostels for hillwalking or climbing are also sparse on the islands. In the Outer Hebrides there are none well located with the possible exceptions of the SYHA hostel on North Uist (at Lochmaddy), where there are few hills, and the Gatliff Trust hostel in Harris (at Rhenigadale) which is useful for only a handful of lesser hills in the south-east. In the Inner Hebrides the only hostels are those belonging to the SYHA on Skye, where the Glenbrittle hostel close to the Cuillin is heavily used, and on Arran, where neither of the two SYHA hostels (at Lochranza and Whiting Bay) is suitably placed for the hills.

Guest house and bed and breakfast accommodation is usually plentiful on the popular islands, especially those to which vehicle ferries exist, and is occasionally well located for the hills; guest houses can also be found readily in the Northern Isles. Up-to-date information on guest houses and private residences offering bed and breakfast is available for the Long Isle from the Outer Hebrides Tourist Board offices at Stornoway and Tarbert, for Skye from the Isle of Skye and South-West Ross Tourist Board offices in Portree and for the Northern Isles from the appropriate Orkney or Shetland tourist organisation. Where such accommodation exists, this is indicated for a given island with a note of location and telephone number of the relevant tourist office. Addresses of self-catering cottage and caravan accommodation, available on many of the islands, can also be obtained from Tourist Board publications.

Few official camping areas are to be found on the islands, but excellent hill and coastal camping is normally to be found. This may be restricted to designated campsite areas on some of the small popular islands, but usually permission for remoter camping in the hills can be easily obtained. Such permission should always be sought locally, from farmers or crofters, or from estate lodges where these exist. Often the response is accompanied with helpful directions to the best or preferred camping places. On the remoter islands camping is often excellent (for those well equipped), and may be the only solution for an extended stay. Where permission for camping is required - as it is at times along with permission to visit an island - from such bodies as the Nature Conservancy Council or the National Trust for Scotland, this is indicated appropriately for a given island. For those choosing to camp or bivouac during the months of June to August some form of midge repellent is almost essential. Campfires can help but precautions against heath fires in dry weather are mandatory. It should be remembered too that deadwood and often drift-wood can be scarce; carrying one's own fuel supply may be necessary.

For some of the remoter islands, or remoter parts of the popular islands, the problem of access can only be solved by visiting in one's own or a chartered boat.

Looking North from Bagh a' Ghallanaich on Muck to the hills of Rhum

For those fortunate enough to combine hillwalking or climbing with sailing (or motor craft) the question of accommodation may not arise; but extreme care should always be exercised in approach as well as anchoring and lying-off Scottish island shores. The seas and reefs can be treacherous and the weather can change unpredictably. Thorough consulting of the Admiralty's *West Coast Pilot* or the appropriate volume of *Directions and Anchorages* for the west coast of Scotland, published (for example) by the Clyde Cruising Club, is essential.

Access to the Hills

Relatively unrestricted access for walkers and climbers to Scotland's mountain areas has been a long-enjoyed freedom. It can be kept as such only by a combination of tolerance and responsibility. Almost all the land on the islands is privately owned. Frequently the owners or their tenants are engaged in earning a living from the land, and in many cases they provide employment. The land may be under sheep, cattle, deer, grouse or forestation. The owner or tenant may employ shepherds, cattlemen, stalkers, gillies, ponymen; others are employed in maintenance of stock, tracks, gates, fences, buildings and plantations.

     The visitor - whether tourist, walker, camper or climber - can injure island and Highland life by carelessness. An estate's management, its culling of livestock and the operation of its stalking or grouse-shooting for financial return, require it to control the access in some seasons. Information on landowners and estates, with names and addresses to contact, can be obtained from the booklet *Heading for the Scottish Hills*, published jointly by the Mountaineering Council of Scotland and the Scottish Landowners' Federation, (1988).

The normal season for deer-stalking is from the beginning of September to the end of October. Although stag-hunting usually finishes around 20th October, the culling of hinds continues until mid-February. The season for grouse-shooting is 12th August to 10th December. Before taking to the hills or the grouse-moors during these seasons, it is essential to enquire at the estate office or nearby farmhouse to ascertain whether stalking or grouse-shooting is taking place. The passage of a single walker can sometimes clear a glen of its deer for that day, or a moor of its grouse. The deer may not move back for weeks so that a season's stalking can be affected. For those running hill farms, which are often marginal enterprises, the venison exports could be crucial.

Sheep grazings, too, must be respected. Dogs should never be taken on the hills or moors during the lambing months and must be carefully controlled at all other times. Ewes, especially when pregnant, can easily be injured if forced to run. If a sheep is found on its back, approach quietly and bring it to its feet (by grasping its horns and twisting gently). If a sheep is trapped on a ledge, report it to a farmer or shepherd; do not attempt a rescue, since a sheep approached by a stranger may jump off and be injured or killed.

Much damage to plants, trees, birdlife and wildlife can be done by leaving litter or causing fires. It is vitally important to observe the countryside code: guard against fire; fasten all gates; keep to paths across farmland; avoid damage to walls and fences; keep dogs under control; leave no litter; safeguard water supplies; protect wildlife and plantlife; respect the life of the countryside. On many of the islands Sites of Special Scientific Interest have been designated by the Nature Conservancy Council. These sites are protected, under the Wildlife and Countryside Act of 1981, from damage being caused to plantlife, wildlife and birdlife, or to special features of interest. Hillwalkers and climbers should excercise particular care wherever such areas have been designated. For many islands or island groups, important sites of special interest are identified in this guide.

Weather

Island weather is, virtually by definition, maritime. Extremes of cold in winter and heat in summer seldom occur on any of the Scottish islands. The Gulf Stream (the remarkably fast moving warm current from the Gulf of Mexico) is deflected as it approaches the west coast of Europe by the North Atlantic Drift to the shores of the British Isles. It strongly affects the weather pattern around the Western Isles of Scotland. The seas there never freeze, except rarely at the heads of sea-lochs that penetrate far inland; while frozen seas are common elsewhere at these latitudes (as for example on the east coast of Canada).

Over the islands the air temperatures in winter are frequently kept above freezing by the influence of the surrounding sea, even when cold air is being fed to the area by an air flow from the north. Many of the islands go for a whole winter without frost at sea-level. Altitude however can have a huge influence. The complete absence of hills on Tiree, for example, causes it to record some of the highest hours of sunshine for the British Isles and lowest rainfall; while the Cuillin of Skye can experience the same severe winter conditions as mainland hills. Likewise, the islands in summer have land temperatures that are never truly high and only in still conditions does the air temperature then rise to values found on the mainland. The sunniest months are generally May and June. July and August are warmer but wetter. Average winter temperature is about 5°C and in summer is around 13°C. Rainfalls average 127 centimetres in the west; rather less in the north.

In winter a major consideration for climbers is the chill factor caused by the almost constant winds over some of the islands. Gales are recorded in the Outer Hebrides for some 50 days in the year, and for more than this in the Northern Isles. The winds, especially in the Western and Northern Isles, produce stunted plants and distorted trees, contributing generally to the erosion. The prevailing directions are from south-east through west to north-west, with northerly winds not uncommon in winter.

Mountain Rescue

Rescue from the hills or mountains of an island can be a complex undertaking. Only on Skye (at Glen Brittle, Sligachan, Portree and Broadford) and on Arran (at Brodick) are mountain rescue posts and facilities to be found. In the event of an accident it is essential - as for anywhere on the mainland - that one of the party reaches a telephone as soon as possible to contact the police (999), who will alert the emergency services. This can be done from public or private telephone or, where such exist, coast-guard station or lighthouse. It is worth noting - because of the remoteness of some islands - that these days many cruising boats and yachts, and always fishing and other commercial vessels, carry radio telephones; if any such craft is moored or anchored (and manned) nearby, it may be possible to seek help from its crew in sounding the alarm.

The police or coast-guard, once contacted and when provided with the essential information, will quickly put into action the necessary rescue service. (Note that a grid reference is the most accurate and unambiguous way of giving the location of an injured person). Speed in reaching a telephone is the rule; time should not be lost in trying to reach and locate a mountain rescue post even if these exist, unless at closehand. Police can be contacted from any telephone (999). HM Coastguard Marine Rescue Centres are stationed at Greenock (0475-29988), Oban (0631-63720), Stornoway (0851-2013) and Lerwick (0595-2976).

GEOLOGY (DNW)

The islands of Scotland are formed from a remarkable variety of rocks. This may not seem surprising given the diverse nature of the islands. Nevertheless, the range of rocks they display is extraordinary in terms of both type and age. The Isle of Arran in particular is probably unsurpassed worldwide for the great variety of rocks it exhibits within a limited area. As a consequence it has become a very popular location for geological fieldwork courses.

Although the islands taken together have a very complex history, most of them can be placed into one of three broad groups. The islands belonging to the first group, as represented by the Outer Hebrides, are formed mainly from extremely ancient Precambrian rocks. Those in the second group, of which Islay and Jura are typical, are built mainly of metamorphic rocks formed during the Caledonian mountain building episode. Those in the third group are built mainly of very much younger Tertiary igneous rocks, and include Mull, Skye and the Small Isles. The chief exception to this grouping is the island archipelago of Orkney. There the islands consist almost entirely of sedimentary rocks of intermediate age.

The Lewisian Complex

Nearly all of the Outer Hebrides, as well as Coll, Tiree and South Rona, consist of rocks loosely described as Lewisian gneiss. Smaller outcrops also occur on Skye, Raasay, Rhum, Iona and Islay. These rocks include some of the oldest so far known in Scotland or indeed in western Europe.

Rocks belonging to the Lewisian complex consist chiefly of banded gneisses. These were derived from a variety of pre-existing rocks by deformation and metamorphism deep in the earth's crust. They incorporate various intrusive igneous bodies, including basic dykes, granite sheets and pegmatite veins. Although they form a very complex group, even the layman should be able to distinguish dark basic masses such as amphibolite, and broad, coarsely crystalline veins of pink pegmatite.

At least two ancient metamorphic episodes can be identified within these gneisses. The earliest, the Scourian, has been dated by radiometric methods as 2,900-2,300 million years old. The subsequent episode, known as the Laxfordian, has been dated at 2,300-1,700 million years.

The entire complex was uplifted and deeply eroded before the deposition of Moine and Torridonian sediments began some 1000 million years ago. The Hebridean region remained relatively undisturbed during the subsequent Caledonian orogeny, or mountain building episode, except for the development of the Outer Hebridean thrust zone. This zone is marked by a broad tract of eastwardly dipping crushed rocks and extends for 200 kilometres along the eastern seaboard of the Long Isle from North Lewis to Barra. It accounts for the line of hills with west-facing scarps in the Uists.

Torridonian

Handa, the Summer Isles, Scalpay, and Soay consist mainly of Torridonian rocks, as do significant parts of Rhum, Skye and Raasay. Outcrops on Islay, Oronsay and Colonsay, which were formerly regarded as Torridonian, are now believed to belong to the much younger Dalradian (see below). The age of similar exposures on Iona remains uncertain.

In marked contrast to the crystalline Lewisian rocks, the Torridonian are predominantly red and grey sandstones, conglomerates, siltstones, and shales. Only where these rocks were caught up in subsequent Caledonian thrust sheets, as on Skye, have they been slightly metamorphosed.

The greatest thickness of Torridonian sediments was deposited about 800 million years ago when the Hebridean area lay about 30 degrees of latitude south of the equator. Greenland was a near neighbour and also an upland region at that time. Many Torridonian sediments are believed to have been deposited as extensive alluvial fans by rivers which flowed from south-east Greenland. Easily recognisable fossils could not be expected in such ancient rocks, but traces of primitive microfossils have been found in a number of places.

Moine and Dalradian

The sedimentary and volcanic rocks, which were to be strongly deformed and metamorphosed during the Caledonian orogeny, began accumulating more than 1000 million years ago. The oldest of these rocks, which are assigned to the Moine Series, underwent an initial metamorphism about 1000 million years ago (Grenvillian orogeny), and possibly also about 750 million years ago (Morarian orogeny). Some of the Moine rocks were originally deposited at the same time as the Torridonian sediments - probably as offshore deltas supplied by the Torridonian rivers.

The later Dalradian rocks, on the other hand, originated as a more varied group of marine sediments, which included limestones, quartz sandstones and mudstones. They were deposited from about 700 million years ago onwards, and were not metamorphosed prior to the Caledonian orogeny. A peculiar and widespread boulder bed is well exposed at Port Askaig on Islay. This was formed during a glacial episode about 670 million years ago when an ice-sheet advanced into a shallow sea. The boulders are thought to have been deposited when the ice-sheet grounded and started to melt.

The Moine and Dalradian rocks accumulated on the north-western side of what has been termed the Proto-Atlantic (or Iapetus) Ocean. When this ocean began to close about 500 million years ago, all of these rocks suffered major deformation and metamorphism during the early phase of the Caledonian orogeny. As a consequence siltstones, mudstones, limestones and quartz sandstones were changed respectively into schists, slates, marbles and (meta)quartzites.

The Caledonian Mountain Chain was formed where two rigid plates in the earth's crust collided with each other during the closure of the Iapetus Ocean. This vast chain extended from Scandinavia and Greenland, across Great Britain to Newfoundland and the eastern side of North America. Continental drift and erosion have since fragmented and worn down this chain, which at one time must have been similar to the present-day Andean chain in South America.

During the Caledonian orogeny most of the Hebridean area formed part of the North American plate and acted as a stable block against which the Moine and Dalradian rocks were squeezed. The rocks of the so-called Hebridean craton are separated from the metamorphosed Moine and Dalradian rocks by the Moine Thrust zone, which runs from Whiten Head on the north coast of Sutherland down through the north-west Highlands to the Sleat peninsula of Skye.

As a result of the thrusting, which took place some 430 million years ago during the climax of the Caledonian orogeny, Moine and Lewisian rocks were pushed several tens of kilometres over the rocks of the Hebridean craton. In many places, slices of Lewisian, Torridonian and Cambrian-Ordovician strata, from the craton, were caught up in the base of the thrust.

The largest outcrops of unquestioned Moine and Dalradian rocks in the islands occur on Jura, Islay, and the islands of Shetland. Smaller exposures occur on Arran, Gigha, Skye and Mull, and possibly Colonsay and Oronsay.

A remarkable thickness of Dalradian quartzite, estimated at some five kilometres, is found on Jura. This rock was originally deposited as clean quartz sand by tidal currents flowing to the north-east, ie parallel to the shoreline of a landmass which lay to the north-west.

The rocks of the Sleat peninsula of Skye, because of their involvement in the Moine Thrust zone, have a particularly complex structure. The rocks of Shetland have also suffered severe dislocation; on Unst and Fetlar, by thrusts striking north-north-east to south-south-west and on the Mainland, by north-south trending tear faults. It has been suggested that the latter are continuations of the Great Glen fault.

At the close of the Caledonian orogeny many large granite intrusions were emplaced throughout what are now the Highlands of Scotland. Sizeable bodies of granite in Shetland and the Ross of Mull also date from this time.

Cambrian - Ordovician

The only significant outcrops of Cambro-Ordovician rocks on the islands occur on Skye. They were originally deposited at about the same time as the Dalradian rocks, but because they were laid down on the Hebridean craton, they escaped subsequent metamorphism. They were however involved in complex Caledonian thrusting, and at a much later date, during Tertiary times, limestones were thermally metamorphosed to marble in the vicinity of large igneous intrusions.

The Cambro-Ordovician exposures on Skye do not form features of interest to the mountaineer, although the marble quarries at Torrin, for example, are conspicuous when travelling from Broadford to the head of Loch Slapin.

Old Red Sandstone (Devonian)

As the violent upheavals of the Caledonian orogeny gradually waned, terrestrial deposits of Old Red Sandstone were laid down. Among the islands important deposits occur on Orkney, Shetland and Arran.

Torrential rivers carried vast quantities of pebbles and sand into the subsiding trough of the Midland Valley and other basin areas. Sands and limy muds were deposited in the great 'Orcadian Lake' that formed over Caithness and Orkney. This shallow freshwater lake teemed with fish as is evident from numerous fossil remains. At times the lake dried up, at least locally, and at others it extended south to Moray and north to the Shetlands. Later, it was filled in with alluvium carried by rivers flowing from the south-west. Upper Old Red Sandstone deposits are particularly thick on Hoy, where at St John's Head they form a sea-cliff almost 350 metres high - one of the highest vertical rock faces in Britain.

Widespread volcanic activity also took place during the Old Red Sandstone period. The famous Old Man of Hoy consists of red fluvial sandstones, but it rests on a base of volcanic ash and basalt.

The Great Glen fault, which cleaves the Highlands in two, has undoubtedly had a very long and complex history of movement. Significant displacement is known to have taken place along this major fault in Old Red Sandstone times. The direction of movement is still a matter of geological dispute, but the land north-west of the Great Glen almost certainly slid horizontally many tens of kilometres relative to the rest of Scotland. The same kind of movement is occurring today along the San Andreas fault in California.

Carboniferous-Cretaceous

Only rocks of minor importance, from a mountaineering point of view, are represented on the islands for the period from the beginning of the Carboniferous (350 million years ago) to the end of the Cretaceous (65 million years ago). The largest outcrops are Permian-Triassic sandstones and mudstones on Arran and Lewis, and Jurassic shales and sandstones on Skye and Raasay; but they do not form any high ground of note.

However, the small sea-cliffs of Jurassic marine sandstones around the Strathaird peninsula of Skye offer some climbing possibilities. They exhibit large-scale cross bedding and constitute the thickest sequence of rocks of their particular age in north-west Europe.

Great Britain crossed the equator during the Carboniferous period, and continued to drift steadily northwards thereafter. When the desert sandstones on Arran were deposited some 270 million years ago Scotland lay at about the same latitude as the present-day Sahara.

Exploration for oil in the North Sea in recent years has revealed that major volcanic activity took place there in Middle Jurassic times. It occurred along part of a rift zone which started to develop between Great Britain on the one hand, and Norway and Denmark on the other. In fact several such incipient rift zones have been detected in the continental shelf around the British Isles. These rifts were associated with the initial opening of the North Atlantic which eventually occurred during late Cretaceous times. Part or all of the British Isles might easily have moved off with Greenland or North America if the final line of opening had been different.

Tertiary

When Greenland and Europe began to separate in the early Tertiary, intense igneous activity broke out down the west coast of Scotland and in north-east Ireland. Vast quantities of basalt lava poured out from fissures and volcanoes and piled up, flow upon flow. Whether these eruptions occurred along a line of weakness that could have become the line of opening of the North Atlantic is not clear. Similar igneous activity certainly took place along the actual line of opening, as is recorded in the rocks of East Greenland and the Faeroes, which now lie on opposite sides of the new ocean. Sea-floor spreading is still taking place today from the oceanic ridge system that runs through a volcanically active part of Iceland. The rate of spreading has been calculated to be about two centimetres per year.

In the Hebridean area sizeable quantities of basaltic lava occur on Skye, Canna, Eigg, Muck, Morvern and Mull. The flows were erupted onto a land surface and must at one time have been much more extensive than appears today. Lavas of more than 1800 metres thickness can be identified on Mull. These have been traced on the seabed and found to merge with the lavas of Morvern, Muck and Eigg. A similar link has been found between the lavas of Skye, Raasay and Canna.

Sometimes the interval between eruptions was sufficient for the surface of the lavas to break down and form soil, and for forests to become established. There are remarkable leaf beds and even fossil trees preserved within the lava sequence on Mull.

The igneous activity subsequently became concentrated around complex intrusive centres. In Scotland these occur on Skye, Rhum, Ardnamurchan, Mull, Arran, St Kilda and Rockall. Elsewhere in Britain several centres developed around Newry in Northern Ireland, and also one as far south as Lundy in the Bristol Channel. A number of submarine complexes are also believed to exist on the continental shelf west of Scotland.

The complexes often have nearly circular outlines. They consist of arcuate or ring-like intrusions grouped concentrically around one or more neighbouring centres, usually some ten to fifteen kilometres across. They have complex and varied histories. Collapse structures known as calderas can be recognised, as can features called explosive vents, ring dykes, cone sheets and sills.

The bulk of the intrusions are of basic and ultrabasic igneous rocks such as gabbro and peridotite, but there is a notable number of more acidic intrusions such as granite. Basalt is formed by the rapid cooling of basic magma at or near the earth's surface, whereas coarsely crystalline gabbro is formed by much slower cooling of the same material deep in the earth's crust.

St John's Head, a 350 metre cliff of Old Red Sandstone on Hoy

A third phase involved the intrusion of extensive north-west to south-east trending dyke swarms. These are closely associated with the igneous centres. Dykes crossing the Mull centre for example can be traced as far as the north-east coast of England.

Volcanic activity in the Hebrides had passed its peak by about 55 million years ago, and had ceased completely by the middle Tertiary. No Tertiary rocks are found on land in the Hebrides after this time. Meanwhile the Alps were being formed in Europe, and earth movements associated with this orogeny caused some folding in south-east England. General uplift and some faulting took place in Scotland.

Quaternary

The final sculpting of the rocks which make up the islands took place in the last two million years. It was during this time that vast ice-sheets built up and receded many times over northern latitudes around the world.

The earth has generally been free of ice, even at the poles, during much of the greater part of geological time. However, at least three glacial episodes or 'ice ages' are known to have occurred at widely spaced intervals. The first occurred in late Precambrian times when the boulder bed on Islay was deposited. During the second ice age in the Permo-Carboniferous period Britain lay near the equator outwith the glacial area.

The most recent glacial episode had a profound influence upon the shaping of Scotland's scenery. A massive ice-sheet developed over the whole country, probably on several occasions. At times of less extensive ice cover separate ice-caps developed on the more mountainous islands. Glaciers carved out the familiar corries, glens, rock-basin lochs and fjords we see today. The floor of Loch Coruisk on Skye for example was gouged out by glacial ice to some 30 metres below present sea-level.

The last glaciation finished about 10,000 years ago. Among the features of interest formed on the islands in late glacial and post-glacial times are the massive rotational landslips in northern Skye, and the raised beaches of the Inner Hebrides.

Where the ice was thickest over the Central Highlands it caused the greatest depression of the land surface. As the ice melted the land began to rebound. Striking examples of raised beaches are displayed on Islay and Jura. However, such features are absent from the Outer Hebrides, Orkney and Shetland because they lay far away from the main region of ice accumulation and so experienced little of this isostatic rebound.

NATURAL HISTORY (DJF)

It hardly needs saying that the forms of plantlife found on the islands are directly related to their geology, through the nature of the top soil. Lime-rich soils, for example, arise from rocks rich in calcium carbonate and acidic soils from granite and gneiss. The geological structure, however, by determining the general nature of ground cover (moorland, peat, sand, or bare rock) plus habitat, also affects the bird and wildlife to be found. Weather has an obvious influence, but weather too inter-relates with geography and thus geology.

This complex inter-dependence is not of course confined to Scotland but the rich variety of geological rocks and structures, found especially in the islands, is reflected by an unusually wide variety of plant and bird species in relation to the land area covered.

Plantlife

Many factors besides geological structure and climate affect plantlife on the islands. It would be impossible, even if a full chapter of this guide was given to island flora, to cover more than a fraction of botanical species. As it is, some mention is made here, for each island or group, of unusual or unique species of plant to be found. For several of the islands a wider mention is made in the text.

As a general rule most islands have different plant forms from nearby mainland regions. Islands close to mainland Scotland usually have large areas of heath, peat bog and rock, and carry relatively few plant species. In addition, exposure to Scottish weather conditions reduces the possibilities of tree and shrub cover, and hence also the protection given to potential plants, thus diminishing further the variety of plants. On the other hand, well-sheltered islands like Arran and Gigha, which also benefit more from the warmth of the Gulf Stream, are rich in unusual plants, including varieties of primula found elsewhere in Britain only in its southern islands.

Despite the difficult climatic conditions of many of the outlying islands, some species of plant always appear to survive. The narrow rocky gannetry of Sula Sgeir, barely a kilometre in length, lying more than 60 kilometres north of the Butt of Lewis, has seven species of plant. To its north again, Rona, two square kilometres in area, supports between 40 and 50 species; while Hirta, the largest of the St Kilda group and ten square kilometres in area, has around 140 species. Shetland, on the other hand, whose archipelago totals 1000 square kilometres, over a hundred times the land area of Hirta, barely supports three times the number of native species of plant found in St Kilda.

Hirta has around 450 native species and 250 or so of 'aliens'; ie, naturalised species which now reproduce outside their original artificial habitat. Some of the latter are hortals (garden escapes) and others the result of commerce and trade (accidental introduction). Naturalised aliens generally increase in number the further south an island is located; the result both of climate and of land-owners introducing extensive garden displays of exotic plants.

Surprisingly, among Scottish islands there are few endemic plants (species known only in that place); while in the British Isles overall there are 20 or more endemic species. Shetland has an endemic hawkweed, its golden and orange flowers forming a colourful feature on the rock ledges of the islands. The hawkweeds, however, are a special case; they reproduce without pollination, like brambles, and small populations of mutations easily arise.

More common than endemic species are island specialities, or subspecies, of which several of interest occur on the Scottish islands. These include a unique subspecies of spotted orchid (*dactylorhiza maculata*) on Rhum, and a subspecies of the common spotted orchid (*o. fuchsii*) sometimes known as the Hebridean orchid (*hebridensis*) found in Shetland, as well as in the Outer Hebrides and a few of the Inner Hebrides - Skye, Coll and Tiree.

On most of the islands the presence of Man has had a profound effect on plantlife. The digging of peat without replacing the fertile top layer effectively scalps the land, leaving bog or even bare rock. Many of the islands are known, from pollen analyses, to have developed forests after the ice ages. Even St Kilda appears to have had birch and hazel. Trees everywhere were cut for building and fuel and this devastation, along with a change to a wetter climate, helped the land to become denuded of forests. Only in the last century has re-planting shown that trees can survive on several of the northern and outer islands. Grazing, too, has taken toll of the vegetation.

In Shetland intensive grazing and burning of scrub has probably been occurring for over 5000 years. However, a selection of maritime plants is to be found in the northern and western islands, including sea campion, sea sandwort and pearlwort, buck shorn and sea plantains, thrift (sea pinks) and saltwort; and among the ferns, sea spleenwort, royal fern (where the sheep and cattle cannot reach) and Scottish lovage.

In the Western Isles especially, the Atlantic beaches are fringed with machair. This is the Gaelic word for short springy turf that grows on, and stabilises, the sand just inland from the extensive dunes along many of the western and northern coasts of the islands. The machair in spring and summer usually provides a spectacle of tiny flora, unrivalled elsewhere in the islands. The machair is particularly fine in the Uists, where it is often cultivated on a shifting system and once left fallow then displays a succession of differently coloured dominant species of flower: daisies, pink in the rain and white when open in the sun, yellow buttercups, and silverweed whose silvery leaves are followed by golden blooms. The fleshy roots of the silverweed once formed a famine food of the Highlands and Islands, before potatoes were introduced.

The machair plants also include white clover, birdsfoot trefoil, kidney vetch, wild pansies, yellow pepperwort, corn marigold, marsh orchids, red clover and purple tufted vetch and even scarlet poppies. The marshy and boggy regions that adjoin the machair support bogbeam (an unusual bloom seen in May), butterfly orchids, a vivid pink ragged robin which is often thick on the ground, dark green marsh cinquefoil and slender green mare's tail.

Almost every island group in the north and west has its special floral display: extensive drift of birdsfoot trefoil, white clover and eyebright behind the sand dunes of Orkney; kingcups in spectacular quantities on the generally desolate moorlands of Lewis and Harris; thrifts carpeting the western shores of the Barra Isles; but generally little except sphagnum moss, sedges, grass and heather between the peat and rock of the Outer Hebridean eastern coasts.

The complex geology of the Inner Hebrides causes surprising variations in flora, even between neighbouring islands; rare ferns in the limestones of Skye, large woodlands of ash in the Sleat peninsula, with many thickets of beech, hazel, oak and willow elsewhere on Skye and Raasay. The Cuillin of Skye hold an assortment of arctic alpines (known only in the sub-arctic zone and the European Alps), which can be found there even at sea-level. Skye is also the only habitat in Britain of the alpine rockcress. White globe flower, mountain sorrel, catsfoot (mountain everlasting), meadow rue, purple saxifrage, moss campion and tufts of roseroot are all to be found on Skye, as on Mull, and some even in Shetland, Orkney and St Kilda. The sandstones of Colonsay and Oronsay provide a soil basis that causes their sedge and heather moors to be interspersed with natural woodlands of birch, hazel, oak, rowan and willow.

Arran, in its turn, has rare whitebeams; Rhum has rare alpine saxifrage; Islay rare primroses; Orkney and Shetland a rare purple-flowering Scottish primrose. The list is endless. The islands abound in botanical interest.

Birdlife

The islands of Scotland have the most spectacular colonies of seabirds in Europe. The most common is the herring gull, which is found widely on populated islands as well as on mainland shores, a result of its amazing ability to coexist with man. The most rare is the sea-eagle which has been successfully re-introduced by man as a result of outdoor laboratory activities, such as those by the Nature Conservancy Council on the island of Rhum.

The increase in population of various members of the gull family over the past fifteen to twenty years has been dramatic. They are nowadays seen even well inland, on playing fields and rubbish tips, as common as blackbirds or starlings. Herring gulls and black-backed gulls have taken over on many of the inhabited islands of the south, for example in the Firth of Clyde and the Solway Firth, where man's domestic and chemical pollution (as well as the increase in gull predation) has driven away the seabirds that once nested there, particularly those of the auk family. A herring gull will steal fish from the mouth of a parent puffin before it can feed its young, while the greater black-backed gull will pounce on a puffin, in the air (puffins are ungainly in flight) or as it emerges temporarily blinded from its burrow, and despatch and devour it on the wing. In the south-west, only on Ailsa Craig in the Firth of Clyde has a colony of puffins and other auks survived together with a stronghold of gannets.

The gulls are a similar menace on the east coast where, in the Firth of Forth, they prey on the puffins of Craigleith, and even harry the huge gannetry on the neighbouring Bass Rock. The Royal Society for Protection of Birds plays an active role in studying and monitoring the colonies of birds on these islands in the Firth of Forth and Firth of Clyde.

On its west and north coasts, Scotland is fortunate in having many uninhabited or sparsely inhabited remote islands, which make wonderful sanctuaries for seabirds, free from man and the predatory gulls. The most spectacular of all is Stac Lee of the St Kilda group which houses the largest gannetry in the northern hemisphere and probably the largest in the world (over 100,000 pairs now nest there). The remoter islands make natural unfenced reserves for seabirds, often with ideally structured cliff-faces for nests, protected by treacherously rough seas. It is this combination of ideal habitat and natural protection that allows, for example, nearly seventy percent of the world's entire population of razorbills to nest on Scotland's islands.

The St Kilda group has more seabirds, in both number and species, than any other island group in Britain; although smaller, less remote but little visited archipelagos like the Treshnish Isles can be as spectacular for varieties of seabird, including kittiwakes, guillemots, fulmars, razorbills, puffins, skuas and gannets. Razorbills will also be found nesting among the bouldery mountain slopes of some of the Inner Hebrides, along with petrels and Manx shearwaters.

Although seabirds dominate, the islands have at the same time many inland nature reserves, as on Rhum and North Uist, with splendid displays of resident, and migrant, moorland and heathland nesting birds. Of note, among these are corncrakes of which a few are found everywhere, and choughs found only locally on such islands as Islay, Colonsay and the Uists. Summer visitors include wheatears and whinchats; winter visitors range from innumerable curlews to occasional woodcocks. A list for every island would be endless.

There are also fresh-water National Nature Reserves, such as Loch Driudibeg on South Uist, which make ideal habitats for every kind of waterfowl, including important breeding grounds for the native grey lag goose. The Northern Isles have only one large gannetry, on Sula Sgeir off the Butt of Lewis, but many large colonies of fulmars, kittiwakes, and guillemots on their steep sandstone and granite cliffs, as well as shags and cormorants nesting on outlying reefs. In Shetland, though, there are already signs of seabird disturbance arising from off-shore oil activity. The seas are lit at night by the light from oil-platform flares, and the oil spillage at Sullom Voe in the early eighties took a severe and ominous toll of seabirds, despite heroic work by the Royal Society for Protection of Birds.

Wildlife

Just as the vegetation of the islands is affected by their geological structure and climate, so is the wildlife they support affected by the vegetation. Also important in the development of unique species of some mammals is isolation, a factor which has been especially important to the wildlife of some of Scotland's remote islands.

Originally, however, mammals on the islands have mostly found their way there as a result of some form of human activity. Even the indigenous and uniquely primitive Soay sheep of the St Kilda group, which have been on Hirta for at least a thousand years, have been traced to a Neolithic domesticated stock-route and must have somehow been brought there by Man. They owe their survival in virtually unchanged genetic form to their island isolation. Hirta has also nurtured its own rodent species, the St Kilda mouse.

In more recent times, Soay sheep have been introduced to Ailsa Craig and to one or two of the Inner Hebrides and outlying islands. They are dark brown, smaller and hardier than their mainland cousins, almost goat-like and equally at home on steep cliff-slopes. Although these qualities have been nurtured splendidly on the islands of St Kilda, the origin of the Soays before they appeared on Hirta is unknown.

Orkney, too, has its own strain of sheep; a small short-tailed breed found on the most northerly of the islands, North Ronaldsay. They live largely on seaweed and their meat, as a result, is dark and rich in iodine. Some years ago the Rare Breeds Survival Trust arranged for the transport of a small flock of these sheep to a small tidal island off Guernsey, where there is ample grass in addition to seaweed. Their numbers have now multiplied to over a hundred, and at every ebb of the tide - it is reported - they make their way over the greasy boulders, to graze the kelp. As with Soay sheep, the origin of this breed before they appeared on North Ronaldsay is unknown.

Feral goats graze in many of the islands - again brought there by Man. They were either released by passing mariners or by the islanders themselves for the purpose of providing milk. Their origin has been traced to the far corners of Europe and Asia. Goats do untold damage to the land wherever the pasture is sparse; though, ironically, they help the shepherd in some instances, by grazing the choicer grass of the cliff-ledges, so reducing the incentive of the less-agile sheep to wander into danger.

Many of the islands also have red deer. The original population of deer was almost exterminated (as in most of Europe) by persecution and the destruction of their forest habitat. Fortunately the red deer were re-introduced to many of the Scottish islands - albeit in the name of sport - during the 19th century. These days, it is pleasing to note, the economics of estate management is maintaining their numbers by restricting the hunting to an annual cull. Elsewhere, the red deer - as on Rhum - are protected for ecological research.

Rhum's management programme also supports a few dozen Rhum ponies, serving as pack animals for bringing in deer carcasses from the hills. The ponies, or small horses, were at one time the product of breeding Highland mares with Arab sires. Similarly the more famous Shetland pony is a result of selective breeding, although their exact origin is less certain.

Rabbits, like sheep and goats, were originally brought to the Scottish islands by farmers. Myxomatosis wiped out a large part of the rabbit population during the 1950's but they survived on many of the isolated islands. On others they have been reintroduced either intentionally or unwittingly. Rodents can be found on most of the

A meadow of wild flowers below Beinn Mhor, South Uist

Gannets on the Bass Rock

islands. In addition to the St Kilda mouse, the ecological isolation has produced a Rhum mouse, an Orkney vole, and other unique breeds. None forms a separate scientific species - they can all breed with their mainland cousins to produce fertile young.

Otters are common, especially in the Northern Isles, and seals are virtually ubiquitous throughout the Scottish islands. The grey seals prefer the more isolated islands of the west coast; the common seal is far more prevalent in the east. Other mammals of the sea, porpoises, dolphins and whales, frequent the islands. Occasionally the tell-tale dorsal fins of large numbers of porpoises or dolphins will be seen close inshore, attracted either by a shoal of mullet or mackerel.

Marine Life

Beach and marine life provide an added interest to an island visit. Many an off-day can be enjoyed combing beaches for their splendid array of unusual shells and brightly coloured seaweed and inshore invertebrates. Their study can add also to the pleasures of coastal bouldering.

An enormous variety of beach-life is to be found; all of it withstanding an exceptional range of conditions, from extreme cold to intense heat, plus pounding seas and strong tides. The shores are swept twice a day by seas rich in plankton, bringing food to the living organisms sometimes during daylight and sometimes during the dark of night. The seaweeds lower down the beach, having longer periods in which to feed, are larger and more luxuriant and brightly coloured; those higher up the beach suffer longer periods between feeding, plus greater extremes of drying, heating or cooling, and are more straggly and weedy. Above the latter, covering the rocks beyond the highest tidal reaches of the sea, are thinly spread lichens; greasy underfoot when damp but giving sound footholds once dried by wind or sun.

The most luxuriant of the lower seaweeds is the brown wrack, *laminaria*, whose strongly anchoring stalk is known as 'holdfast'. In the depths below the lower beaches are the reds and blues of the weeds and shellfish that grow in perpetual sea but with sufficient penetration of life-assisting sunlight. The remarkable clarity of the seawater around Scotland's shores, especially its island shores, makes the cut-off of sunlight penetration unusually deep - as much as twelve or even fifteen fathoms.

The extensive weeds of the lower shores (*laminaria, saccorhiza* and *fucus*) are loosely called kelp, a word derived from the ash formed from burning these various brown seaweeds. In the 18th century the kelp industry in Orkney alone accounted for the seasonal (summer) employment of as many as 20,000 men and women. The weed, after drying in the sun, was burnt in shallow pits and then broken up by sprinkling with water while hot. Some twenty tons of wet seaweed produced one ton of grey ash from which soda ash and potash were extracted for use in the manufacture of glass, soap and fertilisers. The kelp industry declined at the end of the century but was revived around 1812 after the discovery of iodine. The new industry, however, had its difficulties in Scotland; nearly 90% of the iodine can be lost if the untreated weed is washed by rain.

In the Hebrides, where there was no development of a kelp industry as such, huge basket-loads of kelp and short-fronded wrack from the middle shore were harvested after storms by the crofters for manure. Free from crop-weed and harmful fungi, seaweed manure provides excellent food as well as fibre, especially for the sparse soil of the Outer Hebrides.

Most seaweeds are edible. The bladdery seaweeds from the middle to lower shores are an important source of organic alginates, used as a gelling agent in foods and confectionery. Among these wracks, quantities of dulse (*rhodymenia palmata*), which grows from the disc-shaped holdfasts of the lower shores, has in the past been eaten widely in Scotland, especially in the outlying islands. Chewed fresh or dried and boiled in milk, it makes a wholesome dish. Seaweed cakes of laver (*pophyra umbilicalis*) are common even today in remote communities; rolled in oatmeal and fried, they form a nourishing staple or simply a tasty addition to the breakfast plate.

In, under and around the weeds, and under every rock at low tide, are to be found shellfish and other invertebrates. Limpets of every hue, razor shells, glistening mussels, winkles, oysters, clams, dog whelks, sea urchins, richly coloured starfish, sea-anemones and many more. All are attractively coloured. Many are highly nutritious.

One of the largest groups are the gastropods (or marine snails) which live in the open on the rocks, exposed to the full force of the seas. Of these, the limpets are the most common, with their flattish conical shells and the extraordinary muscles of their feet clamping them to the rock, defying their removal by human hand, unless one can catch them unawares. Periwinkles and dog whelks, which can be found in huge numbers at low tide, do not have the tenacity of the limpets. The dog whelk is a carnivorous sea snail; attaching itself to the shell of its relatives, it bores a hole and eats the meat of its prey. The shell of the whelk itself changes colour, as it feeds from its captive, to a mauvey pink or brownish black. The dye it secretes, purpurin, was used as a writing ink by the monks and by the Romans to colour their togas.

Numerous bivalves, including cockles and razor shells, spend at least part, if not all, of the tidal cycle buried in the sand or mud of the sea floor. The razor shellfish burrow rapidly and are consequently difficult to catch. They can even escape often from their shells as one attempts to grasp them. Their taste and food value make them an attractive prize.

Starfish, which also burrow quickly, are not good to eat. Highly coloured, they too are carnivores, devouring cockles whose shells they force open by the suction of their feet. The lobster fishermen say a starfish in the creel means no lobster. The list of sea invertebrates is endless. Brightly coloured jellyfish can be found on beaches as the tide recedes. The variety known as 'by-the-wind sailor' is deep blue around the edges, and about ten centimetres in diameter. The delicate blue Portuguese Man o'War, a frequent visitor from the far side of the Atlantic, is usually battered and windblown by the time it reaches our island shores; however, its sting, which is the method it uses to capture small fish in the ocean, is still powerful - and should be avoided.

SOCIAL HISTORY (DJF)

The islands of Scotland were peopled long before historical records began. The range of pre-historic relics to be found is remarkable. In few other places in the world is there such a wide variety, and the best preserved remains in Europe of Neolithic man are found on Scottish islands.

Pre-history

The earliest settlers in the Hebrides came from the South, probably some thousands of years before Britain was separated from the European Continent by the opening of the English Channel. Their numbers were small, no more perhaps than a few hundred overall, but the evidence of their settlement is clear in the remains of their tools (stone hammers, antler mattocks, harpoons and fish-hooks made of bone) found on Arran, Jura, Oronsay, Rhum, Skye and Lewis.

Some 2000 years later came the Mesolithic (early Neolithic, Stone Age) farming people. They brought domesticated cattle and goats, and seed grain. Being cultivators of the land, they sought fertile islands and settled in Islay and the Uists, and in Orkney in larger numbers. The largest concentration of prehistoric monuments in Europe is to be found in Orkney, with the remains of the earliest known domestic settlement - dating from 3000 BC - on Papa Westray.

The finest archaeological relic anywhere of these farming settlers is also in Orkney, at Skara Brae on Mainland. At the time the spectacularly preserved homes of Skara Brae were built, in the bay of Skaill, the sea was some fifty feet lower than at present. The site was discovered by chance in 1826 when the sands covering the ten or so now-excavated houses were blown from the bay in a freak hurricane. To-day a concrete wall protects the well-preserved remains from storm waves at high water and it is a matter of speculation whether further sites lie out to sea underwater.

Evidence of colonisation by Neolithic man, one thousand years later, can be found throughout Scotland's islands. Here again Orkney possesses the most impressive monument in all Europe, at Maes Howe on Mainland. Skara Brae appears to have been abandoned around 2400 BC while Maes Howe dates from about 2800 BC at the culmination of Neolithic building in Europe.

The Scottish islands also have many examples of structures found only in Britain, the stonehenges of Callanish in Lewis, Lochbuie on Mull, Kilchatten on Bute, and Stenness and Brodgar in Orkney. These important and puzzling stone circles, spectacular in size and mathematical precision (reportedly astrological, but unconfirmed), are widespread among the islands. The sepulchral standing stones of Callanish are the finest, the next in importance being those in Orkney. On Tiree there are two small stone circles, and on Arran as many as ten.

Shetland, surprisingly, has no stone circles nor standing stones. However two of the most impressive and complete remains of brochs in all Scotland are found in Shetland, on the island of Mousa and at Clickimin on Mainland. They are believed to have been built by the Picts of whom little is known except that they arrived in the northern and north-westernmost islands around 100 AD and fled from or were

The standing stones at Callanish in Lewis

overwhelmed by the Vikings towards the end of the 1st century. Another Pictish broch, in good state of preservation, can be seen at Carloway in Lewis. It is characteristically double-walled and massively strong, a beehive-shaped fortress.

Meanwhile the Celtic peoples had been drifting north in huge numbers since around 600 BC, leaving the first - recognisable if unintelligible - inscriptions on stone. That some pre-Celtic and Pictish language existed is undisputed, but it has never been fully deciphered. The best preserved example is probably a memorial message on a four-sided granite pillar on the island of Gigha. A later, more distinctive development of these writings was called Ogam, consisting of a baseline with groups of cross-strokes or strokes to either side. Presumably such inscriptions were easily cut or notched on wooden sticks for communication, but surviving texts are mostly funeral inscriptions on stones.

The Gauls, of Indo-Aryan origin, from Central Europe where iron had been discovered, were also on the move at the time, migrating from lands overrun by the Romans. Some, the Gaels, drifted into northern Ireland, or Dalriada as it was then called, and their language gave rise to the Gaelic which spread with them around 500 AD to the western islands and mainland of Scotland, displacing the Pictish probably spoken there. The Picts left no records despite their knowledge of Ogam, but expressed themselves visually in artistic pictures carved on stone - the eagle often their characteristic symbol. Fine examples can be seen on Burra in Shetland and on several islands in Orkney.

Iona Cathedral

History

The Celtic Church was meanwhile developing an organized faith. St Patrick, and later St Columba, brought Christian missions (with the Gaelic language and the name of Scots) to the islands of Arran, Bute, Islay, Jura, and mainland Argyll. In 563 AD St Columba and his followers landed in Iona, and established the monastery there which for 150 years was to be the national church of Scotland. Particularly fine examples of carved and engraved Celtic (and Kildalton, or sub-Celtic) crosses are now to be seen on Iona, Islay, Oronsay and Raasay (though none surprisingly on Skye, nor Harris or Lewis). The monks of the Celtic Church also founded a fine abbey on the small island of Lindisfarne - Holy Island, the 'Cradle of Christianity' - on the east coast just south of the border.

The Romans too were moving north at this time and by 700 AD disputes between the authority of Rome and the Celtic Church caused the Columban monks of the latter to abandon Lindisfarne and seek and find new settlements in Ireland and on the more remote islands in the west. Their monasteries and abbeys, such as that on Iona which St Columba managed to distance from some of the disputes (even wars) between settlements, were fine centres of craftsmanship and religious instruction; offering sanctuary and dispensing Law and medical care, especially after the Romans abandoned Scotland, until the terrifying Vikings arrived from the north around the year 800 AD.

The Vikings, or more correctly Scandinavians, for they came too from Sweden and Denmark, launched their murderous raids from the sea; plundering the Celtic and Columban settlements, and before that the Pictish settlements further north. By their incomparable seamanship, their invention of the keel and rudder, they soon made the Scottish islands their own. They left little by way of relics, but hill and place names throughout the Hebrides, not to mention Orkney and Shetland, provide ample evidence of their presence which lasted almost 400 years.

Norse settlements have been unearthed at Jarlshof near the southernmost tip of Shetland, and at Underhoull on its northernmost island of Unst. The Jarlshof settlement was huge, but the relics of substance there are of the earlier ages; Celtic bronze (from Ireland) and the remains of a fine Pictish broch. In Shetland and Orkney the Pictish society — its language and culture — were obliterated by the Viking settlements. Probably the Picts took refuge on the Scottish mainland, in the hills across the Pentland Firth, joining the Scots from the west to form the Kingdom of Picts and Scots. Orkney became the base from which the murderous King Magnus of Norway, according to the Norse sagas, dispatched his marauding raids on Lewis, the Uists, Skye, Mull, Tiree, Iona and later Islay and Argyll.

The Viking empire ended, as many before and since, with wars among the leaders. Earl Haakon of Orkney murdered King Magnus on the island of Egilsay in 1117. The Gaelic-speaking Scots absorbed the Picts by 1200 and began before that to ravage the isles in a quest to oust Haakon and his supporters. Haakon's island territories included Skye; the name of Kyleakin derives from the Straits of Haakon, the sound through which he led his long-ships around the Mull of Kintyre as far as Arran and the Cumbraes, retaking lost islands. One of the Scots chiefs, Somerled, who was married to a sister of the notorious Godred, an earlier Norse King of the Isles, defeated Haakon at Largs. The Norwegian fleet withdrew to Orkney where Haakon died and Somerled became the first Scottish Lord of the Isles, making the Parish of Kildalton in Islay his home and fortress.

The Outer Hebrides were the last to see the end of Scandinavian settlement, as late as the mid 1200's. The Faeroe Islands, originally plundered from the Celtic monks around 825, is Scandinavian today. The familiar complex web of history over the next five centuries involved raids, treaties, marriages, treacheries and corruption with many of the islands changing sides frequently. Somerled's grandson, Donald of Islay, giving his name to the clan Donald, succeeded to the Lordship of the island mini-Kingdom, as did several generations of MacDonalds. The Donald territory grew to encompass Sleat of Skye, the Uists and Benbecula. Vassal clans arose, mostly by marriage, partly by favours. The McLeans of Duart were granted a large part of Mull, Coll and Tiree; the Clan Iain, most of Jura plus land in Islay and Mull; the MacLeods of Lewis, Harris and much of Skye; Clan Neil, Barra, South Uist and Gigha; the McPhees, Colonsay; the MacKinnons also part of Mull and Skye.

The clan chiefs built fine castles, which are there today on many of the islands. A council of Hebridean chieftains met once a year in northern Islay to discuss problems and to administer justice publicly. In this manner the Lords of the Isles gave firm rule from Islay for 300 years, but the Donalds always distrusted the

Kiessimul Castle, the ancient stronghold of the Macneills of Barra

Scottish mainland Kings for their introduction of the Norman feudal system from England. The Celtic lords, with their heritage of freemen, frequently flouted the Royal authority from Edinburgh until the Stewart King, James IV, broke the Donald lordship but left the Isles without a supreme Head able to enforce law from Islay. Consequently, clan soon fought with clan, chieftain plotted with and against chieftain, while the isles-folk suffered appalling hardship and cruelty.

In this period of lawlessness, in which churches were burnt and many of the clergy were driven from the islands, the Hebrides became the scandal of the Scottish realm; a troublesome territory to which James VI was especially sensitive when he succeeded to the English crown in 1603. He despatched an expedition (in 1608) which, by the trickery of inviting the Hebridean chiefs to a council at Castle Aros on Mull, made them prisoner to the man on his flagship, which brought them to Edinburgh. A year later they were released on conditions, to which they were forced to agree, drawn up by Andrew Knox, the Reformed Church Bishop of the Isles, at a council on Iona.

Thus was the social and economic life of the Hebrides stabilized — by statutes that destroyed the islanders' capacity for clan feuding. Relative peace came to the islands, with only minor insurrections, confined mainly to Islay; from one such minor feud Argyll and Islay fell to the Campbells. The clans were in fact brought together in one common cause in 1745, when the young Prince Charles Edward Stewart landed on Eriskay. It was a cause doomed to failure at Culloden the

The Islands today; a crofting township at Loch Pooltiel, Skye

following year, but one that effectively ended clan warfare for ever. In that same year kelp manufacture began in the Northern Isles and the herring industries of the Western Isles were soon to follow.

The new prosperity in the islands was shortlived, for the social system linking chieftain to his people had disintegrated with the clan system. In the first half of the 19th century new profit-seeking 'lairds' were turning their land to sheep. The Clearances had begun. Communities were being cleared mercilessly, with the clergy unable or unwilling to denounce the evictions. Missions from the Free Church emerged, to recapture the faith of the island folk; only Barra and South Uist stayed Catholic, as today. The crofters remained without rights of tenancy until the Holding's Act of 1886 - by which time the profit-seekers had turned from sheep, for producing wool, to deer, for providing sport. The social upheaval and misery continued, aggravated by potato blights, and then by the decline of the fishing industries through lost menfolk from two world wars and the heavy competition of today's technology. It is a sturdy people that remain on the islands.

PART ONE

ARRAN TO ARDNAMURCHAN

Graham E Little

CHAPTER 1

ARRAN AND THE ISLANDS
OF THE FIRTH OF CLYDE

Arran and its neighbours form the southernmost group of islands along the west coast of Scotland. They are situated in the open outer reaches of the Firth of Clyde between the Ayrshire coast and the Kintyre peninsula, Arran occupying a central position and the other islands grouped round it.

Among these islands, and indeed among all the Scottish islands, Arran is outstanding for its character, variety and interest, not only for climbers, but for all who appreciate the many qualities of the Scottish islands. Its mountains are certainly the most striking feature of the island, a splendid group whose jagged outline rivals the Cuillin of Skye, but which on closer acquaintance turns out to be much more amenable to hillwalkers of modest ambitions.

The other islands of the Firth of Clyde inevitably suffer by comparison. Bute and the Cumbraes are not mountainous, but very much resorts for summer holiday makers, although Bute has enough by way of low hills and moorland to satisfy many a walker. The rocky peak of Ailsa Craig rising steeply from the southernmost reaches of the Firth might be thought from its appearance to be a rock climber's paradise, but surprisingly this is not as yet the case. Finally, Sanda and Davaar are two small islands lying close to the Kintyre peninsula which are of interest principally to explorers of Scotland's coastline, but not her mountains.

ARRAN

MAPS : Ordnance Survey   1:50,000 Sheet 69
        Bartholomew   1:100,000 Sheet 44
        Harvey Mountain Map 1:40,000

PRINCIPAL HILLS
EASTERN GROUP

Goatfell	874m	991 415
North Goatfell	818m	990 422
Mullach Buidhe	829m	993 427
Cioch na h-Oighe	661m	999 439

Beinn Nuis	792m	955 399
Beinn Tarsuinn	826m	959 412
Beinn a'Chliabhain	675m	970 407
A'Chir	745m	966 421
Cir Mhor	799m	972 431
Caisteal Abhail	859m*	969 443
Ceum na Caillich	727m	976 443
Suidhe Fhearghas	660m*	986 451

WESTERN GROUP

| Beinn Bharrain | 721m | 901 427 |
| Beinn Bhreac | 711m | 906 443 |

ACCESS

Ardrossan to Brodick. Passenger and vehicle ferry operated by Caledonian MacBrayne. Crossing time : 55 minutes.

Claonaig (Kintyre) to Lochranza. Passenger and vehicle ferry operated by Caledonian MacBrayne. Crossing time : 30 minutes.

TRANSPORT

In summer bus services rendezvous with the ferry at Brodick Pier, taking circular routes around the north and south of the island. In winter these services are limited, with no Sunday service. Car and bicycle hire is available, as is a good taxi service (particularly useful in winter). Taking one's own bicycle or car for a longer stay is recommended

ACCOMMODATION

Ample hotel, guest house, self-catering and bed and breakfast accommodation exists at all the population centres. Contact the tourist information centre in Brodick (telephone 0770 2140). Brodick and Corrie both make good bases for the eastern hills. There is a campsite in lower Glen Rosa (grid reference 000 377) and more attractive camping, although without facilities, is available in lower Glen Sannox (grid reference 010 453) for a nominal charge. Bivouacking in the hills is another option, and howffs are available in several locations. Youth hostels are situated at Lochranza and Whiting Bay, although they are not ideally placed for access to the hills.

GENERAL DESCRIPTION

Arran, 32 kilometres long and 15 kilometres wide, and scarcely two hours journey from Scotland's industrial heartland, is an island of many attractions and contrasts. It is both a popular holiday resort, and a mountain wilderness which, among the Scottish islands, is second only in extent and grandeur to Skye. The name Arran is said to mean high island or kidney shape, and both versions are equally appropriate. Its dramatic mountain outline has captured the imagination of many artists and fired the enthusiasm of generations of mountaineers. The island dominates the Firth of Clyde and the entrance to Loch Fyne, being beautifully cradled to the west by Kintyre (from which it is separated by the Kilbrannan Sound), to the north-east by the Isle of Bute and to the east by the Ayrshire mainland. Only to the south is Arran exposed to the prevailing weather. Its glens and lower hills reflect this uniquely sheltered location with a richness of vegetation and general prosperity unparalleled in the Western Isles.

With the exception of Skye and Bute, Arran is the most frequented tourist resort of all the islands covered in this guide. That it has retained much of its natural charm and beauty speaks volumes for the resilience of both its inhabitants and its scenery. It is said that at the height of the season the natural population is swelled tenfold by all manner of incomers. Fortunately only a small minority of these are bound for the hills, the rest being fully occupied with the many other attractions that the island has to offer. In winter Arran is left largely to its own devices, the influx of summer visitors having left, and the residents adopted a less hectic pace of life; whilst the mountains attract only a few enthusiasts.

There is a marked contrast in character between the northern and southern parts of Arran which is principally due to differences in their geology. In the north, a sequence of Dalradian schists and Old Red Sandstone sediments is intruded by a huge mass of Tertiary granite. Further south, Permo-Triassic and Carboniferous sediments predominate, although igneous rocks are also important and include numerous dykes and sills, as well as a ring complex in the centre of the island.

The high mountains of the north are all carved from the Tertiary granite. This outcrops as a circular body some twelve kilometres in diameter, and consists of a coarse outer granite intruded by a finer-grained inner one. The finer granite occurs mainly west of Glen Iorsa and forms lower and more rounded hills, whereas the highest and most spectacular mountains (including Cir Mhor and Goatfell) lie further east on the coarse granite.

In the south, thick sills intruded into the Permo-Triassic rocks have produced many flat-topped hills and craggy headlands. Numerous dykes trending north-north-west cut through all the earlier igneous and sedimentary rocks. This 'swarm' of dykes is particularly well exposed along the south coast around Kildonan, where individual dykes stand out as walls from the softer sandstones. In the north where the dykes cut through harder granite, they have eroded out to form crumbling gullies and dramatic notches on the ridges, the Witch's Step being a striking example of the latter.

The influence of glaciation on the sculpting of the granite mountains is obvious. Classic examples of aretes, corries and U-shaped valleys can be recognised. Arran also possesses an extensive series of raised beaches varying in height from eight to thirty metres above present sea-level. A good example can be seen along the shore between Brodick and Sannox where a raised sea-cliff pierced by many former sea-caves and now draped in luxuriant vegetation lies several hundred metres back from the present shoreline. The eight metre raised beach provides a convenient level for the coast road which encircles the island.

With such a wealth of different rock types, and so many fine examples of igneous and glacial features, it is no wonder that Arran has become a Mecca for geologists.

Arran likewise has many features of archaeological and historical interest. Examples include the great Neolithic chambered cairn of Carn Ban near the head of the Kilmory Water and the fine standing stone circles of Machrie Moor, the gaunt keep of Lochranza Castle and the warm red sandstone pile of Brodick Castle, surrounded by rich gardens (bequeathed to the National Trust for Scotland). The Torrylin Cairn, the Auchagallon Stone Circle and the fort on Torr a' Chaisteal at Corriecravie are also worth a visit.

The southern half of the island, rising to 512 metres at Ard Bheinn, holds little of interest to the mountaineer, being dissected moorland, now extensively afforested, although some enjoyable walks can of course be found. The fine double cascade of Glenashdale Falls is worth a visit and can be approached from Whiting Bay by a forestry road on the north side of the valley. Several sections of the southern coastline provide excellent excursions. The grand thrust of Bennan Head at the southern extremity of the island with its natural prehistoric dwelling, the Black Cave (25 metres high at the entrance and 40 metres long) is a good example. Likewise the coastline north of Blackwaterfoot provides many features of interest from a lichen-draped wall of columnar quartz-felspar porphyry to the cave-riddled white sandstone cliffs further north. The largest cave, usually called King's Cave, contains a wide variety of graffiti, some of considerable antiquity.

The north of Arran has, until recently, escaped the blight of commercial coniferous afforestation, but regrettably the slopes above Corrie and the upper flanks of North Glen Sannox are now ploughed and planted, destroying the natural drainage pattern and ensuring an unnatural blanket of afforestation in years to come. In complete contrast, the Glen Diomhan National Nature Reserve, about 3 kilometres south-east of Catacol, was established in 1956 to conserve two species of rare whitebeam. These trees are found wild in north Arran but nowhere else in Britain.

THE HILLS

The peaks and ridges of Arran are arguably the most shapely of all the granite mountains in Scotland and although, with few exceptions, they do not provide the technical challenges of the Cuillin of Skye, they rank as some of the finest island mountains. Regrettably, an aspect of this popularity is the serious erosion that has taken place, not only on the tourist path up Goatfell but along all the ridges, deep trenches having been worn into the turf and gravel by the passage of many thousands of climbers.

The coarse grey granite produces mountain features unique in the islands; cyclopean buttresses with their characteristic vertical and horizontal fracture lines, vast boilerplate slabs, deeply eroded basalt dykes and great, dank, vegetated north faces.

Arran, like many of the islands, has traditionally been a place for summer

Cyclopean buttresses and boilerplate slabs on the flank of A'Chir

hillwalking. In winter, however, its hills have much to offer, their scars often masked and their virginity briefly renewed. Although snow rarely achieves a build-up comparable to that on the mainland mountains, good conditions are not uncommon, although due to the maritime influence they tend to be short-lived. On the other hand the peaks are more often cloud-free than their mainland counterparts. The increased seriousness of the Arran hills in winter should not be underestimated, as the bare granite slabs loose their fine frictional quality under a coating of ice and powder snow. Good, firm neve snow is something of a rarity.

The convenient configuration of the eastern peaks lends itself to ridge walking circuits of various lengths, the great glens of Rosa and Sannox effectively splitting this group into two halves. The pass between these two glens, called The Saddle, links the two halves of the group.

Access to the heart of the eastern group of hills is best achieved by one of two routes; from Brodick by the path up Glen Rosa, or from Sannox by the path up Glen Sannox. Both paths lead eventually to The Saddle. From Brodick one can drive, cycle or walk to Glenrosa farm, a distance of two kilometres. From there a good track leads up the glen for a further two kilometres to the footbridge across the Garbh Allt. Beyond there the path, though always obvious, becomes very eroded and boggy in places up the west side of the Glenrosa Water. At the foot of Coire Daingean the path divides, the main branch continuing up Glen Rosa and the other one leading north-west up the Fionn Choire below the splendid Rosa Pinnacle to reach quite easily the

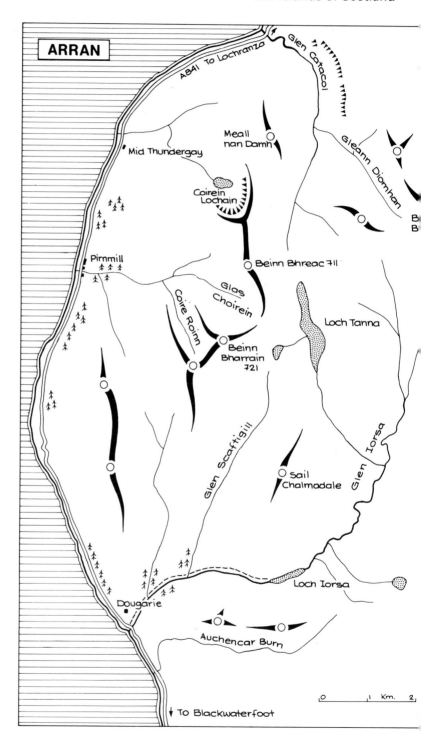

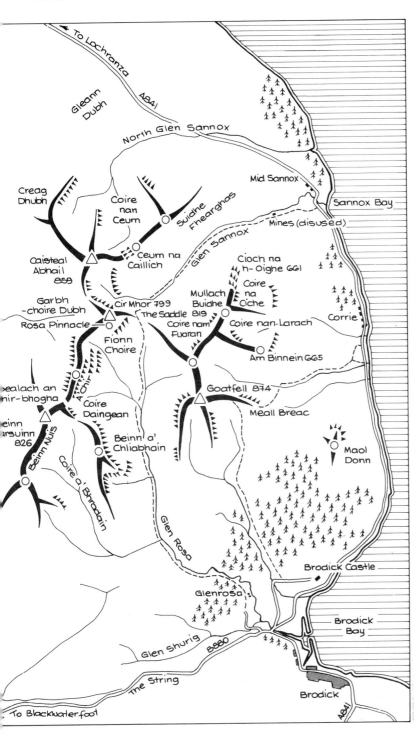

col between A'Chir and Cir Mhor. The path up Glen Rosa continues to climb easy slopes due north to The Saddle, nine kilometres from Brodick.

From Sannox Bay a narrow road on the south side of the Sannox Burn leads to a disused barytes mine in one kilometre. A path continues along the burn for three kilometres and then climbs steeply south to reach The Saddle. The last part of the ascent is particularly steep up an eroded dyke where loose rock and rubble is liable to be dislodged, and the path leads to a point about 100 metres north-west of the true col.

The four most popular excursions are:

1. A circuit of the peaks flanking Glen Sannox from Cioch na h-Oighe to Suidhe Fhearghas via Cir Mhor.
2. A circuit of the peaks flanking Glen Rosa from Goatfell to Ben Nuis via Cir Mhor.
3. The classic ridge traverse from Ben Nuis to Suidhe Fhearghas.
4. A traverse of the ridge from Goatfell to Cioch na h-Oighe.

Various shorter or longer combinations can be selected and for the very energetic a traverse of the whole group is possible, giving approximately 2,500m of ascent and taking about twelve hours for the round trip from Brodick.

The western group of hills provides a ridge traverse ideal for a short day. Although the two groups are widely separated, the ascent of all the main hills of Arran in a single day is feasible, but daunting.

THE EASTERN GROUP

Goatfell (Gaoth Bheinn - Gaelic - *the hill of the wind*) (874m)
Goatfell is by far the most prominent hill in Arran, not only because of its height, but also its position, rising directly above the Firth of Clyde behind Corrie, and separated from the other high tops by the long drop to The Saddle. It is the dominant feature of the view north-westwards from Brodick. Goatfell has a north-south summit ridge, with a prominent east ridge dropping from the summit towards High Corrie. Just less than a kilometre north of the summit, at North Goatfell, the main ridge divides, one branch dropping steeply to The Saddle and the other one leading north-east to Mullach Buidhe and Cioch na h-Oighe.

Goatfell is undoubtedly the most frequently ascended hill on Arran and possibly throughout the islands. In summer, the 'tourist route' to the summit from Brodick well justifies its name, all manner of ill-clad individuals making their holiday pilgrimage to the top of the island's highest peak. This route, commencing at the sawmill one and a half kilometres north of Brodick on the A841 road (grid reference 012 377) follows a well signposted track which crosses the road to Brodick Castle. Further on a left fork is taken and the track narrows to a well maintained path which leads through a delightful tunnel of rhododendron before breaking out onto more open ground to reveal the graceful grey cone of Goatfell framed in the vee of the afforested foreground valley. The path to the summit is obvious and well cairned across the shallow corrie, and reaches the east ridge of the mountain at 630m. The ascent can be enlivened by leaving the path where it enters the corrie and ascending the rocky south ridge.

An alternative and only slightly less popular route leaves the A841 road near the most southerly houses of Corrie. After passing the charming whitewashed cottages of High Corrie it follows the north bank of the Corrie Burn to a height of 400m, then crosses the burn to gain Meall Breac and continues up the east ridge to its junction with the previous route.

Ascents or descents on the Glen Rosa side of Goatfell are not recommended, being tedious and in places dangerous due to vast areas of steep, bare granite slabs.

The flat rocky summit sports a triangulation pillar, a viewpoint indicator and several perched boulders. The near and distant views are very fine and according to the indicator, Skiddaw in the Lake District is visible in ideal conditions, a distance of 169 kilometres. Everyone reaching the summit must be impressed, as was Sheriff Nicolson, by the "terrible congregation of jagged mountain ridges and fantastic peaks" and "the long sweep of Glen Rosa, so symmetrical, so green, so deep, and yet so near".

The north ridge of Goatfell, called Stacach, leads towards North Goatfell over three castellated tors which, if taken directly, offer good rock climbing to a moderate standard, the northerly one being the hardest. They can however be easily outflanked on either side by narrow tracks to a cairn on the col (761m) between Goatfell and North Goatfell. From this point a path bypasses the summit of North Goatfell on its east face.

North Goatfell (818m)

Although somewhat lower and less imposing that its neighbours, this is an important peak, being the junction of the main ridges. The highest point is not well defined, the slabby summit being long, narrow and fairly level. At its north-west end is the junction of the paths from the nearby Mullach Buidhe col (748m) and the more distant Saddle (432m) via the north-west ridge. This ridge, which involves some scrambling in its upper half, is characterised by extensive areas of granite in an advanced state of decay, forming slopes of ochre coloured gravel and grotesquely wind-sculptured rock statues. The lower part of the ridge is grassy and gives impressive views into Coire nam Fuaran with its array of weird rock buttresses and pinnacles.

Mullach Buidhe (*yellow top*) (829m)

A bulky hill with an array of minor tops, of which the southerly one is the highest. Two curving spurs jut out to the east, the southern one culminating in the minor peak of Am Binnein (665m), enclosing in a 'lobster claw' the lonely recess of Coire nan Larach. Both spurs provide enjoyable ascent routes from Corrie. From the northern end of Mullach Buidhe the path follows a wide ridge due north down to a col at the head of Coire na Ciche. From there a gravelly gully, harbouring a rotten pinnacle, gives a scrambling descent to the corrie. This col however is not the lowest point between Mullach Buidhe and Cioch na h-Oighe; it lies one hundred metres further north at an altitude of 670m. The west face of Mullach Buidhe is a maze of

Goatfell and Cir Mhor from the south ridge of Caisteal Abhail

slabs, gullies, buttresses and boulders, and a descent on this side should be avoided.

Cioch na h-Oighe (*the maiden's breast*) (661m)

Though of relatively low altitude, this superb little mountain vies with Cir Mhor as Arran's finest peak and is arguably Scotland's finest under 700m. In profile it is more of a ridge than an individual peak, although the name undoubtedly applies to the upthrust of the ridge at its termination. (The highest point of 692m is in fact further along the ridge, at grid reference 997 436). When viewed from lower Glen Sannox, Cioch na h-Oighe appears as a very sharp and well-defined peak, and its Gaelic name is seen to be very appropriate.

Coire na Ciche (the devil's punchbowl) is no less impressive than its parent mountain, a perfect miniature corrie bounded to the west by the 250m high vegetated rock wall that comprises the south-east flank of Cioch na h-Oighe, and to the east by a wide boulder-strewn ridge merging into the north slopes of Mullach Buidhe. It has a natural beauty and powerful tranquillity.

Various guidebooks have presented a distorted picture of the ascent and traverse of Cioch na h-Oighe, either making no reference to technical difficulty or warning the inexperienced mountaineer not to attempt it. In normal conditions, if the correct line is taken, following a fairly well marked path, an ascent from the north presents little more than a few short sections of scrambling up slabs which should

Looking down from Cioch na h-Oighe to Sannox

be within the capability of the average hillwalker. In winter, however, the difficulty of this ascent can increase considerably and it should not be attempted without the appropriate experience and equipment.

Commencing from the car park at South Sannox (grid reference 016 454), a road and then a track is followed for one kilometre up Glen Sannox to a ford over the Allt a'Chapuill. A path following the west bank of this burn leads to just below the lip of Coire na Ciche (grid reference 003 440) at a small cairn. The path now strikes north-west below the slabby face of Cioch na h-Oighe for 500 metres gaining height gradually to join the north ridge at an altitude of 400m. It then follows the ridge by the line of least resistance between rocky outcrops to the narrow airy summit. The narrow towered ridge leading to the sandy col at the head of Coire na Ciche is quite exposed, requiring care and offering some moderate rock climbing if the crest is strictly adhered to. These minor difficulties can however be outflanked on the west. The potentially serious consequences of a stumble on this ridge are tragically recorded by a grey granite plaque in the corrie (below the start of Ledge 4), being a memorial to W Norman Frazer McGregor "Who lost his life mountaineering and was found on this spot July 24 1929".

Views from this ridge down lower Glen Sannox to the pale sands of Sannox Bay with the foreground profile of Cioch na h-Oighe's great blank shield of granite, called The Bastion, are particularly dramatic. The five ledges that diagonally cross this face, although varying in difficulty, cannot be recommended as ascent routes.

As with the ascent of Cioch na h-Oighe, the traverse of its summit ridge is a much more serious proposition under winter conditions when snow-plastered rock and cornices may be encountered, providing a splendid climb for the experienced mountaineer (Grade II).

Beinn Nuis (*hill of the fawns* or *the face mountain*) (792m)
Beinn Nuis is the most southerly of the long ridge of granite peaks to the west of glens Sannox and Rosa. Its east face is an imposing 150m precipice, seamed by deep gullies, which is well seen when approaching Brodick by boat. The usual route of ascent is from Brodick via Glen Rosa, and this can be the start of a longer traverse northwards to Beinn Tarsuinn and A'Chir.

Leaving the track up Glen Rosa (qv) shortly before the Garbh Allt Bridge where a water pipe spans the Glenrosa Water, a path climbs diagonally across the hillside to the west to reach the Garbh Allt at a small dam. From there continue up this steep little burn for one kilometre either by a path (often very wet) on the grassy north bank, or by a narrow rocky (but usually drier) path on the steep south bank. Then bear north-west across the fairly level lower part of Coire a'Bhradain, still following a path to reach steeper slopes leading to the south-east ridge of Beinn Nuis. Easy walking up this ridge leads to the summit cairn. A granite tor, known as Caisteal an Fhinn, lies 200 metres west of the summit.

Beinn Tarsuinn (*the transverse* or *traverse mountain*) (826m)
A wide, easy angled grassy ridge joins Beinn Nuis to Beinn Tarsuinn with a col at 709m. The path skirts several bald rock towers flanking Coire a'Bhradain to the east; the Flat Iron Tower to the south of the col, and the Full Mead Tower to the north being the most distinctive. Beinn Tarsuinn is well named, its several minor tops being traversed before the summit is reached. From there fine contrasting views unfold, the serrated ridge from Goatfell to Cioch na h-Oighe to the east, westwards to the rounded spine of the hills beyond desolate Glen Iorsa, and north to the grey rock comb of A'Chir. Beinn Tarsuinn's most striking feature is without doubt the huge, nearly vertical rock wall known as the Meadow Face which rises for nearly 200m from a sea of slabs at the head of Coire a'Bhradain, buttressing the mountain's east face. The impressive form of this wall can be well appreciated from the col between Beinn Tarsuinn and Beinn a'Chliabhain. The descent down the north-east ridge to the Bealach an Fhir-bhogha (*pass of the bowman*) can be somewhat confusing in the mist as Consolation Tor and other rocky sections make the true ridge difficult to follow. All obstacles can, however, be avoided by keeping to the west side of the ridge and following the path.

The Bealach an Fhir-bhogha (684m) is not the lowest point between Beinn Tarsuinn and A'Chir, and it is not (in the normal sense of the word) a col. It does however provide easy access from Coire a'Bhradain to Glen Iorsa and is also the point where the ridge from Beinn a'Chliabhain joins the main ridge. A 40m high cyclopean wall drops to the north-east of the bealach with yet another rock wall below, forming the headwall of Coire Daingean. A link path, traversing between these walls, bypasses the Bealach an Fhir-bhogha and connects the A'Chir col with the ridge leading to the Beinn a'Chliabhain col (at grid reference 963 412). Under heavy snow this link path becomes quite exposed. In bad weather navigating in this area can be very difficult and great care should be exercised due to the proximity of numerous crags.

Beinn a'Chliabhain (*hill of the little cradle* or *hill of the sword*) (675m)

Although lower than its neighbours, Beinn a'Chliabhain, with its long north to south summit ridge, dominates middle Glen Rosa and is one of the best viewpoints on the island. Although the northern and western flanks are quite slabby, it boasts none of the great rock features so characteristic of the surrounding mountains.

Its convenient location makes Beinn a'Chliabhain an ideal climb for a short day, a starting point for a circuit of Coire a'Bhradain or the easiest approach to the A'Chir ridge from the south. The hill can be most easily climbed from the path on the north bank of the Garbh Allt (qv), striking north along another path over Cnoc Breac. The col (595m) between Beinn a'Chliabhain and Beinn Tarsuinn can be approached from Coire a'Bhradain to the south without difficulty. The ascent of the north side of this col from Coire Daingean is steeper, but not unduly difficult.

A'Chir (*the comb*) (745m)

This justly famous ridge, over one kilometre in length, is the most interesting on Arran and ranks with the finest in the country. Vast granite slabs fall to the west whilst its eastern flank is buttressed by steep walls falling into Coire Daingean and Coire Buidhe, creating a true knife edge arête on some sections. Its difficulty has been the subject of much debate and comparison, and although easier than the hardest sections of the Skye Cuillin, it should not be underrated. The easiest direction is from south to north as the most difficult sections are descended rather than ascended and route finding is fairly obvious. Much variation is possible, but if the easiest line is taken the rock climbing standard is mostly about moderate. If the true ridge is adhered to, the grade is considerably harder.

The easiest route to the summit of A'Chir is the south-west ridge, whose foot is reached either from Beinn Tarsuinn or Beinn a'Chliabhain (qv) or by a steep climb from the head of Coire Daingean. The ridge itself gives an easy scramble over the succession of rounded towers which form the crest of the slabby face overlooking Coire Dangean.

The true summit of A'Chir is a huge square granite block which offers no easy ascent route. Some ingenuity or rock climbing ability is required to reach the top; the south side is the easiest.

Continuing northwards, the most problematic section of the traverse is at the *Mauvais Pas* (or *Le Mauvais Pas* to the linguistically accurate). This section lies about 300 metres north of the summit. After a steep step in the ridge, turned on the west flank, a narrow cleft in the ridge, across which one can step without difficulty, is reached. Beyond this lies a short, level section terminating in a vertical rock wall dropping to a little col. The correct route is to descend the right (east) side of the

On the A'Chir ridge

ridge roughly mid-way between the gap and the termination (small cairn and faint arrow), initially by a steep 5m high wall with good holds, then a grassy ledge becoming a rock trench cutting across an exposed wall. The final section is a short chimney giving access to the col. In ascent this chimney is awkward (Very Difficult and polished). The section immediately north of this col is particularly good, and the ridge continues with decreasing difficulty towards Cir Mhor. The whole ridge can be outflanked on the west side by a well-defined path skirting the base of the crags.

The A'Chir ridge gives a superb and challenging winter traverse, the slabby nature of the rock making even the easier-angled sections difficult under unconsolidated snow. It is certainly more difficult than the Aonach Eagach in Glen Coe and

Cir Mhor from Beinn a' Chliabhain

will normally be around Grade III, taking about two to three hours. The crux is probably the Mauvais Pas, the trench banking up with snow and greatly increasing the exposure, but several other sections can be equally difficult.

Cir Mhor (*the great comb*) (799m)
It is hard to avoid superlatives when describing this magnificent peak which ranks as one of Scotland's finest and features so widely in climbing literature. All the ingredients of ideal mountain form are present, from its classic symmetrical shape, so well appreciated from almost any angle, to its position of splendid isolation at the very centre of the Arran Hills.

The summit of Cir Mhor is a short and narrow rocky ridge with a distinct feeling of space all around, with the U-shaped glens of Sannox and Rosa stretching away to the sea and the splendour of the remaining Arran peaks all about. The mountain possesses two equally striking, yet markedly contrasting rock faces; to the north a vast damp and sombre pile, to the south the clean cut architecture of the Rosa Pinnacle and its flanking ridges.

When viewed from the northern half of the A'Chir ridge or from the path up the Fionn Choire, the separate rock features of the south face can be clearly distinguished. Dominant is the Rosa Pinnacle, rising from a sea of grassy slabs into a great upsweep of perfect grey granite. Its lower west flank is a vast expanse of clean arching slabs, (many fine rock climbs) topped by a big roof; its upper east face

The Rosa Pinnacle

is a much steeper cracked wall overlooking Sub Rosa Gully. To the east of this gully (not a recommended line of ascent or descent) lies the low, whaleback buttress taken by the route *Prospero's Peril* (Severe). West of the Rosa Pinnacle, beyond the repulsive fan-shaped scoop of Green Gully, is a vertical walled buttress on which is the classic little rock route *Caliban's Creep* (Difficult, but not designed for the over-stout climber). Further west, beyond a deep, wide, boulder-filled gully (which can be ascended with care) is the blocky *Cubic Ridge* (Difficult).

The north-east face is less distinctive in structure, being a mass of steep, vegetated slabs and walls cut by a variety of damp gullies. The westernmost gully is appropriately named West Gully with the larger and deeper Western Stone Shoot to its east. Neither can be recommended in summer, being loose and unpleasant, but in good winter conditions they provide pleasant snow climbs, at about Grade II. Near the east side of the face is the obvious Gully A, blocked by two enormous chockstone constrictions, and as yet unclimbed. Although there are one or two good rock climbs, this side of Cir Mhor is essentially a place for winter climbing.

The ascent of Cir Mhor from either Brodick or Sannox is probably best made by first climbing to The Saddle by one of the paths described on page . From the Saddle the climb is steep, though straightforward if the path is followed up through mixed terrain with rock outcrops to end abruptly at the summit. An enormous granite block, the Rosetta Stone, sits just south of the summit, its ascent and descent being an exercise in nerve and friction. The return to Brodick can be varied by descending the broad easy south-west ridge to the A'Chir - Cir Mhor col at 591m and then dropping down into the Fionn Choire where there is a good path. The direct return to Sannox is best made by The Saddle.

As noted above, the ascent of the south-west ridge is easy. This is the natural route of ascent if one is traversing from A'Chir. The north-west ridge of Cir Mhor, by which one would make the ascent if coming from Caisteal Abhail, is also easy. The west face of Cir Mhor above the head of Garbh-choire Dubh is fairly bouldery but not craggy, and it is quite easy to traverse horizontally across this face between the cols at the lower ends of these two ridges. A well-defined path marks the line of this traverse.

Caisteal Abhail (*stronghold of the ptarmigan*) (859m)

This complex mountain, popularly known as The Castles, throws out four ridges from its castellated summit. The north-westerly one forms a great arc enclosing Garbh-choire, with the minor top of Creag Dubh near its termination. Due north a bold spur thrusts out, dividing Garbh-choire to the west from Coire nan Ceum to the east. Near its termination, on the east flank, lies Cuithe Mheadhonach (*central stronghold*), an imposing grey cyclopean wall. The narrow east ridge leads over several minor tops (the highest being 760m) to the great cleft of The Witch's Step, slabby buttresses falling to the north along its full length. To the south is a gentle curving ridge leading to the col at 624m between Caisteal Abhail and Cir Mhor.

Caisteal Abhail is probably most frequently ascended from Sannox by the north-east ridge over Suidhe Fhearghas and Ceum na Caillich, an excellent route

Cir Mhor and Caisteal Abhail from North Goatfell

which is described below. (See Suidhe Fhearghas). The ascent up Glen Sannox to the col at its head between Cir Mhor and Caisteal Abhail is not recommended as the climb to the col is steep and rocky.

From Brodick a long, but perfectly easy route of ascent goes up Glen Rosa and the Fionn Choire to the A'Chir - Cir Mhor col, then north across the west face of Cir Mhor and finally up the easy south ridge of Caisteal Abhail to its summit.

From Lochranza one can walk up the path in Gleann Easan Biorach for three kilometres and reach the north-west ridge of Caisteal Abhail near Creag Dubh.

Suidhe Fhearghas (*seat of Fergus*) (660m)
Ceum na Caillich (*the witch's step*) (727m)
These two tops lie on the long north-east ridge of Caisteal Abhail, the ridge which provides the best ascent of that mountain. The south flank of this ridge drops very steeply into Glen Sannox; so steeply that ascents of this side tend to be extremely tedious. The north side of the ridge drops much more gently into Coire nan Ceum.

Suidhe Fhearghas is the most northerly of the main granite hills of Arran, and although easy of access it is a marvellous viewpoint. The vast and complicated rock structure of the north-east face of Cir Mhor, and the general configuration of the Sannox hills can be well appreciated from its summit. Legend has it that King Fergus the First ascended the hill to survey his kingdom, and sat on the summit to dine in state.

One kilometre to the south-west towards Caisteal Abhail is Ceum na Caillich. Strictly speaking the name applies to the striking gash (667m) that is such a prominent feature of Arran's mountain skyline. The name, however, is more often used for the fine little pointed rock peak to the east of the gap. Deep gullies fall to the north and south from the gap, but due to their loose nature they cannot be recommended as approach routes to the ridge except in conditions of firm snow, when they may give enjoyable climbs of about Grade I or II.

The normal route of ascent of Suidhe Fhearghas and Ceum na Caillich and the onward traverse to Caisteal Abhail starts at the bridge over the burn in North Glen Sannox at grid reference 994 468. A path leads south up the flank of the glen to reach the north-east ridge and then easily to the summit of Suidhe Fhearghas, a distance of two kilometres. The ridge from

Ceum na Caillich, the Witch's Step

there to Ceum na Caillich drops to 577m at the col, and provides over one kilometre of delightful walking with glorious views of the Firth of Clyde and the Ayrshire coast.

The descent from Ceum na Caillich to the gap is steep and difficult (in hillwalking terms). Climb down rightwards, on the north side of the crest, by a little gully or chimney to reach the top of a smooth slab above the gap. Descend this slab with caution and friction, keeping close to its inner edge where it forms an open chimney in which jamming gives some security. It is possible to avoid these difficulties by leaving the ridge a short distance north-east of the rocky top of Ceum na Caillich, and traversing rightwards along turfy ledges on the north-west side of the peak to reach a point about 10m below the gap.

From the gap there is a short steep climb to reach the more level ridge which continues over a small bump and a few little tors to reach the summit of Caisteal Abhail.

THE WESTERN GROUP

This group of hills, completely separated from the eastern group by the wide Glen Iorsa and much intervening moorland, comprises a horseshoe shaped ridge, whose eastern flank presents a regular smooth slope, its western side being more craggy, with bold projecting spurs. Although composed of a similar, though finer-grained granite, to their eastern counterparts, they have in general succumbed more to the forces of erosion and present a softer outline. They give an enjoyable traverse, providing easy walking with fine views and some interesting mountain features. The round trip from Pirnmill is ideal for a short day, taking four to five hours. The traverse can be conveniently tackled in either direction, but probably the most rewarding start is up the north-west ridge of either the south or north top of Beinn Bharrain.

Beinn Bharrain (*barren mountain*) (721m)

This is a fine hill possessing two distinct tops nearly one kilometre apart. The north-east one(also known as Mullach Buidhe) is the higher, the south-west one the more impressive. They both have well-defined ridges to the north-west enclosing the narrow recess of Coire Roinn. An ascent of either of these two ridges is most enjoyable. The one leading to the north-west top is of particular interest and character as it is rocky and narrow, and provides exposed scrambling for several hundred metres. (First known ascent by W Naismith and partner, July 1910). Under snow this ridge gives a splendid ascent (Grade II). If this route is chosen, a detour to ascend the south-west top (717m) is a must as it is guarded by easy though impressive granite slabs and tors. The easterly tor is known as Caisteal na h-Iolaire (castle of the eagle) and presents a short vertical wall to the north-west.

From the triangulation pillar on the summit of Mullach Buidhe a wide ridge drops to the north-east to Bealach an Fharaidh (574m) and exhibits fine examples of soil slip terracing.

Beinn Bhreac (*speckled hill*) (711m)

The ascent of Beinn Bhreac from Bealach an Fharaidh is an easy but exhilarating stroll, the long clear waters of Loch Tanna glinting alluringly to the east, and beyond that the outline of the main Arran ridges. A nearly level section followed by a stony whaleback ridge leads to the large summit cairn.

The broad ridge continues in descent for one kilometre to a minor top of 653m. From there two options are open, either to descend via the north or the west-north-west ridge which form the enclosing arms of Coirein Lochain. If the former is taken, a good path can be gained crossing the col to the south of Meall Bhig and descending to Mid Thundergay. If the latter is taken the same path can be joined lower down. However, a visit to the pale gravel beaches and crystal clear waters of the Fhionn Lochan is highly recommended. This lochan is unique in Arran, and a place of great atmosphere often enhanced by the haunting screech of red throated divers.

This outing can be pleasantly extended by including an ascent of the steep and isolated Meall nan Damh (570m) and thence to Catacol Bay via its north ridge. This hill is particularly prominent when viewed from Claonaig in Kintyre.

PATHS AND WALKS

The path from Brodick to Sannox through Glen Rosa and Glen Sannox gives the finest excursion of its kind in Arran; a superb walk of 14 kilometres through the heart of the mountains. A good day should be chosen to fully appreciate the atmosphere and contrasts of these two fine glens and their surrounding granite peaks. The route up Glen Rosa has been described on p . There is a short section of slight difficulty on the north side of The Saddle, the pass between the two glens, and care is required when descending from The Saddle towards Glen Sannox. Do not attempt to descend north from the lowest point of the col, but look for a small cairn about 100 metres north-west of that point. This cairn indicates the start of the descent route to an eroded dyke which is descended either directly or by its right flank with a little scrambling. Great care should be taken as there is much loose rock and rubble which can be easily dislodged.

Continuing the descent down Glen Sannox, the path quickly improves and the option of paths on either the left or right bank of the Sannox Burn is available. As in Glen Rosa, beautiful pools may tempt the overheated walker to take a refreshing plunge, although the water can rarely be described as other than icy.

In lusher, lower Glen Sannox the old barytes workings are worth inspection, and the path becomes a well-defined track. Shortly before the main road is reached, at grid reference 016 454, there is an ancient gargoyle carved on a sandstone pillar built into the graveyard wall. A bus (infrequent) or taxi (convenient phone box at roadside) assists the return to Brodick.

Another classic path walk is around the Cock of Arran in the north-east, from Lochranza to North Sannox via the isolated cottage of Laggan. It provides a non-taxing and very scenic excursion of about ten kilometres. An alternative start takes a well-defined path starting at grid reference 946 502, crossing the ridge then joining the previous route at Laggan. Two kilometres before reaching North Sannox the famous Fallen Rocks can be seen, the result of massive rock face exfoliation.

Glen Catacol gives a delightful walk, the path fading into boggy ground just before Loch Tanna is reached. A very good circuit, mostly on established paths, is to branch off Glen Catacol, ascend Gleann Diomhan to a col at 407m, skirt around the south flank of Beinn Bhreac (573m) then descend Gleann Easan Biorach to Lochranza.

Glen Iorsa looks a tempting walk but in fact gives very hard going over hummocky and marshy terrain, a popular breeding ground for midges - not recommended. Coastal walks in the south of the island can make a pleasant change from the hills.

ROCK CLIMBING

Guidebook: *Climbers Guide to Arran, Arrochar and the Southern Highlands*, by K Crocket and A Walker (Scottish Mountaineering Club, 1989).

The vast amount of literature devoted to Arran rock climbing speaks volumes for its distinctive and addictive nature. Arran granite however is not, as is often claimed, totally unique in Scotland, having parallels in the Cairngorms and other scattered localities in the west. However, the island setting certainly imbues it with a strong, individual flavour unmatched elsewhere in the British Isles. It is not the easiest of rock to adapt to, "holds usually materialise where least, and vanish where most expected". It is often damp, disintegrating or vegetated and not infrequently a combination of all three. Despite these drawbacks, the sheer quantity of exposed rock and general steepness of the crags ensures plenty of attractive and relatively clean lines. Friction is excellent, although when wet the abundant lichen growth can cause problems. The Arran rock climber learns to live with the turf 'caterpillars' that abound (providing easy walk-offs on some routes) and at times is even grateful for the occasional grass hold.

Quality climbs now abound in every grade and Arran's finest routes compare favourably with the best in the country. Even the shorter routes have a mountaineering feel about them, no doubt partly due to the surrounding mountain grandeur. Access to even the most remote crags is within the scope of a day, although the pleasures of bivouacking in one of Arran's numerous howffs should not be missed, providing the opportunity for a longer day on the rocks.

The nature of the routes varies from slab climbing, with good friction, to strenuous steep faces, often presenting holdless cracks and blank walls. Spring is normally the best time for rock climbing, although even in the wet days at the end of the year good sport may be had if the right route is chosen. The harder routes, however, require a few days of dry weather for pleasurable ascents.

A good introduction to Arran rock can be found on the fine clean routes on the south face of Cir Mhor, particularly the much celebrated classics of *Sou-Wester Slabs* (Very Difficult), *South Ridge Direct* (Very Severe) and *West Flank Route* (Hard Very Severe), on the Rosa Pinnacle, although many less well-known quality climbs abound.

The array of slabby buttresses in Coire Daingean, on the east flank of the south-west ridge of A'Chir, provides a good selection of middle grade routes. The classic *Pagoda Ridge* (Severe) and its harder neighbour *Mosque* (Hard Very Severe), both on the highest buttress, are perhaps the best routes in the corrie.

For the higher grade climber, Arran's premier location is *The Bastion* on the east face of Cioch na h-Oighe, an 80 metre high, nearly vertical granite wall with many high quality routes in the 'E' grades. A delectable girdle of the upper Bastion is taken by *Tidemark* (Severe), although it has been claimed that the crux is reaching the start of the route, for the way lies over steep friable granite and loose vegetation.

Blinder, Brobdingnag, Brachistochrone and *Bogle* are an alliteration of long, daunting extreme routes on the Meadow Face of Beinn Tarsuinn (named after the

Climbers on Sou-Wester Slabs on the Rosa Pinnacle

small but prominent patch of turf at its base). This is no place for the novice.

A cluster of small buttresses outcrop on the south-east flank of Caisteal Abhail, high above Coire na h'Uaimh. They provide a variety of middle grade routes of indifferent character. At the top of this corrie is a belt of steep slabs of minor interest, the direct version of the delightfully named *Slapstick Wall* (Severe) being about the best route.

High on the hillside above Glen Rosa great expanses of slabs plate the western slopes of Goatfell. Numerous routes are recorded although it is possible to climb almost anywhere when the rock is clean and dry. The smaller South Slabs are the cleanest with the evocatively named *Blank* (Severe) of greatest merit.

The striking cyclopean wall of Cuithe Mheadhonach, Arran's most recently developed mountain crag, lies on the west flank of Coire nan Ceum. Routes are mainly in the upper grades and of high quality. For character, *Fuoco* (Very Severe) can be recommended; for controversy, *Achilles* (E3) is a must.

Outwith the main mountain area, rock climbing is available at Torr Nead an Eoin (schist) overlooking Lochranza, Maol Donn (sandstone) south of Corrie, sea-cliffs to the north of Blackwaterfoot and the remarkable *Black Cave Pillar* (Hard Very Severe) at Bennan Head in the south. Roadside bouldering (granite) around Corrie can give sport on an off day, the Cat Stone at grid reference 020 444 being the best. Considerable scope for exploratory rock climbing still exists on Arran.

HOLY ISLAND AND PLADDA

Surprisingly Arran has just two satellite islands, the larger and more accessible being Holy Island, its three kilometre long spine almost blocking the mouth of Lamlash Bay and thereby creating a fine, sheltered natural harbour. During the Second World War it was used as a base for the Atlantic Fleet and in recent years has been the venue for a major sea angling competition. In the summer months a regular ferry operates from Lamlash, but a more traditional approach is to swim from Kingscross Point (grid reference 056 283) to the lighthouse at the south-east point of the island.

In earlier times the Irish monk St Molios, chose a cave on Holy Island as his residence (still visible at grid reference 058 297) with, for the 6th century, every modern convenience. He is reported to have lived to the age of 130.

A coastal circuit of the island, about half by path, makes a good outing and an ascent to the highest point of Mullach Mor (314m) is a must if only to appreciate the grand view of the northern Arran peaks. The northern ridge gives the least steep approach; other flanks of the hill are rocky and precipitous, particularly to the east, and should not be descended. The feral goats are surprisingly indifferent to man's presence considering the 'sporting' cull to which they are occasionally subjected. The east facing Creag Liath at grid reference 062 293 should provide some good rock routes up to about 30m.

Pladda, lying over one kilometre south of Kildonan, often with turbulent intervening seas, attains a height of just 20m. It is a haunt of seals and bird life, including common and arctic terns, shelduck and rarer migrant visitors.

BUTE

MAPS *:*   Ordnance Survey   1:50,000 Sheet 63
             Bartholomew   1:100,000 Sheet 44

PRINCIPAL HILLS
  Windy Hill   278m   043 698
  Kilbride Hill   256m   030 694

ACCESS
Wemyss Bay to Rothesay. Passenger and vehicle ferry operated by Caledonian MacBrayne. Crossing time : 30 minutes.
Colintraive (mainland Argyll) to Rhubodach (north-east Bute). Passenger and vehicle ferry operated by Caledonian MacBrayne. Crossing time : 5 minutes.

Public bus service, taxis, car and bicycle hire (Rothesay).

ACCOMMODATION
Good choice of hotels, guest houses and self-catering at Rothesay, Port Bannatyne and Kilchattan, plus other more rural accommodation. Information from the Tourist Office, Rothesay, telephone 0700 2151.
    There are no organised campsites. Permission to camp should be sought at Bute Estates Office, Rothesay or ask locally.

GENERAL DESCRIPTION
The island of Bute, 25 kilometres long by ten at its widest, closely hugs mainland Scotland and indeed was probably connected at its northern extremity until relatively recently. Both to the north-west and north-east the narrow sea passage of the Kyles of Bute give it island status, whilst to the south it thrusts into the Firth of Clyde between northern Arran and the Cumbraes.
    It is tempting to dismiss Bute as a mere tourist resort of no interest to the lover of wild and lonely places, but just as in the heart of Glasgow lie green parklands, so on Glasgow's traditional holiday isle there can be found pockets of emptiness and beauty more characteristic of Scotland's farther flung islands.
    The link between Glasgow and Bute is, however, more than just compara-tive, as the visitor disembarking at Rothesay will readily appreciate. The grand red and blond sandstone houses with their elaborate ornamentation were built by the same Victorian craftsmen as were responsible for much of Glasgow's finest architecture, and funded by the same wealth from a prospering merchant city. Rothesay now possesses an air of decaying gentility.
    The Highland Fault line cuts through the middle of Bute, giving higher ground and igneous rocks to the north, although even this area is Lowland in character. The southern half of the island is primarily sandstone, with basaltic intrusions in the extreme south, and provides much rich agricultural land.

Looking south from Dunagoil across the Sound of Bute to Arran

Bute is rich in antiquities and the exhibits from several excavations can be seen in the museum at Rothesay, as can the island's wildlife and more recent cultural heritage. Nearby are the imposing remains of Rothesay Castle, built in the 12th century by the Norse King Magnus Barelegs, but now rather incongruous in its urban setting. The still occupied Kames Castle dating from the 14th century, five kilometres north-west of Rothesay, is a classic tower house, although the miniature castle half a kilometre north of this must rank as the ideal fortified residence.

Numerous chambered cairns and Iron Age forts litter the island, the fort at Dunagoil (occupied 200BC to 200AD) in the south being perhaps the most impressive with its atmospheric location and vitrified ramparts. An ebbing tide reveals fine red sands in the bay nearby.

Bute was greatly favoured in Monastic times. Evidence of this ranges from the simple, lonely hut of St. Ninian's Chapel of the 6th century (grid reference 034 612), on its eponymous peninsula, to the extensive complex around St Blane's Church (grid reference 095 534) lying in a slight valley and surrounded by a stand of mature mixed woodland. Although the church itself is Norman (12th century) with gables still standing, a nearby circular structure, built from enormous stone blocks, is probably a monastic cell dating from the 6th century.

The island of Inchmarnock to the west of Bute, rising to a height of 60 metres, has its own monastic relics, although its greatest archaeological treasure is a Bronze

Age lignite necklace, dating from circa 1500BC, found in 1953 and now displayed in the museum at Rothesay.

THE HILLS

The broad heather and yellowing grass-streaked hills in the north of Bute are divided into two groups by the deep valley of Glen More with the highest tops to the east. All the hills can be ascended with ease and are of limited interest other than providing fine views over to the peaks of Arran.

The triangulation pillar-crowned summit of Windy Hill (278m), the island's highest eminence, is about one hour's walk from Kames Bay. Kames Hill (268m) (grid reference 052 693), the south-east outlier of Windy Hill, gives the best viewpoint looking across Ettrick Bay. The most enjoyable ascent of Kilbride Hill (256m) to the west is via its southern ridge.

A long, broad ridge lies to the west of Glen More giving a good 7 kilometre walk, with the highest point of Torran Turach (227m) about mid-way.

None of the island's central hills are of any note although the small hills in the extreme south are worth climbing, particularly the conical St Blane's Hill (123m) (grid reference 095 526) with its very steep grassy slopes and basalt crag-flanked summit ridge. From the summit triangulation pillar a bird's-eye view of the curiously named farm of Plan and the surrounding farmland can be had, as well as a fine aspect of Little Cumbrae to the south-east. An opportunity should also be taken to explore the very rocky and indented southern coastline.

The highest hill in the south is the ridge of Torr Mor, rising to 149m at grid reference 103 532.

PATHS AND WALKS

A fine walk can be had around the north-western corner of Bute. Starting from the road end in the west, a quiet coast-hugging track is followed through mature oak woods to Kilmichael. A slight detour can be made to visit a chambered cairn and a small chapel giving good views down the Kyles of Bute. Although no continuous path is evident, a pleasant walk along the shore via Buttock Point at the northern tip of the island leads to the road end at Rhubodach. Allow about four hours.

Other coastal walks, particularly in the west, make enjoyable excursions.

ROCK CLIMBING

The only crags of any consequence lie in the south of the island, although they are more of a visible than a tangible attraction. The Hawk's Nib area, at grid reference 113 532, is about the best.

GREAT CUMBRAE AND LITTLE CUMBRAE

MAPS :   Ordnance Survey   1:50,000 Sheet 63
                                      1:25,000 Sheet 428 (NS05/15)
              Bartholomew   1:100,000 Sheet 44

PRINCIPAL HILLS

GREAT CUMBRAE
   Barbay Hill   127m   167 570
LITTLE CUMBRAE
   Lighthouse Hill   123m   142 514

ACCESS

Largs to Cumbrae (slipway at grid reference 183 586 on Great Cumbrae). Passenger and vehicle ferry operated by Caledonian MacBrayne. Crossing time : 10 minutes. A boat to Little Cumbrae can be hired at Millport.

TRANSPORT

A round-island bus meets the ferry, although given the size and road network of Great Cumbrae a bicycle is the ideal form of transport. Walking can be recommended for Little Cumbrae.

ACCOMMODATION

Ample hotel and guest house accommodation in Millport. Self-catering also available, details from Largs Tourist Office, telephone 0475 673765.

GENERAL DESCRIPTION

Both islands lie less than three kilometres from the Ayrshire coast opposite the southern end of Bute, providing superb views of Arran and the eastern coastline of Bute. Their similarities extend no further than this. Whereas Great Cumbrae is a fertile, well developed tourist haunt with the cathedral 'city' of Millport fronting its sheltered southern bay, Little Cumbrae is a rugged, infrequently visited island.

Barbey Hill (127m), the highest point on Great Cumbrae, can be reached by a narrow winding road to its summit.

To the east of Millport lies a marine research station with a museum and aquarium open to the public. Various interesting rock outcrops occur on the island including The Lion rock at grid reference 179 549, a basalt dyke thrusting through the old red sandstone.

A worthwhile day can be spent exploring Little Cumbrae. On the highest point stands an ancient lighthouse where a coal fire was kept burning in an open grate. A path crosses the island from opposite the square keep on Castle Island to the lighthouse complex on the west coast, with a 'Rest and be Thankful' at its highest point.

Various antiquities are worth inspection, including the remains of St Vey's Chapel, whilst the raised beach cliffs in the south provide entertainment for rock climbers and cave enthusiasts. As with Ailsa Craig, the island possesses some intriguing names, many referring to the marshy hollows that are a feature of the island, others more obscure. No self-respecting mountaineer could possibly leave Little Cumbrae before ascending Hill of Hills (grid reference 146 520)!

AILSA CRAIG

MAPS : 1:100,000 and 1:50,000 maps are of little value except to indicate the island's relationship to the mainland.
 The Ordnance Survey 1:25,000 or even better, 1:10,000 (parts of NX 09 NW and NS 00 SW but published as one sheet) are more relevant to the complex, closely packed nature of the topography.

HIGHEST POINT
    The Cairn   338m   019 998

ACCESS
A boat can be hired from Girvan (Telephone 0465 3219). Regular day trips are run during the summer months. Crossing time : approximately 1 hour.

ACCOMMODATION
The island can easily be explored in a day, but camping by the lighthouse or caves for bivouacking are available if required.
 It is a wise precaution to take spare food as unexpected extended stays due to bad weather are not unknown.

GENERAL DESCRIPTION
Ailsa Craig, affectionately known as Paddy's Milestone, is the archetypal island mountain; a symmetrical cone of primitive rock thrusting from the sea 14 kilometres west of the south Ayrshire coastline (16 kilometres from Girvan). It is the most southerly island dealt with in this guide, yet a symbol of great natural grandeur. Ailsa Craig is the Lowland's answer to the big stacks of the Hebridean seas.
 Only one kilometre in diameter and girdled by precipitous cliffs, it presents a front of impregnability; only to the east of the island is this hostile appearance relaxed where a complex of lighthouse buildings squat on the nose of grassy shingle. As well as for its classic profile, Ailsa Craig is famous for having been once the only source of curling stones which were exported throughout the world. The impressive quarried cliffs in the south of red, fine grained Reibickite (a micro-granite) were the source of many thousands of top quality stones. Other quarries produced grey stones. The remains of the narrow gauge railways serving these quarries are still visible.
 Ailsa Craig is also a well known bird sanctuary supporting a vast and varied

Ailsa Craig: Stranny Point and Water Cave

population including a large gannet colony, puffins, guillemots and kittiwakes. Despite its barren appearance, the island is surprisingly rich in flowers, particularly on the upper slopes.

The names of Ailsa Craig's natural features are of interest to the philologist and folk lore enthusiast alike, varying from the delightful and obvious *Spot of Grass* and *Nettley Howe* to the more obscure *Doras Yett* and *The Bourtrees*.

A coastal circuit of the island is a must, and apart from some awkward exposed sections on both sides of Water Cave (a miniature Fingal's Cave) in the south-west, best negotiated at low tide, it is a spectacular but easy walk. The stupendous 120m high wall of Barestack in the north-west is in its central section so steep and ledgeless that even nesting sea-birds avoid it - one of the most impressive sights in the islands.

An ascent to the highest point of Ailsa Craig by a well-defined zig-zagging path presents little difficulty, and continuous interest is maintained. At 110m the square roofless wall of a small castle can be inspected. The coat of arms of the Hamilton family (three stars) has been carved on a stone set in the wall. The path then meanders below crags before following the shallow valley of Garraloo to the miniature Garra Loch. The sensation of height gained as one ascends this path is as dramatic as on any hill, the pier and lighthouse quickly assuming a toy-like scale. The path heads due north across great 'roof tile' rock slabs, passing below the

A distant view of Ailsa Craig from Davaar

summit on its east and then switching back to make the final ascent to the natural stone triangulation pillar from the west. As can be expected the view is panoramic, the atmosphere unique in the Clyde.

ROCK CLIMBING

Difficult as it is to believe, no rock climbing has yet been recorded on the island although it is certain that the potential has long been recognised. Its total neglect can only be partly explained by the island being relatively difficult of access, a bird sanctuary and the subject of extensive quarrying. Loose, vegetated and bird-possessed rock does abound, but gigantic, relatively clean walls thrust uncompromisingly from the boulder beaches to a height of over 100 metres. The potential for hard rock climbing is immense, although in deference to the resident bird population and rough winter seas, it may well be restricted to a couple of months in late summer.

SANDA

MAPS :   Ordnance Survey   1:50,000 Sheet 68
             Bartholomew   1:100,000 Sheet 43

HIGHEST POINT
            Unnamed   123m   730 043

ACCESS
Boat by arrangement from Southend. Telephone 058 683 621.

GENERAL DESCRIPTION
Two kilometres in length by one wide, and lying three kilometres south of the southern tip of the Kintyre peninsula, Sanda is a surprisingly fertile island with ample evidence of earlier occupation and agriculture. Other than the manned lighthouse on a rocky stack-like headland in the south, there are now no inhabitants, although the dwelling near the jetty is still intact. A path links the two.

A ruined chapel with crosses, reputed to house the grave of St. Ninian, can be inspected at grid reference 727 045.

Numerous cave-riddled crags fringe the island and a pleasant few hours can be spent exploring these. The island's highest point, with the inevitable triangulation pillar, is easily ascended from the west and provides wonderful seascape views.

DAVAAR

MAPS : Ordnance Survey 1:50,000 Sheet 68
  Bartholomew 1:100,000 Sheet 43

HIGHEST POINT
            Unnamed   116m   757 199

ACCESS
On foot. (See General Description).

GENERAL DESCRIPTION
Lying at the entrance to Campbeltown Loch, on the west coast of Kintyre, Davaar only attains full island status when the tide is near full or when high seas are running. For much of the time it is linked to the mainland by a dog-legged spit of shingle, over one kilometre in length, called The Dhorlin (Doirlinn). The spit is a favourite haunt of waders and duck, particularly eider. Offshore the white darts of diving gannets can be seen and occasionally the sinister black hull of a nuclear submarine.

Davaar, covered in a patchwork of heather, bracken and short cropped grass, one kilometre at its widest, presents bold red cliffs of micro-granite to the south and east, backed by easier angled slopes to the north and west.

The only dwelling on the island is the lighthouse complex in the north, now unoccupied.

A traverse of the island's coastline makes an enjoyable expedition taking a leisurely three hours from the mainland.

The southern cliffs, the haunt of remarkably tame feral goats, are eroded into a variety of coves, ribs and caves above a boulder beach. The deepest cave, with two entrances (grid reference 760 199), contains the celebrated crucifixion painting, the work of the local artist Alexander MacKinnon. This life-sized figure of Christ was painted in 1887 and retouched by the artist in 1934, making effective use of the irregularities of the rock face to produce a three dimensional effect. The combination of artistic merit and incongruous setting produce a strangely moving vision.

The highest point of Davaar, flat and crowned with a triangulation pillar, provides fine and contrasting views in all directions. To the south-east, far across the sea, is the symmetrical profile of Ailsa Craig, its high western cliffs shining chalk white in the sunlight; to the west, at the head of the loch, the urban sprawl of Campbeltown looks more like some transported section of the Glasgow conurbation. An ascent to the highest point can be made in about twenty minutes from the Davaar end of The Dhorlin.

ROCK CLIMBING

Over one kilometre in length, with a southern aspect and reaching a maximum height of 60m, Davaar's cliffs have, surprisingly, received little attention. Despite their high angle and the conscientious grazing by a troop of agile goats, much of the rock is draped in grass, sea thrift, campion and lichen with blue splashes of wild hyacinth in the spring. Major routes would require extensive 'gardening' but scope for clean, shorter climbs exists. One hundred and fifty metres east of the 'crucifixion' cave a rib, pierced by an arch low down, gives an interesting exposed climb with a strenuous start (Severe).

CHAPTER 2

ISLAY AND JURA

These two large islands lie side by side in the wide entrance to the Firth of Lorn, the Kintyre peninsula to their east and Mull to their north. In character they are markedly different, Islay being for the most part low-lying, with only a few modest hills and high moorland in its south-east corner and some fine coastal cliffs elsewhere. Jura is quite the opposite, rugged and almost entirely hilly, an island wilderness with the distinctive Paps of Jura providing one of the best known outlines of the Western Isles, and giving one of the roughest of hill traverses. Both Islay and Jura are reached by ferry from Kennacraig in West Loch Tarbert.

    The small green island of Gigha can logically be included in this chapter, lying as it does between Islay and the Kintyre peninsula at the southern end of the Sound of Jura. It is reached by ferry from Tayinloan, 20 kilometres south of Kennacraig, so a visit to Gigha can be conveniently combined with a longer sojourn on its two bigger neighbours.

ISLAY

MAPS *:*   Ordnance Survey   1:50,000 Sheet 60
          Bartholomew   1:100,000 Sheet 43

PRINCIPAL HILLS

Sgorr nam Faoileann	429m	432 606
Glas Bheinn	472m	429 592
Beinn Bheigeir	491m	429 564
Beinn Bhan	472m	403 562

ACCESS

Air: Glasgow to Islay Airport (seven kilometres north-west of Port Ellen) Loganair, telephone: Port Ellen (0496) 2022

Sea: Kennacraig (Kintyre) to Port Askaig or Port Ellen. Passenger and vehicle ferry operated by Caledonian MacBrayne. Crossing times: 2 hours and 5 minutes and 1 hour and 50 minutes, respectively.

TRANSPORT

Good bus service from Port Askaig to Port Ellen. Most of the villages are in fact served by bus. Car and bicycle hire also available at Port Ellen.

Looking north across the Sound of Islay to the Paps of Jura

ACCOMMODATION

Numerous hotels, guest houses and caravans are available.
Telephone: Tourist Information Office, Bowmore (049 681) 254 (April to September) for details. "No camping" signs are prominently displayed in the south-east but, given the right approach, camping should be available over most of the island. There are several caravan sites, but no formal campsites.

GENERAL DESCRIPTION

Islay (pronounced *Ila*), the Queen of the Hebrides, is the most southerly of the main Hebridean islands and is separated from neighbouring Jura by the narrow Sound of Islay, barely one kilometre wide, between Port Askaig and Feolin Ferry. At this point the differences between Islay and Jura are strikingly displayed, from the mature wooded policies of Dunlossit House on the former, to the lone white cottage with its barren backdrop on the latter.

Islay has as many similarities with nearby Ireland as it has with Scotland. Indeed the Antrim coast, as can be well seen from the Mull of Oa on a clear day, is as close as the Scottish mainland. During the period between the 6th and 9th centuries Islay was in fact part of the Kingdom of Dalriada, ruled by the Scots, a race from the northern part of Ireland. Subsequently and for many centuries, Islay became the seat of the Lord of the Isles, the remains of this centre of power still being visible as crumbling ruins on an island in Loch Finlaggan.

As with many of the islands, Islay's diversity of scenery is, to a great extent, due to its geological structure; the hard quartzites forming barren uplands, mica-schist and limestone producing the rich agricultural land of the interior. The great indentations of Loch Gruinart to the north and Loch Indaal to the south almost divide Islay into two separate islands; the low lying neck of marshy ground joining the heads of these sea-lochs forming a tenuous link.

Perhaps Islay's main claim to fame rests upon its production of whisky, the island's eight distilleries producing malts of great character and distinctive peaty flavour. Four of these distilleries, Ardbeg, Lagavulin, Laphroaig and Port Ellen, lie along a six kilometre stretch of the island's southern coastline. It is doubtful if such a close concentration of distilleries exists anywhere else in the world. Sadly many of the distilleries are now closed or operating on short time.

Cheese production is also of some importance to the island's economy, its recently claimed aphrodisiac properties no doubt doing much to increase exports.

Islay is perhaps equally famed for the diversity of its wildlife, both resident and migratory. The sight of great skeins of geese thrashing the skies above Loch Gorm is an unforgettable experience; the unmistakable flash of the red beak and legs of the rarer chough as it glides over the cliffs of Oa equally so.

The island is also rich in antiquities, a profusion of standing stones, brochs and Celtic chapels covering all but the highest ground. Arguably the most notable antiquity is the Kildalton Cross (grid reference 458 508), believed by many authorities to be the finest of all Celtic crosses. Although beautifully carved, its proportions somehow offend the eye, not so much by the obvious twist of one arm of the cross, but more by its top-heavy nature. If the shaft were longer (perhaps it once was) it would probably have even more aesthetic appeal. Many fine carved graveslabs can be inspected within and without the adjacent roofless chapel, most impressive of all being the high relief of a knight, with longsword and dagger, set in a window alcove. Another slimmer, and perhaps equally attractive cross, surrounded by carved graveslabs, exists at Kilchoman (grid reference 216 632).

Much of Islay's agricultural land, and indeed its many villages are sheltered from the worst effects of winter storms by the surrounding headlands. These bold coastlines, particularly that of the Mull of Oa to the south-west of Port Ellen, are of great interest to the lover of wild and rugged scenery. This spectacular coastline, part schist, part pink quartzite, takes the full force of the Atlantic swell and is weathered into a fantastic array of coves, bays and stacks. Its most prominent landmark is the American monument (grid reference 270 415) a tall, solid pointed stone tower commemorating the lives lost in the wrecks of the transporters *Tuscania* and *Otranto* in 1918. Part of the inscription reads:

'On Fame's Eternal camping ground
Their silent tents are spread
While Glory keeps with solemn round
The bivouac of the dead'

To the south-east of the monument lies Dun Athad, an iron age hill fort. Although there are better preserved examples in Scotland, few can equal its superb situation or impregnable position. The 108m high stack, on which the dun is built, is connected to the mainland by a grassy neck and the remains of ramparts and wall footings are clearly visible. A large population of multi-coloured feral goats inhabit the Oa coastline, their surefootedness on the steep crumbling crags being remarkable.

The western coastline of the Rhinns and the extreme north-west coastline of Islay also provide good walking with dramatic scenery. The latter, in particular, a continuation of Jura's west coast, is a beachcombers' paradise with extensive raised beaches, boulder-filled coves and numerous caves (see Walks).

Islay has surprisingly few satellite islands of any consequence. In the north-west, a short distance off Ardnave Point, lies Nave Island (height 34m) which holds the ruins of an ancient chapel, but perhaps of greater interest is a remarkable, narrow, cliff-flanked, defile called Sloc na Maoile that virtually cuts the island in two. Lying one kilometre offshore south of the Laphroaig Distillery is the curiously named Texa. It also possesses a ruined chapel, and attains a height of 48m at Ceann Garbh.

THE HILLS

From a brief glance at a map it would be easy to conclude that Islay is of little or no interest to the mountaineer, and indeed compared to neighbouring Jura the hills do lack stature and distinctive form. However, they more than compensate for these failings in providing marvellous rough walking and a seemingly limitless panorama of sea and distant island peaks.

The main hill group lies in the south-east of the island and can be tackled from a base at Bridgend or Bowmore to the west or from the Claggain Bay area in the east. A complete traverse of these hills from Port Askaig to Port Ellen is well worthwhile, involving one to two days' hard walking and taking best advantage of the variable ferry service from the island's two ports. This itinerary is dealt with in the individual hill descriptions, although shorter excursions can of course be undertaken. The hills of Islay are composed of the same band of hard quartzite that comprises most of Jura, and although much rock outcrops, there is a total absence of cliffs other than coastal. The similarity also extends to the red deer population, and it is said that these hardy beasts often brave the fast tide race to visit their neighbouring island relatives. Deep glens run eastward from the hills to the coast whilst extensive heather-clad moorland extends in other directions.

In the far north of Islay there is a similar, though lower lying hill area culminating in Sgarbh Breac, (364m) (grid reference 406 766) which can conveniently be ascended from Bunnahabhainn.

Sgorr nam Faoileann (*rocky peak of the beach*) (429m)
This aptly named rocky peak, the most northerly of the main Islay hills, is of some character and commands a marvellous view up the Sound of Islay. Numerous ribs of white and rose tinged quartzite rupture the thin peat and heather cladding. The obvious line of ascent, from the north-west, is to gain its west shoulder via a path commencing at Storakaig (grid reference 404 619) and thence, by a short scramble,

reach the summit cairn. To the south lies a flat grassy col at 258m with springs, where the now faint line of the aforementioned path, leading to Proaig on the east coast, can be traced. A tumbled stone dyke links the flanks of Sgorr nam Faoileann and Glas Bheinn to the south.

Glas Bheinn (*grey hill*) (462m)
Broken ground leads from the 258m col to a broad stony ridge which gives pleasant walking to a cluster of rocky hummocks, the most southerly being the actual summit of Glas Bheinn. From the north-east flank of this hill a wide ridge runs east to the rounded, heather-clad Beinn na Caillich (*hill of the old woman*) (337m) which overlooks McArthur's Head and its lighthouse (so distinctly seen from the ferry).

A short, nearly level ridge flanked by glaciated slabs runs south from the summit, with a cluster of lochans in the corrie to the west. Some 500 metres along this ridge broad spurs branch west and east, whilst after a steepish slope the main ridge continues south.

Beinn Bheigeir (491m)
The northern slopes of Beinn Bheigeir, the highest hill on Islay, carry extensive scree cover although tongues of grass and heather allow a steep but trouble-free ascent. The summit is crowned by a triangulation pillar surrounded by a circular dry stone wall. On a clear day, particularly in spring, the views from this hill are magnificent. To the north, in the foreground, lie the barren hills of Islay with the distinctive Paps of Jura behind. In the background are the islands of Mull, Rhum and Skye, their serrated skylines floating on the Hebridean sea; a promise of many great mountain days. To the south-east the bold peaks of Arran rise behind the spine of Kintyre, and to the west is a rolling brown landscape with Ireland beyond.

The south-east ridge of Beinn Bheigeir is nearly level for one and a half kilometres and gives a splendid high level walk with an easy descent to Claggain Bay at its termination. This of course makes a convenient route of ascent taking one to two hours.

Beinn Bhan (*fair hill*) (472m)
This hill, with its prominent cairn, is the highest point of an extensive, undulating, heather-clad plateau to the west of Beinn Bheigeir. At the southern end of this plateau lies the cairned top of Beinn Uraraidh (456m) casting scree down its south-west slopes towards its namesake loch.

Although the uplands in this area are not particularly inspiring, many distinctive lochs and lochans maintain interest and aid navigation on a southward hike. The contemplation of indulgence in the local malts should maintain the flagging spirit en route to Port Ellen.

ROCK CLIMBING
Other than a few minor outcrops in the north and west, Islay's rock climbing potential is on coastal cliffs. Surprisingly, considering the amount of rock available, very little has been recorded. The Mull of Oa produced a couple of routes in the early seventies, including the easy though enjoyable seaward ridge of Dun Athad, and

obviously has much more to offer, although in places the quartzite cliffs (maximum height of 150m) are vegetated and loose. An enormous ochre coloured rock scar below Beinn Mhor (well seen from Dun Athad) is proof enough of their unstable nature. To the north of the American monument there are schist crags and stacks (maximum height of 70m) which would give some worthwhile routes. The west coast of the Rhinns also has some interesting though shorter crags.

PATHS AND WALKS

Islay is criss-crossed by old footpaths, many of them, through lack of use, now fading back into the moorland.

From the roadend at Ardtalla (grid reference 466 546) a good path runs north to the McArthur's Head lighthouse via the derelict cottage of Proaig. This gives a fairly easy coastal walk of around ten kilometres return. A more demanding alternative is to take the path branching west at Proaig, which although faint in places, can be followed across the col between Glas Bheinn and Sgorr nam Faoileann and thence down to gain a minor road, by Storakaig, at grid reference 400 624. This is undoubtedly the island's finest hill path and is about eleven kilometres in length from Ardtalla.

Another fine walk starts at Carnmore House (grid reference 350 456) one kilometre west of Port Ellen. An iron gate, on the south side of the road, gives access to a well-defined path through delightful mature mixed woodland leading to the sands of Kilnaughton Bay. The path then runs along the eastern side of the Oa, well above the shore, passing the beautiful sandy cove of Port an Eas to the farm of Inerval. Numerous tumbled ruins can be seen along the four kilometres of its length, the lichen covered stones thrusting above brambles and bracken telling of crofting communities long dead. From Inerval a track leads on for another two kilometres to the deserted farm of Stremnishmore from which point the cliff tops of the Oa can be reached.

An energetic and enjoyable day can be had by starting from Bunnahabhainn and walking around the rough headland of Rubha a'Mhail, then returning via the Doodilmore and Margadale River valleys.

JURA

MAPS :   Ordnance Survey   1:50,000 Sheet 61
            Bartholomew   1:100,000 Sheet 43

PRINCIPAL HILLS

Scrinadle		508m	505 778
Corra Bheinn		575m	526 755
Beinn Shiantaidh		757m	513 747
Beinn an Oir	} Paps of Jura	785m	498 749
Beinn a'Chaolais		733m	488 734
Glas Bheinn		562m	500 699
Dubh Bheinn		530m	489 682

ACCESS

Kennacraig (Kintyre) to Port Askaig (Islay). Passenger and vehicle ferry operated by Caledonian MacBrayne. Crossing time: 1 hour and 50 minutes.
Port Askaig to Feolin Ferry (Jura). Passenger and vehicle ferry operated by Western Ferries. Crossing time: 10 minutes (booking not required).

TRANSPORT

Apart from private transport, 'Charlie's Bus' fulfills all the island's transport requirements (taxi, post bus, school bus, delivery van etc.). Although its exact schedule is somewhat unpredictable, it does tend to form a linking service with the Caledonian MacBrayne ferry. Contact Craighouse Hotel or Post Office or Charlie MacLean (telephone 049 682 221) direct. Bicycles are not available for hire, but taking one over should be considered as it allows greater flexibility.

ACCOMMODATION

Jura Hotel, Craighouse (telephone 049 682 243) provides the only all-year round accommodation. There are no official campsites on the island and the estate's policy seems to be to discourage camping, although limited camping along the coasts is tolerated. A discreet approach is recommended.
        Bunkhouse accommodation is available at Lagg, although without transport this is not an ideal base.

GENERAL DESCRIPTION

Jura (from the Norse *dyr oe*, meaning *deer island*), 44 kilometres long and twelve kilometres at its widest, lies parallel to Kintyre and the long promontories and sealochs of mainland Knapdale, echoing their north-east to south-west orientation. To the south and west Jura is shielded by Islay and Colonsay, only to the north-west is it exposed to the full force of Atlantic weather, although the Paps, being by far the highest hills between Arran and Mull, seem to attract storm and rain clouds like 'iron filings to a magnet'. Loch Tarbert, deeply indenting the west coast, virtually divides the island into two equal parts.

The Paps of Jura from the crofting township of Ardfernal

Despite the close proximity of Islay and Jura and the common band of quartzite that comprise their uplands, they have little else in common. Jura possesses virtually none of its neighbour's rich agricultural land or flora and has a permanent population of only about two hundred, although in the mid-19th century the island supported over six times this number. Even the malt whisky, from its sole distillery at Craighouse, has a different flavour. Jura does however possess, perhaps because of its other limitations, a uniquely wild character.

The public road system is delightfully simple, being a single-track ribbon of tarmac connecting Feolin Ferry in the south to the main centre of population at Craighouse, with its sheltered harbour, then closely following the east coast for much of the way to the tiny settlement of Ardlussa. From there a poor road to just beyond Lealt degenerates into a rough track to the lonely outpost of Kinuachdrachd, passing the now empty Barnhill, the one-time residence of Eric Blair (better known as George Orwell). It was at Barnhill in 1948 that he completed the prophetic novel *Nineteen Eighty Four.*

Like the road, a thin strip of schist runs up the east coast providing the island's only agricultural land, and in the south creating a chain of small islands and sharp promontories. Ninety percent of the island is quartzite, the largest area of this ancient metamorphic rock in Scotland, giving rise to a barren, mottled brown moorland devoted almost exclusively to deer farming with a few small coniferous plantations at its eastern fringes. An estimated 4,000 red deer live on Jura.

The Paps of Jura from Dubh Bheinn

Being relatively inhospitable, Jura possesses few antiquities, the lone four metre high standing stone Camus Stac (grid reference 464 648) is one of the few prominent relics of the past.

On the beach below Jura House, at the southern tip of the island, the phenomena of the singing sands can be experienced, similar to the better known example on Eigg.

Jura supports perhaps as many adders as it does deer, the north-west being their favourite habitat. Although not supporting the same diversity of birdlife as Islay, golden eagles, ravens and choughs are a common sight in the hills.

The Gulf of Corryvreckan (also spelt Corrievreckan) lies between the northern tip of Jura and Scarba to the north. It is perhaps one of Scotland's best known natural phenomena, though the few who have made the effort to hike to An Cruachan, the hill overlooking the Gulf, whilst impressed by the general panorama, have been disappointed with the undramatic nature of this narrow strait. However, when a strong westerly wind opposes a high spring tide the Gulf's fame can be fully appreciated as the great constriction boils and churns, its overfalls and whirlpools creating an awesome spectacle. The Great Whirlpool, known to the Hebrideans as *the hag*, which forms close under the Scarba shore, is said to be the second largest whirlpool in the world and is caused by a submarine rock peak. Its great turbulence causes surf to cream and foam along the black rocks of Scarba, and according to folklore has been the graveyard of numerous vessels. The name Corryvreckan is

Corryvreckan and the northern wilderness of Jura

said to be derived from *Bhreacain*, a Norwegian prince or Irish merchant whose ships were engulfed in the whirlpool. A cave at grid reference 684 005 is claimed to be his burial place and once contained a stone coffin. The cave is 50 metres long and its entrance is protected by low walls.

THE HILLS
The majority of Jura is hill-land, and the so-called Paps of Jura clustered together in the southern half of the island form its dominant feature, their distinctive high domes clearly recognizable from adjacent islands and the mainland. The famous Scottish artist William McTaggart painted a classic view of the Paps in 1902 which can be viewed in the Kelvin Art Gallery in Glasgow. On Jura itself very few viewpoints allow all the Paps to display their individual form, normally one of the group being masked by its foreground neighbour. Although there are only three high Paps (over 700m), Corra Bheinn is often referred to as the 'fourth Pap', but its stature and situation scarcely compare with its three bigger sisters.

A traverse of the three main Paps is a popular hill day and the round trip can be conveniently undertaken from Craighouse, giving just under 1500m of ascent. A more energetic traverse includes Corra Bheinn, adding an extra 200m of ascent, whilst the ambitious may also include the two hills above Craighouse in the circuit.

The Bens of Jura fell race, an annual event held in late May, involving an ascent of seven hills (Aonach-bheinn included, Scrinadle and Beinn Mhearsamail excluded) has been completed in under three and a half hours return, from Craighouse. A more conventional traverse on foot would take over eight hours for the round trip. Whatever one's speed, the silver-grey block scree of Jura's hills demands care and concentration, being in places very unstable.

Although the main mountain interest on Jura is concentrated in the south, an opportunity to visit the magnificent north-west should not be missed. Classic steep-faced little mountains such as Rainberg Mor (454m) (grid reference 566 877) and Ben Garrisdale (365m) (grid reference 633 945) are to be enjoyed by a connoisseur not preoccupied solely with height. Attaining a maximum height of 467m at Beinn Bhreac (grid reference 598 908) this great rock-strewn emptiness is one of Scotland's finest wilderness areas. It is a land of the red deer and wild goat, of raised beaches, rocky defiles, inaccessible coves, arches and caves, banks of pale sea-smoothed boulders flung high above the shore by winter storms: a land of glistening trout-filled lochs, of adders, clegs, ticks and midges. It is virtually devoid of paths, fences or walls, affording splendid rough walking with ever-changing views.

Access into this area can be effected via any of the eastward draining glens, the Lussa River valley being the most central. Shorter, wilder glens drain westward from the watershed. The isolated cottage of Glengarrisdale (grid reference 644 969), best reached via the lochs at the headwaters of Lealt Burn, is central to a fascinating stretch of coastline.

To stand on one of this coastline's remote rocky shores at sunset and to gaze out across the glassy sea to the soft outline of Mull is to know a rare satisfaction.

Scrinadle (508m)

This curiously named hill is the most northerly of Jura's main group, its eastern slopes forming the western flank of Glen Batrick. From the summit cairn excellent views can be had of Loch Tarbert and northern Jura. It also provides an unusual prospect of the Paps. Immediately to the south lies the classic glaciated feature of Loch an Aircill, comfortably nestling in a mountain corrie.

Being a long way from the road and detached from the Paps, Scrinadle is infrequently ascended. The most satisfying line of ascent is from Glenbatrick Lodge (grid reference 517 800) (accessed via 'Evans' Walk', see p 80) up Sron Bheithe and over its subsidiary northern top, but a more direct route is up the east face above Glen Batrick. Alternatively, it can be approached from the south-east, leaving the A846 road two kilometres north-east of Leargybreck and following the path to Glen Batrick for five kilometres before climbing the east side of the hill. This route can be used as the start of the complete traverse of all the Jura hills - a very long day.

A third, and very long, route to Scrinadle starts at Feolin Ferry and goes north by the track past Cnocbreac and then across much rough moorland to ascend the west flank of the hill.

Corra Bheinn *(rough mountain)* (575m)

This mini Pap, with its multi-topped summit ridge (the south-eastern one is the highest) is most easily approached by following the path leading to Glen Batrick,

THE PAPS OF JURA

0   1   2   3 Km.

N

Loch Tarbert

Glenbatrick

Lagg

Glen Batrick

Scrinadle 508

Loch an Aircill

Loch na Fudarlaich

Corra Bheinn 575

Beinn an Oir 785

Beinn Shiantaidh 757

Sloc Brodach

PAPS OF JURA

Loch an t-Siob

Corran R.

Beinn a'Chaolais 733

Gleann Astaile

Beinn Mhearsamail

Inver Cottage

Gleann Iubharnadeal

Glas Bheinn 562

Port Askaig

Feolin

Small Isles

Keils

Dubh Bheinn 530

Craighouse

Sound of Jura

JURA

Sound of Islay

A846

Ardfin

Brosdale Island

ISLAY

Beinn an Oir from Beinn a' Chaolais

and branching off near Loch na Cloiche to climb the hill's broad south-east ridge. On the wide pass between Corra Bheinn and Beinn Shiantaidh lies a complicated group of shallow lochans much beloved by wading birds. The descent from the summit to this pass is about 210m, initially quite steep.

Beinn Shiantaidh (*holy mountain*) (757m)

If Corra Bheinn is not being included in the day's itinerary, then an ascent of Beinn Shiantaidh is best undertaken from the bridge over the Corran River (grid reference 544 721). Starting on the true right bank of the river, its boggy valley can be avoided by striking north-westwards past a conspicuous plantation and over a vague shoulder. The right bank of the river is regained in its upper reaches and followed to its outflow from Loch an t-Siob. The river is crossed and gradually steepening ground is ascended for about one kilometre until the south-east spur of the hill can be gained. This gives a steep climb linking heather patches between jumbles of quartzite scree for about 365m (600m from the loch) to the large summit cairn. On the south side of the cairn is a box containing a well-used visitors' book. The views, as from any of the Paps, can be breathtaking. The descent down the initially narrow west ridge is steep and rocky, requiring care, particularly in winter.

Beinn an Oir (*mountain of the boundary* or *mountain of gold*) (785m)

This is the central, highest and probably the most interesting of the three Paps. When seen from the west (particularly from Port Askaig) its distinctive features are two deep scree-filled gullies which form a V-shape for the full height of its west face above the scree fan. From the col to the east, reached either from Beinn Shiantaidh or Loch an t-Siob, the ascent of 300m can be made less arduous by gaining a slight line of weakness that cuts diagonally up across the slope from left to right (the alignment of an eroded basalt dyke). This ends at a rocky defile on the north-east ridge. The ridge is then followed pleasantly to the summit. The last section of this route, above two dry stone enclosures, follows a cleared pathway which was constructed by the Ordnance Survey during early triangulation work. A circular stone wall surrounds the triangulation pillar on the summit and can provide welcome shelter from the wind.

The 400m descent of the ridge southwards to the col between Beinn an Oir and Beinn a'Chaolais is over fairly complex rocky ground, and after the first obvious section the presence of a minor spur to the south-east can be confusing, particularly in the mist. Additionally, to the west lies a series of steep crags overlooking the corrie of Na Garbh-lochanan. The best line is a series of zig-zagging grassy ramps, but no path exists.

Beinn a'Chaolais (*mountain of the sound*) (733m)

When viewed from Beinn an Oir, the striking dipping strata on the upper north face of Beinn a'Chaolais is a dramatic reminder of quartzite's sedimentary origin and of the geological forces that have subsequently altered, tilted and uplifted this product of an ancient sea bed.

An ascent of the north-east side from the col at 375m involves the usual dodging of unstable scree, although the final section is over easy mossy ground to an undistinguished summit.

If a descent to Feolin is desired, a rough bulldozed track can be reached by descending easy slopes to the south-west and thence to the ferry via Inver Cottage. The descent to Craighouse is much longer and can be extended by taking in Glas Bheinn en route. Just below the summit of Beinn a'Chaolais on its east flank is perhaps the only section of scree running on the island (normally the block scree is too large). Lower down the Beinn Mhearsamail col is quickly gained and this hill can be skirted to its east or west, leading over undulating ground to the head of Gleann Astaile. Beinn Mhearsamail (506m) is quite a rocky hill, although an easy climb. It is totally overshadowed by its larger, higher neighbours.

To reach Craighouse from the flat col at the head of Gleann Astaile, cut across the head-streams of Abhainn Mhic-ill-Libhir bearing south-east, then cross a low ridge and follow the southern bank of the stream leading to Cill Earnadail (an ancient graveyard at grid reference 524 687). From the graveyard follow the track, turning right to the crofting settlement of Keils just over one kilometre from Craighouse.

Glas Bheinn (*grey mountain*) (562m)

A sprawling stony hill which together with its western outlier Aonach-bheinn (499m) forms the south flank of Gleann Astaile. From its summit cairn all the Paps display their separate identity and good views can be had of the east coast.

Dubh Bheinn (*black mountain*) (530m)

Dubh Beinn is of similar character to Glas Bheinn, although it is crowned by a natural stone triangulation pillar surrounded by a crude stone wall. To its west lie four kilometres of mottled, nearly featureless grassy moorland stretching to the coast, a favourite winter haunt of large herds of red deer.

Both Glas Bheinn and Dubh Bheinn are of limited interest to the mountaineer other than for their unfrequented nature and their relative proximity to Craighouse, making them useful for a short day out. Keils, to the north of Craighouse, is the best starting point, although much intervening broken moorland must be crossed before the hills can be reached.

ROCK CLIMBING

Although in places extensive areas of outcropping rock occur, there are few significant mountain crags. Those that do exist tend to be broken and vegetated, offering little opportunity for rock climbing. One exception is a 70m high face on the south-west flank of Beinn an Oir (grid reference 496 746), its right-hand side being fairly clean with scope for several routes. Other smaller crags exist higher on this face.

Coastal cliffs abound to a maximum height of 50m, although most are smaller, providing endless opportunity for exploratory work on both quartzite and basalt (dykes). It is doubtful, however, if any top quality climbing will be discovered on the island.

PATHS AND WALKS

Jura contains remarkably few well-defined paths, although many intermittent alignments created by deer may be followed over the moors and hills. One notable exception is the 'made' path leading from the A846 to Glenbatrick known as 'Evans' Walk'. It is just over eight kilometres in length, leaving the main road at grid reference 550 731, and reaching a height of 265m at the pass above Loch na Fudarlaich. It then passes a chain of inter-connected lochans before descending into Glen Batrick, following the west bank of the river to the isolated lodge at the mouth of Loch Tarbert. A lonely and enchanting spot. Unfortunately, unless one is prepared to take to the hills or face up to many kilometres of rough coastal walking, the path must be retraced, since Glenbatrick is indeed 'the end of the road'.

A short section of path also links the A846 with the head of Loch Tarbert, commencing at grid reference 605 828. Its alignment is marked by small standing stones, and it gives a useful access point to the watery wilderness to the north of Loch Tarbert.

GIGHA

MAPS :   Ordnance Survey   1:50,000 sheet 60
          Bartholomew   1:100,000 sheet 43

HIGHEST POINT
Creag Bhan   100m   647 509

ACCESS
Tayinloan to Gigha. Passenger and vehicle ferry operated by Caledonian MacBrayne.
Crossing time: 20 minutes.

TRANSPORT
Bicycles may be hired at the General Store and Gigha Hotel. Cars are unnecessary
as no point on the island is more than six kilometres from the jetty. Walking
recommended.

ACCOMMODATION
Gigha Hotel and self-catering cottages - telephone Gigha (058 35) 254.

GENERAL DESCRIPTION
Of all the main Hebridean islands, Gigha (probably Norse derivation meaning *goat
island*, but sometimes translated as *the good isle*) is perhaps of least interest to the
mountaineer, being low-lying and well cultivated, with an air of quiet affluence.
Indeed, this green island is not really a place for energetic pursuits, more a relaxing
retreat.

Nine kilometres long, three at its widest and surrounded by numerous
outlying islets and reefs, Gigha lies four kilometres off the Kintyre peninsula and
parallel to it. Its lone road runs down nearly the full length of the island and its only
settlement of any consequence, Ardminish, sits astride the road close to the jetty.
The island's population is around two hundred.

Gigha's main claim to fame are the gardens of Achamore House (open 1st
March to 31st October) which were established by Sir James Horlick between 1944
and 1962, taking advantage of the favourable aspect and climate to introduce many
exotic species. The gardens, now run by the National Trust for Scotland, exude an
air of great tranquility, having struck that fine balance between over-cultivation and
a more natural state. The many paths provide delightful strolls though mature,
mixed woodland with small 'islands' of flowering rhododendrons and azaleas.

Close to Achamore lie the ruins of Kilchatton Church, sometimes called St.
Cathan's Church (grid reference 643 481) with a fine carved red sandstone arch and
an extensive collection of carved grave slabs, although not on a par with those on
Oronsay. On a hillock, one hundred metres to the north-west, stands the famous
Ogham Stone, a slim pillar of native rock. Apparently the notches cut in the west and
southern edges of this pillar are a near unique example of a Celtic 'shorthand'

indicating the name of some Dalriadic warrior. The visitor may be forgiven if he is left unimpressed. Other curious stones and inscriptions exist on the island.

Gigha is rich in bird life and wild flowers with orchids, bluebells, stitchwort, primroses etc., growing in profusion, and despite the ever-present circling buzzards, it supports a thriving rabbit population, perhaps due to the absence of such predators as fox and weasel, and a ban on shooting.

Although extensively cultivated between the distinctive bracken covered ridges, the island does have its wilder side; the rocky Eilean Garbh (not quite an island) in the north and the western coastline with its small, cave-riddled cliffs and rocky coves. Sandy beaches provide safe swimming on the east coast.

THE HILLS

Creag Bhan (*pale rock*) (100m)
Creag Bhan, the only hill of any consequence on the island, is a spine of pale epidiorite; its glaciated slabs burst through a ragged garb of gorse and heather, making it quite a unique little hill. The north end of the ridge, when viewed from Tarbert, appears as a little rock peak. From the triangulation pillar at the south end of the ridge, a bird's-eye view of most of the island can be had and Jura's Paps look particularly fine to the north-west.

An ascent of the hill can be effected from any direction, avoiding cultivated fields and bramble tangles.

ROCK CLIMBING

None has been done and the scope is very limited. The rock is good and even though the coastal crags attain a maximum height of only 20m, they provide good bouldering for the frustrated climber on a family holiday.

CARA

Cara, one and a half kilometres in length and half a kilometre wide, is the only one of Gigha's satellites with any great character or elevation, and lies one kilometre south of its parent island. Boat hire to Cara is available from Ardminish or Tayinloan.

The island is bleak and uninhabited, its only signs of past habitation being an empty house and the hollow shell of an ancient chapel. The highest point of 56m (grid reference 638 433) is at its southern tip where a steep, clean cliff 35m high forms an impressive rampart enjoying the maximum available sunshine and the promise of good rock climbing. Fresh water is available for camping.

CHAPTER 3

THE ISLANDS OF THE FIRTH OF LORN

The south-western end of the Great Glen, that prominent fault which slices from south-west to north-east across the Highlands of Scotland, forms the Firth of Lorn, a beautiful stretch of water leading from the narrows of Loch Linnhe out to the Atlantic Ocean between the headlands of Mull and Jura.

Throughout its length the Firth of Lorn is dotted with small islands and tiny rocky islets and reefs. At its mouth between Jura and the Ross of Mull is Colonsay with its small neighbour Oronsay. About thirty kilometres north-east up the Firth lies a group of little islands off the Argyll coast - Scarba, the Garvellachs, Luing, Shuna and Seil to name a few. A further ten kilometres north-east Kerrera lies just offshore from Oban, and to its north the island of Lismore divides the Firth into two narrow sounds, the Lynn of Morvern and the Lynn of Lorn, which unite north of Lismore at the other Shuna Island to form Loch Linnhe.

Altogether, with its multitude of islands and rocky islets, the fringe of great sea-cliffs and rocky headlands along the southern coast of Mull and the backdrop of mountains in Jura, Mull, Appin and Morvern, the Firth of Lorn is one of the grandest waterways along the west coast of Scotland, and one much frequented by yachtsmen. Although none of the Firth's small islands can be described as mountainous, and only Scarba has on it a hill, Cruach Scarba, of respectable height, climbers should not eschew visiting them for they offer walking and scrambling of great character and delight. Those with small boats or canoes will find endless scope for exploration, but should beware, for in the narrow channels and sounds between some of these islands the tides and currents are extraordinarily strong and fast. Not for nothing is the Gulf of Corryvreckan renowned for its whirlpools and tide-race.

COLONSAY AND ORONSAY

MAPS :   Ordnance Survey   1:50,000 Sheet 61
            Bartholomew   1:100,000 Sheet 43

PRINCIPAL HILLS

Carnan Eoin	143m	409 984
Beinn Bhreac	139m*	375 971
Binnein Riabhach	120m	364 963
Beinn nan Gudairean	136m	388 949
Carn Mor	135m	372 947
Beinn nan Caorach	126m*	365 941
Beinn Eibhne	98m*	378 903
Beinn Oronsay	93m	350 892

ACCESS
Oban to Scalasaig. Passenger and vehicle ferry operated by Caledonian MacBrayne.
Crossing time : 2 hours.

TRANSPORT
Occasional post bus. Taxi available from Scalasaig Hotel. Bicycles for hire.

ACCOMMODATION
Scalasaig Hotel (Telephone Colonsay 316), plus bed and breakfast and self-catering.
Camping discouraged, but ask locally. Good, though windy sites on the west
coast.

GENERAL DESCRIPTION
Lying fourteen kilometres west of Jura, Colonsay, together with its close neighbour
Oronsay (connected at low tide) and their surrounding skerries, epitomise the finest
aspects of the Western Isles. Despite their isolated windswept situation, they exude
a prosperous, harmonious atmosphere; a near perfect balance between rich
agriculture and classic untamed scenery, albeit on a small scale. In their combined
length of sixteen kilometres and maximum width of six kilometres they pack more
variety than perhaps any other Scottish island of comparable size.

Unlike most Hebridean islands, Colonsay escaped the ravages of the
Clearances and consequently exhibits little of the degeneration so characteristic of
the policies of less enlightened lairds. An unusual respect for their own laird is well
testified by the seven metre high needle of pink granite, erected by the people of
Colonsay on Cnoc na Faire Mor, the hill to the south of Scalasaig, commemorating
'The Right Honourable Lord Colonsay, Born 1793, Died 1874'. This easily accessible
site provides superb views of the coast with Islay and Jura beyond.

A curious aspect of Colonsay's human population, still relatively unaffected
by incomers, is the very high incidence of twin births, as high in percentage terms

as anywhere in the world, and the result, it seems, of social, cultural and genetic factors or perhaps plain chance. As with many islands, the population has been steadily falling to its present level of about one hundred and fifty.

Two kilometres north-east along the coast from the pier lie the ghostly ruins of Riasg Buidhe, a one-time fishing community, now reduced to the gaunt roofless shells of over a dozen houses; a most atmospheric place.

The sycamore-fringed village of Scalasaig has the island's only pub, post office and shop. A circular road links the island's main settlements with short offshoots to the north and south. Despite being only seventeen kilometres in length, it has three separate 'A' road designations.

Although much of Colonsay's coastline is rocky, most notably the west coast so beloved of the dark brown feral goat population, it also possesses some superb beaches. They range in character from the famous kilometre long golden sands of Traigh Ban at Kiloran Bay in the north-west, to the sheltered coves of white shell sand in the south-east.

To the south of the exotic palm-studded grounds of Colonsay House (similar to Achmore, Gigha) with its peaches and figs ripening in the sun, lie a chain of three lochs, all named Loch Fada (to save confusion). Visitors may be forgiven for thinking that they have eaten the wrong species of mushroom - yes there are black swans!

The island abounds in standing stones, ruined chapels, crosses and duns, but whilst of passing interest, none are of exceptional note.

A visit to Oronsay is a must on any trip to Colonsay. If one is prepared to paddle across the mud flats (known as The Strand) it is possible to spend a few hours on Oronsay either side of low tide. Timing is fairly crucial unless one is prepared for a longer stay, or to get more than one's feet wet. The best direct route across the flats is from a marker post on a small promontory on the east side of the bay (grid reference 372 903) to a prominent standing stone on a rocky islet just off the northern tip of Oronsay (grid reference 366 897). Only the unadventurous would go to the trouble of hiring a boat.

Oronsay is mostly a flat and windswept island of about six square kilometres given over to grazing, and fringed by sandy bays interspersed by flat rock reefs. Sheltered below Beinn Oronsay lie the famous priory and infamous farm; the latter being of stone plundered from the former. Despite this, the 13th century Priory of St Columba, built on the site of a much earlier Celtic monastery, remains in amazingly good condition, with the small cloisters still intact. It is perhaps, next to Iona's abbey, the most famous ecclesiastical antiquity in the Scottish Islands. Nearby stands a superb tall cross with a crucifixion scene depicted on one side. The roofed building within the walled priory contains a very fine collection of mediaeval carved grave slabs. For the ghoulish, a jumble of human bones lie behind the altar in the main room.

The south tip of Oronsay reluctantly trails into the sea, providing an ideal breeding ground for the grey seal which gather in their hundreds in the autumn to pup. The main skerry, Eilean nan Ron (*seals' island*), a nature reserve, is indeed most appropriately named.

THE HILLS

Despite attaining a maximum height of only 143m, Colonsay is a remarkably rugged, almost mountainous island. Many of its hills display a Torridonian grandeur (indeed the rock is of the Lower Torridonian strata) and they are not, as on other islands, all concentrated in any one area.

Carnan Eoin *(Ian's cairn)* (143m)

The highest top on Colonsay lies among a cluster of hills in the north of the island. The large, well constructed cairn, crowning its rocky summit is in fact slightly higher than the adjacent triangulation pillar. The sands of Traigh Ban are seen to great effect from there. An ascent of Carnan Eoin from the Kiloran Bay side gives some interesting scrambling. Its satellite hills are Beinn Bheag (109m), Beinn Bhreac (122m) and Cnoc Inebri (96m), to the north-west, north-east and south respectively.

Beinn Bhreac *(speckled hill)* (139m)
Binnein Riabhach *(tawny hill)* (120m)

These two similar west coast hills swell from moorland to their east and are thus unimpressive on that side. Their west flanks however, present a different prospect, being near continuous rock walls dropping to narrow, level grassy shelves, before plunging again into the sea. To the north of Binnein Riabhach the impressive ravine of Aoineadh an t-Sruth leads to the shore. Both hills are accessible from the A870 in about half an hour, and can be conveniently included in a coastal traverse.

Beinn nan Gudairean (136m)

An unexceptional roadside hill one kilometre north-west of Scalasaig. Its summit has a triangulation pillar and offers good views over the island.

Carn Mor *(big hill)* (135m)

Sitting above Lower Kilchattan, with Dubh Loch nestling to its south, this is the highest point on the rocky scarp that bounds the south side of the valley containing Loch Fada. It is easy of access. The scarp line terminates in the craggy Meall a'Chaise to the south.

Beinn nan Caorach *(hill of the sheep)* (126m)

This miniature mountain, when seen from the south or west, displays a facade of a grandeur totally disproportionate to its modest height. Although the actual summit is ill-defined and backed by bleak moorland, the hill's rock flanked south-west spur provides interesting and exposed ridge scrambling. Half a kilometre to the south lies a similar, though smaller spur, the westward termination of Sliabh Riabhach.

Beinn Eibhne (98m)

Although of modest height, even by Colonsay standards, Beinn Eibhne is well worth an ascent due to its isolation and vantage position. From its minor western top of Am Binnean Crom, named after the curious rock protuberance pierced by a natural hole and buttressed by steep crags to the south-west, a bird's-eye view of The Strand to the west can be enjoyed. To the east, across the sea, lies the mottled brown spine of Jura with its distinctive Paps.

Beinn Oronsay (93m)

When seen from the flat expanse of southern Oronsay, the island's eponymous hill, with its 'impregnable' southern rock face seems to be as worthy of the name Beinn as peaks ten times its size. Seen from the summit triangulation pillar, the low grassy promontories and scattered skerries of Colonsay's southern shore, with the lone house of Ardskenish, have all the essence of the Hebrides. This summit is a good place to sit and contemplate, as perhaps the monks of the priory to the south did many centuries ago.

ROCK CLIMBING

Although virtually nothing has been recorded, Colonsay has a wealth of potential rock climbing on both inland and coastal crags with the former, unusually, offering the most scope. Short cliffs (up to 30m) around Port nam Fliuchan and to the north of Kiloran Bay provide excellent 'cragging' with a variety of arches and caves giving additional interest, although vomiting fulmars can add unwelcome difficulties.

Carnan Eoin and its satellites are very rocky with interesting scrambling on their west faces. The northern end of this group sports an overhanging 30m scoop of friable metamorphic rock known as Creag Bhan (grid reference 415 989) which might give exciting climbing.

The west flanks of Beinn Bhreac and Binnein Riabhach are long, seaward facing vegetated crags rising to a maximum height of 80m. The northern end of the former has a clean buttress and the centre of the latter a very steep wall, both approached from the south. The gullies breaching these crags also have some clean flanking walls.

From Carn Mor round the flank of the hill to the farm of Machrins, numerous crags buttress the moorland to the east, most impressive of all perhaps being the south-west spur of Beinn nan Caorach whose crest gives a fine scramble. Considerable rock climbing scope exists in this area.

In the south-east an impressive little crag at grid reference 375 902 overlooks The Strand and although heavily lichened, should provide good routes.

The long, lichenous crag on the south side of Beinn Oronsay, remarkably like a gritstone edge, sports some fine looking lines including a big hanging corner. Being of sound rock (gneiss?), 25m high and south-facing, it presents considerable potential.

PATHS AND WALKS

Numerous coastal walks are available, although there are few defined paths. An old path links Scalasaig with Lower Kilchattan, passing just south of Carn Mor, which is a useful short cut when heading for the west coast. A pleasant and non-taxing walk from Scalasaig involves leaving the A870 at grid reference 359 940. A track is then followed across the rabbit-infested golf course (doubling as an occasional airstrip) to its junction with the coast at grid reference 351 922 where a path through the dunes leads to the windswept peninsula of Ardskenish. A return to Scalasaig can eventually be made via the track to Garvard across Traigh nam Barc and then the A869; a round trip of about thirteen kilometres.

SCARBA

MAPS :   Ordnance Survey   1:50,000 Sheet 55
            Ordnance Survey   1:25,000 Sheet 365 (NM60/70)
            Bartholomew   1:100,000 Sheet 47

PRINCIPAL HILL
   Cruach Scarba   449m   690 044

ACCESS

By private hire from Black Mill Bay, Luing. Telephone: Luing 211 or 213. Landing place at Poll na h-ealaidh (grid reference 720 060).

GENERAL DESCRIPTION

A wild and little visited island, Scarba (probably from the Norse meaning *rough isle*) lies one kilometre north of Jura and two kilometres to the west of the south end of Luing. There are no permanent inhabitants, although Kilmory Lodge and the small cottage in the south-east are occupied from time to time (the latter as an Outward Bound type training centre). A fair population of red deer roam the island, and golden eagles are frequently seen.

Its sixteen square kilometres are primarily formed of the same primitive quartzite as that found on Jura and Islay, although Scarba is even more rugged than its larger neighbours, with much outcropping rock and many fine coastal features.

Although popularly associated with Jura, the great whirlpool that forms in the Gulf of Corryvreckan more truly belongs to Scarba. Its power can be well appreciated from above the boulder-choked cove of Camas nam Bairneach in the south-west, its roar at times competing with the wind for supremacy. The much narrower strait to the north, between Scarba and Lunga, is perhaps an equally impressive sight as the tide funnels through Bealach a' Choin Ghlais (usually referred to as the *grey dog*), foaming and churning around Eilean a'Bhealaich beneath the ivy-draped crags of the constricting headlands.

In the east below Kilmory Lodge there are dense woodlands of oak, birch and rowan, whilst scattered across the hillside above are the remnants of an earlier Scots pine forest. In contrast, the west of the island is a wilderness, with great cliffs dropping to a rugged lonely shore and steep craggy hillslopes behind. The waterfall forming a great black streak down Creag an Eas (grid reference 685 050) should not be missed; its single leap of one hundred metres down a crumbling, vegetated wall is a spectacular sight after heavy rains. Its base can be reached by a rough path to the south leading down through a gap in the cliffs. The coastal cliffs, particularly those in the south, offer those with troglodytic tendencies many happy hours of exploration.

The two islands to the north of Scarba, Lunga and Eilean Dubh Mor, have no permanent resident and access is the same as for Scarba. Lunga, with its rugged central ridge spine culminating at Bidein na h-Ionaire (100m), is the largest and most interesting of the group.

Scarba from the Garvellachs

THE HILLS

It is appropriate that the highest point on the island should be called **Cruach Scarba** as the whole island can almost be regarded as one large hill. Numerous small lochans nestle between bare quartzite ribs, and the highest point is marked by a triangulation pillar. Views to the north from the summit are wonderful, a wide flotilla of islands sailing into the distance.

The summit can be most directly gained by branching off the path (see below) at grid reference 704 045 and following a tumbling dry stone wall to a loch at a height of 380m and thence heading due west.

ROCK CLIMBING

No rock routes of any consequence have yet been recorded on the island although, given the considerable extent of coastal cliffs, some climbing is certainly available. However, much of the rock suffers from a mantle of vegetation and the doubtful security characteristic of most quartzite.

PATHS AND WALKS

From the landing place a track leads to Kilmory Lodge. Beyond the Lodge it splits, the left-hand branch leading to an un-named cottage in the south-east, the other bifurcating after a short distance. The left-hand fork of this track ascends the hillside, narrowing to a path at about 200m. This path, initially well-defined, traverses south-west across the hillside passing above Loch Airigh a'Chruidh, then it swings west and fades away just beyond a cairn at grid reference 686 035. The path, a fine walk in its own right, gives access to the west and to grand viewpoints above the Corryvreckan.

Good coastal walks are available in the east and around the northern headland of Rubh a'Chuil but, although very rewarding to follow, much of the remainder of Scarba's coastline requires a certain scrambling and route finding skill.

LUING

MAPS :   Ordnance Survey   1:50,000 Sheet 55
              Bartholomew   1:100,000 Sheet 47

HIGHEST POINT
Cnoc Dhomhnuill   94m   743 131

ACCESS
Vehicle and passenger ferry operated by Strathclyde Regional Council from Cuan (Seil). No vehicle and limited passenger service on Sundays, otherwise frequent service. Crossing time : 5 minutes.

TRANSPORT
Bicycle is ideal, a car is a luxury.

ACCOMMODATION
Guest house and bed and breakfast in Cullipool and elsewhere. Camping should not be a problem, but ask locally.

GENERAL DESCRIPTION
Separated from Seil by the fast tide race of the Cuan Sound, Luing is a scenically uninteresting island with bracken covered ridges in the north and more agricultural land in the south. The villages of Cullipool and Toberonochy are, however, quite attractive.

As with Seil, to the north, Luing was also extensively quarried for slate. Some interesting carved slate grave slabs and unusual graffiti can be seen at a ruined roadside church at grid reference 744 091. A fine basalt dyke, Stac na Morain, lies one kilometre north of Cullipool.

The island's highest point, **Cnoc Dhomhnuill** (94m) is but a short walk to the east from Cullipool.

Numerous islands, both large and small, are scattered around Luing. A heavily wooded Shuna (highest point 90m) lies to the east, the bare Torsa (highest point 62m) to the north-east and the strange little low island of Belnahua, with its ruined village and flooded slate quarry, two kilometres to the west.

SEIL AND EASDALE

MAPS :   Ordnance Survey   1:50,000 Sheet 55
             Bartholomew   1:100,000 Sheet 47

HIGHEST POINT
    Meall a'Chaise   146m   753 178

ACCESS

Over Clachan Bridge (grid reference 784 197) often grandiosely referred to as the 'Bridge over the Atlantic'.

    To Easdale there is a passenger ferry from the village of Ellanbeich on Seil (usually and quite confusingly also referred to as Easdale), run by Strathclyde Regional Council. Crossing time : 5 minutes. On demand - sound klaxon.

TRANSPORT

Take own car or bicycle.

ACCOMMODATION

Ample, in the form of hotels, guest houses and bed and breakfast. Campers may encounter problems.

GENERAL DESCRIPTION

Only just an island, by a matter of thirty metres, Seil is linked to the mainland by a classic hump-backed stone bridge, designed by Thomas Telford and constructed in 1792.

    Seil is quite heavily populated and largely given over to farming. In former times its primary industry was slate quarrying both on mainland Seil and on the island of Easdale. Vast quarries were excavated to a depth of 75 metres. In November 1881 a great storm caused the seas to broach the protective walls and to flood the quarries with great loss of life and the creation of the present island of Easdale. This obsolete industry still dominates the area with vast piles of spoil, flooded pits, and the island museum displaying the life of the 'slate people'. The modern industry of tourism has made its own contribution to the despoilation of the area with its blight of particularly tasteless facilities.

    Fine views of the Garvellachs and Mull's south-eastern coastline can be had from Seil, the indicator on Easdale island's highest point being a particularly good viewpoint, which also affords a bird's-eye view of the attractive cottage village below.

THE HILLS

Meall a'Chaise (146m) can be ascended from Ellanbeich in about twenty minutes and commands panoramic views. The island some two kilometres to the north-west is Insh Island.

ROCK CLIMBING

Although the cliffs north of Ellanbeich are most impressive and rise to a height of

60m, they are alarmingly loose, especially in their higher reaches. Few routes have been recorded.

PATHS AND WALKS

Good walking along the raised beaches in the west. An impasse at grid reference 745 182 prevents a northwards coastal walk from Ellanbeich, even at low tide.

GARVELLACHS

MAPS : Ordnance Survey   1:50,000 Sheet 55
                                 1:25,000 Sheet 354 (NM61/71)

HIGHEST POINTS

Eileach an Naoimh	77m	638 097
Garbh Eileach	110m*	673 124

ACCESS

Boat hire from Cullipool. Telephone Luing (085 24) 282

GENERAL DESCRIPTION

The Garvellachs, often called the 'Isles of the Sea', form a seven kilometre long chain lying on a north-east to south-west orientation between Scarba and Mull in the middle of the Firth of Lorn. Their topography can be equally well appreciated from the ferry to Colonsay or from the summit of Cruach Scarba. The group consists of two main islands, two lesser ones, A'Chuli and Dun Chonnuill, plus a scattering of skerries.

The islands are mostly composed of limestone which explains the verdant, flower-decked slopes above the great cliffs that front their western aspects.

Although now uninhabited, it is evident that the group, particularly Eileach an Naoimh (*rock of the saints*), has a long history of ecclesiastical occupation. The well-preserved remains of a 6th century chapel, a monastery, an underground cell and two beehive cells can be inspected. One of the latter has been restored, standing to a height of around three metres. It is said that St Columba would retire to Eileach an Naoimh when the going became too hectic on Iona. Dun Chonnuill, the most northerly island, holds the remains of a dun and fort, both in a nearly impregnable position.

At the north end of Eileach an Naoimh lies the splendid natural arch, An Clarsach (*the harp*).

Garbh Eileach, the largest of the group, presents a very steep 100m high cliff to the north-west, split by a deep cleft, the Bealach an Tarabairt, which is reported to have good rock climbing on its flanking walls. A good, sheltered landing place can be found at the obvious inlet on the south-east coast.

KERRERA

MAPS : Ordnance Survey 1:50,000 Sheet 49
Bartholomew 1:100,000 Sheet 47

HIGHEST POINT
Carn Breugach 189m 815 278

ACCESS
Passenger ferry from jetty three kilometres south-west of Oban on the Gallanach Road (coastal road), (bicycles transported, space permitting), operated by Strathclyde Regional Council. Regular service, also on demand. Crossing time : 5 minutes.

TRANSPORT
Take a bicycle or walk.

ACCOMMODATION
Self-catering (details from Tourist office, Oban), camp or stay on the mainland.

GENERAL DESCRIPTION
Despite Kerrera's proximity to the hubbub and mainstream tourism of Oban, it has remained a peaceful backwater offering the jaded promenade stroller a taste of alternative tourism and of course an easy 'tick' for the confirmed isleophile.

Eight kilometres long and tucked in tight to the mainland, Kerrera affords Oban a relatively sheltered harbour and large clusters of yachts are often seen in Ardantrive Bay, an even calmer sanctuary. The island has a very hilly appearance with crags bursting through the pervasive mantle of bracken. A rough road almost circles the centre of the island, its ends at Ardmore and Barnabuck being linked by a pleasant path.

Perhaps Kerrera's main claim to fame is Gylen Castle, the 'fairy tale' Renaissance stronghold of the MacDougalls, perched on a rocky headland in the south of the island (grid reference 805 264). It is reached by a path from Lower Gylen. The walls still stand to full height, the north one having some interesting carved relief. An intriguing Glasgow-style 'close' gives access through the castle to the cliff girt top of the headland (pierced by an arch below). The mood of the castle varies dramatically with the weather, looking formidable on a grim day.

THE HILLS
An ascent to the triangulation pillar on Carn Breugach can be made in about thirty minutes from the jetty on the south-east side of the island, although this can be quite trying when the bracken is at full height. Views down the Sound of Kerrera are fine. Although not high, the whole interior of the island is very hummocky, making walking fairly hard work.

ROCK CLIMBING
Rock type varies from hard metamorphosed sandstone to conglomerate and

crumbly basalt. Unfortunately the highest crag on the island is in the last category. Facing west at grid reference 789 274, this vertical 60m high crag awaits the attention of future climbers less fastidious in their tastes than the present generation. Many of the smaller outcrops might provide some sport, although scarcely worth a special visit.

PATHS AND WALKS
There are several coastal walks with caves and coves to explore. A walk out to the monument at the north tip of the island, via Ardantrive, is enjoyable.

LISMORE

MAPS :   Ordnance Survey   1:50,000 Sheet 49
             Bartholomew   1:100,000 Sheet 47

HIGHEST POINT
Barr Mor   127m   814 388

ACCESS
Oban to Achnacroish. Passenger and vehicle ferry operated by Caledonian MacBrayne. Crossing time : 50 minutes.
Port Appin to Lismore (jetty at north end of the road). Passenger ferry (bicycles transported, space permitting). Operated by Strathclyde Transport. Crossing time 10 minutes.

TRANSPORT
Car hire available - contact shop/post office, telephone Lismore 272. The ideal form of transport is a bicycle, although no bike hire is available on the island.

ACCOMMODATION
Isle of Lismore Guest House, telephone Lismore 207 (grid reference 860 434). Also some bed and breakfast houses.

GENERAL DESCRIPTION
Lismore, the 'Great Garden', lying at the mouth of Loch Linnhe where it opens into the Firth of Lorn, is indeed appropriately named; a 16 kilometre long spine of ancient grey limestone supporting a luxurious green mantle. Although low lying, it commands superb mountain views in all directions from the hills of Mull in the southwest to the great peaks of Glen Coe with the high, usually snow-capped dome of Ben Nevis beyond. The views are particularly majestic in the late spring and contrast sharply with the flower-decked ground of Lismore. Several varieties of orchid, rock rose, eyebright, yellow iris, field gential, ragged robin, cranesbill and numerous other species, grow in profusion. In the 16th century Lismore is said to have been almost completely masked in deciduous woodland; now only a scattering of ash, oak, sycamore and horse chestnut remains.

The population of around one hundred and twenty is primarily involved in farming, the island supporting a large number of healthy sheep and beef cattle. Curiously there are no rabbits or foxes on the island. Predictably, in the last century Lismore was a producer of lime and several complete kilns can be found to the west of Port Ramsay in the north, at Port Kilcheran in the east and on Eilean nan Caorach.

Antiquities abound, many in dramatic coastal settings, a visit being worthwhile for the views alone. Achadun Castle (grid reference 804 392) dating from the 14th century, commands a good view of Duart Castle on Mull. Castle Coeffin (grid reference 853 437), of unknown age, is a most evocative thrust of ivy-covered masonry fingers set on a natural rock stack. The atmosphere of this classic ruin is marred only by the vast despoilation of a 'super quarry' at Glen Sanda, on the oposite side of the Lynn of Morvern. An ancient tidal fish trap lies below the castle to the south. On the opposite side of the island (grid reference 867 429) lies the much older but well preserved Pictish broch of Tirefour Castle.

Like Iona, Lismore was a centre of early Christianity, Saint Moluag founding his mission there in the 6th century, although no structural trace now remains. However, the present parish church has incorporated several features dating from a 14th century cathedral into its internal walls.

Several small islands lie scattered around Lismore's coast including Eilean na Cloiche (*island of the stone*) in the east with its curious prominent wart of rock; Eilean Musdile with a lighthouse, off the southern tip; and the largest, Bernera Island, in the west, which is accessible on foot at low tide.

Three kilometres north-east of Lismore, close to the mainland, lies Shuna Island. Rising to a height of just 71m, its soft outline is marred only by the regular dark green of several coniferous plantations. A ruined castle lies near the south end. Two kilometres to the east of Lismore the rich island of Eriska lies across the mouth of Loch Creran. It is reached by a road bridge on its south side.

Mention must also be made of Eilean an Stalcaire, the smallest island in this guide, and occupied by the castle that has graced a thousand calendars. Castle Stalker, sitting at the mouth of Loch Laich, leaves little room on this island for anything else.

THE HILLS

Barr Mor (127m) literally *big top*, is the only hill of any note on Lismore, and a pleasant ascent to its short-cropped grassy dome can be made from any direction. The summit, crossed by a dry stone dyke, is the site of an ancient cairn and cist and affords fine views in all directions. From the summit the high ground runs southwestward, eventually to narrow into the ridge of Druim Mor with its precipitous western flank.

ROCK CLIMBING

The grey Silurian limestone of Lismore, visually very attractive with its streaks of cream, rust and ochre, appears to offer some scope for rock climbing and indeed routes are mentioned in the previous edition of this guide. However, when not extensively vegetated the rock tends to be of variable quality, occasionally sound

Looking south-west down the Firth of Lorn from Gylen Castle on Kerrera

with good holds, but more often brittle with softer bands. The highest cliffs are in the south-west and opposite Eilean na Cloiche in the south-east near a prominent cave. The striking 50m high pillar below Druim Mor at grid reference 794 368 proves on close inspection to be less attractive than it appears from a distance.

PATHS AND WALKS

Due to extensive agricultural use (with the exception of the extreme south) little good inland walking is available, although this is more than compensated for by the abundance of fine coastal walks, usually between the cliffs of the raised beach and the shore. Indeed the whole island can be circumnavigated in this fashion, rarely following established paths. The roughest section is below Druim Mor, in the south-west, where jumbles of boulders must be negotiated.

CHAPTER 4

MULL

AND ITS NEIGHBOURING ISLANDS

Situated due west of Oban and the inner reaches of the Firth of Lorn, Mull lies close to the mainland of Morvern to the north-east, being separated from it by the long and narrow Sound of Mull. The irregular shape of Mull is said to resemble a crouching dog with its neck at Salen.

Although an island of many contrasts, Mull gives an immediate impression of greenery, due no doubt to its hills and moors being predominantly grassy rather than heathery, and having several extensive coniferous plantations as well as natural deciduous woodlands. Its central part is entirely mountainous, with Ben More dominating a dozen or more lower hills. Along the coastline there is a great variety of scenery which is at its most impressive where high basalt cliffs plunge into the sea, nowhere more spectacularly than round the Ardmeanach peninsula.

Among the many neighbouring islands, Iona has its special religious significance, Staffa its famous Fingal's Cave while the Treshnish Isles are probably best known as landmarks for sailors along the west coast.

MULL

MAPS : Ordnance Survey   1:50,000 Sheets 47, 48 and 49
           Bartholomew   1:100,000 Sheet 47

PRINCIPAL HILLS
WESTERN GROUP

Ben More	966m	525 330
A'Chioch	867m	534 333
Beinn Fhada	702m	540 349
Beinn nan Gabhar	572m	542 361
Beinn a' Ghraig	591m	541 372

CENTRAL GROUP

Cruachan Dearg	704m	568 332
Corra-bheinn	704m	573 322

Beinn a' Mheadhoin	602m	586 313
Cruach Choireadail	618m	594 304
Beinn Talaidh	761m	625 347

EASTERN GROUP

Sgurr Dearg	741m	665 339
Mainnir nam Fiadh	757m	676 353
Dun da Ghaoithe	766m	672 362
Beinn Thunicaraidh	648m	660 368
Beinn Mheadhon	637m	653 378
Beinn Chreagach Mhor	579m	631 390

SOUTHERN GROUP

Ben Buie (South Top)	717m	604 270
Creach Beinn	698m	642 276

ACCESS

Oban to Craignure - vehicle and passenger ferry operated by Caledonian MacBrayne. Crossing time : 45 minutes. The ferry (vehicle and passenger) for Coll and Tiree also calls in at Tobermory.

Lochaline (Morvern) to Fishnish - vehicle and passenger ferry operated by Caledonian MacBrayne. Crossing time : 15 minutes.

Mingary (Kilchoan, Ardnamurchan) to Tobermory - passenger ferry operated by Caledonian MacBrayne. Crossing time : 45 minutes. No winter service.

TRANSPORT

Given the size and complex topography of Mull, if a long stay is planned it is recommended that private transport be taken to the island. For a short stay, car and scooter hire is available at Craignure and Tobermory and an adequate bus service, connecting with the ferry, links the main centres of population. For the fit and enthusiastic, a bicycle is probably the ideal way to explore the island.

There is a grass airstrip two kilometres east of Salen, adjacent to the Glenforsa Hotel.

ACCOMMODATION

The main tourist centre is Tobermory, but hotels are also situated at Dervaig, Salen, Glen Forsa, Craignure, Kinloch (at the head of Loch Scridain), Bunessan and Fionnphort. Considering the size of the island, guest house, bed and breakfast and self-catering accommodation is fairly limited and it is wise to book in advance: contact tourist information centres at Tobermory (0688) 2182 (limited winter opening) or Oban (0631) 63122.

Wild camping is generally accepted and numerous good coastal sites are available. It is prudent however, particularly during the stalking season, to obtain local permission.

There is a youth hostel at Tobermory.

GENERAL DESCRIPTION

Mull, the second largest of the Inner Hebrides after Skye, presents a diversity of scenery which is possibly unequalled by any other Scottish island. Its coastline is deeply indented by Loch na Keal and Loch Scridain in the west and Loch Buie and Loch Spelve to the south, which together with many minor bays and inlets account for the estimated 400 kilometres of its coastal extent. It is this very coastline that vies with the mountains as Mull's most striking feature, varying from towering cliffs of crumbling basalt to idyllic sandy coves hemmed in by pink granite bluffs. This contrast can be readily appreciated by driving along Mull's extensive, often twisting, road system although this is no real substitute for exploration on foot. To quote from the first edition of this guide: "Mull has much wild beauty, many a bold sea cliff and lonely waterfall, and is nowhere tame or uninteresting". The notoriously high rainfall does much to enhance the island's numerous waterfalls, but less for the visitor's spirits.

Mull has a population of about 2200, mostly living in Tobermory and Dervaig in the north of the island, whilst other significant population centres exist at Salen and Bunessan. Farming, forestry and tourism are the main sources of employment. In the early 19th century Mull supported a population of around 10,600.

North of Salen, Tobermory itself, Mull Little Theatre, The Byre (folk museum) and the overrated Calgary Bay are all of tourist interest whilst the north-west coast, although quite attractive and offering fine mountain views, does not bear comparison with its southern counterparts. The waterfall of Eas Fors (grid reference 444 422), a half Gaelic, half Norse name literally meaning *waterfall waterfall* , although not particularly high, is notable both for its volume and its straight drop into the sea at high tide. Its spectacular form can only really be appreciated from the shoreline or from a boat.

The southern part of Mull has a wealth of magnificent coastal scenery. The spectacular Gribun cliffs, towering above the B8035 road (beware of falling rocks) can be appreciated without leaving one's car. Further along the coastline and accessible via a signposted path from Balmeanach lies the celebrated Mackinnon's Cave (grid reference 440 322) described by Dr Johnson as "the greatest natural marvel" he had ever seen. It can be entered at low tide with ease, but a more sporting high tide alternative involves either some boulder hopping followed by a short rock climb (Very Difficult), just beyond the waterfall, or a bracing swim. A torch is required to explore the inner chamber. The cave is about 180 metres long and 30 metres high at the entrance. As with many island caves, it is associated with a phantom piper and a hairless dog.

The Ardmeanach headland, with its evocative area called The Wilderness, epitomises the best of Mull's wild scenery and gives a superb coastal circuit (see walks). It offers spectacular waterfalls, great terraced lava flows, numerous caves, rosettes of columnar basalt, herds of feral goats and the famous although disappointing McCulloch's Fossil Tree (grid reference 402 278). Part of this area is owned by the National Trust for Scotland.

In complete contrast is the red granite tip of the Ross of Mull at the relatively low lying termination of the long peninsula that juts out towards Iona. Its scenery is reminiscent of more remote Hebridean islands, bare and windswept, with a scattering of croft houses; only the sheltered pockets of deciduous woodland make it distinctively Mull. Its coastline is a delight to explore, pink craggy bluffs, secluded bays with perfect white and golden sands lapped by a limpid, turquoise sea. The rocky island of Erraid, accessible on foot at low tide, is barely two square kilometres in area yet has a wealth of scenic interest. Robert Louis Stevenson is said to have written Kidnapped in one of its terraced granite cottages. Above the cottages lies an old observatory with the islands highest point, Cnoc Mor, 75m, above that.

Just north of Fionnphort at Torr More disused granite quarries can be inspected, many roughly hewn blocks are still stacked, forever awaiting transportation. This superb pink rock was used to construct Iona Cathedral, the Albert Memorial and the Skerryvore Lighthouse.

The fossil leaf beds, sandwiched in bands between basalt sheets, at the low lying headland of Ardtun are of considerable geological interest. This lava probably welled from a vast volcanic crater to the east of Ben More during the Tertiary period.

Carsaig Bay, gained from Pennyghael by a narrow twisting road is, despite its dirty grey sands, an enchanting spot with its fine, mature woodland and ancient stone jetty. The coastline to the south-west is both varied and spectacular (see walks) with much of geological interest along the foreshore. Near the Nuns' Pass, two kilometres to the west, the white sandstone cliffs are pierced by a wide cave where stone, quarried close by, was fashioned into ornamental graveslabs by Iona's monks. The wild rock scenery of Carsaig Arches lies four kilometres further along the coast at Malcolm's Point, and should not be missed. A headland of columnar basalt is tunnelled by one arch, whilst nearby a tall pinnacled stack is pierced by another. Beyond is a huge isolated table of rock known as Leac na Leum (slab of the leap). A large herd of majestic, great horned, white goats can often be seen browsing along this coastline.

At the head of Loch Buie the remarkably preserved, although apparently unsafe, 14th century ivy covered keep of Moy Castle stands on a bulge of coastal rock, commanding excellent views down the loch. Two larger although perhaps less romantic castles lie to the south of Craignure. Both Torosay and Duart are open to the public. A unique miniature railway links Craignure and Torosay Castle.

Mull's coastline is rich in birdlife with the gaunt grey figure of the heron, fishing the shallows, a common sight. Equally characteristic are the buzzards, often displaying a marked preference for perching upon telegraph poles. Golden eagles are not uncommon and occasionally the white tailed sea eagle can be spotted on hunting sorties from Rhum. A prolific and less attractive form of fauna is the midge which, in late summer and autumn, can greatly detract from the pleasure of the hills.

There is much semi-natural woodland, a mixture of oak, birch and ash, often wind-blasted along the coast. Vast areas of the island are now given over, perhaps regrettably, to commercial soft wood production.

The Mull coastline, looking west from Carsaig Bay towards Malcolm's Point

THE HILLS

The mountains of Mull cover much of the central part of the island, rising to a maximum height of 966m at Ben More, with many peaks over 600m. They afford excellent hillwalking and have none of the badly eroded paths that scar the hills of Arran and Skye. Indeed, apart from Ben More, the hills are infrequently ascended and therein perhaps lies much of their charm.

The main Mull hills break conveniently into four groups: the Western Group (to the west of Glen Clachaig), the Eastern Group (to the east of Glen Forsa), the Central Group (between the previous two and to the north of Glen More) and the Southern Group (south of Glen More). For the sake of convenience Ben Talaidh is included in the Central Group although in reality it stands in splendid isolation between the Central and Eastern Groups. Salen is probably the best base from which to tackle all but the Southern Group. The highest hill in the north of the island is Speinne Mor (444m) at grid reference 499 498, to the north-east of Loch Frisa.

To fully appreciate the vast extent of Mull's mountain groups one must leave the island and take a more distant viewpoint, say from the coastal road between Lochaline and Drimnin (B849) on the mainland. From there most of the hills are visible, the extensive mountain panorama dominated by the vast bulk of Ben More and the distinctive cone of Beinn Talaidh, the other hills forming a softer backdrop.

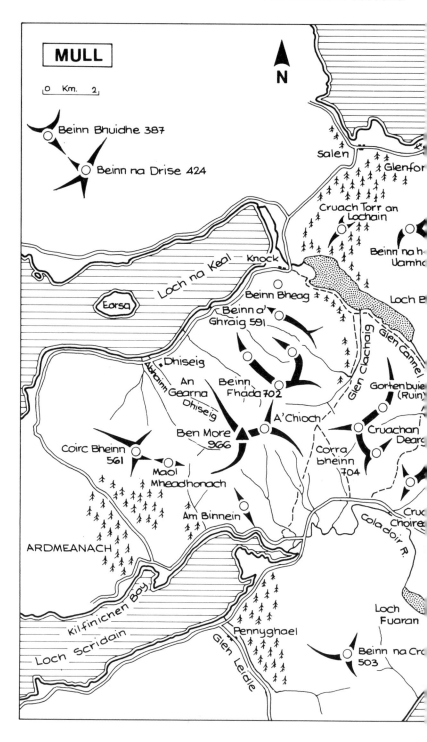

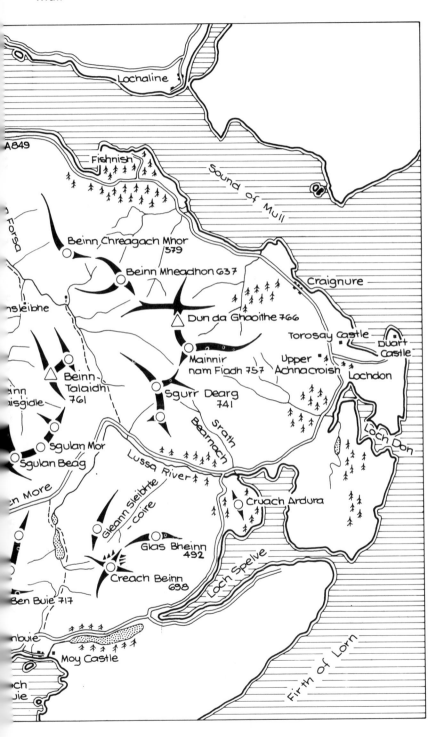

A distant view of Ben More across the Sound of Mull from Morvern

Due to the magnetic nature of the rock, a compass is unreliable on many of Mull's hills.

THE WESTERN GROUP

Ben More totally dominates this group from most viewpoints, although its lower neighbours should not be underrated. A traverse of all the hills in the western group gives a good day which can be conveniently shortened by excluding Beinn nan Gabhar and Beinn a'Ghraig. For preference a clear day should be chosen as the splendid views over Loch na Keal and Ulva to the Treshnish Isles will greatly enhance the experience.

Ben More (*the big hill*) (966m)
A'Chioch (*the breast*) (867m)
The only island Munro outwith Skye, Ben More is the most westerly of Mull's main hills. Its massive grey bulk, together with its fine satellite peak A'Chioch, forms a distinctive profile. An aerial view gives the impression of a great propeller, radiating ridges twisting around a central nose cone. Much of the upper slopes are covered in a mantle of angular scree that emits a metallic 'clinking' sound under the climber's boot. The north-east corrie is quite craggy and often carries snow patches into the late spring.

Ben More from A'Chioch

The most frequently used approach is up the north-west ridge from Dhiseig on the southern shore of Loch na Keal. There is a well-defined path up the lower grassy slopes on the south-west of the Abhainn Dhiseig, and higher up as the grass gives way to screes numerous small cairns show the way to the summit. Alternatively, one can climb up the grassy spur of An Gearna, but there is no path until the previous route is joined high up on the north-west ridge. As can be expected, the summit views are panoramic; an endless collage of sea and island, the mountains of Rhum and Skye prominent to the north, the Paps of Jura to the south.

An approach from the south is roughly the same distance although perhaps rather less attractive, this side of Ben More having been likened to a great slag heap. From the bend in the B8035, at grid reference 530 297, Am Binnein and Maol nan Damh must first be ascended before the south ridge of Ben More is gained.

Without doubt the most aestheticaly attractive ascent of Ben More is via the east ridge over A'Chioch. Commencing at the col between Beinn Fhada and A'Chioch, readily gained from Loch na Keal, via Gleann na Beinne Fada, or from Glen Clachaig, the bare summit of the shapely A'Chioch is quickly breasted by an elegant, narrowing ridge. From here an excellent view to the south of the meandering Coladoir River and delta can be enjoyed.

The connecting ridge from A'Chioch to Ben More appears impressive and has quite misleadingly been compared to the Aonach Eagach and Liathach. Most of it provides a splendid airy walk, with an interesting scramble over shattered rock just below the summit of Ben More. In good winter conditions the whole ridge becomes a delightful and rarely enjoyed snow arete (Grade I/II).

Beinn Fhada (*the long hill*) (702m)

Although somewhat dwarfed by its neighbours, Beinn Fhada, which forms a long curving ridge, has great character. The ideal approach is from Loch na Keal along the south bank of the Scarisdale River to where it flows out of a fine little gorge. From there a spur of regular slope leads to the north-west top (563m). A fairly narrow ridge of one and a half kilometres gives an enjoyable traverse to the higher, cairned, south-east top, with classic views of Ben More and A'Chioch, particularly attractive in the early morning summer light. A small lochan lies a short distance to the west of the summit.

Beinn nan Gabhar (*hill of the goats*) (572m)

A superficially uninspiring lump of a hill where red deer are more likely to be seen than goats. It is tempting and easy to by-pass it en route from Beinn Fhada to Beinn a'Ghraig.

Beinn a'Ghraig (591m)

A grand and quite rocky little hill which obscures Ben More from viewpoints at the head of Loch na Keal. The summit spine is capped by grey basaltic tors, with the speckled ochre screes below belying the granitic body of the hill. An ascent from Knock, over Beinn Bheag, gives a strenuous hour's walking. A fine bird's-eye view of Loch Ba is the reward.

THE CENTRAL GROUP

Mull's central hills form a great horseshoe around the head of Glen Cannel and flank the northern side of Glen More. The area is bounded by Glen Clachaig to the west and Glen Forsa to the east. With the exception of Beinn Talaidh, these hills are infrequently ascended, even by Mull standards. Great herds of red deer can often be seen wandering across the high cols and browsing along the wide grassy ridges. If approached from Loch Ba, the complete circuit, including Beinn Talaidh, gives an energetic and rewarding day with ever-changing views. The striking braided channels of the Glencannel River with the oak fringed Loch Ba beyond are of particular note.

An ideal starting point for the circuit of these hills is the remote and ruined farm of Gortenbuie (grid reference 593 344) which is reached by a rough seven kilometre track along Loch Ba, starting at Knock - a hard walk but an enjoyable and challenging mountain bike ride. Ascents from the Glen More road to the south are much shorter and more direct, but lack the character of the northern approach.

Cruachan Dearg (704m)
Corra-bheinn (704m)

Although separated by a distance of one kilometre, with a drop in height of 130m between them, it is logical to describe these twin peaks together. Their fine shapely mountain form can be appreciated from almost any direction, ironically only when viewed from each other's summit do they fail to impress. From the head of Loch Scridain they appear as balanced upthrusts at the termination of a high level ridge, whereas from the old burial ground in Glen Cannel they display more individual form, the steep darker, upper slopes of Corra-bheinn (a gabbro cap) having a forbidding character.

Both hills throw out ridges to the north-east. The one from the small cairned conical top of Cruachan Dearg drops to the minor top of Cruachan Beag (601m) and lower down widens out to form a great hill expanse, with easy slopes dropping northwards to the shores of Loch Ba. The lower slopes of both hills support lush grasses with a fine mix of wild flowers, the delightful bog asphodel growing in profusion. On the northern slopes of Corra-bheinn (below the gabbro) foxgloves grow, including a rare white variety.

The upper slopes of Corra-bheinn display much outcropping rock and scree, with the summit crowned by a cylindrical triangulation pillar. A direct ascent from Glen More involving 650m of fairly uniform slope can be quickly accomplished. A descent to the col between Corra-bheinn and Beinn a'Mheadoin is best achieved by following the summit ridge of Corra-bheinn north-eastward for 250 metres to a slight dip, and then descending a grassy ramp to the east. The vague alignment of a path crosses this col linking Glen Cannel and Glen More.

Beinn a'Mheadhoin (602m)

A fairly uninteresting hill although the north-west ridge is of some character, giving a pleasant ascent. From the summit its neighbour Cruach Choireadail is seen to good effect.

The Ben More group seen across Loch na Keal from Ulva ferry

Cruach Choireadail (618m)

This fine rugged peak, with warts of outcropping rock studding its upper slopes, forms the north flank of Glen More at the turning of the glen. The southern top is the highest, with very stony ground between it and the lower top of Cruachan Beag (596m) half a kilometre to the north-east. A wide hog-back ridge carpeted with springy turf extends for several kilometres to the east-north-east over the rounded minor tops of Sgulan Beag and Sgulan Mor, terminating at Maol a'Ghearraidh (522m). The col of Mam Bhradhadail (424m) separates this top from Beinn Talaidh. From Sgulan Beag a broad lochan-dotted spur, at right angles to the main ridge line, extends to Beinn Chaisgidle (504m), an ideal viewpoint from which to appreciate the grand setting of Loch Ba.

Beinn Talaidh (*hill of the cattle*) (761m)

Beinn Talaidh, pronounced 'Talla' is, after Ben More, Mull's most distinctive peak, its smooth symmetrical cone easily identified from a great distance and from almost any direction. An often present trail of summit cloud gives the mountain the character of an active volcano. This appearance, together with its considerable bulk and isolation, causes it to dominate Glen Forsa.

On the Ordnance Survey 1:10,000 mapping the triangulation pillar (base) is given the height 761m although a spot height of 763m is shown a short distance to the south-west, outwith the 760m contour ring, on the site of an old cairn. The former height is the true natural summit altitude and the latter is erroneous.

The eastern group of hills and Beinn Talaidh seen beyond Salen

The shortest distance from a road to the summit is from the south, starting at the big bend in the A849 road (grid reference 642 328) via the curving spur of Maol nam Fiadh. The most popular ascent route, however, is from the north, and given vehicle or bicycle access to Tomsleibhe (grid reference 617 372), the climb can be accomplished in a couple of hours. However, if the six kilometre forestry road from the A849 road east of Salen has to be walked, it becomes a day's outing. A most satisfying route is via the north ridge, initially steep although grassy, the angle eases higher up. The upper slopes, above about 500m, carry a mantle of scree. Due to its central location, an expansive view of all Mull's peaks can be had. A steep north-eastward descent to the col (498m) gives access to the gabbro-torred outlier of Beinn Bheag (537m), whose north ridge leads back down to Tomsleibhe.

An ascent of Beinn Talaidh can conveniently be included in a traverse of the Central Group.

THE EASTERN GROUP

The hills flanking the east side of Glen Forsa are in general smooth contoured with little exposed rock and are somewhat reminiscent of the Southern Uplands. A series of broad backed tops rise progressively from north-west to south-east achieving maximum height at Dun da Ghaoithe (766m) and terminating at Mainnir nam Fiadh. The west side of the glen is dominated by Ben Talaidh (described in the Central Group) whilst at the head of the glen stands the comparatively rocky peak of Sgurr Dearg.

A forestry road has recently been pushed up Glen Forsa to grid reference 633 365 which, although speeding up access, definitely detracts from the remoteness of the glen. Extensive afforestation has taken place, with more planned.

Although of a rounded nature, these hills boast deep corries, separated by narrow grassy ridges (particularly on the Glen Forsa side), many of which provide easy access to the main ridge.

Beinn Chreagach Mhor (579m)

This is the first significant top on the sprawling hill mass that extends from the coast on the north side of Glen Forsa. It presents a bold, craggy front to the south. A direct ascent from Glen Forsa gives ample opportunity for rock scrambling. To the east lies a col at 500m occupied by Loch a'Mhaim.

Beinn Mheadhon (637m)
Beinn Thunicaraidh (648m)

These inelegant, broad backed, rounded hills lie on the south-easterly ridge progression. The west ridge of Beinn Mheadhon, from the ruin at Rhoail, is probably the best approach.

Dun da Ghaoithe (*castle of the two winds*) (766m)

Crowned by a large cairn, this shapely and delightfully named hill is the third highest on Mull. It is linked to Mainnir nam Fiadh by a high level, surprisingly dramatic, turfy ridge. Ptarmigan inhabit these tops some 300m below the level of their mainland counterparts. The west ridge, flanking the south side of Coire nam Fuaran, gives an enjoyable ascent from Glen Forsa. The most direct approach is from the east, starting at the road bridge over the Scallastle River (grid reference 703 383) and gaining the wide spur of Maol nam Damh.

Mainnir nam Fiadh (*fold of the deer*) (757m)

Lying at a ridge junction, this top commands spectacular views. It can be independently approached from the east by gaining the prominent mast on Moal nan Uan, 429m (via a track from Upper Achnacroish), then ascending the long narrowing eastern ridge. The summit has a large cairn whilst a cylindrical triangulation pillar lies slightly lower to the south-east.

A linking traverse to Sgurr Dearg involves a steep descent firstly to the south-west, then south, over scree patches. This leads to a green col at 500m with a distinctive T-shaped stone and turf dyke.

Sgurr Dearg (*red peak*) (741m)

Although undoubtedly rocky, the redness of this fine hill is more illusory. From the Sgurr Dearg-Mainnir nam Fiadh col a short ascent leads to a levelling off where the long spur of Beinn Bheag juts out to the south-east. From this point the ridge becomes quite airy above boulder-strewn Coire nan Clach. Some 50m below the top a six metre rock step threatens to bar the way, but it can be climbed without undue difficulty. In winter this little wall can be more daunting.

From the summit long spurs thrust out to the north-west and south and both are confusingly called Beinn Bhearnach. The southerly one forms an independent top of 633m at its termination. This top can be quickly gained from the Glen More road to the south-west.

Sgurr Dearg can also be climbed from the A849 road at the shore of Loch Spelve. The going up Srath Bearnach is quite rough over tussocky grass until easier ground is reached higher up on the south-east ridge of Beinn Bheag or the slopes of the southern Beinn Bhearnach. The ascent of Sgurr Dearg up its south ridge from Beinn Bearnach avoids the short rock step mentioned above.

THE SOUTHERN GROUP

Lying to the south of Glen More are the two fine hills of Ben Buie and Creach Beinn, which together with the surrounding high ground comprise a hill area quite different in character from that to the north. Their dark, rugged appearance is due to extensive areas of outcropping rock, a mixture of gabbro, rhyolite and granophyres. The two hills are separated by the deep valley of Gleann a'Chaiginn Mhoir. Lochbuie is an ideal starting point and an ascent of both hills can be effected in a short day.

Creach Beinn (698m)

Beautifully situated above the idyllic, oak fringed Loch Uisg, Creach Beinn presents a complex south face deeply cut by gullies, with much bare rock in its upper reaches. It throws out a long twisting ridge to the south-west terminating above Lochbuie. This ridge provides perhaps the most interesting line of ascent, although the numerous false tops can be frustrating. From the triangulation pillar on its rounded summit, splendid views out over Loch Spelve to the mainland can be enjoyed, and to the north-east lies the lesser hill of Glas Bheinn (492m). A descent of 550m to the west, initially rocky, leads to the path running through Gleann a' Chaiginn Mhoir.

Ben Buie (717m)

This is a grand twin-topped mountain with a bold, craggy eastern face, well seen from Lochbuie. Numerous interesting ascent routes are available, the shortest being from Gleann a'Chaiginn Mhoir to the east. However an approach from Glen More via the rocky spur of Creag na h-Iolaire has its moments and in combination with a visit to strange, crystal clear Loch Fuaran, an ascent from the west can also be recommended.

The southerly and highest top is crowned with a well made cairn. The northerly top, only 3m lower, lies half a kilometre to the north. To the north-east, framed between Creach Beinn and Sgurr Dearg lies Duart Castle with Lismore and the high mountains of Lochaber beyond. The north-west face is deeply incised by vertical walled gullies (eroded dykes) with falls and deep cauldrons which give good sport to the competent rock climber. West of Loch Fuaran lies some wild, rarely visited hill ground, culminating at Beinn na Croise (503m) (grid reference 559 251). Deep, short glens run south-eastward into Loch Buie with new afforestation to the north of this area.

PATHS AND WALKS

In the north of the island, particularly along the north and west coasts, there are many enjoyable walks. Inland, the path from Kilninian through the hills to the B8073 road east of Calgary gives an easy excursion. A walk down the western shore line of Loch Frisa can also be recommended, particularly if carrying a fishing rod.

In the south, several defined paths pass over high cols and give good exercise and fine views, though transport can be problematic. The best is probably from Knock to Ardvergnish (at the head of Loch Scridain) via Glen Clachaig. Reaching a height of 332m at the pass between A'Chioch and Cruachan Dearg (cairn) this twelve kilometre walk takes three to four hours. A similar, although less frequently used, path climbs over the pass between Corra-bheinn and Beinn a'Mheadoin. Also commencing at Knock, the track is followed along the south side of scenic Loch Ba to the ruin of Gortenbuie. A fairly vague path then leads over to Glen More. Another classic path, five kilometres long, runs through Gleann a' Chaigainn Mhoir linking Glen More to Lochbuie.

Fine coastal walks abound, a few following defined paths, the majority not. Without doubt the most famous is that around the Ardmeanach Peninsula, the complete circuit giving an arduous yet rewarding day ranking as a Scottish classic. Although a track runs from the B8035 road at Kilfinichen Bay (grid reference 490 286) to Burg, most of it is not suitable for normal vehicular access. Thereafter the two critical sections of the walk are finding the steel ladder giving access to the foreshore (grid reference 405 272) and avoiding the deep, sea cut gulf of Sloc nam Ban (grid reference 431 313) by ascending 150m above the coast. This whole coastline has a wealth of interesting features (see General Description). The complete walk from Kilfinichen Bay to Balmeanach is 20 kilometres and will take about eight hours (five from Burg), and it should not be tackled without adequate hillwalking equipment.

Another classic walk is from Carsaig Bay to the Carsaig Arches and back along a rough coastal path. The round trip of 12 kilometres takes about four hours and is never without interest (see General Description). There is also a good walk along the path from Carsaig Bay to Lochbuie, eight kilometres.

Numerous other good walks, both hill and coastal will be found. The ultimate challenge would undoubtedly be a complete coastal circuit of the island. Allow several weeks for this marathon.

ROCK CLIMBING

Considering the extensive amounts of exposed rock on Mull, it is quite inconceivable that there should be no good rock climbing on the island. Sadly, many of the big coastal cliffs are composed of crumbling basalt and the mountain crags seem invariably to be damp, vegetated and broken. Clean, attractive rock walls do exist in the hills but they are usually of limited height, offering good sport but hardly justifying a special visit or route recording. The best areas are on the flanks of Ben Buie, low down on the south flank of Cruach Choireadail and a 40m high slabby face at grid reference 577 330, on the north side of Corra-bheinn (all gabbro). Another possibility is a crag just east of the south end of Loch Ba. The slabby crags in Coire

Staffa

Ghaibhre (Beinn Talaidh) are vegetated and often wet, offering little appeal.

Good coastal cragging on small stacks is available at Quinish and Croig in the north with the added bonus of superb views of Skye and the Small Isles. There is a fine little roadside 'edge' at the junction of the B8073 road and the Ulva ferry road. A north facing 15m high dolerite sill near Ardchrishnish (grid reference 425 234) provides good sport in dry conditions. Indeed there are numerous small crags scattered around the island, although without doubt the best are the beautiful pink granite walls of Erraid and around the tip of the Ross of Mull. Although reaching a maximum height of only 20m, this magnificent clean rock will provide the confident solo climber with many days enjoyment punctuated by the delights of deserted sandy coves and crystal clear water. The main stack of the Carsaig Arches gives a variety of routes, the easiest being the landward side 35m, (Very Difficult) although rather loose near the top.

Recent rumours tell of huge clean, coastal gabbro walls with immense rock climbing potential. The enthusiast can be advised to reach for a geological structure map, as an unaided search of the coastline could be a time-consuming affair.

IONA

MAPS *:*   Ordnance Survey   1:50,000 Sheet 48
                                        1:25,000 Sheet 341 (NM22/32)

HIGHEST POINT
   Dun I   101m   283 252

ACCESS
Fionnphort to Iona. Passenger ferry operated by Caledonian MacBrayne. Crossing
time : 5 minutes. Regular seven day service. Also occasional cruises from Oban,
telephone 0631 62285.

ACCOMMODATION
Two small hotels and some bed and breakfast accommodation - details from tourist
offices at Tobermory (0688) 2182 or Oban (0631) 63122. Some accommodation is
also available at the Abbey. Camping along the shore is another option.

GENERAL DESCRIPTION
Iona has the reputation of being an island of peace and great beauty. The first-time
visitor is rarely disappointed and it has become the annual objective of many a
modern day pilgrimage. Despite being completely overrun by visitors at the height
of the tourist season, this nine square kilometres of rock, sand and machair,
detached from the Ross of Mull by but one kilometre of sea, remains unspoiled. It
manages to retain an air of tranquility against all the odds.

   In 563 AD Saint Columba landed at the south tip of the island and from that
day on it has occupied an important place in the Christian world. The present day
Abbey, probably built on the site of Columba's original monastery, dates from
around 1200 AD, with later medieval additions, and it was extensively restored
during the early part of this century. The whole complex is open to the public and
the church is very much a vital part of community life. St Martin's Cross (9th century)
and a replica of St John's Cross (10th century) stand to the west of the Abbey. The
latter, a very fine example of a Celtic ring cross, similar in style to the Kildalton Cross
of Islay, was blown down and smashed by gales in 1957. The magnificent medieval
MacLean's Cross lies just north of the village at a bend in the road. In the heart of
the village are the remains of a 12th century nunnery.

   Scenically Iona also has much to offer. To quote W H Murray: "What Iona
does have is a purity of light and colour that seems to excel that of other islands".
It is perhaps born of a juxtaposition of pale beaches of finest shell sand, backed by
thick green swards; of numerous outcrops of ancient, contorted gneiss; and of an
open aspect to the Atlantic with its purifying breeze. Yet there is even more than this;
some other magical element, beyond definition.

   The whole of Iona's much indented coastline is worth exploring. Two
features of particular interest are the old marble quarry (a green streaked variety)
in the extreme south-east of the island (not easy to locate) and the spectacular
Spouting Cave at grid reference 262 230. Catch it at high tide on a stormy day.

Dun I (pronounced *'Dun Ee'*) (101m)
By far the highest eminence on the island, this fine miniature mountain is predictably an excellent viewpoint, both of the immediate vicinity and of the dark Wilderness
coastline with the soft high hills of Mull beyond. There is a triangulation pillar just
to the east of the summit. The north face is a vertical rock wall.

ROCK CLIMBING
Iona, like Coll, possesses a wealth of perfect gneiss; enough rock to keep the
enthusiastic 'boulderer' busy for many days. The best areas are in the south-west
and on Eilean Didil, although the north face of Dun I presents an unclimbed 20m high
face. A traverse around the south and west coastline would involve much pleasant
rock climbing.

ULVA AND GOMETRA

MAPS : Ordnance Survey 1:50,000 Sheet 47

PRINCIPAL HILLS

ULVA	Beinn Chreagach	313m	403 402
	Beinn Eolasary	306m	389 403

ACCESS
By ferry, across the narrow Sound of Ulva, although there is no scheduled service.
The ferry, which is privately operated, is available from Tuesdays to Saturdays
inclusive from 9.00 a.m. to 5.30 p.m. It may be called from Ulva to the Mull side by
making the appropriate signal. Gometra is linked to Ulva by a bridge across the
narrow channel Am Bru.

GENERAL DESCRIPTION
Ulva, only just a separate island, is by far the biggest of Mull's outliers. Its small
population is concentrated in the east, the houses sheltered by the surrounding
mixed woodland. The remainder of the island is wild and bracken covered, with
distinctive stepped basalt terracing, creating a strange pyramid like effect. A rough
road runs around the north of the island and onto Gometra. On the south side is a
big bay scattered with islets. Ulva was the birth place of the explorer David
Livingstone and at one time carried a population of over 500. Now it is largely given
over to sheep.   Gometra, similar in character to Ulva, gives fine views of the
Treshnish Isles and both possess some interesting, rocky coastline.
        Several smaller islands lie to the south of Ulva; the oddly named Little
Colonsay (52m at Torr Mor), Inch Kenneth (49m at A'Chrois) with its ancient chapel
and curious house, and in the mouth of Loch na Keal the rugged Eorsa (99m high).

THE HILLS
Ulva's two main hills lie in the west of the island and provide good viewpoints. A
spring ascent is recommended as later in the year the bracken grows to head height.
Beinn Chreagach (313m) is topped by a triangulation pillar, as is the highest point
on Gometra.

STAFFA

MAPS :   Ordnance Survey   1:50,000 Sheet 48
                                           1:10,000 Sheet NM 33 NW

HIGHEST POINT
    Meall nan Gamhna   42m   323 351

ACCESS
Frequent summer ferry service from Fionnphort, telephone Iona (068 17) 373, 338 or 382. Also from Ulva ferry, telephone Dervaig (068 84) 242, weather permitting. A natural landing site in the north-east of the island is often used.

GENERAL DESCRIPTION
Staffa is without doubt the best known of all Scotland's smaller islands, its romantic fame inextricably linked with Mendelssohn's *Hebridean Overture*. From its 'discovery' by Sir Joseph Banks in 1772, it became an increasingly important part of the 'grand tour', such notables as Keats, Turner and Queen Victoria paying their respects; although the ubiquitous Dr Johnson and Boswell failed to land. There are numerous old prints of Staffa, many displaying a degree of artistic licence.

One kilometre in length, Staffa lies twelve kilometres to the north of Fionnphort, although its nearest neighbours are Little Colonsay and Gometra. It is an uninhabited grassy, flat-topped island ringed by spectacular columnar basalt cliffs and pierced by numerous caves. At the southern tip lies the world famous Fingal's Cave (grid reference 324 350), 68 metres long and 20 metres high. Access can easily be gained along the natural walkway called The Causeway leading from the old jetty at Clamshell Cave (grid reference 326 352).

Heavily corroded iron stanchions lead from the mouth of the cave into the interior, a relic of its Victorian showcase days. The booming of the sea inside the cave is an awe-inspiring sound.

The big cave to the west of Fingal's Cave is Boat Cave and beyond that McKinnon's Cave (incorrectly positioned further north on O.S. mapping). Between these caves lies The Great Face, where the hexagonal columns are at their most impressive, rising from a tufa base to a height of 20 metres and capped by a weird contortion of micro-columns.

It is doubtful if any serious rock climbing has yet been done, although scope exists if the glassy nature of the rock and the loose overhanging finishes can be overcome.

TRESHNISH ISLES

MAPS : As for Staffa
Also Ordnance Survey 1:25,000 Sheet 315 (NM24/34)

HIGHEST POINT
Bac Mor or Dutchman's Cap	86m	243 387
Lunga (Cruachan)	103m	278 420

ACCESS
As for Staffa.

GENERAL DESCRIPTION
This ten kilometre long string of uninhabited volcanic islands and skerries, on a south-west to north-east axis, lies some seven kilometres to the west of Gometra. The central, highest and largest island is Lunga with the remains of once occupied black houses near its northern tip. Much of the coast is fringed by low cliffs, the home of innumerable shags, razorbills, guillemots, puffins, kittiwakes, fulmars and many other varieties of seabird. The lush grass above the shore line attracts many winter visitors including barnacle geese. Off the west coast, below Cruachan, lies the impregnable cliff girt Dun Cruit, 30m high and separated by a sea channel barely six metres wide. A worthwhile although remote climbing objective.

To the north-east of Lunga, beyond a profusion of treacherous rocks, lies the flat Fladda (26m high) and beyond that the twin rocky islands of Cairn na Burgh More (35m) and Cairn na Burgh Beg (22m) are the most northerly island of the group. Both hold the remains of castles, that on Cairn na Burgh More dating from the days of the Lords of the Isles. It is recorded that during a clan feud the MacLean of Lochbuie was imprisoned in this castle with only the ugliest woman in Mull for company. However, Lochbuie rose to the occasion and gave her a son who later won back his heritage.

Separated from the rest of the group, at the southern tip of the chain, lies Bac Mor or Dutchman's Cap as it is descriptively known. Its dome is the cone of an ancient volcano, its brim a lava platform forming a very distinctive landmark. The smaller Bac Beag lies to the south, linked by great shelves of rock and covered in tidal pools, into which the sea foams and cascades.

The whole group is a popular breeding ground for the Atlantic seal, although the only safe anchorage for man is just to the north of Lunga.

CHAPTER 5

COLL AND TIREE

Inexplicably, both Coll and Tiree were omitted from the previous edition of the Islands Guide. Certainly, they cannot be regarded as being of great interest to climbers and hillwalkers, but in this respect they are no different from some other islands included in this book. On the other hand, like all the islands, they have their own individual characteristics which make them worthy of exploration.

As with many neighbouring 'paired' islands, they are markedly different in character. Coll is a rugged island, for the most part bare rock and heather. Tiree is green and agricultural, the product of wind-blown sand which has created a fertile plain across much of the island. The two islands share a common underlying rock and have similar climates. The latter is popularly, but quite erroneously, supposed to be characterised by record hours of sunshine, but this is only true for the months of May and June. Later in the year sea-fog and drizzle are more common. On the other hand, the wind seems to blow continuously and dominate the weather pattern of both these islands.

COLL

MAPS : Ordnance Survey   1:50,000 Sheet 46
Bartholomew   1:100,000 Sheet 47

PRINCIPAL HILLS

Ben Hogh	104m	181 580
Ben Feall	66m	145 548

ACCESS

Sea : Oban to Arinagour (Coll) via Tobermory (Mull). Vehicle and passenger ferry operated by Caledonian MacBrayne. Crossing time 3 hours and 15 minutes (ferry calls at Tobermory en route).

TRANSPORT

Car and bicycle hire can be arranged through the Isle of Coll Hotel, Arinagour. Telephone (087 93) 334. Taxi service also available.

ACCOMMODATION

Isle of Coll Hotel, telephone (087 93) 334, is the only hotel on the island. Self-catering cottages are available, telephone Oban (0631) 63122. Camping behind the churches to the north of Arinagour is permitted. Elsewhere, permission should be sought locally.

GENERAL DESCRIPTION

Coll, nineteen kilometres in length and six at its widest, and forming the rough outline of a fish, is at first acquaintance a barren island, its bare ribs of Lewisian gneiss bringing to mind the low, rocky hill country of Sutherland. On closer acquaintance however, the island's great beauty is revealed.

The population is about two hundred, mostly concentrated in the village of Arinagour with its whitewashed, terraced cottages, shops and post office. This is a popular centre for the yachting fraternity, Loch Eatharna providing a sheltered anchorage. Many ruined crofts can be seen around the island, with a concentration near Bousd in the north-west, and they tell of a once much greater population. Coll's economy depends on farming and tourism, together with a wealth of outside interests. The pheasants, bred for sporting purposes, are thick on the ground around Arinagour.

The beaches of Coll's west coast are arguably the finest in the Hebrides. Although not attaining the length of those on Harris and the Uists, they are of the finest shell sand in superb rock-hemmed settings and many are rarely frequented. Long surf edged breakers pound these beaches even on the calmest of days and, together with the numerous islands and reefs that fringe Coll's coastline, provide spice to marine pursuits.

Despite the virtual absence of trees, Coll supports a fair heron population whose scraggy nests are built on the scrubby growths of loch islets (often crannogs).

The narrow neck of land in the south-west between Feall Bay and Crossapol Bay is of note, being covered with enormous sand dunes, rising to a height of 50m and providing habitats for a wide variety of birds. To the east of this area, at the end of the B8070 road, lie two castles. The most northerly is an ugly Victorian pile; the southerly is the classic compact 15th century stronghold of the MacLeans now fully renovated and used as a private residence.

THE HILLS

Whilst in no sense can Coll be called mountainous, and even the term hill may be stretching a point, the numerous rocky undulations are of some interest and greatly add to the island's scenic attraction. The northern half of Coll, like a miniature northern Jura with its abundance of lochs, is a dissected moorland plateau rising to 79m at Meall na h-Iolaire (grid reference 267 617). Its eastern coastline is saw-edged with narrow coves and headlands, and provides a good walk. Although the southern part of the island is much more cultivated, the higher ground is quite rocky, particularly along the north-west coast.

Ben Hogh (104m)

The highest point on Coll, crowned by a triangulation pillar, can be ascended from

Clabhach, to the north, in ten minutes. The hill's north-western flank is fairly rocky and a perched boulder called Clach na Ban-righ (*rock of the queen*) sits upon its northern shoulder. This product of glaciation is probably the island's best view point.

Ben Feall (66m)

Although many higher tops exist on Coll, Ben Feall, being a rocky headland surrounded by sea, sand and dunes, has a relatively grand stature, and is well worth climbing. A track just north of the road junction at Arileod (grid reference 160 548) gives easy access in about twenty minutes.

PATHS AND WALKS

Good walks abound, both coastal and inland. A walk out to the western tip of Coll, initially by the path to Crossapol, can be recommended.

ROCK CLIMBING

Hundreds of little crags present the enthusiastic boulderer with enough steep and perfect rock (gneiss) to satisfy even the most demanding appetite. Although the highest are only about 20m, all are of good quality. Of particular note are Creag nam Clamhan (*crag of the buzzard*) at grid reference 237 622, and the beautiful pink coastal cliffs in the west. A long crag at grid reference 143 549 on Bean Feall would probably repay a visit.

GUNNA

This small island, lying between Coll and Tiree and rising to a hight of 36m at grid reference 097 512, has no mountaineering interest. Being small, uninhabited and the haunt of much bird life, it does possess its own attractions and is a must for any 'island-baggers' list.

TIREE

MAPS :   Ordnance Survey   1:50,000 Sheet 46
            Bartholomew   1:100,000 Sheet 47

PRINCIPAL HILLS

Carnan Mor	141m	967 401
Beinn Ceann a'Mhara		
Mullach Mor	103m	938 410
Beinn Hough	119m	948 462

ACCESS

Sea : Oban to Scarinish. Vehicle and passenger ferry operated by Caledonian MacBrayne. Crossing time: 5 hours (ferry calls at Tobermory and Coll en route).
Air : Glasgow to Tiree, daily flight (except Sundays) operated by Loganair (telephone 041 889 3181).

TRANSPORT

A post bus connects with ferry sailings. Car hire is available (telephone 08792 644 or 555). Also bicycle hire (telephone 08792 428). Cycling is a real pleasure, despite the wind. Taking a bicycle over on the ferry is inexpensive and should be considered.

ACCOMMODATION

Two hotels, Tiree Lodge (telephone 08792 368) and Scarinish (telephone 08792 308) plus a few guest houses and self-catering (telephone Oban [0631] 63122). No official campsite, but camping in the many areas of grassed-over dunes seems acceptable, although finding fresh water can be a problem.

GENERAL DESCRIPTION

The majority of Tiree (*land of corn*) is level, low-lying and under agriculture; indeed its central part, known as The Reef, is so flat that as one approaches by boat the houses seem to rise out of the sea. Its extensive, relatively rich agricultural land is the result of a covering of wind blown shell sand. In spring this machair is thickly carpeted in flowers.

Eighteen kilometres in length, in roughly the shape of an axehead, the island supports a population of around eight hundred, and many crofts are still active, although an increasing number are being used as holiday homes. Good examples of black houses and white houses (built using mortar) can be seen. Many have been converted with distinctive tarred roofs replacing the original turf and thatch.

Tiree is virtually treeless and surprisingly devoid of rabbits, although hares are common. Birdlife is rich and diverse, from wintering geese (several varieties), whooper swans and duck that favour the marshy fringed, shallow lochs to the terns (little, arctic and common) that nest around the coast. Tiree is also rich in antiquities,

Landscape of Tiree at Vaul Bay

particularly duns, brochs and cupmarked rocks. One doubly remarkable rock, the Ringing Stone, situated on the north coast at grid reference 026 487, emits a metallic, vaguely musical note when struck with a small stone and is covered in ancient cup-shaped depressions (many obviously enlarged by recent over-enthusiastic stone ringers). Being composed of augite, its dark colour distinguishes it from the surrounding boulders and its present location is no doubt the result of glacial action, it having probably been carried from Rhum.

The broch of Dun Mor on the coast north of the crofting settlement of Vaul (grid reference 042 492) is the best preserved on Tiree with twin circular walls still standing to a height of nearly two metres (providing a wind-break and perfect sun trap). Its ease of access and splendid setting make it a must on any itinerary. The shells of two ancient chapels can be seen to the rear of the Lodge Hotel at Kirkapol. The largest and most recent (14th century) has some interesting carved grave slabs.

At Hynish in the south stands a stone tower constructed in 1843 of local stone, which was used as a shore base and communications point during the construction of the Skerryvore lighthouse on an isolated reef 17 kilometres to the south-west of Tiree. The lighthouse itself, designed by Alan Stevenson, is 42m high and was built of red granite from the Ross of Mull. The tower at Hynish was turned into a museum in 1984 and graphically illustrates the construction of Skerryvore. A key to the museum is available from the centre house in the adjacent terrace.

Although Tiree is fringed with long, wide beaches of finest shell sand, they perhaps lack the character of those on Coll. However, Tiree does possess a short section of fantastic coastal cliff scenery, in the south-west, at Ceann a'Mhara. Its dramatic rock walls and birdlife can be well appreciated by traversing in along flat rock slabs from the north.

THE HILLS
Although predominantly flat and regarded more for its fine windsurfing than landward pursuits, Tiree does indeed possess three hills whose stature is effectively enhanced by that very flatness.

Carnan Mor (141m)
Tiree's highest hill, accessible by a tarmac road from the west, is crowned by a radar station complex including a great white globe, likened to a giant golf ball, which is visible from almost any point on the island. An alternative and more pleasant ascent route is to follow a substantial dry stone wall from grid reference 957 401. The upper slopes are covered in heather clumps and rock outcrops. The minor top, Ben Hynish (126m), lies half a kilometre to the south.

Beinn Ceann a'Mhara (103m)
Although the lowest of Tiree's main hills, Beinn Ceann a'Mhara is without doubt the most rugged. It occupies most of its namesake headland whose westerly precipitous flank is sea-bitten into a fantastic display of fretted pink gneiss.

The northerly top, known as Mullach Mor, is the highest although the southerly one (90m), close to the cliff edge, is cairned. Quite inexplicably, until recent mapping, the southerly top has always been depicted as the higher.

The whole of this headland is dotted with wild flowers, in particular purple-blue puffs of cornflower, and is a delight to explore.

Beinn Hough (119m)
Beinn Hough is a surprisingly dramatic twin-topped swelling above the surrounding plain dotted with houses. The northern top is the highest, crowned with a triangulation pillar and concrete hut; the southern top, Beinn Mhurstat (113m), with its assortment of masts, is reached by a road from the south. The view across the patchwork of fields below to distant islands is expansive.

PATHS AND WALKS
Although the centre of the island is not particularly attractive to the walker, the long pale beaches of fine shell sand (Traigh Mhor is three kilometres long), the extensive grassy dunes and the flat, rocky coastline will give many hours of pleasant walking. The more energetic may consider a complete coastal circuit.

ROCK CLIMBING
It is hard to believe that any rock climbing is possible on the flatness of Tiree, but the island holds many surprises.

PART TWO

THE ISLAND OF SKYE

D. Noel Williams

INTRODUCTION

Skye is without a doubt the most popular of all the islands with mountaineers. This is partly because it is so readily accessible from the mainland, but principally because it boasts the most magnificent mountain group to be found anywhere in the British Isles — the Cuillin. It has been said that the Cuillin exercise a magnetic attraction not only upon a compass needle, but upon all climbers who ever come under their spell. Be that as it may, there is much more to Skye than the Cuillin, and the many other delights of the island can prove just as attractive in their own way.

Skye is the largest and most northerly major island in the Inner Hebrides. Its eastern end lies close to the mainland at the mouth of Loch Alsh. Only some 700 metres of water intervenes in the strait of Kyle Akin and less than 500 metres in the strait of Kyle Rhea. The island is 78 kilometres long from north to south (Rubha Hunish to the Point of Sleat), and 67 kilometres wide from east to west (Rubha na Caillich to Neist). This bald statement, however, does not convey the remarkably convoluted nature of the island's coastline. It is not possible to walk anywhere on the island for more than 60 kilometres in a straight line, and yet the coastline is more than 570 kilometres in length.

Four major promontories extend from the main body of the island. The northern ones— Duirinish, Waternish and Trotternish — were named by the Norse invaders. The *nish* ending in each case is a derivative of *nes* meaning promontory or headland. Sleat in the south constitutes the fourth major promontory, and two less well defined ones can be identified on the south-western side of the island — Strathaird and the rather straggly Minginish.

Another way of visualising the outline of the island is to imagine that more than a dozen major sea-lochs bite into it. In fact, no part of the island is further than seven kilometres from the sea. Surprisingly, the most distant point from any shore lies in the heart of Trotternish.

The superlative Cuillin are tucked away in the southern part of the island. When there is cloud on the tops, it would be easy to tour the island and not know they were there. The Red Hills are much more obvious since the main road from Broadford to Portree skirts around their base. They are sometimes referred to as the Red Cuillin, although they bear no resemblance in either shape or colour to the sharp and jagged peaks of the true Black Cuillin.

The highest hills outwith the Cuillin and Red Hills are situated on the easternmost part of the island just above Kylerhea. The most impressive hills elsewhere are in Trotternish where the longest continuous ridge on the island has its high point on The Storr. In the west, Macleod's Tables are the loftiest eminences in Duirinish, and are notable for their remarkably flat tops.

The coastline is long and varied. Most of the largest sea-cliffs consist of crumbly basalt, but where dolerite sills occur in the west and north there is good climbing. Countless sea-caves and natural arches are dotted around the coast. They offer great scope for exploration, especially by canoe. There are also numerous small sea-stacks, some of which make good climbs. Reaching them is often an adventure in itself.

Several other islands lie close to Skye. The largest, Raasay, is situated on the east side of the island opposite Portree. South Rona lies just to the north of Raasay, and Scalpay to the south. Tiny Longay and Pabay are nearby. On the opposite side of the island, Soay lies due south of the Cuillin, and Wiay is the largest of the several small islands in Loch Bracadale. Only Raasay is served by a scheduled ferry from Skye.

The island has been divided into five separate areas for the purposes of the guide.

i)	Sleat and South-East Skye
ii)	Strathaird and The Red Hills
iii)	Minginish and The Cuillin
iv)	Duirinish, Waternish and Central Skye
v)	Trotternish

These areas are described in detail after the general information for the whole island which now follows.

MAPS: Ordnance Survey   1:50,000   Sheets 23, 32 and 33
                   Bartholomew   1:100,000   Sheets 50 and 54
(Larger scale maps are listed in the relevant chapters).

ACCESS

At the time of writing of this guide, approval has just been given for the building of a road bridge to Skye, spanning the strait between Kyle of Lochalsh and Kyleakin. When this bridge is built access to Skye will be improved, but several years will probably elapse before any bridge is completed. In the meantime access depends on the existing ferry services which are listed below.

Car Ferries

Skye is served by three ferries from the mainland as well as one from the Outer Isles. All but one are operated by Caledonian MacBrayne (Telephone 0475-33755).
Mallaig to Armadale. The shortest driving route from the south, via the famous 'Road to the Isles'. During the summer season only, there are five crossing daily from Monday to Saturday inclusive. It is advisable to make reservations for cars. There is a reduced winter service for passengers only. Crossing time: 30 minutes.
Glenelg to Kylerhea. The oldest and most scenic route. A small independent car ferry which operates only in summer from 9.00 to 17.00. No Sunday service. Crossing time: 4 minutes. Telephone Glenelg (059982) 224/344
Kyle of Lochalsh to Kyleakin. The most frequent service and also the busiest. There may be queues during the summer months. Operates seven days a week, Monday to Friday 06.00 to 23.15, Saturday 06.30 to 23.15, Sunday 10.15 to 21.15 (10.15 to 18.45 in winter). Roll-on roll-off vehicle and passenger service. Two ferries operate simultaneously at peak times. Crossing time: 5 minutes.
Lochmaddy to Uig, and Tarbert to Uig. Island hoppers can cross to Skye from Tarbert (Harris) and Lochmaddy (North Uist) during the summer months. It is

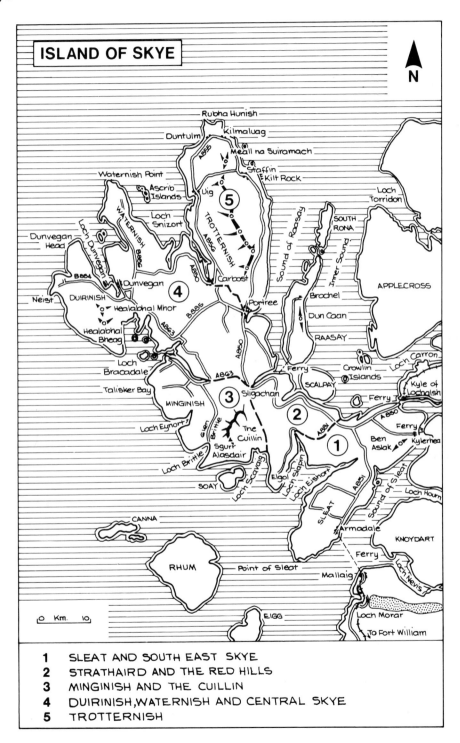

ISLAND OF SKYE

N

1   SLEAT AND SOUTH EAST SKYE
2   STRATHAIRD AND THE RED HILLS
3   MINGINISH AND THE CUILLIN
4   DUIRINISH, WATERNISH AND CENTRAL SKYE
5   TROTTERNISH

advisable to make reservations for cars. One or two crossings each day except Sunday. Crossing times (from both Tarbert and Lochmaddy): 1 hour 45 minutes.

Trains
The Mallaig ferry can be reached by train from Glasgow via Fort William, and the Kyle of Lochalsh ferry can be reached by train from Inverness. British Rail, Fort William: Telephone 0397-3791 British Rail, Inverness: Telephone 0463-238924.

Coaches
Scottish Citylink Coaches and Skye-Ways Express Coaches operate joint services daily (including Sunday) to Portree from Glasgow via Fort William, and from Glasgow via Perth and Inverness. The journey from Glasgow to Portree (via Fort William) takes just over seven hours. Both services cross on the Kyle of Lochalsh ferry and call at Broadford, Sconser and Sligachan. Some services continue to Uig. Scottish Citylink Coaches: Telephone 041-332-9191. Skye-Ways Express Coaches: Telephone 0599-4328.

Flights
There is an airstrip five kilometres to the east of Broadford, but there are no longer any scheduled flights to and from the mainland. Telephone Broadford (04712) 261.

TOURIST INFORMATION OFFICES
The main tourist information office is in Portree (Telephone 0478-2137). Two additional information centres are open in the holiday season at Broadford (Telephone 04712-361/463) and Kyle of Lochalsh (Telephone 0599-4276).

TRANSPORT
There are good main roads from Kyleakin to Portree, Uig and Dunvegan. Most others are single track with passing places. Roads on Skye are continually being improved. For example, the Storr to Staffin road on the east side of Trotternish has been much improved in recent years.

Information about bus services, self-drive car hire and boat hire can be obtained from the tourist information offices mentioned above.

Most parts of the island are served by bus in some way. The main operator is Highland Scottish Omnibuses (Telephone 0478-2647). Details of the different operators are liable to change, but W.J. Sutherland, for example, runs a service from Portree to Fiscavaig via Sligachan, Drynoch, the Glenbrittle road junction, Carbost and Portnalong. The journey takes one hour, (Telephone 047842-267).

Postbus services run between Broadford and Elgol, Dunvegan and Glendale, and Dunvegan and Gillen (Waternish). Details of these services can be found in the Scottish Postbus Timetable or from the main post office in Portree, (Telephone 0478-2533).

ACCOMMODATION
Information about the various accommodation facilities on the island is available from the tourist information offices mentioned above.

Camping
The two most important camp sites as far as hillgoers are concerned are situated at Sligachan opposite the hotel and in Glen Brittle beside the beach.

Other sites with facilities exist at Breakish by Broadford, Torvaig just north of Portree, Staffin, and at Edinbane by Loch Greshornish.

Opportunities for wild camping by the roadside are rather limited, but camping at Loch Coruisk and in the Cuillin corries is possible.

Caravans
Most of the camp sites will also accept caravans. Sites exclusively for caravans exist at Braes and Dunvegan. Caravan rent is possible at many of the villages, crofts and cottages on Skye.

Huts
Coruisk Memorial Hut (JMCS, Glasgow Section).
Situated on the shore of Loch na Cuilce, 100 metres north-west of the outflow from the Scavaig River. Access by boat from Elgol or Mallaig, or on foot from Sligachan or Strathaird. Accommodation for nine.

Glen Brittle Memorial Hut (BMC and MC of S). Situated at the roadside in Glen Brittle, about 300 metres north of Glenbrittle House. Accommodation for sixteen. Resident warden April to September.

Reservations for places in these two huts should be made through club secretaries or direct to the custodian (in the case of associate members of the BMC and MC of S.

Self Catering Accommodation
A house and two cottages, situated opposite the Sligachan Hotel, are available all year round for groups on a self-catering basis. Telephone 047852 303.

Details of other self-catering accommodation can be obtained from the tourist information offices.

Youth Hostels
There are youth hostels in Glen Brittle, Armadale, Broadford, and Uig.

Bed and Breakfast
Numerous establishments offer bed and breakfast accommodation.

Hotels
There are many hotels and boarding houses on the island. The most convenient for the Cuillin is at Sligachan. Telephone 047852-204.

MOUNTAIN RESCUE
Skye is one of the few islands with full mountain rescue facilities. There are rescue posts in Portree, Broadford, Glen Brittle and Sligachan. As usual, the simplest advice in the event of an accident is to contact the police who will then set a rescue in motion. Dial 999 or contact the police station in Portree (Telephone Portree 2888). Telephones are situated at such key places as Glenbrittle House (also a rescue post), Sligachan Hotel, Elgol, Torrin and Broadford.

Bla Bheinn from Ord on the shore of Loch Eishort

CHAPTER 6

SLEAT AND SOUTH-EAST SKYE

The area described in this section consists of all the ground to the south-east of Strath Suardal, i.e. the Broadford to Torrin Road. It includes the long arm of the Sleat peninsula as well as the easternmost part of the island around Kylerhea.

MAPS :   Ordnance Survey   1:25,000 Sheets NG 50, 60/70, 61/71, and 62/72
                                 1:50,000 Sheets 32 and 33

PRINCIPAL HILLS

Sgurr na Coinnich	739m	762 222
Beinn na Caillich	733m	770 229
Ben Aslak	610m	751 191

GENERAL DESCRIPTION

The south-eastern section of Skye does not display such dramatic relief as other parts of the island. It does, however, harbour the highest hills outwith the Cuillin and Red Hills. All three ferries from the mainland land there, and so it is the first part of the island that most visitors experience.

Very different impressions of the area are gained from the three separate roads which lead from the landing points of the mainland ferries. The road from Kyleakin to Broadford follows the relatively flat, northern coastal fringe, and simply provides the quickest route to the remainder of the island. The road from Kylerhea is the most spectacular. It climbs steeply between the highest hills in the area, and then makes a long descent down Glen Arroch to join the Kyleakin to Broadford road opposite Skye Airport. The single track road from Armadale is the longest. It runs along the east side of the Sleat peninsula and eventually joins the Kyleakin to Broadford road at Skulamus just east of Broadford. It also extends south to Aird of Sleat from where a track and path lead to the lighthouse at Point of Sleat.

The area is set apart by its rocks which are generally very much older than those forming the bulk of the island. The most widespread rock is Torridonian sandstone, but there are also large amounts of Lewisian, Moinian and Cambro-Ordovician strata. These were all involved in very complex Caledonian thrusting. Some additional rocks occur in the north-western part of the area, where Jurassic sediments are intruded by acidic sills, and Cambro-Ordovician limestones are intruded by a Tertiary granite mass.

The bulbous finger of Sleat is linked to the northern part of the area by a neck of land little more than two kilometres wide. It has a character all of its own. The name Sleat is derived from sleibhte meaning extensive tracts of moorland. This is an apt description for the peninsula, since it consists mainly of lochan-strewn moor and lacks any noteworthy hills. Halfway down the peninsula a loop road goes over to Ord, Tokavaig and Tarskavaig on the north-west coast. This makes a pleasant excursion. The most rugged ground occurs where there are outcrops of Cambrian quartzite on the ridges called Sgiath-bheinn an Uird and Sgiath-bheinn Chros-savaig. The interior of the peninsula, however, is more likely to interest the naturalist than the hillwalker.

There are fine ash woods on the Cambrian limestones around Tokavaig. Further south at Coille Dalavil above Loch a'Ghlinne there is a mature wood of beech and Scots pine, which was planted in the middle of the 19th century. Below the big trees there is a natural understorey of birch, hazel, willow, rowan, ash and oak. This diverse woodland supports the richest wildlife on Skye apart from the sea-cliffs.

In a restored part of Armadale Castle, at the Clan Donald Centre, there is an exhibition and museum. It is set among fine woodland gardens. The remains of several other castles or duns are scattered about the coast. One of the few sandy beaches on the island is to be found in Tarskavaig Bay.

The road which leads south from Skulamus to the Sleat peninsula separates the northern part of the area into two distinct regions. To the east lies the hilly ground overlooking Kyle Rhea, to the west lies the gentler terrain surrounding Glen Suardal. The hills overlooking Kyle Rhea may not have a particularly distinguished form, but they do offer superb panoramic views. They are conveniently ascended from the high point on the road leading from Kylerhea to Glen Arroch.

It was at Kylerhea that the drovers used to cross over to the mainland with their cattle in the 18th and 19th centuries. The beasts were made to swim across, linked nose to tail, during slack water. The leading animal was towed from the stern of a rowing boat. Many thousands of cattle crossed annually in this way.

The area west of the Skulamus to Kinloch road is bounded to the north-west by Strath Suardal. On the north coast of this block of land is the busy little town of Broadford. It lies on the through route to the rest of the island. The area is penetrated in its eastern half by a road which leaves Harrapool on the east side of Broadford and leads over to the hamlet of Heast by Loch Eishort. On the west side overlooking Loch Slapin, a track runs from Kilbride down to Suisnish above Rubha Suisnish.

At one time there were settlements at both Suisnish and at Boreraig further east, but they were 'cleared' in the 1850s. The inhabitants would not go voluntarily, and had to be evicted by a body of constables. Three men who resisted were sent for trial in Inverness, and although found not guilty, were still subsequently evicted along with their families. Today, the deserted village at Boreraig imparts a haunting atmosphere to this section of coast.

There is much dolomitic limestone around Strath Suardal. In places it outcrops as limestone pavement containing numerous narrow crevices or grikes. Lime-loving plants of interest to the botanist can be found growing within these grikes. In the vicinity of the large granite intrusion of Beinn an Dubhaich, the limestone has been thermally metamorphosed to marble. Several quarries have been worked there over the years. A wide range of calc-silicate minerals, and so-called skarn deposits, occur close to the granite in association with the marble.

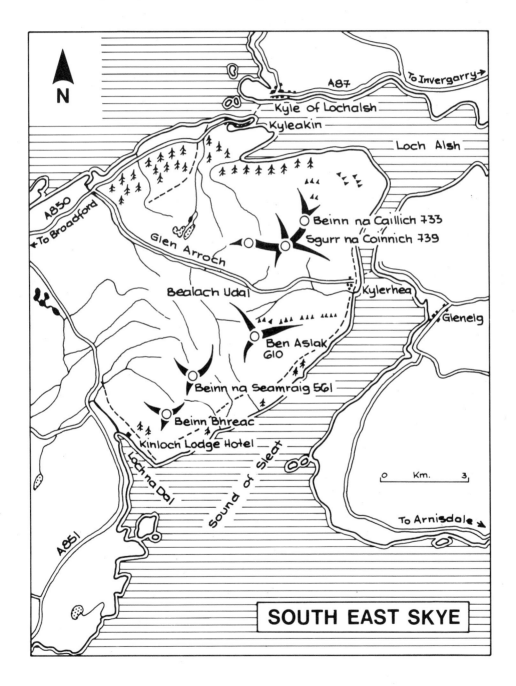

THE HILLS

Sgurr na Coinnich (*peak of moss*) (739m)

As its name suggests, Sgurr na Coinnich is not a rocky peak. In the summer it has a uniformly green appearance when seen from Glenelg. It does make a wonderful viewpoint though, and the hillwalker with an hour or two to spare before the ferry will find its ascent rewarding.

Five corries cut into the peak and separate several broad ridges. There are two minor tops, Beinn na Greine and Beinn Bhuidhe, on the west and south-east ridges respectively. Beinn na Caillich, a top on the north-east ridge, is distinctive enough to be considered a separate peak.

The best starting point for an ascent is undoubtedly the Bealach Udal (279m), since it greatly reduces the height to be climbed. The road leading up to this bealach is steep on the Kylearhea side, but more gentle on the Glen Arroch side.

From the bealach, follow the southern flank of the mountain without any difficulty. There is a lochan near the 700m contour where the broad summit ridge is gained. The views from the summit are extensive. Beinn Sgritheall and Ladhar Bheinn are prominent on the mainland to the south-east.

Beinn na Caillich (*mountain of the old woman*) (733m)

This peak lies one kilometre north-east of Sgurr na Coinnich, from where it is normally ascended via the Bealach nam Mulachag. It has a steepish western face and is a rather more shapely top than its neighbour. There are fine views over Loch Alsh from the summit, where the solitude contrasts markedly with the bustle of the ferry traffic at Kyleakin below.

There is no particular merit in continuing the traverse to the north. To return to Kylerhea the eastern flank can be descended to the shore beside Kyle Rhea, where a path from a light beacon can be followed south to the ferry slipway at Kylerhea. Alternatively, return to the Bealach nam Mulachag and then head south-east over Beinn Bhuidhe, whose steep south-eastern shoulder leads directly to Kylerhea.

Ben Aslak (610m)

This mountain lies on the south side of Kylerhea Glen and is clearly seen from the Kylerhea road. Its sprawling northern face is quite rugged, although its southern flank is uninspiring. The name Aslak is probably derived from aslaich meaning breast - a reference to the mountain's twin peaks.

The Bealach Udal is again the most convenient starting point. A small top called Beinn Bheag can be ascended first, before the broad north-west shoulder of the mountain is followed. Trend slightly right eventually to reach the summit. The eastern top is some 400 metres away and only slightly lower.

A traverse can be made by continuing down the long, easy-angled east ridge. From its foot a path leads to Kylerhea. The alternative traverse, in a south-westerly direction over Beinn na Seamraig (*peak of clover*) to Kinloch Lodge, is unlikely to appeal unless transport can be arranged on the A851.

PATHS AND WALKS

There is some pleasant low-level walking in the north-western part of the area, south of Strath Suardal. Those without their own transport may find it convenient to use the postbus service which runs between Broadford and Elgol. An interesting circular outing starts not far from Cill Chriosd, the graveyard about half way along the strath. A path leads south around the flank of Ben Suardal to some old marble quarries. At one time a miniature railway, known locally as the Broadford Express, ran from the quarries to a pier at Broadford. Traces of it can still be seen.

The path continues past the head of Glen Suardal and then descends on the west side of the Allt na Pairte to the remains of the former settlement of Boreraig by Loch Eishort. It then goes westwards along the coast below tall, sloping cliffs and eventually ascends to Suisnish, where a number of cottages have been renovated. From there a poor path can be taken which heads inland and eventually rejoins the road in Strath Suardal by Loch Cill Chriosd. The total length of this circuit is some 14 kilometres. Alternatively, a vehicular track can be followed northwards from Suisnish to Kilbride on the road to Torrin.

ROCK CLIMBING

There is little to detain the rock climber on this part of Skye. The Sleat peninsula has the most to offer. A little bouldering can be had on some small sea-cliffs of Torridonian sandstone in the vicinity of the ruins of Dunscaith Castle, north-west of Tokavaig. Better climbing, which may be of interest to those using the Armadale ferry, is to be found near the Point of Sleat, where there are some 20m high sea-cliffs. They are reached by walking for four kilometres from Aird of Sleat. The first three kilometres are on a poor track; then a path heads south to the Point of Sleat. The cliffs lie south-west of a small hillock with a spot height of 74m. About half a dozen routes of Severe and Very Severe grade have been done there. They are best tackled outwith the nesting season.

CHAPTER 7

STRATHAIRD AND THE RED HILLS

The mountainous part of the area covered in this chapter is bounded by Strath Suardal to the east, and by Glen Sligachan and Srath na Creitheach to the west. It includes both the Eastern and Western Red Hills, as well as the Cuillin Outliers of Bla Bheinn, Clach Glas and Garbh-bheinn. The lower-lying Strathaird peninsula, which juts out to the south of Bla Bheinn, is bordered by Loch Slapin on the east and Loch Scavaig on the west.

MAPS :   Ordnance Survey   1:25,000 Outdoor Leisure Map 8 THE CUILLIN
                                   AND TORRIDON HILLS
                                   1:50,000 Sheet 32

PRINCIPAL HILLS
THE EASTERN RED HILLS

Beinn na Caillich	732m	601 232
Beinn Dearg Mhor	709m	587 228
Beinn Dearg Bheag	582m	592 219
Beinn na Cro	572m	569 241
Glas Bheinn Mhor	569m	554 257

THE CUILLIN OUTLIERS

Bla Bheinn (Blaven)	928m	530 217
South-west top	926m	528 215
Clach Glas	786m	534 221
Sgurr nan Each	720m	537 227
Garbh-bheinn	808m	531 232
Belig	702m	544 240

THE WESTERN RED HILLS

Ruadh Stac	493m	514 232
Marsco	736m	507 251
Beinn Dearg Mheadhonach	651m	515 271
Beinn Dearg Mhor	731m	520 285
Glamaig	775m	513 300

GENERAL DESCRIPTION

The Red Hills are a remarkable group of rather rounded granite mountains with scree-covered slopes, which dominate the landscape between Broadford and Sligachan. They are divided into the Eastern and Western Red Hills by a line drawn between the heads of Loch Ainort and Loch Slapin. The hills are red and grey in colour and contrast starkly with the much darker and more jagged peaks of the Cuillin and their outliers, which lie to the south and west.

The A850, which is the main road through the island, winds around the northern side of both groups of Red Hills between Broadford and Sligachan. It stays near to the coast apart from a short section just after the head of Loch Ainort, where it climbs over a col to the west of Druim nan Cleochd. Beinn Dearg Mhor, one of the northern members of the Western Red Hills, lies within easy reach of this col.

The only other motoring route in the area is the single track A881 road which heads south-west from Broadford around the south side of the Eastern Red Hills. The first part of the road along Strath Suardal gives little impression of the delights to come. As the head of Loch Slapin is approached near Torrin, superb views are obtained of Bla Bheinn and the other Cuillin Outliers. These hills are all readily accessible from the roadside.

The road then turns south, runs out along the picturesque promontory of Strathaird and eventually leads over to Elgol on the peninsula's western side, from where there is a spectacular though somewhat distant view of the whole Cuillin range. This tiny village has a post office, some small shops, a restaurant, and several bed and breakfast establishments. A twice daily postbus service runs between Elgol and Broadford, and boats can be hired from Elgol to sail across Loch Scavaig to Coruisk. The road down to the slipway at Port na Cullaidh is very steep and narrow, so parking facilities are provided further up the hill. A short spur road crosses over from Elgol to Glasnakille, a crofting community on the eastern side of the peninsula. This locality is famous for its Spar Cave.

Part way along the Strathaird peninsula an important walking route leads over to Camas Fhionnairigh, a bay which lies near the foot of Bla Bheinn's south ridge. There is a bothy on the west side of the bay, not far from the outlet of the Abhainn Camas Fhionnairigh.

Camas Fhionnairigh probably means the bay of the white shieling. The name has been anglicised to Camasunary. A path continues around the coast, via the famous 'Bad Step' on the west side of Sgurr na Stri, to Loch Coruisk and the Cuillin proper. This is described in the Cuillin section.

Srath na Creitheach, which runs north from Camasunary and then north-westwards from Loch an Athain (*loch of the ford*), joins with Glen Sligachan to form a walking link between the north and south coasts of the island. Although this route is almost thirteen kilometres long, the watershed by Lochan Dubha is at a height of only 70m. The Red Hills and the Bla Bheinn group are effectively severed from the main Cuillin hills by this deep defile, which serves as a natural boundary for the area.

Two much shorter glens also cut right across the centre of the area and provide walking routes between the north and south sides of the island's eastern peninsula. Srath Mor links Luib by Loch Ainort with the head of Loch Slapin. It is six kilometres long, although its floor does not rise above 30m. All the Eastern Red Hills, with the exception of Glas Bheinn Mhor, lie to the east of this glen. A little further to the east, Srath Beag provides a more scenic through route between Strollamus and Torrin; it climbs to just over 180m at its highest point.

The Red Hills are formed from various acid igneous rocks which are loosely referred to as granite. They were intruded in Tertiary times shortly after the main Cuillin complex. Three separate centres can be recognised. The first of these developed around Srath na Creitheach, the next in the Western Red Hills and the last in the Eastern Red Hills. The granites postdate the main phase of dyke intrusion on the island. Where dykes do occur they tend to be more resistant to erosion and so stand out in relief. The gabbro intrusions of the Cuillin, on the other hand, are cut by numerous dykes, many of which have eroded out to form gullies. This accounts in part for the more jagged outline of the Cuillin ridges.

Though the mountains of the Bla Bheinn group are physically connected to the Western Red Hills, they originated as part of the earlier Cuillin complex and so display the same characteristics as the main Cuillin peaks. The colour change at the junction between the so-called Cuillin Outliers and the Red Hills (or Red Cuillin) is plainly seen even from a distance. It occurs at a dip in the ridge one kilometre north of Garbh-bheinn.

The Strathaird peninsula is built predominantly of Jurassic sedimentary rocks overlain by Tertiary lavas, all of which dip gently to the west. The lavas form the higher ground to the north-west of the road to Elgol. All the rock types of the peninsula are cut by dykes trending from north-west to south-east.

At various localities around the peninsula there are small sea-cliffs of cross-bedded sandstone, some of which offer opportunities for climbing. In places where the rocks have a significant content of limy material, they weather to produce a curious honeycomb structure.

The Spar Cave at Glasnakille is well worth a visit. Although the entrance to the cave itself lies just above high-water-mark, it is only accessible for a short period at low-tide. A torch is required to explore it. The cave has formed where a basaltic dyke has been eroded out by wave action to produce a deep cleft. Water has percolated through from the neighbouring limy rock and deposited calcium carbonate (spar) over the collapsed rubble on the cave floor. There are several tiny pools of crystal clear water on the floor, and all around the spar deposits glisten in the light. The best stalactite formations were knocked off (in both senses) by 19th century visitors, and at one time a wall and door were built across the entrance in an attempt to protect them. It is to be hoped that modern visitors will be more considerate. The floor slopes up quite steeply at one point, and then drops down to a deep pool beyond which the cave soon ends. The cave is marked on Ordnance Survey maps (grid reference 538 128). It is approached by turning right at the T-junction in Glasnakille. After 200 metres leave the road and head downhill just west of a small building. Eventually follow a dry, shallow gully which leads to the shore some 120 metres south-west of the cave entrance.

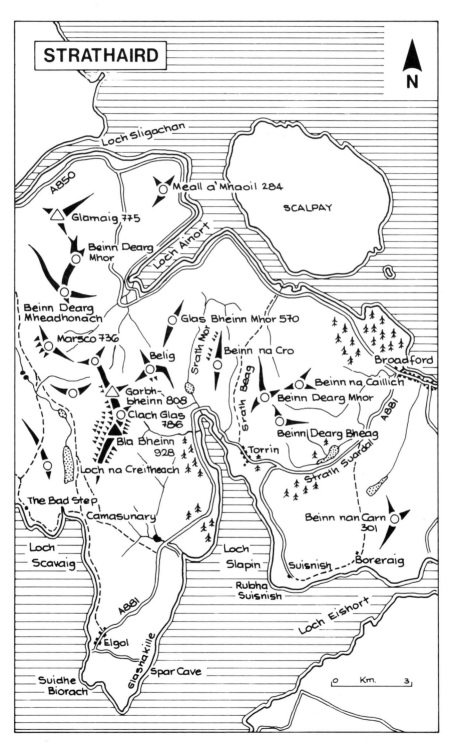

STRATHAIRD

N

Loch Sligachan

A850

Meall a'Mhaoil 284

SCALPAY

Glamaig 775

Beinn Dearg
Mhor

Loch Ainort

Beinn Dearg
Mheadhonach

Glas Bheinn Mhor 570

Marsco 736

Srath Mor

Beinn na Cro

Belig

Broadford

Srath Beag

Beinn na Caillich

Garbh-
bheinn 808

Beinn Dearg Mhor

Clach Glas
786

Beinn Dearg Bheag

Bla Bheinn
928

A881

Torrin

Loch na Creitheach

Strath Suardal

The Bad Step

Beinn nan Carn
301

Camasunary

Loch
Scavaig

Loch
Slapin

Suisnish

Boreraig

Rubha
Suisnish

A881

Loch Eishort

Elgol

Glasnakille

Spar Cave

Suidhe
Biorach

0   Km.   3

THE EASTERN RED HILLS

Beinn na Caillich (*mountain of the old woman*) (732m)
This massive rounded mountain is clearly visible from Broadford. It is the highest
of three peaks which form a horseshoe around Coire Gorm; the other two being
Beinn Dearg Mhor and Beinn Dearg Bheag. It is best ascended from Coire-chat-
achan (the ruined remains of a famous MacKinnon household), which lies some two
kilometres west of Broadford. This is gained either by a path which starts not far
from a Neolithic chambered cairn in Strath Suardal, or by a track which runs
south-south-east from the A850 road one and a half kilometres north-west of
Broadford.
A direct line can be followed from Coire-chat-achan up the boulder-covered
slopes to the summit, but a much more attractive excursion can be made by
completing the full horse-shoe circuit of Coire Gorm. Ascend Beinn Dearg Bheag
(little red mountain) by its east ridge, continue round over Beinn Dearg Mhor, and
so gain Beinn na Caillich by its west ridge. A prominent dyke stands proud on the
south side of the mountain. There are splendid views from the summit.

Beinn Dearg Mhor (*big red mountain*) (709m)
This peak is normally ascended along with Beinn na Caillich during the round of
Coire Gorm. It can be climbed independently from Torrin, either directly by its south-
west ridge, or more pleasantly by Coire Sgreamhach and its south-east ridge,
starting up the path from Torrin to Strollamus. It gives superb views westwards to
Bla Bheinn and the other Cuillin Outliers.

Beinn na Cro (*mountain of the fold*) (572m)
The two deep glens of Srath Mor and Srath Beag lie on either side of this peak and
isolate it from the other Eastern Red Hills. It is best ascended from the road beside
Loch Slapin in the south. The going is easiest on the ridge which overlooks the Allt
an t-Sratha Bhig. If the peak is traversed as far as Gualann nam Fiadh (*shoulder of
the deer*), a return can be made by the path in Srath Beag. The northern part of the
mountain is capped by basalt lavas.

Glas Bheinn Mhor (*big grey mountain*) (569m)
This peak lies close to Loch Ainort and is best ascended from Luib on the Broadford
to Sligachan road. Although it is geologically a part of the Eastern Red Hills centre,
it is physically joined to the Cuillin Outliers. It has the same long, narrow shape as
Beinn na Cro on the opposite side of Srath Mor. However, it is formed from a rather
different granite, which weathers to a dull grey colour; hence the mountain's name.
The remains of a stone wall can be followed up the north ridge to the summit. The
outing can be extended by continuing over Belig and Garbh-bheinn, and then
returning along the Druim Eadar Da Choire (*ridge between the two corries*).

The Cuillin Outliers — Garbh-bheinn, Clach Glas and Bla Bheinn from the west

THE CUILLIN OUTLIERS

Bla Bheinn (Blaven) (928m)

The name possibly means blue mountain (Old Norse *bla = blue*).

Bla Bheinn is a magnificent mountain. Alexander Nicolson, a local Skye man who played a major role in the early exploration of the Cuillin, considered it to be the finest hill on Skye. It is the highest and most southerly peak in a group of hills referred to as the Cuillin Outliers. This group links with the Western Red Hills (or Red Cuillin) to form a more or less continuous chain of hills which stretches from the Strathaird peninsula in the south to Loch Sligachan in the north.

The east side of Bla Bheinn is readily accessible from the A881 Broadford to Elgol road near the head of Loch Slapin. The south ridge and the west flank are within easy reach of Camasunary. The approach from the north through Glen Sligachan is very much longer.

The mountain has twin summits which are less than 300 metres apart, the south-west top being only a couple of metres lower than the main top. The bulk of the mountain consists of gabbro, which has been intruded by inclined dolerite sheets and north-west to south-east trending basalt dykes. In many cases the dykes have been eroded out to form corresponding gullies on opposite sides of the mountain, as has happened, for example, at the dip between the summit and the south-west top.

Bla Bheinn and Clach Glas seen from Torrin across Loch Slapin

The mountain is steepest and most complex at its northern end. The east ridge twists down from the summit and forms the north side of Coire Uaigneich. The lower section of the east ridge is easy-angled on its southern flank, and this provides the normal route to the summit.

Start from the roadside on the west side of Loch Slapin. Cars can be parked at a small gravel quarry just south of the bridge over the Allt na Dunaiche. Follow a path, boggy in places, on the north bank of the Allt na Dunaiche. After one kilometre pass some beautiful wooded waterfalls, and a little further on cross over the stream and head due west.

Cross a tributary stream just below where it emerges from a rocky gorge and climb more steeply south-westwards up Coire Uaigneich (*secret corrie*), first on heather, then on grass. Pass below the triangular area of rock at the foot of the east ridge, which contains C Gully on the left and D Gully on the right.

Once in the flatter upper reaches of the corrie, turn to the right and zigzag up steep grass and rocks on the south flank of the east ridge. The route becomes easier to follow on the scree higher up. Pass the top of the *Great Prow* (740m) which juts from the face on the right, and eventually reach a small top on a shoulder at about 800m. From here the ridge becomes narrower, and curves first left and then right. There is occasional easy scrambling before the angle eases and the summit with its triangulation pillar is reached.

There is an easy but exhilarating walk southwards along the summit ridge

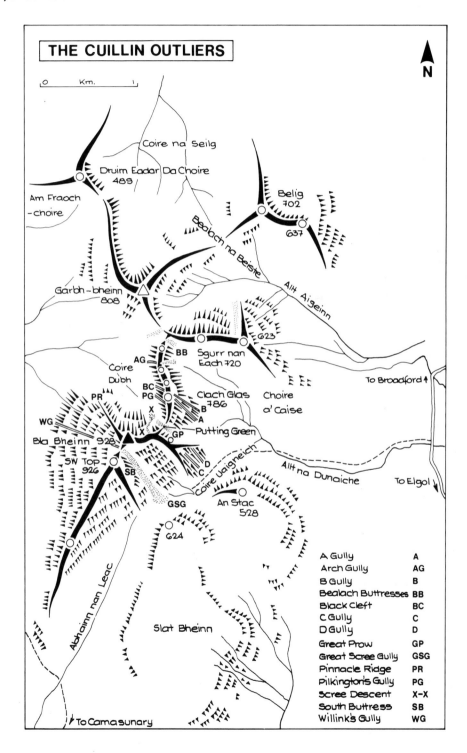

THE CUILLIN OUTLIERS

N

0 Km. 1

Coire na Seilg

Druim Eadar Da Choire
489

Am Fraoch
-choire

Belig
702

637

Bealach na Beiste

Alt Aigeinn

Garbh-bheinn
808

623

AG
Coire
Dubh

BB
Sgurr nan
Each 720

BC
PG
PR

Clach Glas
786
B

Choire
a' Caise

To Broadford ↑

WG

X
A

GP
Putting Green

Bla Bheinn 928

SW Top
926
SB

D
C
Coire Uaigneich

Allt na Dunaiche

To Elgol ↓

GSG
An Stac
528

624

Slat Bheinn

Abhainn nan Leac

To Camasunary

A Gully	A
Arch Gully	AG
B Gully	B
Bealach Buttresses	BB
Black Cleft	BC
C Gully	C
D Gully	D
Great Prow	GP
Great Scree Gully	GSG
Pinnacle Ridge	PR
Pilkington's Gully	PG
Scree Descent	X-X
South Buttress	SB
Willink's Gully	WG

to a col at 896m. The left-hand (east) gully, called the *Great Scree Gully*, gives a quick but unattractive descent route to Coire Uaigneich. The south-west top (926m) is soon reached after scrambling up rocks for 15m out of the col. On a good day the view from the summit ridge is one of the finest on Skye. The main Cuillin range fills the horizon to the west, and the isles of Rhum and Eigg are prominent to the south.

An alternative to returning by the same route is to go south from the south-west top and after a short distance descend the broad south-east ridge on the left. Take care not to stray too far left, as this leads over South Buttress. Continue descending to the bealach at the head of the Abhainn nan Leac. Then turn left and drop down into the upper reaches of Coire Uaigneich and so regain the path used in ascent.

The east ridge is much steeper on its northern side, where there are a number of buttresses which offer some excellent climbing. Part way down the east ridge, a spur drops steeply north-eastwards to link with the south ridge of Clach Glas. The bealach at 695m has become known as the *Putting Green* because of a small mossy flattening on its crest. The prominent rock tower overlooking the bealach on the Bla Bheinn side was named the *Half Crown Pinnacle* by Naismith, but it is also known as *The Horn*. Good route-finding and a high level of scrambling ability are both required to negotiate successfully the route between the Putting Green and the east ridge of Bla Bheinn. This is an important section on the Clach Glas to Bla Bheinn traverse, and is described in detail under the traverse of the whole Cuillin Outliers group.

The Putting Green can be gained from the east by ascending a long and rather unpleasant scree slope, the base of which is reached by continuing west-wards where the normal route to Bla Bheinn (qv) bears south-westwards into Coire Uaigneich. (In descent it is necessary to bear south-east at the base of the scree in order to avoid a steep gully.) A slightly less tedious scree slope on the west side of the Putting Green can be ascended without difficulty from the upper reaches of Coire Dubh.

The east face of the mountain is cleft by the Great Scree Gully, which was ascended by the Willink brothers in 1873. It leads to the col at 896m between the summit and the south-west top. It is a straightforward but uninspiring line, and may be used as a quick descent route. The broad south-east ridge of the south-west top is another uncomplicated ascent route. South Buttress, which lies on its north-east flank overlooking Great Scree Gully, has good climbing. The easiest of all routes to the summit, however, is the long south ridge from Camasunary.

The normal approach to Camasunary starts one kilometre south-west of Kirkibost on the road to Elgol; there is a small carpark just south of this point. Follow the track for rather more than two kilometres to Am Mam (*the pass*). After crossing the pass continue for a further kilometre to a hairpin bend. Then take a path which leads straight on at the bend, rather than descend the track to Camasunary itself.

Leave the path soon after crossing the Abhainn nan Leac, and strike up the hillside. Gain the crest of the ridge from the right (east) side. Follow the ridge over numerous minor bumps, swinging right from time to time to circumvent the tops

Looking up the north ridge of Clach Glas

of gullies on the west face. W H Murray and R G Donaldson had a trying time when they attempted to take a short cut down this western flank after completing the third Greater Traverse in August 1939. (See W H Murray's *Mountaineering in Scotland*).

Some 90 metres beyond the south-west top there is a 15m step down to a col. The ridge then continues easily for a further 175 metres to the triangulation pillar on the main top.

The extensive western flank of the mountain is a little disappointing. It forms a great sweep of rather broken rock overlooking Loch na Creitheach and Srath na Creitheach. It is seamed with gullies, the longest and most prominent of which was descended in part by the Willink brothers in 1873. (They were stopped by a pitch halfway down, and traversed out onto the north-western slope). The broad buttresses on either side of the gully offer easy and reasonably pleasant ascent routes. This gully corresponds with Great Scree Gully on the opposite side of the mountain.

The *Pinnacle Ridge* lies on the north face and can be identified from Loch an Athain to the west. After the first steep 90m it is rather indefinite, but higher up it narrows and becomes more interesting. Much further round on the north face, a large stone chute offers a fast descent route from the north side of the mountain to Srath na Creitheach. The top of it is reached by descending the east ridge from the summit to a small saddle at 795m, where the route from the Putting Green finishes. Go down the stone chute, and take a dog-leg to the right where it joins another stone chute originating from higher up the face. At its foot it merges with the scree slope on the west side of the Putting Green, some 70m below the bealach itself. It is much easier than the north-east ridge, and makes a reasonable ascent route from Coire Dubh.

Clach Glas (*grey stone*) (786m)
Clach Glas is a superb and shapely rock peak which lies some 600m north-east of Bla Bheinn. It is unnamed on the Ordnance Survey 1:50,000 map. The traverse of its north and south ridges constitutes one of the finest scrambles on Skye. Although it lacks the misleading status of its immediate neighbours (Bla Bheinn to the south is a Munro, and Garbh-bheinn to the north is a Corbett), it is the most difficult of the three summits to reach. The technical difficulties need never be more than Moderate, but the almost alpine-like situations are intimidating; Clach Glas is not a peak for the ordinary walker. The mountain is geologically similar to Bla Bheinn; dolerite sheets, concordant with layering in the gabbro, are inclined towards the north-west, and have eroded to form ledges on the east face.

The mountain can be approached on its eastern side from the road around the head of Loch Slapin, and on its western side from Coire Dubh, which lies above Loch an Athain in Srath na Creitheach.

The south ridge of Clach Glas rises from the Putting Green (695m), and once that bealach has been gained it provides the shortest scrambling route to the summit. Although it makes an interesting line of ascent, it is more usually descended during a traverse of the mountain. It is described in detail under the traverse of the Cuillin Outliers.

The turreted north ridge is the mountain's most spectacular feature. It can be reached most readily from the east by ascending a scree chute from Choire a' Caise (*corrie of cheese*). Twin buttresses, known as the *Bealach Buttresses*, lie to the right (north) of this scree chute, and further right again another scree chute marks the western end of the south flank of Sgurr nan Each.

The left-hand scree chute gives a straightforward ascent, and leads to a bealach (at about 630m) at the start of the north ridge. The bealach is not a pass, as there is a deep gully on its western side, called *Arch Gully*, which has a big chockstone pitch halfway up and is graded Moderate. The bealach can be gained from the west by first ascending to another bealach further north (at 636m) between Sgurr nan Each and Garbh-bheinn, and then traversing south across the western end of Sgurr nan Each for 350 metres. Alternatively, a rather more direct rightwards curving line can be taken starting some distance to the left (north) of Arch Gully. The north ridge of Clach Glas is described in detail under the traverse of the Cuillin Outliers.

The east face of Clach Glas consists of steep broken rock crossed by grassy ledges. It is cleft by two long slanting gullies. The left-hand one is called *A Gully*, and the right-hand one, which originates from the lowest rocks of the face, is called *B Gully*. They can be identified from Torrin. The easiest way up this face is a scramble which has become known as *Sid's Rake*. It starts up and left from A Gully, and then slants rightwards across the face to finish at the top of B Gully, some distance north

The Imposter, the knife edge at the top of the south ridge of Clach Glas

of the summit. There is a prominent tower just to the north of the top of B Gully.

The west face has more continuous rock and is also cleft by gullies, the two most prominent of which lie on either side of the summit tower. The left-hand one, the *Black Cleft*, is unattractive and unclimbed. It corresponds with B Gully on the other side of the mountain. The right-hand one is *Pilkington's Gully*. This is the line followed by the mountain's first ascensionists in 1888. It is only a scramble and leads to the crest of the south ridge just below the summit. Here Pilkington's party were alarmed by "a knife-edge of tremendous steepness" above them. By crossing round to the right and pulling up a little gully, it is found that this knife-edge is merely the arete formed by the edge of a moderately angled slab. It can be ascended surprisingly easily and has become known at *The Imposter*. The route finishes abruptly at the summit cairn.

Sgurr nan Each (*peak of the horses*) (720m)
This peak is the high point on a rocky subsidiary ridge which runs out eastwards from the main ridge between Clach Glas and Garbh-bheinn. It is rarely ascended for its own sake, and is usually by-passed during the traverse of the Cuillin Outliers. However, it makes an entertaining detour from the main ridge, and some enjoyable scrambling can be had over its several tops. It is often crossed from east to west as a pleasant approach to the Clach Glas to Bla Bheinn traverse.

Sgurr nan Each is most conveniently ascended by its long, easy south-east ridge from the head of Loch Slapin. The top of a gully is turned on the left shortly before the easternmost top (623m) is reached. No difficulties are encountered on the stretch of ridge which leads westwards to the main top. The north face is rocky but rather broken. A prominent ridge on this face was climbed by Harold Raeburn in 1898.

A number of small tops west of the main summit involve some easy scrambling. At the western end of the ridge it is possible to make an easy descent from a little col (at 668m) immediately north of the Bealach Buttresses by a straightforward scree slope leading south-eastwards into Choire a' Caise.

Garbh-bheinn (*rough mountain*) (808m)

Garbh-bheinn is situated one and a half kilometres north of Bla Bheinn. It is the most northerly of the three peaks on the main chain of Cuillin Outliers. Belig lies one and a half kilometres to the north-east, but is set rather apart, and is in any case largely a basalt rather than a gabbro hill.

Garbh-bheinn does not receive as much attention as its more spectacular companions, Bla Bheinn and Clach Glas. Nevertheless, it is a shapely mountain and a worthy member of the Cuillin Outliers. It is a wonderful viewpoint, and deserves to be climbed more often. Purists tackling the Greater Traverse should include it.

The mountain lies some three kilometres from the A881 road round the head of Loch Slapin, and only marginally further from the A850 road round the head of Loch Ainort. Three ridges radiate from the summit, and all provide suitable lines of ascent.

The well-defined south-east ridge rises from a bealach at 636m, and gives the shortest route to the summit. The bealach can be approached fairly easily from the head of Loch Slapin either by Choire a' Caise or by traversing Sgurr nan Each (as described above).

The north-east ridge is broad and boulder-strewn in its lower reaches, but is not as tedious to ascend as it appears from Belig or Bealach na Beiste. The upper section is much narrower and more interesting, and finishes abruptly at the summit.

The long north ridge of Garbh-bheinn is best approached along the Druim Eadar Da Choire, starting from the big bend in the road at the head of Loch Ainort. Traverse the 489m summit at the top of this ridge, then descend to a bealach at the foot of the north ridge proper. The dramatic change in the rock colour there marks the boundary between the Red Hills and the Cuillin Outliers. Some climbing has been done on the large gabbro buttress situated on the east side of the ridge immediately south of the bealach. The north ridge gives a satisfying line of ascent. Turn left at the rocky summit ridge to reach the highest point.

The broad south-west shoulder of Garbh-bheinn can also be ascended from Srath na Creitheach.

Belig (702m)

The western flank of this mountain is gabbro, but its upper reaches are basalt. It is an attractive little peak, which can easily be included in a round with Garbh-bheinn.

The Cuillin Outliers seen from the west

It is best ascended by its south-east ridge from the head of Loch Slapin. This is described under the traverse of the Cuillin Outliers.

THE TRAVERSE OF THE CUILLIN OUTLIERS

The traverse of the Cuillin Outliers makes a superb expedition. It is best attempted from north to south, thereby leaving the ascent of Bla Bheinn - the only Munro of the group - as the climax of the day. The total distance involved is not excessive (12 kilometres at most), but the second half of the traverse, over Clach Glas and Bla Bheinn, demands a high level of competence in scrambling as well as a head for heights. This latter section is one of the finest ridge scrambles in the whole Cuillin range, and is particularly taxing when undertaken as the final part of the Greater Traverse of the Cuillin.

Start from the roadside at the very head of Loch Slapin and set off towards the south-east ridge of Belig. Cross the Allt Aigeinn and head up the hillside beyond. The ground gradually steepens as the foot of the ridge itself is approached. The lower section of the ridge is grassy and unrelentingly steep. Cattle graze to surprising heights here in the summer months. The ridge eventually flattens off at a long gentle shoulder (637m) which runs from east to west, and there are fine views over Glas Bheinn Mhor to the north. A somewhat narrower and steeper section of ridge then rises north-westwards to the summit of Belig. An old stone wall appears from the right (north-east) and is followed over the summit.

Descend the broken rocks and scree of the broad south-west ridge for some 250m to Bealach na Beiste (456m). This descent is the greatest height loss on the traverse. From the bealach ascend the broad bouldery slope forming the lower section of the north-east ridge of Garbh-bheinn, and continue up the ridge, which is more interesting in its upper section, to the rocky summit.

From the summit of Garbh-bheinn, descend the south-east ridge, with steep ground on the left-hand (east) side, to the 636m bealach. A detour can be made from there along the rocky ridge leading to the highest top of Sgurr nan Each, which lies some 400 metres or so to the east. Otherwise, contour the slope southwards to the next bealach (not a pass) at about 630m. An easy scree chute leads down into Choire a' Caise on the left (east), and the top of Arch Gully lies to the right.

The north ridge of Clach Glas now follows. It presents no great difficulties initially, and some pinnacles are easily turned on the right. Eventually the start of the summit tower is reached at a gap where a broad scree gully slopes down to the right (west). Descend the gully slightly to an obvious weakness in the opposite wall. Climb this to gain access to the slabby west face. A more sporting alternative for the climber is to scale the near vertical wall at the top of the gap by a short pitch of Very Difficult standard. Then slant up a scree-covered ledge, and either go round an exposed edge on the right or climb two difficult parallel cracks in a steep wall to easier ground. Continue up slabs and broken rocks to the 786m summit of this spectacular mountain.

Traverse the airy summit of Clach Glas, and descend the south ridge, firstly down a crack in a slab, then by a narrow arête (the Imposter). Thereafter difficulties are normally turned on the left, sometimes in exposed positions. There are fine views of the Great Prow across the corrie on the left side of the ridge. Eventually reach the Putting Green, the bealach at 695m between Clach Glas and Bla Bheinn.

Good route-finding is required on the complex north-east spur of Bla Bheinn which rises above. Avoid an initial steep section by a path on the left, and then climb a 4m wall. Traverse scree some distance rightwards past a steep chimney to a narrow stone chute. Climb this to an enclosed scree platform. The Half Crown Pinnacle is situated up and left from there.

From the platform gain a narrow boulder-filled gully and climb it for 18m by its right wall. At the top cross some big stones rightwards, and descend slightly to enter the upper section of a large stone chute. Ascend this leftwards to a cairn at a saddle on the east ridge at 795m where the major difficulties cease. Various other routes can be taken onto the east ridge from either side of the col behind the Half Crown Pinnacle.

Turn right and follow the upper section of the east ridge to the summit of Bla Bheinn. There are various options from there. One is to descend the normal route down the east ridge, which initially involves retracing one's steps. Another possibility is to traverse the main summit and descend Great Scree Gully from the dip between the mountain's twin tops. A further option is to continue to the south-west top and descend by the broad south-east ridge. All these routes lead into Coire

Uaigneich from where the path of the normal route is followed back to the road beside Loch Slapin.

THE WESTERN RED HILLS

Ruadh Stac (*red stack*) (493m)
This rather isolated little hill lies just over one and a half kilometres due west of Garbh-bheinn. It overlooks Loch an Athain in Srath na Creitheach. Strictly speaking it belongs to the Srath na Creitheach centre rather than the Western Red Hills. It is rarely ascended, but could conveniently be traversed en route for Garbh-bheinn from the west.

Marsco (736m)
This distinctive mountain holds a commanding position at the head of Glen Sligachan and can be seen clearly from the Sligachan Hotel. The main ridge of the district, which runs from Bla Bheinn in the south to Glamaig in the north, makes a westward diversion to incorporate Marsco, which is separated from the other mountains in the chain by low easy passes on two sides. The spine of the mountain is aligned north-west to south-east. One pass, the Mam a' Phobuill (pass of the people), is situated below the north-eastern flank at about 290m, and the other is situated at the foot of the south-east ridge at 323m. From the latter pass, a broad ridge leads eastwards over the 489m top of Druim Eadar Da Choire to link with the north ridge of Garbh-bheinn and the northern end of the Cuillin Outliers group.

The mountain is formed from a number of different granite, micro-granite and granophyre intrusions. A composite ring-dyke, which cuts across the mountain from west to east, consists of rocks collectively referred to as the Marscoite suite. On the north-western side of the mountain, overlooking Glen Sligachan, the ring-dyke has been eroded to form *Harker's Gully*. On the south wall of this gully is an overhanging rock feature called the *Shelter Stone*. There is also a cap of gabbro on the south-eastern part of the summit.

The easiest ascent route is by the south-east ridge, which is best approached from the A850 road round the head of Loch Ainort. Ascend Coire nam Bruadaran (corrie of dreams) to the bealach at 323m and continue up the easy-angled south-east ridge.

A much longer route from Sligachan goes for three kilometres up Glen Sligachan and then by the south bank of the Allt na Measarroch to the Mam a' Phobuill. From there, head due south up the shoulder on the east side of Coire nan Laogh to join the south-east ridge near a slight saddle at about 630m. A rather more direct route to the summit follows the west side of Coire nan Laogh, but this way is steeper and there are some small crags which may have to be circumvented.

On the west side of the mountain is a feature called Fiaclan Dearg (*red tooth*). Two buttresses there offer some excellent climbing on porphyritic granophyre which is well endowed with holds. This is the only significant climbing crag in the Red Hills.

Beinn Dearg Mheadhonach (*middle red mountain*) (651m)
There are two tops of very similar height on the chisel-like summit of this mountain.
They are separated from one another by some 250 metres of almost level ridge.
From the north top a ridge descends gradually northwards to Bealach Mosgaraidh
to link with Beinn Dearg Mhor, the parent mountain. A long shoulder, the Druim na
Ruaige (*ridge of the chase*), also extends north-westwards towards Sligachan. From
the south top a shorter ridge leads south to Ciche na Beinne Deirge, a small top
which overlooks the Mam a' Phobuill.
    The traverse of this mountain makes a fine hillwalk. It is normally combined
with Beinn Dearg Mhor, and often Glamaig as well. The best approach starts from
the roadside west of Loch Ainort. Leave the road where it crosses the Allt Mhic
Mhorein at a hairpin bed, and head south-west, either on the south bank of the
stream, or along the Bruach nam Bo (*ridge of the cows*). Continue to the saddle at
the top of Coire na Ciche, and then ascend the south ridge directly to the summit.

Beinn Dearg Mhor (*big red mountain*) (731m)
    Beinn Dearg Mhor is a compact mountain, with a main north-south ridge
and a subsidiary north-east spur. To the south it links with Beinn Dearg Mheadhonach at Bealach Mosgaraidh (511m), and to the north it links with Glamaig at
Bealach na Sgairde (415m). It is the most readily accessible mountain in the whole
area, and is easily combined with its neighbouring peaks. Despite the appearance
of its slopes, it gives a most enjoyable ridge walk.
    Both Beinn Dearg Mhor and Beinn Dearg Mheadhonach are composed of
granophyre which weathers to a rusty red colour. This is noticeably different from
the dull grey colour of the granite which forms much of Glamaig, Druim na Ruaige
and the north end of Marsco.
    The quickest and most interesting route to the summit is by the rocky north-
east spur, which forms the south side of Coire nan Laogh. This can easily be reached
from the highest point on the A850 road between Broadford and Sligachan, just
west of Loch Ainort. The best descent route is to traverse the summit to Bealach
Mosgaraidh, and then to drop down into the eastern corrie and follow the stream
to the road. Alternatively, the traverse can be continued to Beinn Dearg Mheadhonach and Ciche na Beinne Deirge, and a return can then be made by Coire na Ciche
and Bruach nam Bo.

Glamaig (775m)
Glamaig overlooks Loch Sligachan, and is the highest and most northerly of all the
Red Hills. The main summit, which lies at the western end above Sligachan, is
known as Sgurr Mhairi. From there a ridge extends for just over one kilometre north-
east to another top at 673m called An Coileach. South of the main summit a steep
scree-covered shoulder drops to Bealach na Sgairde (*pass of looseness* or *scree*),
which links on its south side with Beinn Dearg Mhor.
    On the summit, and to the north and west of it, the mountain is composed
of altered basaltic lavas. These were elevated to their present position by the
incoming granites, which form the bulk of the mountain. Both lavas and granite are

Glamaig (left), Beinn Dearg Mhor and Beinn Dearg Mheadhonach
Beinn Dearg Mheadhonach and Marsco from the north

cut on the south-west flank by a composite sheet of the Marscoite suite.

From Sligachan the mountain appears as an imposing scree-covered cone. A long standing record exists for the ascent of the mountain from this side. In 1899 Major (later General) Charles Bruce, one of the great pioneers of Himalayan climbing, brought a Gurkha by the name of Harkabir Thapa to Skye. Harkabir, or Herkia as he was also called, ran from the door of the Sligachan Hotel to the summit and back in 55 minutes (37 minutes up and 18 minutes down) - a record that despite several attempts still stands.

The mountain is a much finer hillwalk than might be imagined. It is probably best ascended by its north-east ridge from Gleann Torra-mhichaig, starting just north of the point where the A850 road crosses the Abhainn Torra-mhichaig. This route avoids the worst of the scree. An alternative is to start a short distance south-west of Sconser; scramble up the west bank of the Eas Mor and follow the north shoulder (on the west side of Coire na h-Airighe) directly to the summit.

A pleasant circuit of the Western Red Hills, excluding Marsco, can be made from Sligachan, starting from the path on the east side of Glen Sligachan. Ascend Sron a' Bhealain, and follow the Druim na Ruaige to the summit of Beinn Dearg Mheadhonach. From there, follow the ridge northwards over Beinn Dearg Mhor to Glamaig. Descend steep scree westwards from the summit and so return to Sligachan.

PATHS AND WALKS

The route between Sligachan and Camasunary passes through some spectacular country, and is undoubtedly the most impressive low-level walk in the area. It follows the east side of Glen Sligachan to the watershed at Lochan Dubha, and then continues down Srath na Creitheach to the picturesque bay of Camas Fhionnairigh. It is easy, in as much as it involves very little ascent, but it is 13 kilometres long, and the going is rather wearisome at times.

A walk of similar length, but with a better finish, takes the right fork in the path shortly after the watershed, and then crosses the Druim Hain to Loch Coruisk. This is described in the Cuillin section.

The walk from near Kirkibost (on the Elgol road) to Camasunary was mentioned earlier as an approach route to the south ridge of Bla Bheinn. It can be extended around the coast, via the Bad Step on the west flank of Sgurr na Stri, to Loch Coruisk, and from there it is possible to continue round the coast to Glen Brittle (see next chapter). The complete coastal route to Glen Brittle should not be underestimated. It is not devoid of technical difficulty and can become impossible at a number of places after heavy rain. There is no longer a bridge across the Abhainn Camas Fhionnairigh immediately west of the bothy at Camasunary. The lower reaches of this river are tidal and can become very deep at high tide. The stepping stones across the outlet from Loch Coruisk can also become awash. Even in good weather walkers have had their epics (see *Hunger March* in Alastair Borthwick's *Always a Little Further*).

There is also some pleasant walking around the tip of the Strathaird peninsula. The walk from Elgol to Camas Fhionnairigh, best done from south to north, commands superb views of the Cuillin across Loch Scavaig.

ROCK CLIMBING

The climbing in the area does not attract as much attention as it deserves. There are many fine routes on the gabbro cliffs of Bla Bheinn, Clach Glas and Garbh-bheinn, and also the granophyre of Marsco. The crags may not be set in quite such spectacular corries as those in the main Cuillin, but they offer climbing of comparable quality. Only a few climbs are mentioned here. The reader is referred to the SMC climbing guide for fuller details. (*Rock and Ice Climbs in Skye* by J R Mackenzie).

The Great Prow, which protrudes from the north face of the east ridge of Bla Bheinn, is possibly the mountain's best-known rock feature. The fact that it was not climbed until 1968 gives an indication of the neglect that the area has suffered. The original route up the end of the *Great Prow* (115m, Very Severe) is a classic outing with plenty of atmosphere. The crux is on the steep first pitch. It can be quite nerve-racking to observe parties descending the south ridge of Clach Glas from this route. They appear to be in grave danger of plunging off the ridge at any moment.

The impressive wall on the east flank of the Great Prow provides two harder and finer routes. *Jib* (Hard Very Severe) takes a steep corner and chimney line up the left side of the wall, and *Stairway to Heaven* (E4) takes a superb line up the centre of the wall itself. A scree gully on the west side of the Great Prow, known as *Scupper Gully*, provides a convenient descent route.

There are two prominent chimney-gullies (both Very Severe) at the top right-hand end of the north wall - *Clough's Cleft* on the left and *Chock-a-Block Chimney* on the right. A fine route, *Ecstasis* (85m, Very Severe), follows the ramp on the upper wall just left of Clough's Cleft. Right of Chock-a-Block Chimney, and overlooking the Putting Green bealach, is The Half Crown Pinnacle. *The Horn* (Severe) and the *Horn Direct* (Hard Very Severe) climb the east face of this pinnacle. There are many other routes on this side of the mountain.

The other main area of climbing interest on Bla Bheinn is South Buttress, which lies on the left (south) side of the Great Scree Gully on the east face. *Central Pillar* (195m, Severe) climbs the obvious light-coloured pillar on the left side of the buttress. *Birthday Groove* (195m, Very Difficult) lies to its right. Various routes can be climbed to reach a slanting terrace on the right-hand half of the buttress, from where *The Outsider* (65m, Very Difficult) takes an exciting line up the outside edge of a great slab. Further right is *The Hem* (180m, Very Severe), a fine route with three difficult pitches.

On the east face of Clach Glas, a deep-cut gully which starts from the lowest rocks gives the line of B Gully. This long Severe route has a dozen small pitches. Near the top, the left wall may require combined tactics before the bed of the gully can be regained. Starting high up and to the right of B Gully is the line of *Sickle* - a good Very Severe, which follows a prominent line on the steep north wall of Pinnacle Buttress.

Further right again, just north of a low point on the main ridge, are the Bealach Buttresses. These twin buttresses provide interesting ways onto the ridge. The left-hand one is Difficult (135m), and the right-hand one is Very Difficult (120m).

There is much smooth sound rock set at an amenable angle on the west face of Clach Glas. By careful route-finding it is possible to find any number of ways up at about Difficult or Very Difficult standard.

The best climbing on Garbh-bheinn is on a large, 120m high buttress at the northern extremity of the north ridge overlooking Coire na Seilg. More than a dozen routes were completed there in the 1970's. They range in grade from Very Difficult to E1, and are of good quality. The buttress is readily accessible from the road at the head of Loch Ainort.

The only place in the Red Hills where there is any quantity of sound rock is on the west face of Marsco. The rough, almost gabbro-like texture of the granophyre there is due to the weathering out of large feldspar crystals. The prominent buttress seen in profile on the approach along Glen Sligachan is *Central Buttress*. To the right of Central Buttress there is a steep wall and waterfall; to the left, there is an amphitheatre. The original route on the crag is *Odell's Route* (180m, Difficult) which was pioneered in 1943. It starts up the centre of this amphitheatre, follows slabs and grooves to a scree patch and then trends a long way right to the shoulder above Central Buttress, where a final wall gives some of the best climbing.

The first line on Central Buttress itself was Very Difficult, but subsequent variations and neighbouring routes have been of Very Severe and Hard Very Severe grade. Central Buttress faces west-south-west across to Sgurr na h-Uamha, but there is also a north-west buttress which faces Sligachan. This has two Hard Very Severe routes, *The Boojum* and *Teflon*, of about 120m. Both lines visit a cave which lies in the centre of the cliff.

Away from the mountains, there are some short routes on the sandstone sea-cliffs around the Strathaird peninsula. At a headland just over one kilometre south of Elgol, called Suidhe Biorach (*sharp-pointed seat*), the cliff-top has weathered to a very uneven surface. A massive cracked block, shaped somewhat like India, juts out from the upper part of the cliff. Just to the east of this there are two V-shaped grooves, which face out to Rhum, and both give pleasant climbs. The right-hand (eastern) one is *Fertility Right* (25m, Severe); the left-hand one is *Fertility Left* (30m, Very Severe).

CHAPTER 8

MINGINISH AND THE CUILLIN

The area is bounded in the east by Glen Sligachan and Srath na Creitheach, and in the north by Glen Drynoch and Loch Harport. The whole region is known as Minginish. The Cuillin, which lie in the south-eastern part of Minginish, form rather less than half of the area. The hills outwith the Cuillin are described first.

MAPS: The Scottish Mountaineering Trust. The Black Cuillin, Island of Skye. Two different maps of the Cuillin are printed on opposite sides of the same sheet. One map (1:12,500) depicts rock relief, the other (1:15,000) is more schematic.

Cicerone Press	1:20,000 Black Cuillin of Skye (Supplied with the book Scrambles in Skye by J Wilson Parker.)	
Ordnance Survey	1:25,000 Outdoor Leisure Map 8 THE CUILLIN AND TORRIDON HILLS	
Ordnance Survey	1:50,000 Sheet 32	

MINGINISH OUTWITH THE CUILLIN

PRINCIPAL HILLS

Beinn a' Bhraghad	461m	409 253
Beinn Staic	412m	398 236
An Cruachan	435m	381 225
Stockval	416m	350 295
Preshal More	322m	333 300
Preshal Beg	347m	329 278

GENERAL DESCRIPTION

The Sligachan Hotel is strategically placed at the gateway to Minginish. It stands where the roads to Portree and Dunvegan diverge at a bridge over the River Sligachan. The hotel has an important place in the history of the Cuillin because it was a popular base for the early explorers. Nowadays mountaineers are more likely to stay at the camp site across the road. A small shop near the hotel is open seven days a week in the summer.

The A863 road from Sligachan to Dunvegan, through Glen Drynoch, runs along the northern edge of the area. Near Drynoch, almost nine kilometres from Sligachan, the B8009 road cuts off to Carbost along the south side of Loch Harport. Radiating from this road are several subsidiary roads which lead to the southern and western parts of the area.

The first of these minor roads is of most importance to mountaineers. It begins at a sharp left turn, almost three kilometres along the road to Carbost, and leads over into Glen Brittle on the western fringe of the Cuillin. The second minor road forks off to the left just before Carbost and after a short distance divides again; one branch leads south to Glen Eynort and the head of Loch Eynort, and the other west to Gleann Oraid and Talisker. The road into Carbost zigzags up behind the famous Talisker Distillery, and then continues north-westwards overlooking Loch Harport to the rambling and picturesque crofting and fish farming communities of Portnalong and Fiskavaig.

The initial part of the road to Glen Brittle runs across fairly desolate moorland, but from the highest point of the road there are superb views of the north-western side of the Cuillin. The road then descends dramatically into Glen Brittle itself. Strangely, the lower reaches of the glen are not as scenic as might be imagined, given the proximity of the Cuillin. The glen is thickly afforested on its western flank, and the Cuillin peaks, which are often hidden in cloud, are set back to the east.

There is a youth hostel by the bridge over the Allt a' Choire Ghreadaidh some two kilometres from the end of the glen. It is in a rather cheerless location, isolated from other habitation, but it is handy for the mountains. The Glenbrittle Memorial Hut (owned by the BMC and MC of S) is situated nearly one kilometre past the youth hostel. Further on, there are various dwelling places including Glenbrittle House. The road ends at a large camp site by a long beach with black sand. This camp site, some 24 kilometres by road from Sligachan, is by far the most popular base for hillwalkers and climbers venturing into the Cuillin.

Glen Eynort is a steep and narrow little glen, situated only a few kilometres north-west of Glen Brittle. The enclosed community at the end of the glen is largely given over to forestry. The beach here is not attractive, and because Loch Eynort is a crooked inlet there is no view of the open sea. However, there is a pleasant walk through the plantations on the east side of the loch over Bealach Brittle into Glen Brittle.

Talisker lies at the western end of Gleann Oraid, some eight kilometres along the road from the distillery of the same name in Carbost. About half way along this road, on its northern side, lies the long escarpment of Na Huranan. Shortly afterwards the view is dominated on the south side of the road by the craggy northern flank of Preshal More. This massive hump appears ever more imposing as the road descends steeply to the floor of the glen.

Cars should be parked at a junction just before the wooded grounds of Talisker House. From there a track leads in one and a half kilometres to the sandy beach at Talisker Bay. This is an enchanting place to visit on a fine evening. To the east Preshal More is lit up by the setting sun, whilst in the bay itself two small sea-stacks are silhouetted against the sky.

The Old Inn at Carbost is small but homely, and since it is the nearest hostelry to Glen Brittle, it is very popular with mountaineers. Similar friendly service is available at Taigh Ailean (Alan's House) in Portnalong.

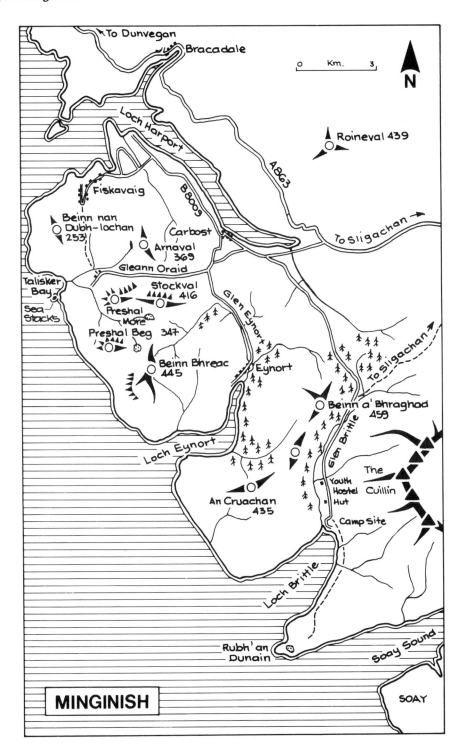

There is a small harbour and jetty at Portnalong. This community was established after the first world war, when families from Lewis, Harris and nearby Scalpay were resettled by the Department of Agriculture. There is now a huge fish farm there.

The greater part of Minginish is built from plateau lavas, which form a green, relatively gentle, and characteristically terraced landscape very different from the Cuillin. Only a handful of hills formed from these lavas rise above 400m.

The sea-cliffs on the south-west coast of Minginish are the most spectacular scenic features of the area outwith the Cuillin. They extend from Fiscavaig in the north to opposite Soay in the south, but are especially impressive between Talisker Bay and the mouth of Loch Eynort, and between there and the mouth of Loch Brittle. Some two kilometres south of Talisker Bay they reach a height of 280m. This whole section of coastline is wild and interesting to explore, and caves and stacks can be found in a number of places. Unfortunately the basalt is inherently loose, so the climbing potential of the cliffs is limited.

THE HILLS
Beinn a' Bhraghad (*hill of the neck*) (461m)
Beinn Staic (*steep hill*) (411m)
An Cruachan (*the small stack* or *conical hill*) (435m)
These three hills are all situated above the forestry plantations on the west side of Glen Brittle. On a clear day they offer in Ben Humble's opinion "just about the finest viewpoint for the Cuillin". Beinn Staic is the most shapely of the three, and lies close to the track which leads over the Bealach Brittle to Glen Eynort. There are footbridges at three different places across the River Brittle. The 1:25,000 map is recommended for finding suitable approach routes through the forest.

Stockval (416m)
Preshal More (322m)
Stockval lies on the south side of the road to Talisker, and is a rather uninteresting hill apart from its prominent western shoulder, which is called Preshal More. This is steep and craggy on three sides, and towers above Talisker House. It is one of the more striking hills in the area.

It can be approached by leaving the road in Gleann Oraid shortly after it crosses to the south side of the River Talisker. Head south-east and climb a steep grassy runnel to the col at the eastern end of the shoulder. In descent it is easier to drop down on the south side of the col, and then to contour around the base of the crags back to the north side.

Preshal Beg (347m)
Some two kilometres to the south of Preshal More, on the opposite side of Sleadale, lies the twin peak of Preshal Beg. As is often the case, this peak is in fact the higher of the two despite its name (beg - small). It is of similar shape to its twin, being steep on three sides, with a flat col at its eastern end. This col gives the easiest line of ascent and is best approached from Talisker House up Sleadale. The hidden south-

The Cuillin seen from the road between Carbost and Glen Brittle

west face is steep and some 70m high. The remains of a broch can be seen on the west side of Sleadale.

PATHS AND WALKS

There is a popular and fascinating walk from the camp site in Glen Brittle, which is suitable for an off day or an evening. It goes out along the east side of Loch Brittle to Rubh' an Dunain (*headland of the little fort*). It is an easy low level route.

There are two parallel paths for the first few kilometres, the lower of which stays close to the shore. The Allt Coire Lagan can be difficult to cross when in spate, but there is a footbridge midway between the paths. Shortly after the paths merge, skirt below Creag Mhor and then turn left into the entrance of a long, narrow trench-like feature, called the Slochd Dubh (*black ditch*), which cuts right across the headland.

When the path becomes difficult to follow, continue in a south-westerly direction for rather more than a kilometre. The remains of a chambered cairn can then be found beside a wall, just north of Loch na h-Airde (*loch of the promontory*). Various items of archaeological interest, including Beaker pottery, have been found there and also in a small cave some 450 metres east of the loch. The sea floods into the loch along a narrow man-made channel at high tide. Immediately to the east of this channel there is a Dun on a rocky knoll, and some 750 metres to the north-east are the remains of the Rhundunan. This was the farm and family home of the

MacAskills before they built Glenbrittle House in the 19th century. On the south side of the headland, east of Slochd Dubh, there are basalt sea-cliffs that rise to more than 100m.

The route from Glen Brittle over to Glen Eynort, though mainly along forest tracks, is pleasant enough, especially if combined with an ascent of Beinn Staic or An Cruachan from Bealach Brittle.

A path also zigzags up beside the Eas Mor (*big waterfall*) on the north side of Gleann Oraid, and crosses over by Huisgill to link up with a surfaced road near Ard an t-Sabhail in the district of Fiskavaig. The remains of a broch can be inspected on an eminence just west of there.

ROCK CLIMBING

There is no climbing of quality in Minginish outwith the Cuillin, the basalt generally being too unreliable. Probably the best climbing is to be found on several small sea-cliffs on the east side of Loch Brittle, which are easily reached from the camp site. A number of traverse lines can be undertaken which vary in seriousness according to the state of the tide.

Some climbing has been reported near the road over to Talisker on a 30m high crag called Na Huranan, which extends for more than 600 metres on the south side of Arnaval. The craggy flanks of Preshal More and Preshal Beg, however, have yet to yield any routes of note.

There are two sea-stacks on the south side of Talisker Bay which are accessible at low tide. The larger one, known as The Fiddler, has been climbed by a number of lines at its western end. Suffice it to say that the routes have not become popular. A girdle traverse has also been done on a crag due north of the road end at Fiskavaig.

THE CUILLIN

GENERAL DESCRIPTION

The Cuillin are an extraordinary range of exceptionally rocky mountains, whose pointed peaks, sharp ridges and deep corries have entranced mountaineers for well over a century. There are larger groups of mountains on the mainland, but none displaying such rugged grandeur and none as difficult to traverse. The Cuillin are arguably the finest mountains in the British Isles, and as such have become a Mecca for mountaineers.

The word Cuillin has been spelt almost a dozen different ways over the years, and in view of this it is perhaps not surprising that the origin of the name remains obscure. One of the more plausible theories is that it has been derived from the Gaelic word *cuileann* meaning *holly*, presumably because of the prickly outline of the range. Another credible origin is the Gaelic word *cuile* (or *cuilidh*) meaning *cellar* or *rocky corrie*; another possibility is that it comes from an old Celtic word meaning *worthless*, a reference to the absence of pasturage in the range; yet another theory is that it comes from an old Norse word, *kjolen*, meaning *high rocks*. The idea that the word has been derived from *Cuchullin*, the name of a legendary warrior, is now generally discounted.

Even though its meaning cannot be explained with any certainty, at least Cuillin is now the generally accepted spelling. Note that this is given in the singular and does not have the word Hills tagged onto it. The Cuillin are similar in this respect to another great range of mountains - The Himalaya.

The main Cuillin ridge is some twelve kilometres long and incorporates, along with its subsidiary ridges, more than thirty rock peaks, including eleven Munros and nine Tops. It lies in a large arc which is concave to the east, with a long straight lateral ridge, called Druim nan Ramh, extending from inside this arc. The huge hollow on the south side of Druim nan Ramh contains a large loch, Loch Coruisk. Situated a little to the east of Loch Coruisk are some much smaller hills, the Eastern Cuillin, which are set apart from the main ridge.

The Cuillin are carved from a large basic and ultrabasic igneous complex some twelve kilometres in diameter, which was intruded in the area east of Glen Brittle and south of Sligachan. The complex consists of a series of arcuate intrusions of gabbro and peridotite. In general, the oldest intrusions occur around the margins of the complex, whilst the youngest are found towards the centre. Many of the intrusions show distinct layering, which is rather an unusual feature in igneous rocks. It is thought to have come about when crystals of certain minerals settled out under gravity from the cooling magma. All this layering is inclined towards the centre of the complex. The intrusions of gabbro and peridotite are themselves intruded by numerous dykes and cone-sheets. The dykes are narrow vertical intrusions, which are orientated north-west to south-east and extend for great distances outwith the complex. The cone sheets, however, are generally concordant with the layering in the main intrusions and usually less than one metre thick. Both the cone-sheets and the layering dip at shallow angles (10-20 degrees) on the margins of the complex, but at increasingly steeper angles towards the middle, so that in the centre of the complex they dip at 50-65 degrees. All these structures dip towards a common focal point some two to three kilometres below Meall Dearg, the small hill that lies at the head of Glen Sligachan.

Thus on Sgurr nan Gillean, for example, at the northern end of the Cuillin ridge, the structures dip towards the south; in the central part of the main ridge they dip to the east; on the Dubh Slabs, on the south side of Loch Coruisk, they dip to the north-east; on Sgurr na Stri (in the Eastern Cuillin) they dip to the north, whilst on Bla Bheinn (in the Cuillin Outliers) they dip to the north-west. The north-eastern sector of the complex was obliterated when the later granites of the Red Hills Centres were intruded.

Gabbro is a coarsely crystalline rock that weathers to give a very rough surface with superb frictional properties. This makes it excellent to climb on, but at the same time causes rapid wear on boots, ropes and fingers. Peridotite has a similar crystalline texture, but a rather different mineralogical composition. It weathers to produce a very distinctive orange-brown rock with a curious sponge-like surface. A major band of peridotite can be traced from An Garbh-choire, across Sgurr Dubh an Da Bheinn, and over the Sgurr Coir' an Lochain ridge.

Most of the dykes and cone-sheets consist of dolerite and basalt. These rocks are chemically similar to gabbro, but cool at different rates. Dolerite cools more quickly than gabbro, and so develops only small to medium-sized crystals. Basalt cools even faster, and so forms very small crystals indeed. Jointing is often present within these intrusions and as a consequence they are generally less sound than gabbro. Their finer grain also makes them more slippery, especially when wet. In many instances the dykes have been eroded more rapidly than the neighbouring gabbro and so form deep chimneys and gullies. The cone-sheets, on the other hand, have in some places proved more resistant and in others less resistant than the gabbro.

It should be noted that a compass is likely to be unreliable in the Cuillin, because of the magnetic nature of many of the rocks. Readings are best taken with the compass held as far away as possible from any rock (at shoulder height); even then readings should be used with caution.

There are three main bases from which the Cuillin can be explored;
i)   Sligachan in the north (camp site, hotel and self-catering cottages);
ii) Glen Brittle in the west (camp site, hut, and youth hostel);
iii) Coruisk in the south-east (hut and wild camping).
See the accommodation section in the introduction to Skye. In addition, it is possible to stay further to the east at Camasunary (wild camping and bothy), but this is perhaps more convenient for the Cuillin Outliers. The bases are all linked by walking routes around the margins of the Cuillin, and these are now described.

Sligachan to Glen Brittle

There is a direct walking link between Sligachan and Glen Brittle, although nowadays it is not often used as such. From the hotel, follow the A863 Dunvegan road westwards for 700 metres, then take a track on the south side of the road towards Alltdearg House. This white-washed cottage is passed on the right by a boggy path. The route then follows the north-west bank of the Allt Dearg Mor (*great red stream*), for a further four kilometres, all the way to Bealach a' Mhaim (*pass of the rounded top*). The distinctive outline of the Basteir Tooth stands out on the skyline to the south. The last section up to the top of the pass is very boggy. The pass presumably gets its name from the rounded top (Am Mam) which lies immediately to the north of it.

The path descends from the bealach on the north side of the Allt a' Mhaim, and leads in three kilometres to the road near the head of Glen Brittle. There is a large forestry plantation on the uphill side of the path for the last half of this descent. Across Coire na Creiche on the left, there are good views of the north-west face of Sgurr an Fheadain, which is split by its famous Waterpipe Gully. It is a further six kilometres from the point where the path joins the road to the camp site by the beach (14 kilometres in total).

Glen Brittle to Coruisk — The Coastal path

There is a route around the southern end of the Cuillin from Glen Brittle to Coruisk, which is sometimes called the 'coastal path'. It continues around the coast to Camasunary. The path is very indefinite in its second half towards Coruisk and is far from easy going. It has been described as "a gruelling tramp". Leave from the east end of the camp site in Glen Brittle, and soon join a path which leads uphill away from the shore. After 500 metres take the right fork in the path, cross a small stream and head towards the base of Sron na Ciche. Cross the Allt Coire Lagan and follow a lower path which eventually passes the mouth of Coir' a' Ghrunnda and Coire nan Laogh. Continue to the foot of Gars-bheinn.

The route up to this point is also used by those starting the main ridge traverse from the south, and it is not too difficult to follow even though there is no path marked after Coir' a' Ghrunnda on the Ordnance Survey Outdoor Leisure map. When the path fades, contour for some distance at a height of about 230m, then follow a long gently rising traverse line to a point overlooking Loch Scavaig.

Go round the shoulder at the south-eastern foot of Gars-bheinn, and cross a small stream called the Allt an Fhraoich at a height of about 280m. Continue northwards along a cairned shelf as far as the Allt Coir' a' Chruidh. Cross this above a waterfall and contour at about 300m until a large crag appears on the left. Then descend, at first by a short line of slabs, all the way to the shore, passing the Mad Burn Buttress en route.

This point can also be reached by taking a much lower line around the south-east shoulder of Gars-bheinn. Slant down to the shore soon after crossing a small stream which flows from a point due south of the summit of Gars-bheinn. Reach Ulfhart Point and continue around the coast following the vestiges of an up and down path. There is an awkward step about one kilometre before the two routes join up again on the shore. This second option is slighty longer, but less complicated than the upper route.

Looking across Loch Scavaig to the Cuillin. The prominent peaks are Gars-bheinn (left) and Sgurr na Stri (right), with Coir'-uisg between them

Shortly after the junction of the two alternative routes, cross two streams, the second of which is called the Allt a' Chaoich (Mad Burn); this can become impassable when in spate. Continue to some rock slabs which dip into the sea. These can be avoided in part when the tide is right out, but otherwise they provide some scrambling interest comparable with the Bad Step further round the coast below Sgurr na Stri. Situated not far from there, below a long rock face, is the Coruisk Memorial Hut. (See the accommodation section in the introduction to Skye.) There are ample opportunities for camping nearby on rather peaty ground. Down at the water's edge some rusty iron steps are fixed to a steep rock slab where boats from Mallaig and Elgol set passengers ashore. This locality is commonly referred to as 'Coruisk', although in fact the huge corrie of Coir'-uisg proper lies out of sight further round the corner to the north-east. (Glen Brittle to Coruisk Hut - 11 kilometres)

Coruisk to Sligachan

The River Scavaig is a remarkably short river which flows for less than 400 metres from Loch Coruisk to the sea. It spills down rock slabs into Loch na Cuilce some 100 metres south-east of the Coruisk Hut. A path leads from the hut across some rock slabs and down a small step to the side of the river. It then turns upstream and eventually leads to some stepping stones near the head of the river by Loch Coruisk.

These stepping stones can become awash after a prolonged spell of wet weather, in which case they can be hazardous or impossible to cross.

Two paths lead off from the other side of the river. The right-hand one leads round the coast to Camasunary and is described below. The one on the left is followed for Sligachan. It skirts around the end of Loch Coruisk and then ascends north-eastwards to a low point on the crest of a broad ridge called Druim Hain. There are wonderful views from the top of this 316m pass, which is situated about three kilometres from the Coruisk Hut.

The path then descends northwards to the head of Srath na Creitheach. It crosses to the other side of the glen just before Lochan Dubha and joins a path which leads north from Camasunary. It continues north along the east side of Glen Sligachan, past the shapely peak of Marsco, all the way to Sligachan itself. The way is fairly obvious, but the going is rather tedious at times. (Coruisk Hut to Sligachan - 12 kilometres)

Coruisk to Camasunary

From the Coruisk Hut, follow the path to the stepping stones across the head of the River Scavaig, as described for the previous route. Take the right-hand path on the far side of the river to a small bay at the head of Loch nan Leachd (loch of the slabs). Continue around the shore for some 400 metres to the famous Bad Step - a steep slab of rock that lies immediately above the sea. A short crack-cum-gangway slanting down the slab gives a fairly straightforward scramble, although some walkers find it unnerving when laden.

Continue along the coast over other rock slabs and cut across the small headland of Rubha Buidhe. Follow the obvious path without any further difficulty until a large bay, Camas Fhionnairigh, and a bothy come into view. Head north until a suitable place can be found to ford the Abhainn Camas Fhionnairigh. This river is tidal and can be difficult to cross at high water or after continous wet weather. (Coruisk Hut to Camasunary - 4 kilometres)

See Chapter 7 section for details of the routes from Camasunary.

It is worth reflecting for a moment on the 'Coruisk Affair' of the late 1960s, when the Army tried to 'improve' the route along this unspoilt section of coast. There was talk of blasting the Bad Step to oblivion. The excuse was that it would facilitate the evacuation of injured climbers. The proposal, which apparently originated from the Inverness-shire Police, was never put to the Mountain Rescue Committee of Scotland. The climbing world objected vehemently, but various construction works went ahead, although the Bad Step itself was not dynamited.

The bridges that were built across the Abhainn Camas Fhionnairigh and the River Scavaig have long since been swept away, and only the vehicular track from near Kirkibost to Camasunary remains as a reminder of this extraordinary escapade. Much of the attraction of this wonderful corner of the Cuillin is due to its remoteness. It would be a tragedy if it should ever became readily accessible.

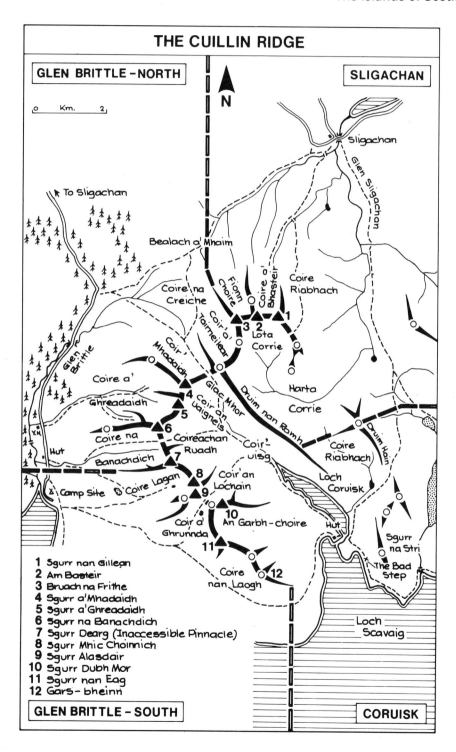

THE CUILLIN RIDGE

GLEN BRITTLE – NORTH

SLIGACHAN

N

0   Km.   2

To Sligachan

Sligachan

Glen Sligachan

Bealach a' Mhaim

Fionn Choire

Coire a' Bhasteir

Coire Riabhach

Coire na Creiche

Coir' a' Tairneilear

Coire a Lota Corrie

1

3 2

Coir' a Mhadaidh

Glen Brittle

Coire a' Ghreadaidh

Glac Mhor

Druim nan Ramh

Harta Corrie

4

Coir' an Uaigneis

5

Coire na Banachdich

6

Coireachan Ruadh

Coir'uisg

Coire Riabhach

Druim Hain

Hut

7

8

Coir' an Lochain

Loch Coruisk

Camp Site

Coire Lagan

9

10

An Garbh-choire

Hut

Coir a Ghrunnda

Sgurr na Stri

11

The Bad Step

Coire nan Laogh

12

Loch Scavaig

1 Sgurr nan Gillean
2 Am Basteir
3 Bruach na Frithe
4 Sgurr a'Mhadaidh
5 Sgurr a'Ghreadaidh
6 Sgurr na Banachdich
7 Sgurr Dearg (Inaccessible Pinnacle)
8 Sgurr Mhic Choinnich
9 Sgurr Alasdair
10 Sgurr Dubh Mor
11 Sgurr nan Eag
12 Gars-bheinn

GLEN BRITTLE – SOUTH

CORUISK

THE CUILLIN PEAKS AND CORRIES

The normal practice in this guide is to describe each peak in an area in turn. This does not work quite as satisfactorily for the Cuillin, because many of the peaks are closely linked to one another along the main ridge with only slight drops between them. The corries bounding the main ridge have a controlling influence on its topography, and also provide most of the important access routes to the ridge itself. The Cuillin are therefore described corrie by corrie, rather than peak by peak. Consequently, in order to obtain a complete description of any particular peak, it may be necessary to consult more than one of the next four chapters.

The majority of climbers reach the Cuillin first at Sligachan, and many then continue to Glen Brittle. For this reason, the corries are described starting at Sligachan and going in an anti-clockwise direction to Glen Brittle and finally to Coruisk. Thus, from the point of view of someone looking at the ridge, they are described from left to right.

The corries are grouped into four chapters according to the starting points from which they are usually approached. These starting points are Sligachan, Glen Brittle and Coruisk. Glen Brittle is further divided into North Glen Brittle and South Glen Brittle. The corries allocated to the former are those that are most easily accessible from the upper reaches of the glen above the Memorial Hut, and the corries allocated to the latter are those most conveniently approached from the camp site.

CHARTER 9
SLIGACHAN

1. Harta Corrie and Lota Corrie
2. Coire Riabhach and Coire nan Allt Geala
3. Coire a' Bhasteir
4. Fionn Choire

CHAPTER10
NORTH GLEN BRITTLE

5. Coir' a' Tairneilear (Coire na Creiche)
6. Coir' a' Mhadaidh (Coire na Creiche)
7. Coire a' Ghreadaidh
8. Coire na Banachdich

CHAPTER 11
SOUTH GLEN BRITTLE

9. Coire Lagan
10. Coir' a' Ghrunnda
11. Coire nan Laogh

CHAPTER 12
CORUISK

12. Coir' a' Chruidh and Coire Beag
13. An Garbh-choire
14. Coir' a' Chaoruinn and Coir' an Lochain
15. Coireachan Ruadha
16. Coir' an Uaigneis and Glac Mhor
17. Coir'-uisg
18. Coire Riabhach

THE PRINCIPAL PEAKS OF THE CUILLIN

To assist the reader in finding information on individual peaks, the table below lists the principal peaks of the Cuillin together with the chapter numbers (9 to 12) and the numbers of the various corries (1 to 18) under which they are described.

The main Cuillin ridge forms a huge C-shaped curve. In order to avoid unnecessary repetition of information, a full description of the main ridge is given only for the corries lying on the outside of this curve. Thus only minimal information about the main ridge is given under Harta and Lota Corries, and under the corries in Chapter 12 (Coruisk). Reference is made to the complete traverse of the main ridge at the end of Chapter 12.

The Northern Cuillin

			Chapter(s)	Corrie(s)
Sgurr na h-Uamha	736m	476 240	9	1
Sgurr Beag	764m	476 246	9	1
Sgurr nan Gillean	964m	472 253	9	1,2,3
Am Basteir	934m	465 253	9	1,3
Basteir Tooth	916m	465 253	9	1,3
Sgurr a' Fionn Choire	935m	464 252	9	1,4
Bruach na Frithe	958m	461 252	9,10	1,4,5
Sgurr na Bhairnich	861m	461 246	9,10	1,5
An Caisteal	830m	461 244	9,10	1,5

The Central Cuillin

Bidein Druim nan Ramh	869m	456 239	9,10,12	1,5,16
Druim nam Ramh	500m	480 217	9,12	1,17
Sgurr a' Mhadaidh	918m	447 235	10,12	6,7,16
Sgurr Thuilm	881m	439 242	10	7
Sgurr a' Ghreadaidh	973m	445 231	10,12	7,16
Sgurr Thormaid	926m	441 226	10,12	7,15
Sgurr na Banachdich	965m	440 224	10,12	7,8,15
Sgurr Dearg (cairn)	978m	444 216	10,11,12	8,9,15
Inaccessible Pinnacle	986m	444 215	11,12	9,15
An Stac	954m	445 215	11,12	9,15

The Southern Cuillin

Sgurr Mhic Choinnich	948m	450 210	11,12	9,15
Sgurr Coir' an Lochain	729m	454 214	12	14
Sgurr Thearlaich	978m	451 208	11,12	9,10,14
Sgurr Alasdair	992m	450 208	11	9,10
Sgurr Sgumain	947m	448 206	11	9,10
Sgurr Dubh an Da Bheinn	938m	455 204	11,12	10,13,14
Sgurr Dubh Mor	944m	457 205	12	13,14
Caisteal a' Garbh-choire	829m	454 202	11,12	10,13

Sgurr nan Gillean from Sgurr a' Bhastair, the Pinnacle Ridge in profile

Sgurr nan Eag	924m	457 195	11,12	10,11,13
Sgurr a' Choire Bhig	875m	465 191	11,12	11,12,13
Gars-bheinn	895m	468 187	11,12	11,12

The Eastern Cuillin

Meall Dearg	364m	492 230	9	1
Druim Hain	347m	493 226	12	18
Sgurr Hain	420m	503 209	12	18
Sgurr na Stri	494m	499 193	12	18

CHAPTER 9

SLIGACHAN

The corries belonging to the Sligachan group lie on either side of the northernmost Cuillin peaks. In general they are most conveniently approached from Sligachan, although some can also be reached from either the head of Glen Brittle or Loch Coruisk.

1. **Harta Corrie** and **Lota Corrie**
2. **Coire Riabhach** and **Coire nan Allt Geala**
3. **Coire a' Bhasteir**
4. **Fionn Choire**

1. HARTA CORRIE (*stone corrie*)
LOTA CORRIE (*wound corrie*)

SURROUNDING PEAKS

Meall Dearg	364m	492 230
Bidein Druim nan Ramh	869m	456 239
An Caisteal	830m	461 244
Sgurr na Bhairnich	861m	461 246
Bruach na Frithe	958m	461 252
Sgurr a' Fionn Choire	935m	464 252
Basteir Tooth	916m	465 253
Am Basteir	934m	465 253
Sgurr nan Gillean	964m	472 253
Sgurr Beag	764m	476 246
Sgurr na h-Uamha	736m	476 240

Harta and Lota Corries are two very fine corries hidden away on the south side of the northern Cuillin peaks. Lota Corrie is effectively an upper level of Harta Corrie, and is separated from it by a broad slabby rock band. The River Sligachan originates in Lota Corrie, and initially flows south, then east, and then north-east before eventually draining northwards down Glen Sligachan.

The western side of Harta Corrie is dominated by the complex peak of Bidein Druim nan Ramh, which lies at the junction between the main ridge and a major lateral ridge running south-eastwards called Druim nan Ramh (*ridge of the oars*).

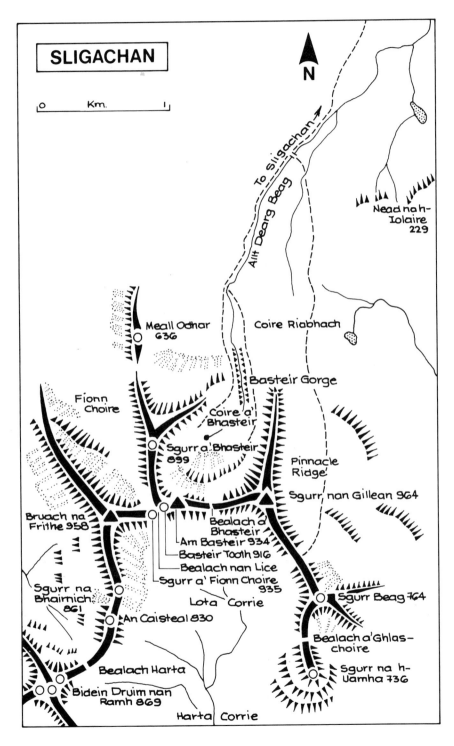

SLIGACHAN

N

Km.

To Sligachan →

Allt Dearg Beag

Nead na h-
Iolaire
229

Meall Odhar
636

Coire Riabhach

Basteir Gorge

Fionn
Choire

Coire a'
Bhasteir

Sgurr a' Bhasteir
899

Pinnacle
Ridge

Sgurr nan Gillean 964

Bruach na
Frithe 958

Bealach a'
Bhasteir

Am Basteir 934

Basteir Tooth 916

Bealach nan Lice

Sgurr a' Fionn Choire
935

Lota Corrie

Sgurr Beag 764

Sgurr na
Bhairnich
861

An Caisteal 830

Bealach a'Ghlas-
choire

Bealach Harta

Bidein Druim nan
Ramh 869

Sgurr na h-
Uamha 736

Harta Corrie

This lateral ridge, and its rather indefinite north-eastern extension to Meall Dearg, form the southern side of Harta Corrie.

Three major peaks, Bruach na Frithe, Am Basteir and Sgurr nan Gillean, are situated on the main ridge overlooking the head of Lota Corrie. A further section of ridge, which curves southwards from Sgurr nan Gillean to Sgurr na h-Uamha, forms the eastern side of Lota corrie.

These corries are infrequently approached from below, although it is fairly common for parties to descend them when returning to Coruisk after completing the main ridge traverse. Harta Corrie, being well off the beaten track, is a delightfully wild place to camp. The approach from Sligachan, by the path on the east bank of the River Sligachan, is a long haul. Leave the main path at Lochan Dubha, and follow the south-east bank of the river to the entrance of Harta Corrie. A short distance up the corrie stands a gigantic boulder (known as Clach Fuileach or *the Bloody Stone*), which offers some shelter and good bouldering.

The approach to Harta Corrie from Coruisk via Coire Riabhach is slightly shorter and more interesting, but involves crossing a broad bealach at 270m between Druim nan Ramh and Druim Hain.

No less than four easy passes can be used to cross or (more likely) gain the ridge from these two corries. The first pass, which has become known as Bealach Harta, is situated on the western side of Harta Corrie about 200m east-north-east of the northern top of Bidein Druim nan Ramh. It links with Coir' a' Tairneilear and is the only easy pass between Harta Corrie and Glen Brittle. At 760m it is the second lowest point on the main ridge, Bealach na Glaic Moire on the opposite side of Bidein Druim nan Ramh being marginally lower. To reach it, walk up Harta Corrie for almost three kilometres and make for a wide stony break which splits the corrie's very slabby western wall. Ascend this, eventually trending right on scree below the summit buttresses of Bidein Druim nan Ramh. Climb a scree chute to gain the ridge.

The other three passes are approached from Lota Corrie. To reach them a way must first be found up the great sweep of rock forming the lip of Lota Corrie. Generally the easiest way goes to the right (east) of a small stream that tumbles down the right-hand side of the rock band.

Once established in Lota Corrie, to reach Bealach nan Lice (which connects with Fionn Choire) and Bealach a' Bhasteir (which connects with Coire a' Bhasteir) follow the main stream to the left of a rocky knoll. Ascend to the back of the corrie, and, just before the angle begins to steepen noticeably, reach the junction of two streams. For Bealach nan Lice, follow the left branch north-westwards to its source, and continue in the same line on scree past the base of the Basteir Tooth. A large knobble of rock stands at the top of the pass. For Bealach a' Bhasteir, take a more northerly course between the two streams up the back wall of the corrie to the lowest point on the skyline. This side of the pass is not well used, and has less scree. It is fairly steep, but is a walk nevertheless.

The fourth pass, called Bealach a' Ghlas-choire, is a low point on a southward extension of the main ridge from Sgurr nan Gillean to Sgurr na h-Uamha. It links with An Glas-choire and Glen Sligachan. Ascend the lip of Lota Corrie as for the previous bealachs, and then immediately after passing a waterfall in the stream turn right and ascend the steep eastern wall of the corrie, mainly on scree. This can be used as a descent route by those returning to Coruisk after traversing the ridge.

Meall Dearg (*red hill*) (364m)
This rounded little hill is situated above the entrance to Harta Corrie and looks down the full length of Glen Sligachan. Its main claim to fame is that it lies, geologically speaking, at the very heart of the whole Cuillin complex; otherwise it is a most undistinguished eminence. It is not a true member of the Cuillin, being part of a later granite intrusion which also formed Ruadh Stac on the other side of Srath na Creitheach. It can be climbed most interestingly and conveniently by its north-east spur from a point just south of Lochan Dubha.

Druim nan Ramh (*ridge of the oars*)
The crest of this long straight ridge can be gained without great difficulty in a number of places from Harta Corrie. The traverse of the ridge to Bidein Druim nan Ramh is described in the Coir'-uisg section.

Bidein Druim nan Ramh (*peak of the ridge of the oars*) (869m)
This complex triple-topped mountain stands at the junction between Druim nan Ramh and the main ridge. The main central summit and its north top overlook Harta Corrie. Short sections of Moderate rock climbing are involved in ascending either of these summits and this puts them out of bounds to walkers. The easiest approach from Harta Corrie is to ascend to Bealach Harta (see Coir' a' Tairneilear), although it is also possible to ascend a gully to a gap, high up on Druim nan Ramh, situated between the central peak and a feature known as the Druim Pinnacle (see Coir'-uisg).

An Caisteal (*the castle*) (830m)
Sgurr na Bhairnich (*peak of the limpet*) (861m)
These two minor tops, between Bidein Druim nan Ramh and Bruach na Frithe, are separated by a deep gash. From Harta Corrie they are best traversed by starting from Bealach Harta. (See Coir' a' Tairneilear).

A more difficult route can be taken from the uppermost part of Harta Corrie to the col between the peaks. Climb the slope on the right-hand (north) side of the steep gully that falls from the col. Eventually traverse a rock wall into the upper part of the gully where it starts to lie back. Then follow the gully easily to the col.

ROCK CLIMBING
The Harta face of An Caisteal is a great slabby mass of rock, cleft by two long gullies into three buttresses. A number of long, pleasant climbs, mainly of Difficult standard, have been done there. The first route was put up by Harold Raeburn in 1905. It follows a line on Central Buttress near to the south (or left-hand) gully. The final third of the buttress is split by several chimneys. All the buttresses have been climbed, but the nature of the rock allows much scope for variation.

Bruach na Frithe (*slope of the deer forest*) (958m)
It would be unusual to attempt this peak from Lota Corrie, because of the long

approach. However, once Bealach nan Lice is reached, it is a simple matter to skirt around the north side of Sgurr a' Fionn Choire, and so gain the start of the easy east ridge. This point can also be reached by slanting left some distance from the top of Bealach nan Lice, below the south face of Sgurr a' Fionn Choire, (see Fionn Choire).

An alternative approach from Harta Corrie is to ascend to Bealach Harta, and then traverse An Caisteal and Sgurr na Bhairnich to the start of the south ridge, (see Coir' a' Tairneilear).

Sgurr a' Fionn Choire (*peak of the fair corrie*) (935m)
This small rocky top lies immediately south of Bealach nan Lice and 340 metres due east of Bruach na Frithe, (see Fionn Choire).

ROCK CLIMBING
Two Moderate climbs have been reported on the steeper sides of this peak; one is on the north-east face opposite Am Basteir, the other on the face overlooking Lota Corrie.

Basteir Tooth (916m)
This strange rock protrusion at the western end of Am Basteir can be approached from Lota Corrie by ascending to Bealach nan Lice, but it is much more easily approached from the north, (see Coire a' Bhasteir). It can only be ascended by rock climbing.

ROCK CLIMBING
There are two important routes on the Lota Corrie face of the Tooth. The more popular climb, *Naismith's Route*, is often included as part of the main ridge traverse. It is only Very Difficult, but many parties are so intimidated by its appearance from Sgurr a' Fionn Choire that they decide to give it a miss. The route is reached from Bealach nan Lice by scrambling along the crest of a rocky ridge to a dip below the western end of the Tooth. Descend a few metres and step across onto the south-west face. Traverse right until it is possible to climb up to a prominent ledge, then continue to the right. (A huge boulder which once stood on this ledge, and which was used as a belay, has now disappeared.) Climb a steep section of face (crux) to gain a chimney. Ascend this until a crack can be followed rightwards to the sloping roof of the Tooth. Go left up easy rock to the summit.

The second route is longer but slightly easier (Difficult). It was climbed by Collie and Mackenzie on the first ascent of the Basteir Tooth in 1889. It follows a leftwards rising traverse line on the flank of Am Basteir rather than on the Tooth proper. Descend some distance from Bealach nan Lice on the Lota Corrie side to near the toe of the buttress. Follow slabs and short chimneys trending left to finish by a steep pitch at the Nick between the Tooth and Am Basteir.

Once on the summit of the Tooth, it is normal practice to scramble down an easy slab to the Nick, and then find a way up onto Am Basteir (see p. 178).

The Basteir Tooth; the climbers are on Naismith's Route

Am Basteir (possibly derived from *basdar*, an obscure Gaelic word meaning *cleft*)
(934m)
This peak is immediately recognisable by the Basteir Tooth which projects from its
western end. The easiest way to the summit is by the east ridge from Bealach a'
Bhasteir, but this pass is very rarely approached from Lota Corrie, (see Coire a'
Bhasteir).

ROCK CLIMBING
The main south face of Am Basteir overlooking Lota Corrie is steep but has no
recorded climbs. However, there is some climbing involved in reaching the main
summit from the Basteir Tooth. The difficulties are short, but very steep. The easiest
way is of Difficult standard, although there is scope for variation. Start by moving
rightwards from the Nick between the Basteir Tooth and Am Basteir. After
ascending a loose gully, most parties climb the left side of a steep chimney, at one
point on overhanging rock. Then a short scramble leads to the airy summit.

Sgurr nan Gillean (*peak of the young men or gullies*) (964m)
This magnificent mountain is normally approached from the north, but it is possible
to approach from Lota Corrie by ascending to Bealach a' Bhasteir which lies at the
foot of the west ridge. Alternatively, the start of the graceful south-east ridge can be
gained by ascending to Bealach a' Ghlas-choire, and then slanting across the scree-
covered western flank of Sgurr Beag. The west ridge is described under Coire a'
Bhasteir, and the south-east ridge is described under Coire Riabhach and Coire nan
Allt Geala.

Sgurr Beag (*little peak*) (764m)
This little top sits on a short, crescent-shaped spur running eastwards off the ridge
between Sgurr nan Gillean and Sgurr na h-Uamha. It can be ascended by its broad
south ridge from Bealach a' Ghlas-choire, or by continuing south from the south-
east ridge of Sgurr nan Gillean. The west flank overlooking Lota Corrie is undistinguished. The peak's finest feature is its south-east ridge, though this is rarely ascended.

Sgurr na h-Uamha (*peak of the cave* or *hollow*) (736m)
This beautifully shaped peak lies some one and a half kilometres south of Sgurr nan
Gillean, and towers above the north side of Harta Corrie. It constitutes the true termination of the main ridge, and although it is significantly lower than Sgurr nan
Gillean, its ascent provides a worthy finale to the main ridge traverse. It is
surrounded on three sides by great sweeps of rock, while on the fourth side the north
ridge gives a difficult scramble. Though the summit itself is rather sprawling, it
provides fine views. Altogether, Sgurr na h-Uamha is a peak to delight the
connoisseur.

The normal route to the summit is a little too difficult for walkers. It follows
the north ridge from Bealach a' Ghlas-choire (*pass of the grey corrie*). This bealach
(640m) is normally reached from the north by the ridge from Sgurr Beag, but it can
also be approached from the west up the steep sidewall of Lota Corrie, or from the

east by the Allt a' Ghlas-choire. On the latter approach, though, it may be necessary to go some distance up Harta Corrie to ford the River Sligachan.

A small top halfway along the north ridge gives some pleasant scrambling. The crux of the ascent, however, is the steep rise immediately after this top. The easiest line is not obvious and is at least Moderate. In ascent it is usual to spiral upwards on the west side of the ridge, although a more direct line can be taken in descent when the way is easier to see.

On the first ascent of the peak in 1887, Charles Pilkington's party found a way up from An Glas-choire by a steep break in the rocks on the north-east flank. They described their route as a "capital scramble".

ROCK CLIMBING
There is some good climbing on the various faces overlooking Harta Corrie. The south-west face is the most impressive. It lies above a tiny side branch of Harta Corrie called Coire nan Clach. A number of routes (up to Severe in standard and 300m in length) have been climbed there. The face is tiered, and the lines are open to variation. The left-hand side of the face is bounded by West Gully (Moderate). On the steepest tier there are a number of overhangs which can be turned by ledges and steep grooves.

One of the earliest climbs on the peak was made on the great slabs of the south face. Another route has been done on a hanging tongue-shaped ridge on the east face (*Aslan's Tongue*, 300m, Severe). The rock is generally good, and most of the routes finish with at least 30 metres of scrambling.

2. COIRE RIABHACH (*grey corrie*)
COIRE NAN ALLT GEALA (*corrie of the white stream*)

BORDERING PEAK

Sgurr nan Gillean	964m	472 253

These two corries are situated, one above the other, on the north-east side of Sgurr nan Gillean above Glen Sligachan. Coire Riabhach is a fairly open corrie lying at the foot of the Pinnacle Ridge (or north ridge) of Sgurr nan Gillean, and facing out towards the Western Red Hills. On its eastern side it harbours a sizeable lochan (Loch a' Choire Riabhaich) which drains into Glen Sligachan. Coire nan Allt Geala forms an upper, southern tier to Coire Riabhach. It lies on the east side of the Pinnacle Ridge of Sgurr nan Gillean, and is a very stony place. The uppermost part of the corrie is bounded by the south-east ridge of Sgurr nan Gillean and by an indefinite ridge running off it to the east.

The main importance of these two corries is that they provide the most popular approach to the south-east ridge of Sgurr nan Gillean. This is the line followed by the so-called 'tourist route' to the summit of the mountain.

Sgurr nan Gillean (*peak of the young men* or *gullies*) (964m)
This magnificent pyramidal peak is among the finest in the Cuillin. There are several

higher peaks in the range, but few that are quite so impressive overall. The mountain's relatively isolated position, at the northern end of the main ridge, helps to accentuate its grandeur. It was first climbed in 1836 by Duncan MacIntyre, a local forester, and Professor James Forbes, an outstanding scientist of the day. The former had made several previous attempts by other routes before the successful ascent. Theirs was the first recorded ascent of a major Cuillin peak.

The mountain has three prominent ridges, all of which offer interesting routes. The south-east ridge, which was climbed by the first ascent party, is the easiest way to the summit. Although it is commonly referred to as the 'tourist route', it is nevertheless a stiff scramble. The west ridge is somewhat harder even though its notorious Gendarme has now departed. The narrow section of ridge on which this pinnacle was once perched remains a formidable obstacle to the timorous. The Pinnacle Ridge, which falls in the direction of Sligachan, is a Difficult rock climb. The latter two ridges are described under Coir' a' Bhasteir.

Despite its popularity, the 'tourist route' should not be underestimated. The long approach to the south-east ridge becomes particularly difficult to follow in poor visibility, and the ridge itself is quite tricky and exposed in places. The route begins a short distance west of the Sligachan Hotel. A path leads in a few hundred metres to the Allt Dearg Mor (*big red stream*). This is crossed by a footbridge near the remains of an old hydro scheme. The next one and a half kilometres are very boggy in all but the driest weather. The path eventually ascends beside the Allt Dearg Beag (*little red stream*). Shorty afterwards cross this stream at a footbridge, and head south on rather better ground to a shoulder overlooking Coire Riabhach. Ignore the faint path that climbs to the right, and instead descend slightly into the corrie.

Stay several hundred metres to the west of Loch a' Choire Riabhaich and continue in a southerly direction. Ascend an obvious scree scar at the head of Coire Riabhach and zigzag up a steeper section to emerge on a shoulder forming the lower edge of Coire nan Allt Geala.

Head due south up this boulder-strewn corrie, with the base of the Pinnacle Ridge on the right. Eventually start curving up rightwards to a steeper band of rocky ground. Find a way through this by a terrace slanting leftwards, and so gain the scree slope flanking the south-east ridge.

Join the ridge at about 790m just before it starts to steepen. The broad crest can be followed without undue difficulty initially, and the easiest line is usually on the Lota Corrie side. Higher up the ridge narrows, and a more direct line must be taken, with hands being required on several steeper sections. An exposed scramble leads to the superb rocky summit - one of the finest viewpoints in the Cuillin.

ROCK CLIMBING

Little more than two kilometres due south of Sligachan, there is a low ridge called Nead na h-Iolaire (*nest of the eagle*). Some surprisingly good climbing can be had on a rather heathery crag on the north-west side of this ridge. The crag is approached by following the first part of the 'tourist route' until across the Allt Dearg Beag. The climbs are fairly short and are suitable for an evening or an off-day.

The extensive eastern face of Sgurr nan Gillean's Pinnacle Ridge is not quite as steep as its western face, and there are no notable routes there. However, some climbing has been done on the front of the first pinnacle or tower overlooking Coire Riabhach. The tower is divided into two sections by a scree shelf. Various lines were climbed on both tiers at an early date. These include the prominent gash of *Black Chimney* on the lower tier, and *Sligachan Gully* on the upper tier. The latter contains a fine cave carpeted with moss, juniper and blaeberries.

Just south of the point where the 'tourist route' joins the south-east ridge a rather indefinite spur descends in an easterly direction to Glen Sligachan. Some enjoyable climbing can be had on the north side of this spur overlooking Coire nan Allt Geala, to the east of the 'tourist route'.

At the base of this same spur, just above the floor of Glen Sligachan, there is a buttress on which a number of climbs of up to 170m (Very Difficult to E1) have been made. The buttress is in two sections separated by two prominent chimneys, and lies on the opposite side of Glen Sligachan from the buttresses on Marsco.

3. COIRE A' BHASTEIR (possibly *corrie of the cleft*)

SURROUNDING PEAKS

Sgurr nan Gillean	964m	472 253
Am Basteir	934m	465 253
Basteir Tooth	916m	465 253
Sgurr a' Bhasteir	899m	464 257

Coire a' Bhasteir is an impressive north-facing corrie which is well seen from Sligachan. It is bounded on either side by prominent pointed peaks - the magnificent Sgurr nan Gillean on the left and the slightly lower Sgurr a' Bhasteir on the right - whilst at its head stands Am Basteir and its distinctive Tooth. In the centre of the corrie lies tiny Loch a' Bhasteir, which feeds the headwater of the Allt Dearg Beag. This stream plunges out of the corrie through the dramatic Basteir Gorge.

The corrie is approached from Sligachan by following the first part of the path to Coire Riabhach (p 180). Two alternative routes can be taken from the bridge over the Allt Dearg Beag. One route stays on the west bank of the stream, and climbs high above the west side of the Basteir Gorge to enter the corrie. The other route crosses the Allt Dearg Beag and follows the Coire Riabhach path for a further 800 metres. Then, instead of dropping down into that corrie, it ascends a broad shoulder initially in a south-westerly direction. Higher up there are occasional short sections of scrambling, and good views of the Basteir Gorge down on the right. The shoulder continues to the base of the first pinnacle of Sgurr nan Gillean's Pinnacle Ridge. However, once past the gorge, the floor of the corrie can be gained by moving onto the right side of the shoulder and then traversing rightwards across awkward scree and rocky ground.

Both approach routes converge some distance up the corrie by Loch a' Bhasteir, an attractive little lochan occupying an ice-scraped hollow in a rocky section of the corrie floor. A crag split by two gullies lies to the south-east of the lochan, but otherwise the backwall of the corrie comprises extensive scree slopes.

The Basteir Gorge itself has been ascended, but it is a difficult excursion and may involve swimming. It is certainly not a recognised approach route to the corrie.

There are two important access points to the main ridge from Coire a' Bhasteir. The first lies at the head of the corrie, between Sgurr nan Gillean and Am Basteir, and is known as Bealach a' Bhasteir. The second lies near the south-west corner of the corrie, and is known as Bealach nan Lice. The latter is situated just beyond the western end of the Basteir Tooth, and strictly speaking overlooks neighbouring Fionn Choire. Both bealachs offer an easy link with Lota Corrie, although they are rarely used as passes.

To reach either bealach, ascend steep boulders and scree behind Loch a' Bhasteir. Then continue on slightly easier scree towards the impending north wall of Am Basteir. The two routes now divide. Bear left and climb steeply up loose scree to reach Bealach a' Bhasteir. For Bealach nan Lice, bear right and follow a path in the scree below the north wall of Am Basteir to the western end of the Basteir Tooth. Continue following the base of a lower rock ridge which leads rightwards, and so reach the knobble of rock that characterises the head of Bealach nan Lice.

Sgurr nan Gillean (*peak of the young men* or *gullies*) (964m)
This superb mountain is one of the most striking peaks in the Cuillin. The most popular line of ascent from Sligachan is the south-east ridge (see Coire Riabhach and Coire nan Allt Geala). However, the mountain presents its best face to Coire a' Bhasteir. The north ridge, which forms a spectacular eastern border to Coire a' Bhasteir, is known as the Pinnacle Ridge because of its four obvious towers. The ridge is not seen to best advantage from Sligachan, being viewed end on from that direction. It has short sections of Difficult climbing and is a superb mountaineering outing, (see Rock Climbing). In the right conditions it makes an outstanding grade III winter climb.

The west ridge, which is ascended from Bealach a' Bhasteir, is a fairly straightforward scramble apart from a very narrow section that until recently was guarded by the famous *Gendarme*. A short distance from the bealach a vertical step on the ridge is turned by a chimney on the Coire a' Bhasteir side. There is a slightly harder and longer chimney just to the left. At the top of the first chimney the ridge narrows alarmingly. A fresh rock scar on the crest marks the position once occupied by the Gendarme. Most of this pinnacle keeled over in 1987. The remaining rock is now reasonably sound, although it is still an exposed little traverse.

An easier way up the west ridge, which avoids the narrow section, is to ascend *Nicholson's Chimney*. This starts some distance left (north) of the two chimneys already mentioned. It should more properly be described as a rake, and follows a rightwards slanting line.

Before and after: The Gendarme on the West Ridge of Sgurr nan Gillean which collapsed in 1987

ROCK CLIMBING

The Pinnacle Ridge is not as difficult, nor as sustained, as it appears from the floor of Coire a' Bhasteir. It is best approached from the more easterly of the two routes into the corrie. From a point overlooking the head of the Basteir Gorge walk south-east to the foot of the first pinnacle and scramble up its north-west face. Continue easily along the crest to the third pinnacle.

The descent from the third pinnacle is the crux, and is achieved by climbing down a Difficult crack on the left (east) side (or by abseil), before moving right into a shallow gully on the west side. Knight's Peak (or the fourth pinnacle) is fairly steep to ascend, and also requires care in descent. It is possible to turn it on the Basteir side. There is a small tower after the last gap, and the final section up to the summit of Sgurr nan Gillean continues to give interesting climbing. The whole ridge is slightly easier in descent, and competent parties sometimes include it as a final topping to the main ridge traverse.

There are numerous routes on the Coire a' Bhasteir side of Pinnacle Ridge, although they seem rather unfashionable these days. They are up to 150m in length and range from Moderate to Severe in grade. All the gullies between the pinnacles have been ascended, that between Knight's Peak and the main summit being on easy scree.

Am Basteir (possibly derived from *basdar*, an obscure Gaelic word meaning *cleft*) (934m)
This fine peak dominates the head of Corrie a' Bhasteir. It has one of the most readily identifiable profiles on the Cuillin skyline, because of The Tooth which projects from its western end. The only route up the mountain that does not involve climbing follows the long east ridge from Bealach a' Bhasteir. It is a good airy scramble, with steep drops on both sides. There is an awkward 3m descent on the crest some distance before the main summit. In descent the natural tendency is to use the Lota Corrie side of the ridge, and then traverse back to the crest further down.

When approaching along the main ridge from the west, if the climbs on the Basteir Tooth (such as Naismith's Route) are too daunting, the east ridge of Am Basteir can be reached without difficulty by dropping about 120m from Bealach nan Lice into

Looking up the east ridge of Am Basteir

Coire a' Bhasteir, skirting below the steep north face along a path in the scree and then ascending to Bealach a' Bhasteir.

The descent from the summit of Am Basteir to the Nick before the Basteir Tooth is Difficult and may necessitate an abseil, (see Harta Corrie and Lota Corrie).

ROCK CLIMBING
There are some climbs on the steep north face of Am Basteir, but the rock is not as good as on the Tooth. The best line (North Face, Difficult) starts up Am Basteir Chimney on the left, and then follows a rising traverse rightwards across the face to finish by a steep pitch near the summit.

Basteir Tooth (916m)
This intimidating fang of rock guards the western end of Am Basteir. It is the most difficult of all Munro tops and can only be ascended by rock climbing. It is commonly bypassed by a path on the north side, (see Am Basteir).

ROCK CLIMBING

The most popular line of ascent is Naismith's Route on the south-west face, (see Harta Corrie and Lota Corrie). The two most obvious lines on the north face overlooking Coire a' Bhasteir are *King's Cave Chimney* (Very Difficult), which finishes at the Nick between the Tooth and Am Basteir, and *Shadbolt's Chimney* (Very Difficult), which lies further right. They both involve subterranean excursions, and lack the elegance of Naismith's Route.

Sgurr a' Bhasteir (possibly *peak of the cleft*) (899m)
This summit, which lies almost 500 metres north of the Basteir Tooth, is the high point on a north to south ridge forming the west side of Coire a' Bhasteir. It suffers by comparison with the other peaks bordering the corrie, but it is certainly the finest viewpoint for the Pinnacle Ridge of Sgurr nan Gillean.

    The most agreeable line of ascent is by the north-east ridge, which rises from the Basteir Gorge. This is approached from the more westerly of the two routes into the corrie. Trend right after gaining some height above the gorge. Some occasional scrambling enlivens the ascent. The final section to the summit is on scree.

    Another approach from the north goes over the small top of Meall Odhar to the north-west ridge. The easiest route, however, is by the south ridge. This is reached without difficulty from the south-west corner of Coire a' Bhasteir, by gaining a dip (868m) in the ridge to the north of Bealach nan Lice.

4. FIONN CHOIRE (*fair corrie*)

SURROUNDING PEAKS

Sgurr a' Bhasteir	899m	464 257
Sgurr a' Fionn Choire	935m	464 252
Bruach na Frithe	958m	461 252

Fionn Choire is a markedly gentler corrie than Coire a' Bhasteir, which lies on the opposite side of the Sgurr a' Bhasteir ridge. Its carpet of grass and flowers makes it the greenest corrie in the Cuillin and also the easiest for walking. It boasts the highest source of easily accessible drinking water in the whole range, a fact worth remembering on sweltering summer days. The water issues from a small mossy spring in the floor of the corrie at a height of about 820m (70m below Bealach nan Lice).

    Sgurr a' Fionn Choire, a small but shapely peak, is set back somewhat at the head of the corrie. Just to its north is Bealach nan Lice, an easy pass that links with Lota Corrie. The principal peak of the corrie, Bruach na Frithe, lies to the west of Sgurr a' Fionn Choire at an important change in direction of the main ridge.

    The usual approach to the corrie is from Sligachan by the path on the north bank of the Allt Dearg Mor to Bealach a' Mhaim, although it is marginally shorter to start from the opposite end of the same path in Glen Brittle. Take a left fork in the path about one kilometre north-east of Bealach a' Mhaim, cross a small stream and

The central Cuillin from Am Basteir; Sgurr a' Fionn Choire on the extreme right

head south over fairly featureless terrain for about 600 metres, keeping the Allt an Fhionn-choire some 100 metres to the left (east).

There is now a choice of routes. Straight on, a well marked route ascends for two kilometres all of the way up the corrie to finish on scree at Bealach nan Lice. To the right, another cairned route ascends a shoulder to reach the north-west ridge of Bruach na Frithe.

Sgurr a' Bhasteir (possibly *peak of the cleft*) (899m)
This peak can easily be ascended from Fionn Choire, either from the dip in the ridge north of Bealach nan Lice, or from the dip in the ridge south of Meall Odhar, (see Coire a' Bhasteir).

Sgurr a' Fionn Choire (*peak of the fair corrie*) (935m)
This small rocky top lies 340 metres due east of Bruach na Frithe, and immediately south of Bealach nan Lice. Although it is often bypassed by a path on its north-west side, it is worth ascending for the excellent view it provides of Am Basteir and its Tooth, which are situated a short distance to the north-east on the opposite side of the bealach. Gullies on the north-west side provide the easiest line of ascent. The best route, however, is the west ridge, which gives a pleasant scramble.

Bruach na Frithe (*slope of the deer forest*) (958m)
This shapely mountain has three ridges, two of which, the south and east, form a

right-angled turn in the main ridge. Its first recorded ascent took place in 1845, when Professor Forbes carried a barometer to the top, accompanied by Duncan MacIntyre. It may have been ascended prior to that date, since it is one of the easiest of the major Cuillin summits for hillwalkers to reach. The same pair had made the rather more difficult ascent of Sgurr nan Gillean some nine years earlier. The summit is a celebrated viewpoint. Being free of crags it has become a popular excursion from Sligachan. It is the only Cuillin peak to sport a triangulation pillar. The easiest line of ascent follows the marked route up Fionn Choire. Just short of Bealach nan Lice head south-west below Sgurr a' Fionn Choire, and gain the very easy east ridge of Bruach na Frithe, which soon leads to the summit. This is also the best descent route from the mountain. It is possible to jog down to Sligachan in an hour.

A more entertaining ascent route from the north is by the north-west ridge. This can be approached, either by heading in a southerly direction from the lower part of Fionn Choire, or by ascending the Sron Tobar nan Uaislean (*shoulder of the well of the gentry*) from Bealach a' Mhaim. The latter approach is more convenient from Glen Brittle. Both routes join where the ridge narrows at about 700m. Some scrambling can be enjoyed if the crest is ascended throughout. An easier option is to follow a path some 30m below the ridge on its right-hand (south-west) side, and then regain the crest some distance below the summit. The last part of the ascent is an easy walk.

The south ridge is described under Coir' a' Tairneilear.

ROCK CLIMBING
Although the summit is devoid of cliffs there are some craggy sections on the western and northern flanks. The largest chimney on the north face was climbed by W.W. King and party in 1908 and graded Difficult.

CHAPTER 10

NORTH GLEN BRITTLE

These corries lie on the west side of the main ridge and are best approached from the upper (north) part of Glen Brittle.

5. **Coir' a' Tairneilear**
6. **Coir' a' Mhadaidh**
7. **Coire a' Ghreadaidh**
8. **Coire na Banachdich**

5. COIR' A' TAIRNEILEAR (*corrie of the thunderer*)

SURROUNDING PEAKS

Bruach na Frithe	958m	461 252
Sgurr na Bhairnich	861m	461 246
An Caisteal	830m	461 244
Bidein Druim nan Ramh	869m	456 239
Sgurr an Fheadain	688m	452 245

The obvious north-west facing corrie seen when descending the road into Glen Brittle is called Coire na Creiche (*corrie of the spoil*). The upper part of the corrie is divided by the peak of Sgurr an Fheadain into two smaller corries - Coir' a' Tairneilear on the left (north-east) and Coir' a' Mhadaidh on the right (south-west).

Coir' a' Tairneilear is not the most prepossessing of Cuillin corries. Its left-hand side is formed by the broad western flank of Bruach na Frithe. At the top left-hand corner of the corrie a prominent notch on the skyline marks the col between Sgurr na Bhairnich and An Caisteal. The right-hand side of the corrie is formed by the spur that runs off the main ridge from Bidein Druim nan Ramh to Sgurr an Fheadain.

The corrie is most readily accessible from the Glen Brittle road, although it can also be reached from Sligachan via Bealach a' Mhaim. Start from the upper reaches of Glen Brittle just below the point where the road emerges from between two forestry plantations. (There is limited parking space near a forest entrance.) Take the path to Sligachan for 250 metres, and once across the Allt an Fhamhair, slant down to the river in the floor of the glen. Follow a path on the north bank of the river past some lovely pools and waterfalls. Keep heading more or less directly

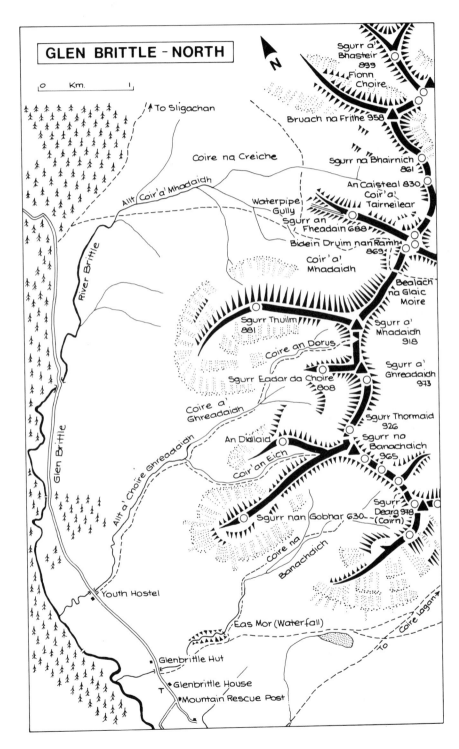

GLEN BRITTLE - NORTH

N

0   Km.   1

To Sligachan

Coire na Creiche

Allt Coir' a' Mhadaidh

River Brittle

Glen Brittle

Allt a' Choire Ghreadaidh

Sgurr a'
Bhasteir
899

Fionn
Choire

Bruach na Frithe 958

Sgurr na Bhairnich
861

An Caisteal 830

Coir' a'
Tairneilear

Waterpipe
Gully

Sgurr an
Fheadain 688

Bidein Druim nan Ramh
869

Coir' a'
Mhadaidh

Bealach
na Glaic
Moire

Sgurr Thuilm
881

Coire an Dorus

Sgurr a'
Mhadaidh
918

Sgurr a'
Ghreadaidh
973

Sgurr Eadar da Choire
808

Coire a'
Ghreadaidh

Sgurr Thormaid
926

Sgurr na
Banachdich
965

An Diallaid

Coir' an Eich

Sgurr
Dearg 978
(Cairn)

Sgurr nan Gobhar 630

Coire na
Banachdich

Coire Lagan

To

Youth Hostel

Eas Mor (Waterfall)

Glenbrittle Hut

Glenbrittle House

T

Mountain Rescue Post

Coire na Creiche

for the corrie, which is situated to the left of Sgurr an Fheadain and its conspicuous Waterpipe Gully. Shortly before reaching the mouth of the corrie cross to the other bank of the Allt Coir' a' Tairneilear. A path which originates from Bealach a' Mhaim also crosses the stream at this point, but then continues round into Coir' a' Mhadaidh.

The only easy pass over the main ridge from Coir' a' Tairneilear connects with Harta Corrie, and consequently has become known as Bealach Harta. It is situated at the very back of the corrie just to the north-east of Bidein Druim nan Ramh. Once above the head of two small streams in the upper part of the corrie, ascend a steep scree slope and then slant right over loose ground to reach the main ridge a short distance north-east of the lowest point of the pass. The easiest line down into Harta Corrie starts on the south-west side of the lowest point. The main ridge may also be gained by ascending a straightforward scree slope to the gap between Sgurr na Bhairnich and An Caisteal, though this is more pleasant in descent.

Coir' a' Tairneilear is often ascended as a roundabout way of approaching Bealach na Glaic Moire, which is situated in neighbouring Coir' a' Mhadaidh, and gives access to Coruisk. There are a number of options on this approach. One is to ascend to Bealach Harta and then skirt down and round to the right on scree below the triple summits of Bidein Druim nan Ramh, until the main ridge can be regained a short distance before the bealach. Another is to take a rather more direct line to the point where the ridge leading from Sgurr an Fheadain abuts against the main ridge. Then traverse round to the right below the western peak of Bidein Druim nan Ramh as for the previous route. Yet another option is to ascend a scree slope from the floor of the corrie directly to a dip on the ridge behind the summit of Sgurr an Fheadain. This ridge can be followed without difficulty, and then the western summit of Bidein turned as before to reach the main ridge.

Bruach na Frithe (*slope of the deer forest*) (958m)
This fine mountain is popularly ascended from the north, (see Fionn Choire). It has an extensive western flank which forms the left-hand side of Coir' a' Tairneilear, but this is loose and unattractive. The south ridge, however, is an exhilarating walk with short sections of scrambling, mainly near the summit. It forms one of the more straighforward sections of the main ridge, and is approached by first traversing Sgurr na Bhairnich.

Sgurr na Bhairnich (*limpet peak*) (861m)
This minor top lies at the start of the south ridge of Bruach na Frithe, and is separated from An Caisteal by a deep gap (764m). It can approached from Coir' a' Tairneilear, either by ascending an obvious scree gully directly to this gap, or more pleasantly by first traversing An Caisteal from Bealach Harta.

From the Caisteal-Bhairnich gap, scramble up scree-covered ledges to a pinnacle, and then turn some small overhangs on the right. Beyond the summit descend to a small col, and from there slant across the Tairneilear face to gain the crest of the south ridge of Bruach na Frithe.

An Caisteal (*the castle*) (830m)
The traverse of this summit is a tricky scramble. It is usually ascended by its south-west ridge from Bealach Harta. A short wall leads to an easy, level stretch of ridge, which is followed by a narrower section requiring care. At one point there is a gap on the crest which must be bridged by a bold stride. Easy scrambling then leads to the summit, some 500 metres from Bealach Harta.

Just beyond the summit, the ridge ends in a huge drop into Harta Corrie, so it is important to return slightly from the summit and to look for a way down on the west side of the ridge. Descend slabs covered in fine scree, and arrive at a steep wall overlooking the Caisteal-Bhairnich gap. Descend on the Tairneilear side at first, and traverse back right until it is possible to make a hard move into the gap.

The scree gully on the left (west) provides an uncomplicated descent to Coir' a' Tairneilear. That on the right is suitable only for climbers (see Harta and Lota Corries).

ROCK CLIMBING
An indefinite line has been climbed on the west face of An Caisteal, but there are more worthwhile climbs on the east face (see Harta and Lota Corries), which can be approached from Coir' a' Tairneilear by crossing Bealach Harta.

Bidein Druim nan Ramh (*peak of the ridge of the oars*) (869m)
All three peaks of this complex mountain overlook Coir' a' Tairneilear, and although

among the lowest of the summits on the main ridge, they are a very tricky group to traverse. Walkers will prefer to circumvent all three by following the base of the summit rocks on the northern side of the mountain. As can be imagined from their names, the west, central and north tops are set in a right angle on the ridge.

The easiest top is the western one (847m), which can be attained without undue difficulty by following the crest of the ridge from Bealach na Glaic Moire. An alternative route is to ascend the bouldery gully that runs up between the central and western tops on the north side of the mountain. This gully can be approached either directly from Coir' a' Tairneilear or by traversing from Bealach Harta. It is topped by a large jammed boulder known as the Bridge Rock. A short steep section out of the gap soon leads to the massive block forming the western summit.

The central peak (869m) is the highest of the three and the most difficult to reach. When traversing from south to north the route up from the Bridge Rock involves short sections of Moderate climbing. The rightward trending line is fairly obvious and includes the ascent of a small chimney. Pull up on a cracked block to reach the airy summit platform of this delightful peak.

In order to continue the traverse towards the north top, retrace your steps for a short distance, then head right and weave a way down a series of delicate slabs on the right-hand side of a rib. This section is Moderate and quite sustained. Eventually reach a steep drop down to the gap before the north top. Some parties abseil here, but by moving across to the right (east) it is possible to find a way down which does not necessitate a rope. Traverse a wall back to the left (west), and make one final awkward move down a short overhanging section to gain the gap.

Climb up and left out of the gap, and surmount a nose to gain the ridge. The north top (852m) is a short distance away. Descend a short drop soon after the summit. Then follow pleasant slabs on the right-hand side of the crest, and so reach Bealach Harta.

Sgurr an Fheadain (*peak of the water-pipe*) (688m)

There is no mistaking this small peak from the road because of the prominent gash, *Waterpipe Gully*, which runs the full length of its north-west flank. It can be ascended by a scree slope from Coir' a' Tairneilear to the gap behind the summit, but a much better line - a scramble known as The Spur - follows the broad slabby buttress left of Waterpipe Gully. It is exposed in parts, but makes a fine approach to the main ridge.

ROCK CLIMBING

First climbed in 1895, Waterpipe Gully is still rated Severe by the easiest line. Like many major gullies it offers an entertaining mixture of climbing, walking and water sport in an expedition setting. At the base of the gully on the left there is a fine rock face on which there are a number of more conventional climbs of various grades.

6. COIR' A' MHADAIDH *(corrie of the fox)*

SURROUNDING PEAKS

Sgurr an Fheadain	688m	452 245
Bidein Druim nan Ramh	869m	456 239
Sgurr a' Mhadaidh	918m	447 235
Sgurr Thuilm	881m	439 242

This corrie is more dramatic than its partner on the opposite side of Sgurr an Fheadain. Its headwall being almost entirely rock, it provides few easy ways onto the main ridge. The south side of the corrie is dominated by the four peaks of Sgurr a' Mhadaidh, whose north-west face offers many climbs. The right-hand side of the corrie is bounded by a long spur that runs out from the main top of Sgurr a' Mhadaidh to Sgurr Thuilm. The latter peak is best climbed from Coire a' Ghreadaidh and is described in the section for that corrie.

The normal approach to the corrie starts from the roadside in Glen Brittle, as for Coir' a' Tairneilear (see P. 193). Follow that route for almost two kilometres, then cross the Allt Coir' a' Tairneilear at a stream junction, and follow the right-hand stream to Coir' a' Mhadaidh.

The only pass from this corrie connects with Coir'-uisg; it is the lowest pass on the main ridge and is called Bealach na Glaic Moire (*pass of the great hollow*). It is guarded by a large band of high slabs, which are split by three gullies. The route to the bealach follows an unpleasant scree slope to the left of the slabs and then slants back rightwards above. (It is marked faintly on the 1:25,000 map.) Route finding can be a problem in mist, and so an approach by Coir' a' Tairneilear is normally preferred.

Sgurr an Fheadain *(peak of the water-pipe)* (688m)
This top is described more fully under Coir' a' Tairneilear. It can be gained from Coir' a' Mhadaidh, either by ascending a scree slope to the gap behind the summit, or by following the scree to the left of the slabs (as for the Bealach na Glaic Moire), and then turning left to join the ridge which descends from Bidein Druim nan Ramh.

Bidein Druim nan Ramh *(peak of the ridge of the oars)* (869m)
This mountain is described under Coir' a' Tairneilear. Only its western top faces Coir' a' Mhadaidh.

ROCK CLIMBING
The three gullies cleaving the slabs at the head of the corrie are best allocated to this mountain. They all give climbs. The right-hand one (*South Gully*), which lies directly under the Bealach na Glaic Moire, is probably the best gully climb on Skye. It is the hardest of the three lines, and is graded Severe.

Sgurr a' Mhadaidh *(peak of the fox)* (918m)
This mountain has four well-defined tops, three of which run in line along the ridge to the south-west of Bealach na Glaic Moire. The fourth and westernmost top, which

On the ridge of Sgurr a' Mhadaidh, looking down to Loch Coruisk

is also the highest, is set back slightly from the others and overlooks neighbouring Coire a' Ghreadaidh. The traverse of all four peaks makes an interesting excursion which requires Moderate rock climbing ability. There are deep gaps between the peaks, and steep flanks on both sides of the ridge preclude any easy alternatives for the walker. The main difficulties are at the western ends of the tops, so the traverse is normally done from south-west to north-east. The easiest lines are generally on the Coruisk side. There are superb views down Loch Coruisk from this section of ridge.

The mountain shows a large and complex rock face to Coir' a' Mhadaidh. From a prominent amphitheatre to the left of centre, two rightward slanting rakes offer the easiest ways to the main summit. The lower one, known as *Foxes' Rake*, is an Easy/Moderate rock climb, but it crosses some rather loose ground. It finishes by a short chimney at a broad notch high up on the north-west ridge. The upper rake is of comparable standard, but of better quality. It is reached by a right-slanting gully from the back of the amphitheatre, and finishes between the third top and the main summit. Neither route is obvious in poor visibilty. The mountain's north-west ridge is a good, hard scramble, normally approached from Coire a' Ghreadaidh, (see below).

ROCK CLIMBING
Numerous high quality climbs of all grades have been made on the north-west face.

Some of them are slow to dry. The face below Foxes' Rake offers some of the best climbing. The routes there are up to 250m long, and include *Thor* (E2), *Quark* (E2), *Megaton* (E1) and *Archer Thomson's Route* (Severe). Further right is *Deep Gash Gully*. On a large crag to the right of the latter is an excellent Very Difficult climb - *Whispering Wall*.

7. COIRE A' GHREADAIDH (*corrie of torment*)

SURROUNDING PEAKS

Sgurr Thuilm	881m	439 242
Sgurr a' Mhadaidh	918m	447 235
Sgurr a' Ghreadaidh	973m	445 231
Sgurr Thormaid	926m	441 226
Sgurr na Banachdich	965m	440 224
Sgurr nan Gobhar	630m	427 224

Coire a' Ghreadaidh is a huge open corrie lying to the west of mighty Sgurr a' Ghreadaidh. It is bounded to the north by the ridge linking Sgurr Thuilm with Sgurr a' Mhadaidh and to the south by the western ridge of Sgurr na Banachdich. All of the water that drains from the corrie flows past the Youth Hostel in Glen Brittle.

The corrie has two subsidiary recesses in its upper reaches. The left-hand (northern) one, high up under the summit of Sgurr a' Mhadaidh, is known as Coire an Dorus. It is not marked on the 1:25,000 map, but is situated beneath an important gap on the ridge called An Dorus (*the door*). Coire an Dorus is separated from the main corrie by a small spur which leads out to Sgurr Eadar da Choire. The right-hand (south-western) recess is known as Coir' an Eich (*corrie of the horse*). It is a minor scree bowl between Sgurr nan Gobhar and An Diallaid - two small tops on the ridges leading west and north-west respectively from Sgurr na Banachdich.

Coire a' Ghreadaidh is approached from the bridge at the Youth Hostel by a path on the south bank of the Allt a' Choire Ghreadaidh. In its lower reaches this large stream flows in a lovely ravine containing pools and waterfalls.

The easiest way over the ridge from the corrie is by An Dorus - the obvious gap at the head of Coire an Dorus between Sgurr a' Mhadaidh and Sgurr a' Ghreadaidh. The west side is straightforward, but the Coruisk side is something of a scramble with more involved route finding. It finishes by joining the lower part of the Bealach na Glaic Moire route. This pass is reported to have been used by the MacLeods during their 'campaigns' in days of old. There is a much narrower gap on the ridge just to the south of An Dorus called Eag Dubh (*black gash*). This is also fairly easy on the west side, but the gully on the Coruisk side has a Difficult pitch in it.

Sgurr Thuilm (*peak of the rounded hillock*) (881m)
This shapely peak offers a fine viewpoint, although its flanks consist mainly of scree

and broken rock. It can be ascended without difficulty by its south-west flank from Coire a' Ghreadaidh. A crag, at about 400m, is turned on the left. Ascend further scree and join the west ridge which leads to the summit. The north-east face is broken and craggy. To continue the traverse, descend the easy, but exhilarating, south-east ridge to the col at the foot of the north-west ridge of Sgurr a' Mhadaidh. If the latter is too daunting (see below), an easy rake can be descended from the col in a south-easterly direction to the floor of Coire an Dorus.

ROCK CLIMBING
A worthwhile HVS route (*Gail*, 65m) climbs the obvious central corner of the main crag on the south-west flank of the mountain. It can be reached in about 45 minutes from the Youth Hostel.

Sgurr a' Mhadaidh (*peak of the fox*) (918m)
Only the main summit of this fine mountain overlooks Coire a' Ghreadaidh. (See Coir' a' Mhadaidh for a description of its other three tops.) The easiest line of ascent is by the short south ridge from An Dorus. A steep pitch above the gap soon leads to easier scrambling. Subsequent difficulties can be avoided on the left (west).

The north-west ridge is longer and considerably harder. It can be reached either by traversing Sgurr Thuilm, or by ascending fairly directly to the Thuilm-Mhadaidh col from Coire an Dorus. Two rock ribs rise impressively from this col. Weave a way up the slabby left-hand one, which is awkward and exposed in places. The large buttress forming the left (north) side of the ridge is rent by Deep Gash Gully.

The ridge then starts to level off and a dip on the crest marks the top of Foxes' Rake (see Coir' a' Mhadaidh). The remainder of the ascent is easy and soon leads to a minor top (900m) on the main ridge. Turn right there, and follow ledges on the right (west) of the narrow crest, reaching the main summit after some 120 metres.

Sgurr a' Ghreadaidh (*peak of torment*) (973m)
South top (970m)
This is the highest mountain on the northern half of the main ridge. It has twin summits some 120 metres apart, which are linked by an exceptionally narrow crest. The traverse of the mountain by its north and south-west ridges makes an excellent scramble. Both ridges are of comparable standard, but there is no easy approach to the col at the foot of the south-west ridge, so the easiest way to the summit is by the north ridge.

The start of the north ridge is reached by ascending to An Dorus. Scaling the short pitch out of An Dorus itself is as hard as anything on the route. A short easy section follows, then a narrow gash is reached cutting across the ridge. This is the Eag Dubh. Descend into it and ascend out by staying more to the left (Coruisk) side. Further up the ridge there sits a huge slabby excrescence known as the 'Wart'. This can be avoided by ledges on the right (west). A final easy rise leads to the main top and the knife-edge of the summit ridge. The whole of the next section leading to the south top is sensationally exposed but the rock is sound.

Descending the south-west ridge from the south top commits the scrambler to continuing as far as Sgurr na Banachdich and, since there is further scrambling on intervening Sgurr Thormain, the timorous would do better to return down the north ridge. The south-west ridge is narrow initially, but then becomes broader and less sound. There is an awkward slabby rib high up, but after that there are no special difficulties to the col before Sgurr Thormaid.

The spur which separates Coire an Dorus from the main'corrie is topped by a small double peak called Sgurr Eadar da Choire (peak between the two corries). The neck behind the spur can be reached by an easy rake from Coire an Dorus, or by a scree slope from the main corrie. More direct ascents of the spur involve at least Moderate rock climbing, as does the continuation up the north-west ridge of Sgurr a' Ghreadaidh.

ROCK CLIMBING
There are several climbs on the large north-west face between An Dorus and Sgurr Eadar da Choire. On the right-hand side of the face, *Hamish's Chimney* (Difficult) provides an interesting route direct to the summit cairn. Three gully lines and a buttress route, mainly of Very Difficult standard, have also been climbed on the rocky west face overlooking the main corrie. There is a harder route (*Gael Force*, HVS) on the south-west flank of Sgurr Eadar da Choire.

Sgurr Thormaid (*Norman's peak*) (926m)
This peak is named after Professor Norman Collie, one of the early Cuillin pioneers. It is in effect the northern top of Sgurr na Banachdich. The cols at either end of it can only by gained from Coire a' Ghreadaidh by unattractive Moderate climbs. A leftward trending gully leads to the north-eastern col. A rake, which passes rightwards beneath a massive overhang on the north-west face, gives access to a gully leading to the south-western col. The latter is known as Bealach Thormaid.

The north-east ridge is a good scramble, notable because of its three 'teeth'. These become progressively harder, with the highest one being Very Difficult if taken direct. However, they can all be avoided on the right (west) by a broken ledge starting from the col. A slab above is best taken direct to the airy summit.

The south-west ridge is a straightforward scramble, with the easiest lines being generally on the north-west side.

Sgurr na Banachdich (965m)
After turning a couple of pinnacles in Bealach Thormaid, the north ridge of this mountain gives an easy scramble on scree. Hold to the west side of the ridge to avoid the steep north-east face.

The main summit is readily gained by its west ridge from Coir' an Eich. This is the easiest route to a major summit from Glen Brittle. Some of the scree in Coir' an Eich can be avoided by moving left (north) onto the An Diallaid ridge. This ridge curves south to join the main west ridge rising from Sgurr nan Gobhar, (see Coire na Banachdich).

8. COIRE NA BANACHDICH (possibly derived from banachdach - *vaccination* or ban-achadh - *wasteland*)

SURROUNDING PEAKS

Sgurr nan Gobhar	630m	427 224
Sgurr na Banachdich	965m	440 224
Sgurr Dearg	978m	444 216

Coire na Banachdich lies due east of the Glen Brittle Memorial Hut and is the most accessible of all the Cuillin corries. It is approached along the south bank of the Allt Coire na Banachdich. A path, which leaves the road 50 metres south of the Glen Brittle Memorial Hut, crosses to the south bank after 300 metres to join with a path starting from Glenbrittle House. Continue along the rim of a deep hollow where the stream crashes over a spectacular waterfall, the Eas Mor (*great waterfall*). Be sure not to take paths forking off to the right for Coire Lagan, but instead continue by the Allt Coire na Banachdich.

The headwall of the corrie is comprised of slabs and cliffs split by terraces. Between the southernmost top of Sgurr na Banachdich and Sgurr Dearg lies an important pass over to Coruisk - Bealach Coire na Banachdich. This is the easiest pass between Glen Brittle and Coruisk, provided the correct route is followed. The west side of the bealach is guarded by a deep black gully (*Banachdich Gully*, Very Difficult), so the normal line of approach goes well to the right, close to the flank of Sgurr Dearg. A scree terrace then slants leftwards below a buttress to the bealach. The Coruisk side is a straightforward scree descent.

The round of the corrie is a popular outing, affording dramatic views eastwards of magnificent Coir'-uisg. It involves relatively uncomplicated scrambling. The only difficulties are on the south ridge of Sgurr na Banachdich. A short distance down on the Coire Lagan side of Sgurr Dearg sits the extraordinary Inaccessible Pinnacle.

Sgurr nan Gobhar (*peak of the goats*) (630m)
This conical top is a prominent feature from the floor of Glen Brittle. It can be approached directly across the moor from the Glen Brittle Hut. The south-western shoulder, being scree-covered, gives the easiest line of ascent. The north and south flanks are craggy, though of little climbing interest; *Goat's Gully* (Difficult) on the south flank was climbed in 1950 but contains much rotten rock. The ridge leading east from the summit is an easy scramble. It links with the easy west ridge of Sgurr na Banachdich to provide the shortest way possible to the main ridge from the west.

Sgurr na Banachdich (965m)
Centre top (942m)
This peak challenges Bruach na Frithe for the title of 'the easiest Cuillin Munro'. The main summit can be ascended without difficulty by its west ridge, either via Coir' an

Eich, or via Sgurr nan Gobhar. The traverse of the south ridge from Bealach Coire na Banachdich is more difficult and involves some pleasantly exposed scrambling over three lower tops.

The first (unnamed) top is situated a short distance north of the bealach and immediately above a shoulder called Sron Bhuidhe, which divides Coireachan Rudha to the east. The second (or south) top lies some 300 metres further north. The whole of this first section is little more than walking. The major difficulties occur on the traverse of the third (or centre) top, which has an awkward descent to the gap before the main summit. The ridge can be avoided by following exposed scree-covered ledges on the left (west), but this is not a particularly attractive option. Descent should not be attempted before the summit is reached. The mountain is precipitous on its eastern side (see Coireachan Ruadha) and although in many places it appears possible to descend into Coire na Banachdich, there is much loose ground there, with cliffs and slabs below.

The summit is a magnificent viewpoint, and marks the halfway point on the main ridge. The western aspect of the mountain offers no climbs of note.

Sgurr Dearg (*red peak*) (978m)

The name Sgurr Dearg is puzzling, because the mountain takes on a reddish hue only when lit by the setting sun. But for the extraordinary blade of rock known as the Inaccessible Pinnacle (see Coire Lagan), which stands proud on the south-east side of the summit, it would be one of the least spectacular peaks on the main ridge. The mountain is a popular objective for walkers from Glen Brittle and offers superb views of the main ridge.

The easiest line of ascent is by the north-west ridge from Bealach Coire na Banachdich. This is no more than a walk up a broad scree slope, with impressive drops to the left (north-east). The west ridge, which forms the south side of Coire na Banachdich, provides a more interesting route. It is reached via the wide shoulder of Sron Dearg. There is some scrambling on the narrow crest after the minor top of Sgurr Dearg Beag (929m), with stupendous views across Coire Lagan to the right.

ROCK CLIMBING

The best climbing in Coire na Banachdich is to be found on two separate buttresses on the north side of Sgurr Dearg's west ridge. The first is known as *Window Buttress* because of the remarkable 'hole' which pierces its summit tower. In the right light, this feature is discernible from the Glen Brittle Hut. The normal route (Window Buttress, Difficult) is one of the most popular climbs on Skye, and there is a well-defined path to its foot from Eas Mor. A number of harder variations are possible. There are also several options from the neck behind the top of the main buttress, including a continuation called *Upper Window Buttress* (Severe).

North-West Buttress lies some 350 metres further up the corrie, and has its base level with the top of Upper Window Buttress. It is distinguished by two prominent black chimneys and has several good routes on sound rock, mainly of Severe standard.

CHAPTER 11

SOUTH GLEN BRITTLE

These corries lie on the south-west side of the main ridge and are best approached from the lower part of Glen Brittle.

  9. **Coire Lagan**
10. **Coir' a' Ghrunnda**
11. **Coire nan Laogh**

9. COIRE LAGAN *(hollow corrie)*

SURROUNDING PEAKS

Sgurr Dearg	978m	444 216
Inaccessible Pinnacle	986m	444 215
An Stac	954m	445 215
Sgurr Mhic Choinnich	948m	450 210
Sgurr Thearlaich	978m	451 208
Sgurr Alasdair	992m	450 208
Sgurr Sgumain	947m	448 206
Sron na Ciche	859m	447 204

Coire Lagan is one of the most magnificent and certainly the most popular of the Cuillin corries. It is ringed by spectacular and varied peaks, including the highest (Sgurr Alasdair) on all the islands. Here a beautiful lochan is set in a rock basin, backed by gigantic stone chutes and superb crags, and all within striking distance of Glen Brittle. The round of the corrie is a classic expedition which involves at least Difficult climbing by the normal route, and hard scrambling even if some of the difficulties are bypassed.

      The corrie can be reached by two well worn paths which originate from Glen Brittle camp site and from Glenbrittle House. These are rather boggy in all but the driest weather, and in places a number of parallel swathes have been worn through the peat. The two routes start to merge after passing either side of Loch an Fhir-bhallaich. Hereabouts another path branches off rightwards for the north-west face of Sron na Ciche, and the terrain starts to become more bouldery. The path steepens as it moves closer to the stream which drains from the upper corrie, and eventually emerges onto ice-scraped slabs cradling a lovely lochan. Walkers will find this excursion alone worthwhile.

Two broad shoulders bound either side of the corrie - Sron Dearg to the north, and Sron na Ciche to the south. Above the headwall of the corrie, in its top left corner, is perched the Inaccessible Pinnacle. Further right is the long steep south face of Sgurr Mhic Choinnich, and in the right-hand corner the Great Stone Chute divides Sgurr Thearlaich from mighty Sgurr Alasdair.

There are two bealachs on the main ridge backing the corrie. The lower of the two, called Bealach Coire Lagan, cannot be recommended as a pass. It is situated well left of centre between An Stac and Sgurr Mhic Choinnich, some 140 metres north-west of the lowest point on the skyline. The Coire Lagan side is not difficult, although it entails a long slog up scree. The Coruisk side, however, is difficult and unpleasantly loose. A more amenable pass is located between Sgurr Mhic Choinnich and Sgurr Thearlaich, and is known as Bealach Mhic Choinnich. The broad gully that falls from it on the Lagan side is best reached by traversing left from part way up the Great Stone Chute. There is some scrambling in the upper section. The main ridge is intimidating just here, but the descent on the Coruisk side is by a straightforward gully. It is then possible, either to continue down Coireachan Ruadha, or to cross the easy ridge on the right (between Sgurr Thearlaich and Sgurr Coir' an Lochain) and descend Coir' an Lochain and thence Coir' a' Chaoruinn.

There is a further important pass over the lateral ridge between Sgurr Sgumain and Sron na Ciche, which connects with neighbouring Coir' a' Ghrunnda; it is known as Bealach Coir' a' Ghrunnda. On the Lagan side it is reached by ascending the Sgumain Stone Chute. This involves some 400m of ascent on boulders and scree beneath the massive north-west face of Sron na Ciche - the greatest and most frequented climbing cliff on Skye. Towards the top of the Stone Chute the route passes to the right of a feature known as the Ladies' Pinnacle. On the Coir' a' Ghrunnda side, slant down leftwards (eastwards) on scree to the north end of a delightful lochan, Loch Coir' a' Ghrunnda. This pass is often used as a way between Glen Brittle and the southern Cuillin peaks, and also between Glen Brittle and Coruisk (when it is used in conjunction with Bealach Coir' an Lochain or Bealach a' Garbh-choire).

The Great Stone Chute originates from a small, high col between Sgurr Thearlaich and Sgurr Alasdair. The col is not a pass, however, since there is a precipice a little way down the Coir' a' Ghrunnda side. From the lochan in upper Coire Lagan a path leads across to the base of the Great Stone Chute. This was once a 400 metres long scree run, but its upper section especially has become badly eroded by the passage of countless feet. An ascent of the chute is laborious rather than difficult, although one needs to be alert to the danger of falling rocks. Care should be taken, particularly when descending the upper part of the chute, not to disturb rocks unnecessarily, because the curving nature of the chute makes it impossible to see parties below. Stones can pick up great speed on the barer upper section.

Sgurr Alasdair (left) and Sgurr Dearg from Sgurr a' Ghreadaidh

Sgurr Dearg and Sgurr na Banachdich (right) from the south

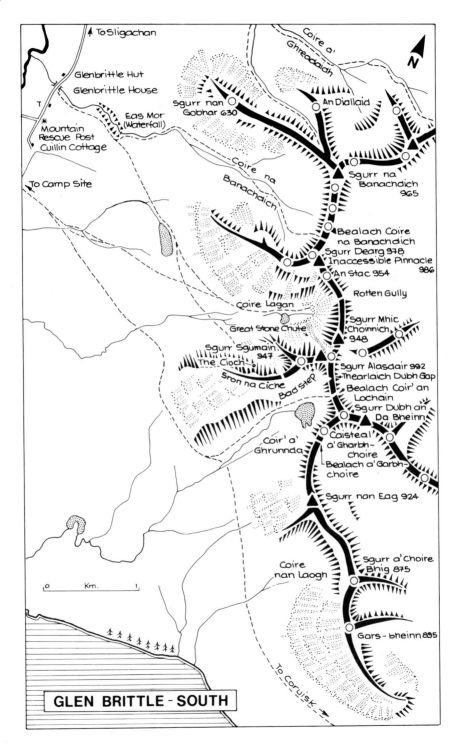

To Sligachan

Coire a'
Ghreadaidh

N

Glenbrittle Hut
Glenbrittle House

T

Sgurr nan
Gobhar 630

An Diallaid

Eas Mor
(Waterfall)

Mountain
Rescue Post
Cuillin Cottage

Sgurr na
Banachdich
965

To Camp Site

Coire na
Banachdich

Bealach Coire
na Banachdich
Sgurr Dearg 978
Inaccessible Pinnacle
986
An Stac 954

Rotten Gully

Coire Lagan

Great Stone Chute

Sgurr Mhic
'Choinnich
948

Sgurr Sgumain
947
The Cioch
Sron na Ciche

Bad Step

Sgurr Alasdair 992
Thearlaich Dubh Gap
Bealach Coir' an
Lochain
Sgurr Dubh an
Da Bheinn

Coir' a'
Ghrunnda

Caisteal
a' Gharbh-
choire
Bealach a' Garbh-
choire

Sgurr nan Eag 924

Coire
nan Laogh

Sgurr a' Choire
Bhig 875

Gars-bheinn 895

0   Km.   1

To Coruisk

GLEN BRITTLE - SOUTH

Sgurr Dearg (*red peak*) (978m)
This is the least serious of the peaks bordering Coire Lagan, and consequently it is a popular objective with walkers. The summit itself is rather uninspiring, although it offers fine views. The Inaccessible Pinnacle (see below) overtops it by some 8m, and immediately draws the eye. The mountain can be ascended by scrambling along its west ridge, (see Coire na Banachdich). An alternative route from the floor of Coire Lagan ascends a long scree slope, almost as far as Bealach Coire Lagan, then moves left and slants up and across the south face of An Stac. Care is needed when using this route in descent, (see An Stac).

ROCK CLIMBING
The south side of the mountain facing Coire Lagan has some good climbing, the best of which is concentrated on South Buttress. This is situated some 120m above the lochan in the upper corrie. The routes range from

The west side of the Inaccessible Pinnacle

Difficult to Hard Very Severe, and offer climbers an interesting approach to the Inaccessible Pinnacle.

Inaccessible Pinnacle (986m)
The famous fin of rock that sprouts from the summit dome of Sgurr Dearg is the second highest peak in the Cuillin. Its base can be reached by walking or easy scrambling from a number of directions (see Sgurr Dearg), but its summit can only be gained by rock climbing. It is the most difficult of all Munro summits, and has been the downfall of many would-be 'baggers'. There is a large perched block on the summit.

ROCK CLIMBING
The easiest and most popular route on the Inaccessible Pinnacle is the *East Ridge*, climbed by the Pilkington brothers on the first ascent in 1880. It is graded Moderate, but is very narrow, and sensationally exposed. The *West Ridge*, which is situated

nearest the summit of Sgurr Dearg, is shorter but harder (Difficult), and is probably more often abseiled than climbed. The obvious crack on the south face (*South Crack*) is a classic Hard Very Difficult. Further left there are three VSs, and just on the other side of the West Ridge is *North-West Corner* (Difficult).

An Stac (*the stack*) (954m)
The name An Stac was probably applied originally to the Inaccesible Pinnacle and not to this fairly minor peak on the south-east ridge of Sgurr Dearg. The top can be reached without difficulty from the summit of Sgurr Dearg by descending below the south face of the Inaccessible Pinnacle.

There are two popular ascent routes from Bealach Coire Lagan. The easiest follows an obvious line of weakness that slants up across the south face. It is little more than a walk. Cross a tiny shoulder, and continue ascending on scree and slabs below the peaks's south-west wall. Eventually rejoin the crest of the main ridge just to the east of the Inaccessible Pinnacle. Turn right and the summit is soon gained. The alternative route follows the east ridge, and is only for climbers or confident scramblers. It involves sustained scrambling in fairly exposed positions, with occasional moves of Moderate standard - an exhilarating route for the competent. The rock is a little loose in places, though not unpleasantly so. There is a splendid view of the Inaccessible Pinnacle from the summit.

When descending to Coire Lagan from the vicinity of the Inaccessible Pinnacle it is important to stay close to the south face of An Stac. At one point it is necessary to ascend slightly and to go round an obvious corner on the left. Beware the tempting scree slope on the right, which ends in cliffs. Just before reaching Bealach Coire Lagan, it is possible to make a descent of the An Stac screes to upper Coire Lagan.

ROCK CLIMBING
A prominent 60m crack cleaving the south face was climbed by Goggs and Russell in 1908.

Sgurr Mhic Choinnich (*Mackenzie's Peak*) (948m)
This fine peak presents a long rocky face to Coire Lagan. It was named in honour of John Mackenzie, a local guide and early Cuillin pioneer. The summit is at the mountain's eastern end, above Bealach Mhic Choinnich. The easiest line of ascent is by the long north-west ridge from Bealach Coire Lagan, but even this is a stiff scramble. From the bealach traverse a minor prominence to reach the lowest point (804m) on the skyline of the upper corrie. The route from there is well worn, and the initial scrambling is very enjoyable. The middle part of the ridge is relatively straightforward, but the upper part involves further scrambling on one of the sharpest sections of the main ridge. There are steep drops on both sides of the basalt slabs that form the crest. The summit itself is comparatively spacious, and a wonderful viewpoint. Unfortunately it is spoilt somewhat by a crudely cemented memorial plaque.

The southern end of the mountain appears formidable from Bealach Mhic

Approaching the Inaccessible Pinnacle along the ridge from An Stac

On the ridge between Sgurr Mhic Choinnich and Sgurr Thearlaich

Choinnich. However, the upper part of the north-west ridge can be reached from this bealach by traversing across the west face above Coire Lagan along an exposed scramble known as *Collie's Ledge*. The route for the most part follows the line of a prominent cone sheet. It starts some 6m above the bealach, and slants round to the left below *King's Chimney* (see below). After rounding the buttress, it continues in the same line to reach the north-west ridge. There is another ledge above Collie's Ledge proper, but it is not continuous. It is also possible to reach the north-west ridge by descending a short distance from Bealach Mhic Choinnich, following less definite ledges below the steep upper section of the west face and then ascending an open gully.

ROCK CLIMBING
On the south side of the summit rocks there is an important 30m Difficult climb known as King's Chimney. It is popular with those traversing the main ridge from the south since it provides a direct way to the summit from Bealach Mhic Choinnich. The route follows a prominent corner capped by an overhang and is reached by scrambling some 20m up from the bealach. There is a loose chockstone in the corner, and at the top the route traverses out onto the right wall.

The Coire Lagan face is generally too broken for satisfactory climbs, but *West Buttress* (300m Difficult), which leads directly to the summit, has some good climbing in its upper section. The final pitch above Collie's Ledge offers an alternative to King's Chimney. A prominent dyke to the left of West Buttress gives the line of another 300m Difficult climb called *Jeffrey's Dyke.*

Sgurr Thearlaich (*Charles' peak*) (978m)
This tricky peak is named after Charles Pilkington who led the first ascent party in 1884. It lies on the main Cuillin ridge, unlike its grander partner on the opposite side of the *Great Stone Chute.* The simplest ascent route involves some easy rock climbing, so it is not a peak for the walker.

The normal way to the summmit is from the col at the top of the Great Stone Chute. The main difficulty lies in getting established on the south ridge. It is usual to start at a short wall just down a little from the top of the col on the Coir' a' Ghrunnda side. After a steep move or two of Moderate standard, some scrambling leads to the crest of the ridge. This is followed without further difficulty to the summit.

The descent of the north ridge to Bealach Mhic Choinnich is more taxing. It is longer, harder and more exposed than the first route, and requires careful route finding. After a narrow section of ridge, a slab on the east side of the crest is descended using small incut holds. Continue to weave a way down mainly on the eastern side and then climb down a final steep section to easier ground. Alternatively, from part way down the ridge, move left and descend a gully that finishes just below the level of the bealach on the Coire Lagan side. The correct gully, however, can be difficult to identify from above.

ROCK CLIMBING
Five gullies have been climbed on the west face, overlooking the top section of the Great Stone Chute. They have been named alphabetically from the left (A to E), and range in standard from Moderate to Very Difficult. They are not popular in summer, although E gully was climbed by the first party to ascend the peak in 1884.

Sgurr Alasdair (*Alexander's peak*) (992m)
The highest peak on Skye is a splendid mountain. It is not as well separated from neighbouring peaks nor perhaps as tricky to ascend as Sgurr nan Gillean, but nevertheless it has a very shapely summit, the views from which are unrivalled. The seaward vistas are magnificent and encompass both the Inner and Outer Isles. A host of mainland peaks can also be distinguished including Ben Nevis.

The peak is named after Alexander Nicolson, a native of Skye and one of the boldest early explorers of the Cuillin. On the first ascent, in 1873, he traversed Sgurr na Banachdich and Sgurr Dearg before gaining the summit by the Great Stone Chute.

The mountain is situated just off the main ridge, on the opposite side of the Great Stone Chute from Sgurr Thearlaich. It is the first summit on a lateral ridge that extends south-westwards over Sgurr Sgumain and Sron na Ciche. The finest rock climbing in the Cuillin is to be found on the Coire Lagan side of this ridge.

The Great Stone Chute offers the easiest line of ascent. From the col at its top, a pleasant scramble up the well scratched east ridge soon leads to the narrow summit. On a fine evening it is delightful to linger there for the sunset, secure in the knowledge that nearby there is an easy descent route to the corrie floor.

The alternative route is by the south-west ridge, which rises from the col between Sgurr Alasdair and Sgurr Sgumain. This col (921m) is the highest pass in the Cuillin. It links with neighbouring Coir' a' Ghrunnda and is known as Bealach Sgumain. It is virtually never used as a pass since Bealach Coir' a' Ghrunnda on the other side of Sgurr Sgumain is lower and more pleasant. The extremely steep scree slope on the Coire Lagan side can be gained by trending right a short distance up the Great Stone Chute. A much more agreeable approach, however, is to ascend the broad south-west flank of Sron na Ciche and then continue over the summit of Sgurr Sgumain.

A short distance above Bealach Sgumain is the famous *Bad Step*. It can be negotiated in a number of ways. If the obvious 6m corner is climbed directly it gives a move or two of Severe standard. An alternative is to climb the wall on the left and then ascend its extremely narrow crest at about Difficult standard. The easiest option, however, is to descend slightly to the right (the Coir' a' Ghrunnda side), and then, as soon as possible, to follow an Easy chimney leftwards back to the crest. Thereafter the ridge is exposed and slightly loose in places, but otherwise no more than an easy scramble.

ROCK CLIMBING
The huge north-west buttress of Sgurr Alasdair is not as steep as it appears. It is reached by first ascending past the narrows of the Great Stone Chute. Two long routes of Difficult standard (*Abraham's Climb* and *Collies Climb*) were ascended here at an early date. They are both somewhat loose. Abraham's Climb gives a good winter climb (III/IV).

Sgurr Sgumain (*stack peak*) (947m)
This broad summit is merely the south-west top of Sgurr Alasdair. It can be ascended without difficulty by its south ridge from Bealach Coir' a' Ghrunnda. The north-east ridge from Bealach Sgumain is also straightforward.

On its Lagan aspect this peak exhibits two broad buttresses, North Buttress on the left and West Buttress on the right, separated high up by an impressive north-west face. An easy rake slanting across the bottom of West Buttress provides a convenient way of reaching the Sgumain Stone Chute from upper Coire Lagan.

ROCK CLIMBING
The North Buttress is a fairly well defined ridge of Moderate standard, which starts above and left of Loch Coire Lagan, and leads directly to the summit. The broad West Buttress is moderately angled, but provides almost 500m of continuous rock climbing up to Difficult standard. A shattered arete leads to a final tower, which can be climbed by one of several lines, including a Severe on the north-west face, or avoided altogether by a terrace on the right.

A number of lower grade climbs on sound rock are to be found on the flank of West Buttress. *Sunset Slab* with the *Yellow Groove* continuation (MVS) is

The great cliff of Sron na Ciche, with the Cioch in the centre

particularly fine. There are also numerous good routes, generally of a slightly harder standard, high up on the north-west face. These include *Frostbite* (VS) and *Grannie Clark's* Wynd (E1).

Sron na Ciche (*shoulder of the breast*) (859m)

The rather undistinguished top at the end of the lateral ridge extending from Sgurr Alasdair is the lowest of all the summits bordering Coire Lagan. Nevertheless, it more than compensates for its modest altitude by throwing down a stupendous face to the north-west. This is the greatest cliff in the Cuillin and easily the most popular with climbers. It stretches for more than 700 metres, and is nearly 300m high.

The broad south-west flank offers the easiest way to the summit. It is normally approached from the Glen Brittle camp site by taking a right fork in the path at a stream early on. The route is nothing more than a walk. It is only a short scramble from the north-east side of the summit down to Bealach Coir' a' Ghrunnda and the head of the Sgumain Stone Chute.

Climbers heading for the north-west face use a well worn path that branches off from the paths to the upper corrie and crosses the Allt Coire Lagan. Two long gullies (Eastern Gully and Central Gully) divide the face into three main sections. An extraordinary rock feature, which projects from a slab halfway up the central section of the face, was christened A' Chioch (*the breast*) by John Mackenzie, who partnered Norman Collie on its first ascent in 1906. Collie had spotted the great shadow cast by this curious tower on a summer's evening several years previously. The Cioch also gives it name to Sron na Ciche.

Experienced scramblers may be able to follow Collie's Route to the summit of the Cioch, but otherwise this whole face is only for climbers.

ROCK CLIMBING

Every climber should try to visit the unique Cioch at some time in his or her career. The numerous ways to its summit range in grade from Moderate to E3. For details of the many and varied routes on the vast north-west face of Sron na Ciche, the reader is referred to the climbing guide published by the SMC (*Rock and Ice Climbs in Skye* by J R Mackenzie). Most climbers should be able to find routes of quality there to match their particular standard, although they probably will not want for company on them.

The names and grades of a few routes may help to indicate the variety of climbing available. *Vulcan Wall* (HVS), *Direct Route* (Very Difficult), *Shangri-La* (Very Severe) and *Team Machine* (E4) lie on Eastern Buttress. *Bastinado* (E1) and *Cioch Direct* (Severe) lead to the terrace below the Cioch. *Arrow Route* (Very Difficult) ascends the slab left of the Cioch, whilst *Integrity* (Mild Very Severe), *Trophy Crack* (E1) and *Wallwork's Route* (Very Difficult) climb the buttress above. *Crack of Doom* (Hard Severe) and *Crack of Double Doom* (Very Severe) lie further right. *Amphitheatre Arete* (Moderate) and *Hang Free* (E2) represent the extremes of difficulty on Western Buttress.

On the Direct Route of the Eastern Buttress, Sron na Ciche

10. COIR' A' GHRUNNDA   (*bare corrie*)

SURROUNDING PEAKS

Sron na Ciche	859m	447 204
Sgurr Sgumain	947m	448 206
Sgurr Alasdair	992m	450 208
Sgurr Thearlaich	978m	451 208
Sgurr Dubh an Da Bheinn	938m	455 204
Caisteal a' Garbh-choire	829m	454 202
Sgurr nan Eag	924m	457 195

Coir' a' Ghrunnda is an impressively rocky place with a powerful atmosphere. Although not as grand as Coire Lagan, it is the better for being less frequented. It would be hard to imagine a finer example of a glaciated mountain corrie. Large ice-scraped slabs are exposed in its floor, and a conspicuous rock band fringes its upper tier in which lies the superb Loch Coir' a' Ghrunnda, the highest body of water in the Cuillin. On the moor below the mouth of the corrie is an obvious terminal moraine.

To reach the lower corrie, start along the Coire Lagan path from the camp site and fork right at the first stream. Head towards the southern end of Sron na Ciche, and once past this take a higher path which turns up to the left. Stay on the western side of the corrie above the stream, and pass below the crags of Sron na Ciche. Some scrambling is involved in overcoming the rock slabs guarding the upper corrie.

The left-hand side of the corrie is formed by the Sgurr Alasdair - Sron na Ciche ridge, which presents a less fiercesome face here than it does on the Coire Lagan side. An alternative approach to the upper corrie is to cross Bealach Coir' a' Ghrunnda, which is situated between Sron na Ciche and Sgurr Sgumain, (see Coire Lagan). The most important feature on the main ridge above the backwall of the corrie is the famous Thearlaich-Dubh Gap. This constitutes one of the most difficult problems on the main Cuillin ridge. The huge western flank of Sgurr nan Eag bounds the right-hand side of the corrie.

There are two bealachs offering ways over the main ridge to Coruisk from the upper corrie. Both can be reached without difficulty from the Loch Coir' a' Ghrunnda by ascending scree and boulders. Indeed it is a straightforward matter to reach all the cols between the surrounding peaks, except the one between Sgurr Alasdair and Sgurr Thearlaich, which is guarded by a steep crag.

The first pass, Bealach Coir' an Lochain, lies to the north-east between Sgurr Thearlaich and Sgurr Dubh an Da Bheinn. The descent into Coir' an Lochain is over rough ground, but is not unduly difficult. However, the lower reaches of that corrie are quite taxing, and so from just below the lochan the normal descent route bears east over the right-hand shoulder into Coir' a' Chaoruinn, (see the Coruisk section).

The second pass is known as Bealach a' Garbh-choire. It is situated on the eastern side of the upper corrie between Sgurr nan Eag and Sgurr Dubh an Da Bheinn. A massive chunky crag called Caisteal a' Garbh-choire sits astride the ridge at this point. The ridge can be crossed at either end of this feature, although it is rather easier at the right-hand (southern) end. The pass itself is straighforward, but it leads into the roughest corrie in the Cuillin, (see An Garbh-choire).

Sron na Ciche (*shoulder of the breast*) (859m)
Sgurr Sgumain (*stack peak*) (947m)
See the Coire Lagan section for a general description of these tops. They can both be ascended without difficulty from Bealach Coir' a' Ghrunnda.

ROCK CLIMBING
There is some climbing interest on the south-east face of Sron na Ciche. The normal path into the lower corrie passes beneath a broad crag which faces Sgurr nan Eag. The crag is divided by a watercourse into two main parts - South Crag on the left and North Crag on the right. The better climbing is generally to be found on South Crag. The routes there include the popular *White Slab* (180m Very Difficult) and its variations (Severe and Very Severe).

Sgurr Alasdair (*Alexander's peak*) (992m)
See Coire Lagan for a description of the route up the south-west ridge.

ROCK CLIMBING
Some fine short routes are to be found on a steep cliff high up in the left-hand corner of Coir' a' Ghrunnda. The cliff extends from below the summit of Sgurr Alasdair rightwards to the gully falling from the Thearlaich-Dubh Gap. The routes on the right-hand part of the cliff finish near the col at the head of the Great Stone Chute. One such route, *Con's Cleft* (Hard Very Severe), is an outstanding climb. The section of crag to the right of the Thearlaich-Dubh Gully is described under Sgurr Thearlaich.

Sgurr Thearlaich (*Charles' peak*) (978m)
The ascent of this peak directly from Coir' a' Ghrunnda is not a practicable proposition for either walkers or scramblers. The col between the summit and Sgurr Alasdair is guarded by a steep crag, and part way up the south-east ridge lies the notorious Thearlaich-Dubh Gap. This is one of the hardest obstacles on the main ridge, and, since it cannot easily be circumvented, it becomes something of a bottleneck at times. It involves Very Difficult climbing. The start of the south-east ridge is reached by ascending to Bealach Coir' an Lochain.

ROCK CLIMBING
The first part of the south-east ridge is a pleasant scramble. After weaving round a minor pinnacle some harder scrambling leads to The Gap itself. When traversing from the south-east it is normal to abseil the very steep 8m wall into the gap. (This is Severe in ascent.) The climb out of the gap up its longer side follows a rather smooth basalt chimney. This is Very Difficult when dry and very treacherous when wet. It is possible to escape into Coir' a' Ghrunnda, by descending the steep gully on the south-west side of the gap, which has only a short section of Moderate

climbing. In winter, when the main ridge is usually traversed from north to south, it is common practice to abseil the longer side of the gap and then to descend this gully, rather than to climb the shorter side.

Soon after the Thearlaich-Dubh Gap, move leftwards off the ridge and ascend scree for a short distance to the top of the Great Stone Chute. The summits of Sgurr Thearlaich and Sgurr Alasdair are close at hand, (see Coire Lagan).

There is some good climbing on the Coir' a Ghrunnda face of the south-east ridge to the right (south-east) of the Thearlaich-Dubh Gully. *Grand Diedre* with the *Direct Start* is an excellent Very Severe.

Sgurr Dubh an Da Bheinn (*black peak of the two ridges*) (938m)
This peak is situated at the junction between the main ridge and an important lateral ridge leading eastwards to Sgurr Dubh Mor and Sgurr Dubh Beag - hence its name. It presents a boulder-strewn flank to Coir' a' Ghrunnda.

The south ridge from Caisteal a' Garbh-choire offers any amount of scrambling over large boulders. Trend right over scree near the top. The summit can easily be avoided by slanting left, but it is worth visiting for its fine views. The north-west ridge from Bealach Coir' an Lochain is also an easy scramble. It is becoming accepted practice on the main ridge traverse to detour along the east ridge from the summit to bag Sgurr Dubh Mor, (see An Garbh-choire).

Caisteal a' Garbh-choire (*castle of the rough corrie*) (829m)
This immense block of amazingly rough rock sits in the col between Sgurr Dubh an Da Bheinn and Sgurr nan Eag. The summit can only be reached by rock climbing, but when traversing the main ridge the whole feature can be avoided on either side without great difficulty. It is possible to maintain height by scrambling along ledges at the base of the west face.

ROCK CLIMBING
The traverse of the summit is an entertaining diversion. It is normally achieved by Moderate/Difficult lines on the southern and north-western sides. The northern end overhangs.

Sgurr nan Eag (*peak of the notches*) (924m)
This huge mountain has a very long and level summit ridge aligned from north-west to south-east. Only the north-western end of the ridge overlooks Coir' a' Ghrunnda. The highest point lies at the south-eastern end which overlooks neighbouring Coire nan Laogh. The mountain can conveniently be ascended by its north-north-west ridge from Bealach a' Garbh-choire. This makes an enjoyable and varied scramble, with the hardest lines generally following the crest and the easiest ways going to the right (west).

The broad western flank of the mountain, which overlooks the lower part of Coir' a' Ghrunnda, is rocky and of minor rock climbing interest. The extensive south-western flank, which lies below the summit ridge, consists largely of scree and boulders. It can be ascended almost anywhere, but is not an attractive option.

Sgurr Dubh an Da Bheinn (left), Gars-bheinn and Sgurr nan Eag

ROCK CLIMBING
There is a sizeable broken buttress on the west flank opposite the South Crag of Sron na Ciche. It has yielded a 200m Difficult climb (*West Buttress*) leading almost to the summit ridge. There is also a two pitch Very Severe hereabouts called *The Stag*.

11. COIRE NAN LAOGH   *(corrie of the calves)*

SURROUNDING PEAKS

Sgurr nan Eag	924m	457 195
Sgurr a' Choire Bhig	875m	465 191
Gars-bheinn	895m	468 187

This open corrie is the most southerly in the Cuillin. It is rarely visited for its own sake, being rather uninteresting and a long way from Glen Brittle. The mouth of the corrie is used as a landmark by parties following the coastal path to the foot of Gars-bheinn prior to starting the main ridge traverse from the south.

The head of the corrie is lined by a great sweep of slabs some 150m high cut by three prominent gullies. There are no easy routes to the cols between the surrounding peaks.

Sgurr nan Eag (*peak of the notches*) (924m)
The southern shoulder and east ridge of this mountain border Coire nan Laogh. It is the first Munro on the southern section of the main ridge, and is easily ascended by its east ridge. The broad col at the foot of this ridge (774m) is normally approached by traversing from Gars-bheinn over Sgurr a'Choire Bhig.

There are plenty of opportunities to enjoy the superb views from the remarkably level summit ridge, which extends north-westwards for more than 400 metres. An enjoyable scramble then leads down the steepish north-north-west ridge to Bealach a' Garbh-choire, (see Coir' a' Ghrunnda).

The south shoulder offers an easy but tedious route direct to the summit from the coastal path.

Sgurr a' Choire Bhig (*peak of the little corrie*) (875m)
This attractive little top lies on a narrow ridge some 500 metres north-west of Gars-bheinn. It is normally traversed by its short south ridge and long north-west ridge, both of which are fairly straightforward but exhilarating walks. The peak's best feature is undoubtedly its north-east ridge, (see An Garbh-choire).

ROCK CLIMBING
The slabs at the head of Coire nan Laogh do not offer any continuous lines of note. Pitches of up to Severe standard can be found. The three gullies cutting the slabs (*West, Central* and *East*) were climbed in 1912. The hardest of these, *Central Gully* (Very Difficult), gives the best climb. It lies beneath the north-west ridge of Sgurr a' Choire Bhig.

Gars-bheinn (possibly *echoing mountain*) (895m)
The southernmost peak on the main ridge is a shapely summit, and a splendid viewpoint, but it is flanked by scree-ridden slopes to the south and west. Walking round to the base of this mountain from Glen Brittle and then slogging up its south-western flank is the most gruelling way of starting a traverse of the main ridge.

A number of bivouac places have been fashioned among the summit rocks. A short distance to the west of the summit there are two minor rocky tops, which could be mistaken for the true summit in thick mist. The north-west ridge leading to Sgurr a' Choire Bhig is narrow, but without difficulty. Once started on, the main ridge is best followed at least as far as Bealach a' Garbh-choire, although the southern shoulder of Sgurr nan Eag does offer a possible descent route.

CHAPTER 12

CORUISK

These corries lie to the east and north-east of the central and southern Cuillin peaks. Water flowing from all of these corries eventually drains into Loch na Cuilce (*loch of the reed*), the innermost part of Loch Scavaig.

12. **Coir' a' Chruidh** and **Coire Beag**
13. **An Garbh-choire**
14. **Coir' a' Chaoruinn** and **Coir' an Lochain**
15. **Coireachan Ruadha**
16. **Coir' an Uaigneis** and **Glac Mhor**
17. **Coir'-uisg**
18. **Coire Riabhach**

Few who stand for the first time on the shore of Loch Coruisk can fail to be impressed by the surroundings. Words alone cannot do justice to the scene. Only by seeing at first hand the bare rock slabs, boulders, buttresses, corries and jagged peaks which soar all around can the special atmosphere of this corner of the Cuillin be appreciated. A visit blessed by fine weather is a magical experience.

The name Coir'-uisg (*corrie of water*) is strictly speaking applied only to the lower part of the great hollow around the head of Loch Coruisk. However, the anglicised form Coruisk is commonly understood to refer to the whole basin enclosed by the southern part of the main ridge and Druim nan Ramh. Magnificent Loch Coruisk, which fills a deep ice-gouged trough in the floor of this basin, is some two and a half kilometres long and nearly half a kilometre wide. Paths, boggy in places, run along both sides, and at the outflow from the south-eastern end of the loch there are stepping stones across the River Scavaig. This river flows for only a few hundred metres before spilling into the sea not far from the Coruisk Hut.

There are several ways of reaching Coruisk. The low-level walking routes from Sligachan, Glen Brittle and Camasunary were described in the introduction to the Cuillin (p. 165-7). In addition there are six recognised passes over the main ridge from Glen Brittle. They are:

1. **Bealach na Glaic Moire** (760m) - see Coir' Tairneilear
2. **An Dorus** (847m) - see Coire a' Ghreadaidh
3. **Bealach Coire na Banachdich** (851m) - see Coire na Banachdich
4. **Bealach Mhic Choinnich** (892m) - see Coire Lagan
5. **Bealach Coir' an Lochain** (855m) - see Coir' a' Ghrunnda
6. **Bealach a' Garbh-choire** (797m) - see Coir' a' Ghrunnda

Of these passes, Bealach Coire na Banachdich is the easiest and An Dorus possibly the hardest.

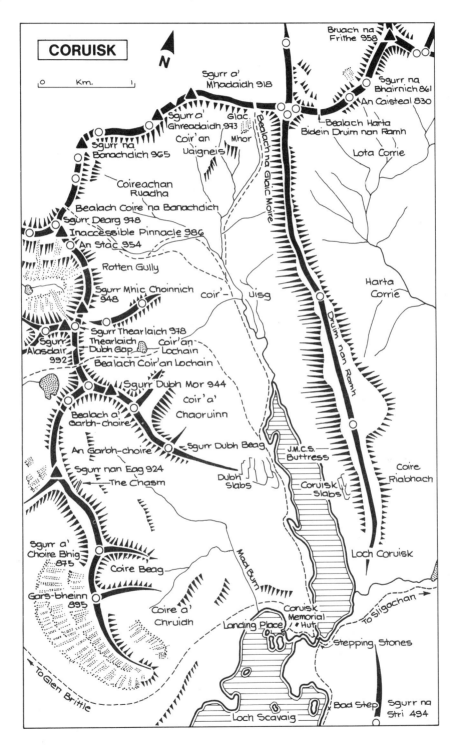

CORUISK

0   Km.   1

N

Bruach na Frithe 958

Sgurr a' Mhadaidh 918

Sgurr na Bhairnich 861

An Caisteal 830

Sgurr a' Ghreadaidh 973

Glac Mhor

Bealach Harta
Bidein Druim nan Ramh

Coir' an Uaigneis

Sgurr na Banachdich 965

Lota Corrie

Coireachan Ruadha

Bealach Coire na Banachdich

Sgurr Dearg 978

Inaccessible Pinnacle 986

An Stac 954

Rotten Gully

Sgurr Mhic Choinnich 948

Coir' - Uisg

Harta Corrie

Sgurr Thearlaich 978

Sgurr Alasdair 992

Thearlaich Dubh Gap

Coir' an Lochain

Bealach Coir' an Lochain

Sgurr Dubh Mor 944

Coir' a' Chaoruinn

Bealach a' Garbh-choire

An Garbh-choire

Sgurr Dubh Beag

J.M.C.S. Buttress

Coire Riabhach

Sgurr nan Eag 924

The Chasm

Dubh Slabs

Coruisk Slabs

Loch Coruisk

Sgurr a' Choire Bhig 875

Coire Beag

Mad Burn

Gars-bheinn 895

Coire a' Chruidh

Coruisk Memorial Hut

Landing Place

To Sligachan

Stepping Stones

To Glen Brittle

Bad Step

Sgurr na Stri 494

Loch Scavaig

The most attractive approach to Coruisk, however, is by sea. Boats can be chartered from Elgol and Mallaig. For the cognoscenti this is the way to visit the Cuillin. There are few more wonderful experiences in the British Isles than to sail into Loch na Cuilce on a fine summer evening.

The Coruisk Hut is situated below a long rock face close to the landing place at the head of Loch na Cuilce. Ample camping space is available nearby on rather boggy ground. After heavy rain the Allt a' Chaoich and the River Scavaig may become impassable (see walking routes around the Cuillin), in which event possibly the best escape route leads to Glen Brittle via the south-west shore of Loch Coruisk, An Garbh-choire, Bealach a' Garbh-choire, and Bealach Coir' a' Ghrunnda.

12. COIR' A' CHRUIDH (*corrie of cattle*)
COIRE BEAG (*little corrie*)

SURROUNDING PEAKS

Gars-bheinn	895m	468 187
Sgurr a' Choire Bhig	875m	465 191

Coir' a' Chruidh lies to the east of the summit of Gars-bheinn, whilst Coire Beag lies to the north, the two corries being separated by the peak's north-east ridge. Neither corrie is of special interest, although both offer access to the main ridge on opposite sides of Gars-bheinn.

To reach Coir' a' Chruidh from the Coruisk Hut follow the coastal path towards Glen Brittle as far as the Allt Coir' a' Chruidh (p. 165), then head uphill in a westerly direction towards the steep flank of the north-east ridge of Gars-bheinn. Turn left (south) to join the south-east ridge of Gars-bheinn at a small rise some 200 metres from the summit.

To reach Coire Beag follow the coastal path until just after the Allt a' Chaoich, then ascend the hillside beside the next small stream. Some distance from a knoll with a spot height of 193m turn left and head south-west. Follow the more westerly branch of a stream which drains from Coire Beag. Slant rightwards along a shelf to gain the upper corrie, and at the head of this follow the left-hand of two obvious scree gullies to a gap a short distance west of the summit of Gars-bheinn.

Gars-bheinn (possibly *echoing mountain*) (895m)
The north-east ridge offers a pleasant scramble and is the most attractive ascent route on the mountain. It is gained by moving left from the normal approach to Coire Beag. The south-east ridge is very remote and rarely climbed. It terminates in a small conical top (686m) which can be reached from the coastal path. The ridge itself is straightforward and has scree slopes on the left overlooking the island of Soay, and craggy ground on the right falling into Coir' a' Chruidh.

ROCK CLIMBING
Rather more than one kilometre north-east of Gars-bheinn, at a height of 150m

The MV Western Isles in Loch na Cuilce

above sea level, there is a diamond-shaped crag called *Mad Burn Buttress*. It can be reached in 20 minutes from the Coruisk Hut and offers several pleasant Severe climbs.

Sgurr a' Choire Bhig (*peak of the little corrie*) (875m)
The north-east ridge of this fine little peak gives a superb hard scramble. It is more interesting than the north-east ridge of Gars-bheinn and is comparable in many ways with the magnificent Dubh Ridge on the opposite side of An Garbh-choire. Follow the approach route to Coire Beag and then trend right. The initial section of slabs can be climbed by a number of lines, and even when the ridge becomes more definite higher up there is much scope for variation. A prominent curving band of overhanging rock is situated to the right of the crest. Near the top a steeper section of rock is normally turned on the right.

ROCK CLIMBING
The north-west ridge of Sgurr a' Choire Bhig curves westwards as it drops to the col before Sgurr nan Eag. On the north side of this ridge there is a long rock face which can be reached by descending a rake rightwards from the col. Two gullies were ascended at an early date, but better lines still remain unclimbed.

13. AN GARBH-CHOIRE (the rough corrie)
SURROUNDING PEAKS

Sgurr a' Choire Bhig	875m	465 191
Sgurr nan Eag	924m	457 195
Caisteal a' Garbh-choire	829m	454 202
Sgurr Dubh an Da Bheinn	938m	455 204
Sgurr Dubh Mor	944m	457 205
Sgurr Dubh Beag	733m	465 204

This magnificent corrie is appropriately named. Above a height of about 500m its entire floor is filled by a jumbled mass of gigantic blocks and boulders, the negotiation of which requires some care and agility. Not only are there sizeable cavities between the blocks, but the blocks themselves consist largely of peridotite, the roughest rock in the Cuillin.

The corrie lies between the three most southerly peaks on the main ridge and a major side ridge which runs off eastwards to Sgurr Dubh Beag, known as the Dubh Ridge. Above the headwall of the corrie, sitting astride Bealach a' Garbh-choire, is Caisteal a' Garbh-choire. The distinctive outline of this squat rock tower can be recognised on the skyline from the landing place near the Coruisk Hut.

There are two approaches to the corrie from the Coruisk Hut. The more direct route is to follow the coastal path over the Allt a' Chaoich and then to ascend beside the next small stream (as for Coire Beag). The alternative is to follow the River Scavaig upstream to Loch Coruisk, go along the path on the south-west shore for rather more than one kilometre, and then turn up a wide depression on the left. Both routes lead to the broad expanse of the lower corrie floor, from where a westerly line leads to the upper corrie.

Bealach a' Garbh-choire, which connects with Coir' a' Ghrunnda, is the only easy pass from the corrie. The approach to it involves clambering over the massive blocks in the floor of the upper corrie (similar to the *clapier* of the Maritime Alps). The going is perhaps marginally easier towards the Sgurr Dubh side. At the top it is possible to pass either side of Caisteal a' Garbh-choire. The left-hand (south) side is straightforward, but the right-hand side involves crawling under a giant block.

Sgurr nan Eag (*peak of the notches*) (924m)
The north-north-west ridge can be gained from Bealach a' Garbh-choire, (see Coir' a' Ghrunnda). The col at the foot of the east ridge (see Coire nan Laogh) can also be gained from the floor of An Garbh-choire, although it is difficult to find a way which does not involve some Moderate slab climbing. The impressive north-eastern flank has no easy routes.

ROCK CLIMBING
There is an important crag on the north side of the east ridge, which can be reached from the col between Sgurr nan Eag and Sgurr a' Choire Bhig. It lies just west of the crag on Sgurr a' Choire Bhig, and is characterised by a deep cleft called *The Chasm*. This classic Very Difficult climb has four short pitches and is highly recommended. It finishes by emerging on the Coire nan Laogh side of the ridge. Snow may linger in The Chasm until well into the summer. It was partially filled with snow when Steeple and Barlow made the first ascent at Easter in 1915.

The Left Edge (E1, 5a) of The Chasm is an even finer, but much more serious route of three pitches. First climbed by Robin Smith in 1957, it remains a bold lead even with modern protection. Among the other routes on the crag is another Smith creation called *Ladders* (Very Severe).

Caisteal a' Garbh-choire (*castle of the rough corrie*) (829m)
For a general description of this feature, see Coire a' Ghrunnda.

ROCK CLIMBING
Steep routes of Very Difficult and above have been climbed on the face overlooking An Garbh-choire.

Sgurr Dubh an Da Bheinn (*black peak of the two ridges*) (938m)
The south ridge can be reached from Bealach a' Garbh-choire, (see Coire a' Ghrunnda).

It is becoming increasingly popular on the main ridge traverse to detour from the summit of Sgurr Dubh an Da Bheinn in order to bag Sgurr Dubh Mor (a Munro). When descending the east ridge of Sgurr Dubh an Da Bheinn it is better to follow the crest, sometimes on the right side, rather than a tempting scree path on the left (north) side. A height loss of some 52m leads to the col below the south-west spur of Sgurr Dubh Mor. This col can also be reached directly from An Garbh-choire by ascending an unpleasantly steep boulder field. An extremely loose gully which lies further right (east) is definitely not recommended.

Sgurr Dubh Mor (*big black peak*) (944m)
Sgurr Dubh Beag (*small black peak*) (733m)
Sgurr Dubh Mor is the highest of the Dubh summits. It is an impressive peak, situated some 250 metres off the main ridge to the east of Sgurr Dubh an Da Bheinn. From the col at the foot of the east ridge of Sgurr Dubh an Da Bheinn pass some pinnacles on the right, and then find a difficult scrambling route up the steep south-west spur. This was the route taken by Nicolson and MacIntyre on the first ascent of the peak in 1874. (They completed their outing by descending the unexplored northern flank in darkness.) The highest point is situated at the western extremity of the narrow, wedge-like summit ridge.

Sgurr Dubh Beag lies a further kilometre to the east, but is unlikely to be approached from the major summit. Instead it is commonly traversed during an ascent of the Dubh Ridge (see below).

The southern flanks of these two peaks are steep and craggy, but do not offer attractive routes.

ROCK CLIMBING
There can be few finer ways to the summit of any mountain in the British Isles than the ascent of Sgurr Dubh Mor by the so called *Dubh Ridge* from the shore of Loch Coruisk.

Virtually nothing but rock lies underfoot for two kilometres horizontally and 900m vertically. Difficulties need never exceed Moderate standard, although a short abseil is normally made on the descent from the summit of Sgurr Dubh Beag. It is an outstanding route because of the excellent quality of the rock and the superb situations. The low level of technical difficulty puts it within reach of experienced scramblers with climbing ambitions.

Two verses, penned by an early SMC member, capture the essence of the outing;

> "Said Maylard to Solly one day in Glen Brittle,
>   All serious climbing, I vote, is a bore;
> Just for once, I Dubh Beag you'll agree to do little,
>   And, as less we can't do, let's go straight to Dubh Mor.

> "So now when they seek but a day's relaxation,
>   With no thought in the world but of viewing the views,
> And regarding the mountains in mute adoration,
>   They call it not 'climbing', but 'doing the Dubhs'."

From the path on the south-west shore of Loch Coruisk, head up towards an obvious broad apron of slabs at the foot of the east ridge of Sgurr Dubh Beag. Ascend a grassy bay to the right of the lowest rocks. After a short distance, experienced climbers should be able to transfer to the slabs on the left. From a large

High above Loch Scavaig on the Dubh Ridge

ledge at 100m, head up right to join a continuation of the slabs. For the next 600m follow beautiful rough slabs set at the perfect angle for 'padding', with only minor steps of steeper rock, all the way to the summit of Sgurr Dubh Beag. At about 470m it is possible to escape down an easy grassy runnel on the left into An Garbh-choire.

Just past the summit, on the south-west ridge, there is a steep drop of 15m where an overhanging section is normally abseiled. It is possible to avoid this manoeuvre by returning down the crest for some distance and following grass and scree ledges on the south side, but the best line is not obvious.

It is a short distance then to the col at the foot of the east ridge of Sgurr Dubh Mor. If retreat is called for at this point, a tricky but feasible escape can be made northwards down steep scree and intervening slabs into Coir' a' Chaoruinn. The An Garbh-choire side of the col is not recommended.

A long section of easy walking leads pleasantly up the east ridge of Sgurr Dubh Mor, until steep rocks are encountered below the summit ridge. A way onto the ridge is normally found by ledges on the south flank. The highest point lies at the far western end.

After scrambling down the steep south-west spur, it is normal to continue onto Sgurr Dubh an Da Bheinn, although there is an easy descent into Coir' an Lochain on the right from the intervening col.

14. COIR' A' CHAORUINN (corrie of the rowan)
COIR' AN LOCHAIN (corrie of the lochan)

SURROUNDING PEAKS

Sgurr Dubh Beag	733m	465 204
Sgurr Dubh Mor	944m	457 205
Sgurr Dubh an Da Bheinn	938m	455 204
Sgurr Thearlaich	978m	451 208
Sgurr Coir' an Lochain	729m	454 214

These two north-east facing corries are separated by the broad north-east ridge of Sgurr Dubh Mor. They both overlook Coir'-uisg, but otherwise have remarkably contrasting characters. The more easterly of the two, Coir' a' Chaoruinn, is the first corrie encountered on the left at the head of Loch Coruisk. It is a long scoop-shaped corrie overlooked by the summit of Sgurr Dubh Beag. The floor of the corrie is at a more or less constant gradient for one kilometre, and only steepens significantly at the headwall. There are conspicuous slabs and waterslides at the entrance to the corrie, but higher up there is much scree. The col between Sgurr Dubh Beag and Sgurr Dubh Mor can be gained by scrambling leftwards at the head of the corrie. The main importance of the corrie, however, is that it provides a convenient approach route into neighbouring Coir' an Lochain, from where Bealach Coir'an Lochain (which connects with Coir' a' Ghrunnda) and Bealach Mhic Choinnich (which connects with Coire Lagan) can be reached.

About half way up Coir' a' Chaoruinn, a fairly obvious grassy rake slants rightwards onto the north-east shoulder of Sgurr Dubh Mor. Continue rightwards until a prominent stream is met which leads up to the superb lochan nestling in upper Coir' an Lochain - one of the most delightfully wild corries in the Cuillin. Despite being overlooked by a busy section of the main ridge that includes the Thearlaich-Dubh Gap, the corrie itself receives few visitors.

A direct line taken straight up the corrie behind the lochan leads over steep rough ground to Bealach Coir' an Lochain. The right-hand side of the corrie is formed by a ridge which runs north-eastwards from the northern end of Sgurr Thearlaich and ends in a spectacular little top called Sgurr Coir' an Lochain. To reach Bealach Mhic Choinnich, continue past the lochan and ascend sharply rightwards to gain an obvious low point on the ridge leading to Sgurr Coir' an Lochain. Turn left and follow the ridge south-westwards for a short distance until an obvious scree gully on the right can be ascended to Bealach Mhic Choinnich.

It is also possible to reach the col between Sgurr Dubh Mor and Sgurr Dubh an Da Bheinn by heading leftwards up scree from the back of the corrie.

Sgurr Dubh Beag (*little black peak*) (733m)
Sgurr Dubh Mor (*big black peak*) (944m)
Sgurr Dubh an Da Bheinn (*black peak of the two ridges*) (938m)

These peaks show a considerable amount of rock on their northern aspects, but no routes of distinction have been reported. The north-east ridge of Sgurr Dubh Mor looks an interesting outing, but is very rarely ascended.

Sgurr Thearlaich (*Charles' peak*) (978m)
There are no easy ways to the summit of this peak.

ROCK CLIMBING
The south-east ridge can be ascended from Bealach Coir' an Lochain, but this entails a crossing of the Thearlaich-Dubh Gap, (see Coir' a' Ghrunnda). An intriguing chimney climb of Difficult standard (*Aladdin's Route*) also leads directly into the gap from Coir' an Lochain.

The north-east ridge provides a less problematic route. Start from the low point on the Sgurr Coir' an Lochain ridge and ascend the ridge (as for Bealach Mhic Choinnich), and then instead of taking the scree gully on the right continue along the crest by Moderate slabby rocks. These abut against the main ridge from where the tricky north ridge can then be followed to the summit, (see Coire Lagan).

Sgurr Coir' an Lochain (*peak of the corrie of the lochan*) (729m)
This superb little top is reminiscent of Sgurr na h-Uamha which overlooks Harta Corrie. It has steep rock on three sides and projects as a nose above Coir'-uisg. It was possibly the last British mountain peak to be climbed when Collie and company ascended it from the north in 1896. All ways up it involve some climbing.

ROCK CLIMBING
The south ridge gives the most straightforward ascent route. Start from the col on the ridge leading north-eastwards from Sgurr Thearlaich. The first part of the ridge is not well defined but it soon narrows, and a fairly level section leads to minor top of 759m. Some distance after this a prominent gap cuts across the ridge. The only difficulty on the route is the descent into this gap, which involves a move or two of Difficult standard. Gullies on either side of the gap give more direct but less attractive routes of similar standard. A short scramble then leads up to the small rocky summit, from where there are wonderful views of the Coruisk basin.

More demanding routes of various grades have been made on the steep overlapping slabs and walls of the north and north-east faces. They have a mountaineering atmosphere and require skilful route-finding. No routes have been reported on the almost vertical west face. Climbers wishing to experience the sensation of pioneering on a secluded crag should not find the approach from Glen Brittle (via Bealach Coire na Banachdich) too onerous.

15. COIREACHAN RUADHA (*ruddy corries*)

SURROUNDING PEAKS

Sgurr Coir' an Lochain	729m	454 214
Sgurr Mhic Choinnich	948m	450 210
An Stac	954m	445 215
Inaccessible Pinnacle	986m	444 215
Sgurr Dearg	978m	444 216
Sgurr na Banachdich	965m	440 224
Sgurr Thormaid	926m	441 226
Sgurr a' Ghreadaidh	973m	445 231

Coireachan Ruadha is the name given to a pair of high corries lying on the north-east side of the main ridge, and partially separated by the small spur of Sron Bhuidhe. They extend from Sgurr Coir' an Lochain in the south to the south-east ridge of Sgurr a' Ghreadaidh in the north, and lie on the opposite side of the main ridge from two very popular corries, Coire Lagan and Coire na Banachdich.

The corries are noteworthy for two reasons. Firstly, they give access to one of the easiest crossing points on the main ridge between Coruisk and Glen Brittle (Bealach Coire na Banachdich), and secondly they offer some good climbing on a number of major crags. They are probably entered more frequently from above by parties crossing the main ridge from Glen Brittle, rather than from below by parties approaching via the head of Loch Coruisk.

When approaching from Coruisk, continue past the head of Loch Coruisk for some two kilometres, and then trend left up rough but otherwise straightforward ground. The main ridge can be gained without great difficulty at three main cols. Bealach Mhic Choinnich lies in the most southerly corner of the corries and is normally approached via neighbouring Coir' an Lochain (qv), although it can be reached by bearing left shortly after passing below Sgurr Coir' an Lochain.

Bealach Coire na Banachdich lies in the centre of Coireachan Ruadha, just south of Sron Bhuidhe. To reach it, head south-west and then west up the line of a stream, mainly on tediously loose scree, and finish up a loose gully bounded by steep rock walls. This is one of the most popular crossing points from Glen Brittle. (See Coire na Banachdich.)

Bealach Thormaid is situated in the northern corner of Coireachan Ruadha between Sgurr na Banachdich and Sgurr Thormaid. It is reached by ascending very unstable scree in a westerly direction. There is no easy descent on the other side. (See Coire a' Ghreadaidh.)

Sgurr Mhic Choinnich (*Mackenzie's Peak*) (948m)
The easiest way to the summit of this fine mountain from Coireachan Ruadha starts from the foot of the gully leading to Bealach Mhic Choinnich. Follow a rightward slanting rake across the east face to a nick on the north-west ridge. There are no recommendable ways to the start of north-west ridge from this side.

Looking across Loch Coruisk to the slabs of Sgurr Dubh Beag

ROCK CLIMBING

Some fine climbs are to be found on the rather intimidating crags of the north-east face. They generally need a few days of good weather to dry out. The usual approach from Glen Brittle is to ascend to the lowest point on the Coire Lagan skyline and then descend the frightening *Rotten Gully*. The approach from the Coruisk side is longer but more pleasant. Among the many classic climbs there are *King Cobra* (Hard Very Severe), *Dawn Grooves* (Very Severe) and *Fluted Buttress* (Hard Severe).

There are also numerous climbs on a large crag known as Bealach Buttress, which lies on the north side of Rotten Gully at a lower level than the main crag.

An Stac (*the stack*)   (954m)
Inaccessible Pinnacle   (986m)
Sgurr Dearg (*red peak*) (978m)

The Coireachan Ruadha faces of these peaks are very steep but unattractive. The only noteworthy route is *O'Brien and Julian's Climb* (Very Difficult) on Sgurr Dearg.

Sgurr na Banachdich (965m)
The south ridge can be gained from Bealach Coire na Banachdich (see Coire Banachdich), but a more interesting approach is to ascend the spur of Sron Bhuidhe. The north ridge can be reached from Bealach Thormaid. (See Coire a' Ghreadaidh.)

ROCK CLIMBING
Immediately north of Bealach Coire na Banachdich are two buttresses known as *The Twins*. The *South Twin* (Difficult) is separated from the *North Twin* (Severe) by a dark gully. Further north, *Midget Ridge* lies below the South Top, whilst *Clouded Buttress* (Severe) lies below the main summit.

Sgurr Thormaid (*Norman's Peak*) (926m)
The south-west ridge can be gained from Bealach Thormaid. (See Coire a' Ghreadaidh.)

ROCK CLIMBING
A good Hard Very Severe climb (*Peridot*) lies on South Buttress which overlooks the Coruisk side of Bealach Thormaid.

Sgurr a' Ghreadaidh (*peak of torment*) (973m)
The easiest way to the summit of this mountain from Coireachan Ruadha is to traverse Sgurr Thormaid from Bealach Thormaid, (see Coire a' Ghreadaidh).

ROCK CLIMBING
The south face is cleft by *Terrace Gully* (Very Difficult), a good climb best left for fine weather, which leads to a large grassy terrace at 700m. Further right lies the *South-East Ridge* (Difficult), a very long climb pioneered by Norman Collie which finishes on the south top.

16. COIR' AN UAIGNEIS (*corrie of solitude*)
GLAC MHOR   (*great hollow*)

SURROUNDING PEAKS

Sgurr a' Ghreadaidh	973m	445 231
Sgurr a' Mhadaidh	918m	447 235
Bidein Druim nan Ramh	869m	456 239

Coir' an Uaigneis is a fine hanging corrie situated to the south-east of Sgurr a' Ghreadaidh and Sgurr a' Mhadaidh. It is guarded by crags and dominates the head of Coir'-uisg. Glac Mhor, a prominent scoop which lies immediately to the east, is more readily accessible.

The main ridge can be reached without difficulty by ascending Glac Mhor to Bealach na Glaic Moire. Follow the most northerly stream at the head of Coir'-uisg that bends north-westwards in its upper section. Stay on the left-hand side of a rocky rib, and pass the spring that issues from the scree some 100m below the col. The other side of the col is less straightforward. (See Coir' a' Mhadaidh.)

It is also possible to reach An Dorus (see Coire a' Ghreadaidh) by slanting west-north-west into Coir' an Uaigneis from part way up Glac Mhor.

Sgurr a' Ghreadaidh (*peak of torment*) (973m)
The north-east ridge can be ascended from An Dorus, but it is rarely tackled from

Loch Coruisk

the Coruisk side because of the protracted approach. The impressive east face is for climbers only.

Sgurr a' Mhadaidh (*peak of the fox*) (918m) The east ridge from Bealach na Glaic Moire gives the most obvious line of ascent, (see Coir' a' Mhadaidh). From Coir' an Uaigneis an easy leftward rising rake, which starts at the foot of a gully between the second and third tops, leads to the col between the third top and the main summit.

ROCK CLIMBING
A number of routes have been made on *Coruisk Buttress* which lies directly below Coir' an Uaigneis. There are also some climbs on the rocks immediately below the mountain's various tops.

Bidein Druim nan Ramh (*peak of the ridge of the oars*) (869m)
See Coir' a' Tairneilear.

The Druim Pinnacle

17. COIR'-UISG (*water corrie*)

BORDERING PEAK

Druim nan Ramh   500m   480 217

Only on its north-eastern side is magnificent Coir'-uisg bounded by a ridge, the Druim nan Ramh, rather than by a higher corrie.

Druim nan Ramh (*ridge of the oars*) (500m)
The ascent of this ridge is a splendid excursion, giving superb views of the whole Cuillin range. The 300m high south-western flank is extremely rocky for much of its length and offers no easy lines for the walker. To reach the foot of the ridge, follow the east bank of Loch Coruisk from its outflow for barely one kilometre, and cross the Allt a' Choire Riabhaich. A Difficult rock band at the south-eastern end of the ridge can be avoided by ascending a gully on the north-east (right) side. Thereafter, follow the broad ridge over the summit of Druim nan Ramh and continue easily for some distance towards the central peak of Bidein Druim nan Ramh. This is the longest, straightest and easiest section of ridge in the Cuillin.

The ridge becomes trickier in its upper section, and there is a gap just before The Druim Pinnacle (752m). Further on it is usual to traverse ledges leftwards across the south-west face of the central peak of Bidein Druim nan Ramh, in order to reach the col between it and the west peak at the Bridge Rock. Since the short ascent to the central peak involves Moderate climbing, walkers should head west from this col to Bealach na Glaic Moire. (See Coir' a' Tairneilear.)

ROCK CLIMBING

There are some pleasant climbs, mainly about Severe standard, on the south-west flank of Druim nan Ramh on both the *Coruisk Slabs* (Grid Reference 485 209) and *JMCS Buttress* (Grid Reference 479 213).

18. COIRE RIABHACH *(grey corrie)*

SURROUNDING PEAKS

Druim nan Ramh	500m	480 217
Druim Hain	347m	493 226
Sgurr Hain	420m	503 209
Sgurr na Stri	494m	499 193

Coire Riabhach is enclosed by a sprawling extension of the Druim nan Ramh ridge which finally peters out at the shapely peak of Sgurr na Stri overlooking Loch Scavaig. The corrie is used as a thoroughfare between Sligachan and Coruisk, (see p. 166), and also offers the most convenient way back to Coruisk from the northern end of the main ridge. The head of the corrie can be gained from Harta Corrie by crossing a broad col at 270m just to the west of a hillock called Meallan Dearg.

Druim Hain (347m)
Sgurr Hain (420m)
The north-eastern side of Coire Riabhach is bounded by a broad, lochan-peppered ridge called Druim Hain, which at its south-eastern end links with the minor peak of Sgurr Hain. The col between these two high points is crossed by the path from Sligachan to Coruisk, from which both can conveniently be ascended.

Sgurr na Stri *(peak of strife)* (494m)
This splendid little hill is the culmination of a broad ridge which extends south-south-westwards from Sgurr Hain. It rises directly from Loch Scavaig and thereby blocks easy access to Coruisk from the east. Although it has a rather indefinite summit, it is well worth ascending for the breathtaking views it gives of the whole Cuillin range. The north ridge gives the easiest ascent route and is merely a walk. A prominent ramp on the north-west flank makes a good scramble. The infamous Bad Step lies below the west face near sea-level, (see p. 167). The east face is rugged but has no notable climbing.

ROCK CLIMBING

There are some pleasant climbs on the superb slabby rock of the west face, which can if desired be started directly from a boat.

THE MAIN RIDGE TRAVERSE

The traverse of the Cuillin main ridge is the finest mountain excursion in the British Isles. From first to last peak is some eleven kilometres, and at no point in that distance does the ridge fall below 750m. However, neither the length nor the altitude of the ridge are exceptional; rather it is the narrowness of the crest, the difficulty of the climbing, the roughness of the rock and the spectacular nature of the bordering corries, that are unmatched by any other mountain group in the country.

The traverse involves sustained scrambling, with several sections also demanding some competence in rock climbing (up to Very Difficult standard). To complete the ridge in a day, starting and finishing at sea level, necessitates a good level of fitness. It is important to carry an adequate supply of water. Two litres is perhaps a reasonable amount on a warm day. In early summer this can sometimes be topped up from snow patches on the northern half of the ridge. Given settled weather, some mountaineers prefer to savour the experience by spending two days on the outing with a planned bivouac.

If the true line on the crest of the ridge is followed, the main technical difficulties when traversing from the south are;

1. The Thearlaich-Dubh gap   (See p. 214)
2. The descent from Sgurr Thearlaich   (See p. 208)
3. The ascent of SgurrMhic Choinnich   (See p. 207)
4. The traverse of theInaccessiblePinnacle   (See p. 205)
5. The tops of Sgurr a' Mhadaidh   (See p. 194)
6. The traverse of Bidein Druim nan Ramh   (See p. 192)
7. The ascent of the Basteir Tooth   (See p. 176)
8. The west ridge of Sgurr nan Gillean   (See p. 182)

The traverse was first completed in a day by L C Shadbolt and A C McLaren in 1911. Some details of times taken on the traverse by various parties (prior to 1952) are tabulated in Ben Humble's *The Cuillin of Skye*, to which the reader is referred.

It is usual to detour from the main ridge to ascend Sgurr Alasdair, and it is becoming increasingly common to include Sgurr Dubh Mor as well. An average time for the traverse from first to last peak is about 12-14 hours. Fell runners capable of leading Hard Very Severe should be able to solo the climbing sections and hence reduce this time dramatically. The present record of 3hrs 49min 30sec (which includes both Sgurr Alasdair and Sgurr Dubh Mor) was set by Del Davies of Eryri Harriers on 12th August 1986. His parter, Paul Stott, took only one minute longer after following a different line on Am Basteir. The record holder believes that someone with a good knowledge of the ridge should be able to better his time by some twenty minutes.

PEAKS AND PASSES
The peaks and passes of the Cuillin main ridge are represented by the two profiles shown on pp. 236-7. Both profiles depict the ridge as seen from its eastern side (i.e. from Druim nan Ramh). The upper diagram shows the southern half of the ridge, and the lower diagram shows the northern half. The names of the corries on the eastern side of the ridge are given on the border below the profile, whilst those of the western (or 'outer') corries are given on the border above the profile.

THE GREATER CUILLIN TRAVERSE
The extension of the main ridge traverse to include the Cuillin Outliers of Clach Glas and Bla Bheinn is a very demanding outing, principally because of the great height that must be lost and regained between the two groups of peaks. It was first achieved inside a day by I G Charleson and W E Forde in 1939. An average time for a fit party (first to last peak) is about 20 hours, though it has been done inside twelve hours.

    An obvious remaining challenge is to extend the Greater Traverse to include the Red Hills bordering Glen Sligachan (i.e. starting and finishing at the Sligachan Inn - all within 24 hours).

WINTER IN THE CUILLIN
The traverse of the main ridge in winter is a magnificent mountaineering expedition (Grade IV), and is certainly the finest winter outing in these islands. It was first achieved by T W Patey, B Robertson, H MacInnes and D Crabb over two days in 1965. The Greater Traverse was done by J G McKeever and N Robinson in April 1988.

    Good conditions for winter climbing in the Cuillin probably occur more frequently than is generally supposed. Although good snow cover is usually short-lived, ice climbing may be possible at any time from November through until May. The quality and quantity of snow and ice on the ridge cannot always be judged properly from sea level, and those prepared to venture out on spec may be well rewarded.

    There has been a gradual increase in winter climbing activity in the Cuillin over more recent years due in part to overcrowding in the classic mainland areas.

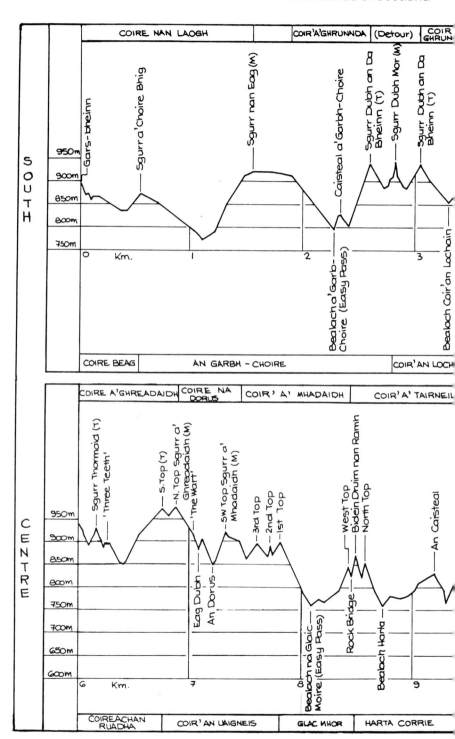

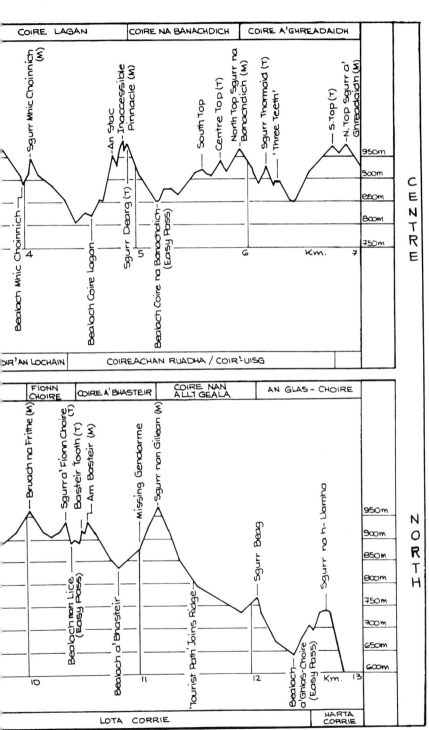

CHAPTER 13

DUIRINISH, WATERNISH

AND CENTRAL SKYE

The area is bounded by Glen Drynoch in the south and by the A850 road from Portree to Skeabost in the north.

MAPS : Ordnance Survey 1:50,000 Sheets 23 and 32

PRINCIPAL HILLS

EASTERN GROUP

Ben Lee	445m	502 335
Ben Tianavaig	413m	511 409

WESTERN GROUP

Healabhal Bheag	488m	225 422
Healabhal Mhor	469m	219 445

GENERAL DESCRIPTION

The main road from Broadford divides in two at Sligachan, from where the A850 continues north to Portree, and the A863 goes north-west past Loch Bracadale to Dunvegan. Two ragged promontories extend from Dunvegan; the northern one is known as Waternish and the western one as Duirinish. The latter is the most attractive part of the area for the hillwalker and climber. Central Skye, which lies between the A850 and A863 roads, forms a major part of the area, but is of no great hillwalking interest being mainly a featureless tract of undulating moorland and rounded hills.

Access to Duirinish is by the B884 road that starts just south of Dunvegan, and leads over into secluded Glen Dale. From there the road continues west and then divides in three. One road runs south to Ramasaig, from where a path continues south-eastwards for some thirteen kilometres to Idrigill Point. The second road turns northwards and serves the community of Milovaig, which overlooks Loch Pooltiel, and the third road continues west to Waterstein and ends at the clifftop overlooking the lighthouse at Neist (*promontory*) - the most westerly point on Skye.

The whole of the area is built from a thick succession of basalt lavas which

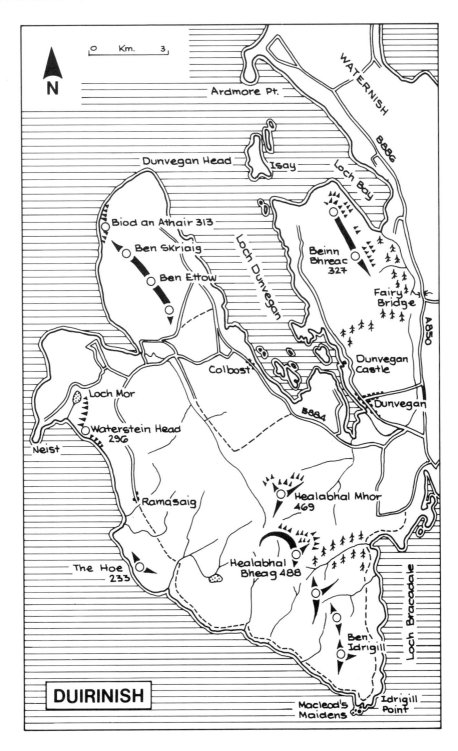

DUIRINISH

form a distinctive stepped landscape. The underlying sedimentary rocks are exposed only in a few places on the coast. The highest hills, Macleod's Tables, lie in Duirinish and are notable for their flat tops. Although several other hills in the southern and eastern parts of the area also exceed 400m, none of them has a shapely summit, with the exception of Ben Tianavaig - the area's easternmost hill - which overlooks the Sound of Raasay.

The coastline of Duirinish compensates to a certain extent for the relatively tame relief of the hills. In the north, near Dunvegan Head, the sea-cliffs are over 300m high. They rise to almost the same height at Waterstein Head just south of Waterstein. Further south, along the remote section of coast to the south of Ramasaig, the cliffs are peppered with dramatic sea caves, arches and geos (steep sided inlets). The basalt on the whole is appallingly loose, and only in the vicinity of Neist, where two dolerite sills occur in the sedimentary rocks underlying the basalt, is there any worthwhile rock climbing.

So called 'coral sand' is an unusual feature on the eastern shore of Loch Dunvegan just north of Claigan. The sand is formed not from coral, but from an encrusting seaweed that grows just offshore. Broken fragments of it get washed up by wave action.

Though the area is of fairly limited mountaineering interest, it has a lot to offer the ordinary walker and visitor. The remains of duns, brochs and souterrains can be found at several localities, though better preserved examples occur on other islands. Dunvegan Castle is not particularly attractive architecturally, much of the present edifice having been added in the 19th century, but it has strong historical associations and is said to be one of the oldest inhabited buildings in Scotland. For several hundred years it has been the seat of the MacLeods. It is open to the public, as are its gardens.

Waternish has no climbing, but is renowned for its bloody history, in particular the atrocity perpetrated there by the MacDonalds of Uist in 1578. A raiding party landed by boat at Ardmore Bay under cover of mist, and then barred and set fire to the church at Trumpan whilst the local inhabitants were worshipping inside. All perished except for one woman who escaped by a window. This is believed to have been an act of revenge for a similar massacre in a cave on Eigg the previous year.

The Braes, which is situated on the east coast opposite the southern tip of Raasay, is famous as the locality where the 'Battle of the Braes' took place in 1882. This was the last battle fought on British soil. It involved local crofters, armed with sticks and stones, and fifty policemen who had been sent from Glasgow to quell a dispute about grazing rights. The incident aroused such strong feelings among the people of Skye that Gladstone eventually had to set up a Royal Commission to investigate the grievances of crofters.

Many craft workshops and several delightful little restaurants have become established in the area in recent years. Portree is a pleasant little town with a fine natural harbour. Originally called Kiltaraglen, it was renamed Port an Righ (*the king's harbour*) after a visit by James V in 1540. It is the principal town of the island.

Neist Point; An t-Aigeach and the lighthouse

THE HILLS
EASTERN GROUP
Ben Lee (445m)
This hill lies on the north side of Loch Sligachan and offers good views of the Cuillin and Red Hills. It can be ascended without difficulty by following the east bank of the Eas Ruadh from the head of Loch Sligachan, or by traversing Meall Odhar Mor from the A850 road two kilometres north of the Sligachan Hotel.

Ben Tianavaig (413m)
The south ridge of this little hill makes a surprisingly enjoyable outing. It is best approached from Camastianavaig which lies just off the road to The Braes. An escarpment is situated on the eastern side of the ridge, and there are fine views of Portree and Raasay from the summit trig point.

WESTERN GROUP - DUIRINISH
Macleod's Tables
These distinctive flat topped hills can be seen clearly from the road near Dunvegan. Their likeness to great natural altars supports the suggestion that their names may be derived from *helgi fjall* meaning *holy fell*. Both hills can be ascended without undue difficulty by doing the round of Glen Osdale.

Healabhal Bheag (possibly *lesser holy fell*) (488m)
This is the higher and more southerly of the two Tables. It probably acquired its *beag*
tag because it has the smaller summit plateau. It is marginally less accessible than
its partner, but offers the finer view. The east-north-east ridge can be ascended from
Orbost, or, alternatively, the southern flank can be approached by walking through
the forestry plantation in Glen Bharcasaig.

Healabhal Mhor (possibly *greater holy fell)* (469m)
The easiest ascent route is the broad east-north-east shoulder from Osdale, but a
more interesting route is the north-west flank which is best approached by following
a path from Skinidin and traversing Beinn Chreagach.

PATHS AND WALKS
The most spectacular walking route in the area lies in the southern part of Duirinish.
It is some 20 kilometres long and follows the coastal path from Ramasaig to Orbost
via Idrigill Point. The outing would be much more popular were it not for the
difficulty of organising transport at both ends.

        Some two kilometres past Ramasaig the path drops down to Lorgill which
lies due east of The Hoe (233m). From there to Loch Bharcasaig by Orbost the
coastline is wild and fascinating. Innumerable caves, arches, stacks, waterfalls and
geos have been fashioned in the basalt cliffs. Near Idrigill Point are three sea-stacks
called Macleod's Maidens. The largest is referred to as the mother, and the lesser
two as her daughters.

ROCK CLIMBING
The only rock climbing in the area is found in Duirinish. No routes of quality have
so far been found on the basalt lavas, although the largest of Macleod's Maidens has
yielded a 65m Severe (*The Old Lady*). It is accessible only at low tide, and is
approached by abseiling from the nearby headland. The spectacular arete at
Waterstein Head has also been climbed (260m, Severe), but the state of the rock has
not encouraged repeat ascents.

        The best climbing is concentrated on the sea-cliffs near Waterstein. This is
a delightful place just to visit, and often has better weather than the mountainous
parts of the island. The climbs, which lie on two parallel sills of dolerite, are
approached from a small car park at the road end overlooking Neist. Situated well
above the sea, one kilometre north of the car park, there is a 30m pinnacle known
as *The Green Lady*. This offers a pleasant route of Hard Severe standard, although
descending from the summit presents a problem.

        The path leading down to the lighthouse at Neist skirts around a small hill
known as An t-Aigeach (*the stallion*), on the north-west side of which lies an
impressive sea-cliff. *Supercharger* (115m, E2) ascends this cliff at its highest point.
The striking arête immediately left of Supercharger has given the hardest climbing
on Skye so far (*Death Pirate*, E6, 6b).

        Several small bays nearby have yielded numerous shorter routes of various
grades (Hard Severe to E4).

CHAPTER 14

TROTTERNISH

Trotternish is the bulbous finger of Skye that lies north of the Portree to Skeabost road. It includes the most northerly point of the island.

MAPS : Ordnance Survey 1:50,000 Sheet 23

PRINCIPAL HILLS

Meall na Suiramach	543m	446 695
Bioda Buidhe	466m	439 664
Beinn Edra	611m	455 626
Sgurr a' Mhadaidh Ruaidh	587m	473 584
Baca Ruadh	637m	474 575
Hartaval	668m	480 551
The Storr	719m	495 540
Ben Dearg	552m	478 504

GENERAL DESCRIPTION

Were it not in competition with The Cuillin and also situated at the northernmost end of the island, Trotternish would undoubtedly be much more popular with hillwalkers, for it harbours some wonderful scenery including the longest continuous ridge on Skye. The area has many hidden delights which can only be uncovered by numerous visits. The Trotternish Ridge forms the 'backbone' of the area and extends for some 30 kilometres from Sgurr Mor in the north to Pein a' Chleibh in the south.

A road starting from Portree encircles the peninsula. It rises to 200m at its highest point to the east of The Storr, but for much of its length it remains at a much lower level and rarely strays far from sea. Only in one place, towards the northern end of the peninsula, does a subsidiary road cross the Trotternish Ridge. It links Brogaig near Staffin in the east with Uig in the west.

A handful of other roads extend from the main loop road, but few penetrate for any distance into the interior of the area. The track that runs west from Lealt on the eastern side of the peninsula is the most important for hillwalkers. It leads to the former diatomite workings at Loch Cuithir about one kilometre north of the distinctive peak of Sgurr a' Mhadaidh Ruaidh. The track is now potholed, though with care it can still be negotiated by car. It gives access to the mid-point of the Trotternish Ridge.

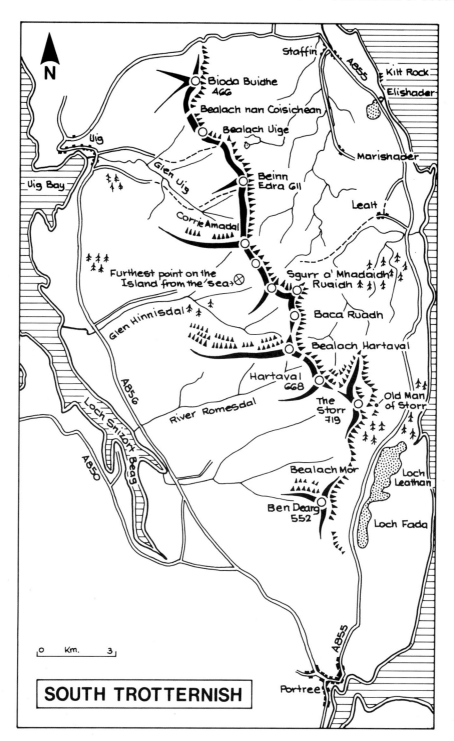

SOUTH TROTTERNISH

Diatomite deposits have been found at several localities in the area, though they are no longer economical to extract. The material is formed from the siliceous remains of microscopic aquatic organisms called diatoms, which accumulated during a warm spell in early post-glacial times. Being inert and highly absorbent, diatomite can be used, for example, in the production of dynamite.

The high ground of the area consists of a thick succession of basalt lavas dipping gently to the west. This accounts for the gentle slopes on the western side of the Trotternish Ridge. The steep escarpment on the eastern side of the ridge, however, has been accentuated by gigantic rotational landslips. Since glacial times numerous vast masses of lava have slipped in an easterly direction over the underlying sedimentary rocks. The most spectacular examples of landslips can be seen at the Quiraing, which lies just north of the Staffin to Uig road. At least five successive landslipped masses can be distinguished in the two kilometres or so between the edge of the present escarpment east of Meall na Suiramach and the sea.

Below The Storr, further south, a similar landslipped area has been made famous by one particularly dramatic pinnacle - the Old Man of Storr. The water dammed in nearby Storr Lochs is fed by pipes to a power station on the beach some 130m below. Steps lead down to the shore where ammonite fossils can be found.

There are further good exposures of the Jurassic rocks underlying the lavas around the coast. Intruded into these shales, sandstones and limestones are some spectacular dolerite and picrite sills. One of the most obvious of these forms the Kilt Rock on the coast south-east of Staffin. The well developed columnar jointing in the sill there is reminiscent of the pleats in a kilt. It formed when the sill contracted as it cooled.

The road that loops round the northern end of the Trotternish peninsula passes close to the ruins of Duntulm Castle. Some three kilometres further north lies beautiful Rubha Hunish, the most northerly point of the island. The western side of the peninsula is less interesting, although Uig is an important ferry port for the Outer Isles.

This is the richest region of Skye for arctic and alpine plants.

THE TROTTERNISH RIDGE

There are more than a dozen separate summits spread out along the 30 kilometres length of the Trotternish Ridge. To traverse them all in one outing is a demanding undertaking, even though for much of the way the terrain underfoot consists of close-cropped greensward which is delightfully easy to walk on. The section south of the Staffin to Uig road is fairly committing, and leaving the ridge before the end normally entails a long walk (either east or west) to the coastal road, as well as difficulties with transport.

It is refreshing to note that the Trotternish Ridge does not receive much traffic, unlike many prominent ridges on the mainland, and consequently shows few signs of wear along its crest. The ridge can conveniently be broken down into three more manageable sections if desired. The first section lies north of the Staffin

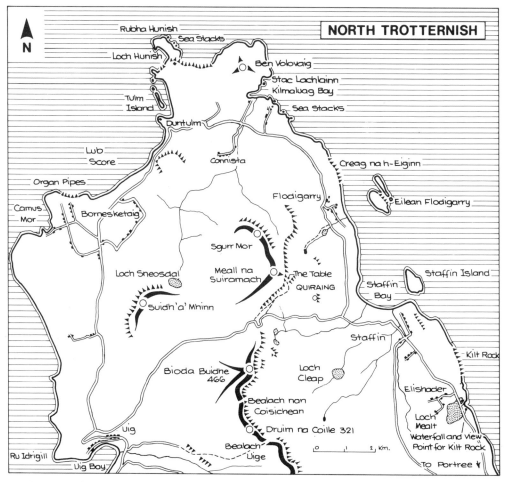

to Uig road. The second section lies south of the same road and extends as far as Bealach na Leacaich, from where an eastward descent leads to Loch Cuithir and the track to Lealt. The third section lies south of Bealach na Leacaich and finishes either near Borve or two kilometres north of Portree on the A855.

Ten relatively easy passes across the ridge are marked as bealachs on the 1:50,000 map.

NORTHERN SECTION

Meall na Suiramach (543m)

This hill is the highest summit lying north of the Staffin to Uig road. It appears rounded and uninteresting from the west, but on its eastern side are numerous major landslips. The normal route to the summit starts from the highest point on the aforementioned road. Ignore a path leading north-eastwards to the Quiraing, and instead head due north up the grassy hillside. Eventually trend north-eastwards to the extensive summit plateau. From the edge of the escarpment, to the east of the summit, there are superb views looking down on the amazing Quiraing. This extraordinary natural fortress was formed where a huge mass of rock slipped a short distance from the main escarpment. Behind the turreted outer wall of the Quiraing lies a remarkably flat, green area known as The Table. This feature is completely hidden from below, but a prominent pinnacle known as The Needle points the way to it, (see Paths and Walks).

The mountain can also be approached from the north starting from Connista near Kilmaluag. Ascend the steep north-western flank of Sgurr Mor (big peak), and continue more easily along the plateau to the main summit. This route is frequently used by parties traversing the full length of the Trotternish ridge in a single outing.

CENTRAL SECTION
Bioda Buidhe (*yellow top*) (466m)
Beinn Edra (611m)
There are no special difficulties on this part of the ridge, although there is quite a steep descent southwards from Bioda Buidhe. Two separate paths originating from Glen Uig in the west lead onto the crest of the escarpment at opposite ends of Beinn Edra. This fine summit is the highest point on the central section of ridge.

The crest narrows slightly for the next two kilometres southwards to Groba nan Each, from where a broad side ridge runs westwards to Ben Brogaskil. However, the main spine continues southwards over Flasvein to Bealach na Leacaich. From there it is a fairly straightforward matter to pick an easterly route down to Loch Cuithir and so gain the track to Lealt. (One kilometre west of Bealach na Leacaich lies the furthest point on Skye from the sea.)

SOUTHERN SECTION
Sgurr a' Mhadaidh Ruaidh (*peak of the red fox*) (587m)
Baca Ruadh (637m)
Hartaval (668m)
The Storr (719m)
Ben Dearg (*red mountain*) (552m)
This is possibly the most spectacular section of the Trotternish Ridge and includes the highest summit on the peninsula - The Storr. When approaching by the road from Lealt to Loch Cuithir, the projecting bulk of Sgurr a' Mhadaidh Ruaidh looks particularly impressive. However, the large buttresses of rotten rock on its north-west face are best avoided. The steep, grassy north-east flank offers a more attractive route. Otherwise the summit can be gained by following the main ridge from Bealach na Leacaich or from an unnamed col to the west of Sgurr a' Mhadaidh Ruaidh.

The traverse of Baca Ruadh is without difficulty, though the descent to Bealach Hartaval is over broken rocks. The traverse of Hartaval then intervenes before the start of the north-west flank of The Storr is reached. Some 230m of ascent leads to the summit, where on a good day there are magnificent views of the whole island. The Old Man of Storr can be seen below, as well as countless mainland peaks and The Long Isle.

The Old Man of Storr, with the Red Cuillin beyond

At this point the road is less than two kilometres away to the east. This allows The Storr to be ascended independently, either from the south by steep grass and scree at the head of Coire Faoin, or from the north-east up Coire Scamadal. The road remains tantalisingly close on the next few kilometres of ridge leading to the final major summit, Ben Dearg. This is ascended by a steep scree slope. A further four kilometres of walking, nearly all in descent, complete the ridge.

PATHS AND WALKS

There is any amount of walking in Trotternish. In addition to the long ridge traverse just described, two routes in particular are very popular. The first ascends from the road just north of Loch Leathan through a forest plantation to visit the extraordinary group of tottering pinnacles on the landslipped area below The Storr. The section of path through the forest can become a quagmire in wet weather, in which case it may be closed. The main attraction is the Old Man of Storr, although the tumultuous landscape in the vicinity of this pinnacle is also fascinating to explore. Ancient stone circles can be seen a little to the south.

The second outing starts from near the high point on the Staffin to Uig road and ventures into the Quiraing - one of the most intriguing of Skye's many scenic splendours. Leave the road not far from a hairpin bend and follow a path that leads horizontally north-eastwards. (A slightly more direct route can be taken by starting lower down the road to the east.)

A broken escarpment develops on the left-hand side of the path and a landslipped mass, Cnoc a' Mheirlich (hillock of the robber) can be seen clearly on the right. The path undulates slightly and after a further kilometre, a prominent pinnacle called *The Needle* can be seen high up to the left. (The obvious landslipped mass on the right at this point is known as *The Prison*.) Head up steeply towards The Needle and pass it on the left. Continue upwards through a breach in the wall of the Quiraing, and eventually find a way up onto an extraordinary flat green surface known as *The Table*. There is no easy way onto the summit plateau of Meall na Suiramach from the Quiraing, so return by the same route.

A delighful circuit can be made by heading north from below The Needle for about one and a half kilometres. On the way countless rabbits can be seen scampering around in the grassy hollows below the main escarpment. A gently rising path eventually leads onto the crest of the ridge on the left. Follow the rim of the escarpment southwards with superb views of the Quiraing and Staffin Bay below on the left. Then descend south-westwards back to the road.

An alternative approach to the northern end of the Quiraing starts half a kilometre south of Flodigarry and follows a track on the north side of Loch Langaig to Loch Hasco.

ROCK CLIMBING

Though some of the basalt cliffs on the eastern side of the Trotternish Ridge rise to an impressive height, especially below The Storr, they have yielded few worthwhile climbs. Three routes have been recorded on the Old Man of Storr (Hard Very Severe

The Kilt Rock

and above), and another on The Needle at the Quiraing, but all of them are on unreliable rock.

By far the best climbing in the area is to be found on the much sounder sills of dolerite which are exposed at various localities around the coast. There has been considerable activity in recent years on the eastern side of the peninsula along a one and a half kilometre section of coast from just north of Loch Mealt to the slipway at Staffin. This includes the well known scenic feature called Kilt Rock.

A number of routes of Severe and Very Severe standard have been done on the walls of the descent gully by Kilt Rock, including *Clandestine* (38m, Hard Severe) and *Staffin Special* (42m, Very Severe). However, the majority of routes on the more exposed faces and buttresses are of E1 and above. Many of the climbs follow steep crack lines, and will appeal particularly to hand-jamming specialists. The routes on Kilt Rock itself are generally approached by abseil and require a 50m rope. They include *Edge of Beyond* (45m, E2) and *Grey Panther* (45m, E1).

Some distance north of Kilt Rock there is a slender column of rock close to the main cliff called *The Chimney Stack*. This has been climbed by two E5 lines (*Shear Sear*, and *Over the Rainbow*) on the south and seaward faces respectively.

Many other climbs can be found hereabouts. For example, more than a dozen routes (mainly HVS - E3) have been done on a buttress set back from the sea just over a kilometre south-east of the slipway at Staffin (Grid Reference 502 672). The approaches to the foot of the routes are less intimidating than at Kilt Rock, though the climbing is of similar excellent quality.

Three sea-stacks (30m high, Severe to E1) have been climbed at the northern tip of Trotternish on the eastern side of Rubha Hunish. Highly skilled antics with a grappling iron were needed to reach the two southernmost stacks on the first ascents.

Many other climbing possibilities exist around the coast, and since the peninsula has drier weather than the Cuillin it is likely to become increasingly popular with climbers.

PART THREE
ARDNAMURCHAN TO SHETLAND

Derek J Fabian

For Dawn

CHAPTER 15

THE SMALL ISLES

Almost every island of the Inner and Outer Hebrides can be said to be unique. Nowhere is this more true than among the group of four that form the Parish of The Small Isles. Each has its own distinct and quite different character.

Rhum, the boldest, and Eigg, the most varied and fertile, are the largest and highest of the group and together are easily the most important of all the islands to the climber outside of Skye and Arran, with the possible exception of North Harris. The Cuillin of Rhum are the most dramatic peaks of the Hebrides outwith Skye, and they even surpass the Skye Cuillin for their boldness of skyline when seen from the mainland. Rhum and Eigg give their names to the title of Sheet 39 of the Ordnance Survey Landranger Series, which usefully covers all four islands of the group. Canna, the furthest north-west, holds the most sheltered harbour and is distinctive for its high plateau. Muck, the southernmost, is climatically and scenically the gentlest, despite a treacherously rocky approach to its shores by sea.

The group forms a shallow south-west facing crescent, measuring some 50-60 kilometres in length and arching north-east towards the southernmost tip of Skye - The Point of Sleat - which lies just twelve kilometres due east of the entrance to Loch Scresort where this cuts deeply through the easterly cliffs of Rhum. At the southern toe of the crescent is Muck, positioned just eight kilometres north of the western extremity of the Ardnamurchan peninsula. Eigg, which lies between Muck and Rhum, and is separated from each by a narrow sound that bears the name of the larger island, is the most fertile. It is rich in farmland and crofts, as well as in flowers and birdlife.

The Isle of Eigg is also distinguished by probably the most impressive tower of columnar pitchstone, An Sgurr (Ordnance Survey spelling), anywhere in the British Isles. This Scuir of Eigg, meaning tooth or tusk of Eigg, is especially impressive when viewed from the shores just north of Galmisdale Bay, in the south-east corner of the island. Here the off-lying Eilean Chathastail shelters a tiny though useful harbour and jetty serving Eigg. It is also the site of a small but important lighthouse that guides vessels rounding the point of Ardnamurchan, and headed north-east, safely past the dangerous shores of Muck and Eigg to the shelter of the Sound of Sleat lying between Skye and the mainland. Eigg has also the largest and finest sandy bay of the group, the Bay of Laig under Cleadale.

253

RHUM

MAPS :   Ordnance Survey   1:50,000 Sheet 39
                                1:25,000 Sheets 233 (NG 30/40) and 261 (NM 38/48)
            Bartholomew   1:100,000 Sheet 50

PRINCIPAL HILLS
THE RHUM CUILLIN

Barkeval	591m	376 972
Hallival	722m	395 963
Askival	812m	393 952
Trallval	700m	377 952
Ainshval	781m	378 943
Sgurr nan Gillean	764m	380 931
Ruinsival	528m	356 940
Beinn nan Stac	546m	396 941

THE WESTERN GROUP

Orval	571m	334 991
Ard Nev	556m	346 986
Fionchra	463m	339 003
Bloodstone Hill	388m	315 007

ACCESS

Kinloch on Rhum is served by passenger ferry (Caledonian MacBrayne) from Mallaig, the nearest mainland port. The ferry serves also Eigg, Canna and Muck; it operates approximately four days per week. Passage time to Rhum is two to three hours depending on whether it calls first at Canna or Eigg. The MacBrayne's steamer is met in Loch Scresort by motor launch which transfers passengers (for a not insignificant charge) between steamer and shore. Non-regular sailings can also be found from Arisaig (Arisaig Marine Ltd; telephone 0687 5678) and charters can be arranged from both Mallaig (Bruce Watt Cruises; telephone 0687 2283) and Arisaig. If the seas are truly calm, which is rare, landings can be made — with reward for the climber — at Harris Bay in the south-west and at Bagh na h-Uamha in the east.

Rhum is owned by the Nature Conservancy Council from whom a wealth of information can be obtained (by writing to the Chief Warden, White House, Isle of Rhum; telephone 0687 2026). Day visitors may land at Loch Scresort without formality. All overnight visitors are asked to report to the Chief Warden and parties must request approval for camping and climbing in advance (through Club Secretaries). Camping at Loch Scresort is only permitted in the designated areas around Kinloch. No rescue services are available on the island and the Nature Conservancy specifically excludes liability or calls on its staff for assistance. Thus, the minimum size of party for climbing approval is four and the maximum fifteen.

Much of the island is actively used for conservation research. Visitors, hillwalking or climbing, are asked to comply with any local restrictions, which can vary daily. Some regions, especially north of glens Kinloch and Shellesder, are at times closed for scientific research. Information on restrictions for a given period can be obtained from the Chief Warden; eg the Kilmory study area is open only on Sundays, but is closed in June and October for deer calving and rutting. Restricted areas may be varied at short notice and an access map is posted in Kinloch for morning consultation. However, that said, and bearing in mind that Rhum is the third largest National Nature Reserve and 'outdoor laboratory' in Britain and has been designated by UNESCO as part of an international network of such reserves, the climber and hillwalker will find a visit to the island more than rewarding and should not consider some restrictions unreasonable.

It may indeed be said that the unique quality of Rhum, with every *val* (Norse for *hill*) and *dil* (Norse for *glen*) resplendent with wild life, has much to owe to the island's history of "forbidden-to-visitors" and to its current ecological protection.

TRANSPORT

In short, none. The only roads on the island are an unsurfaced continuation of the Loch Scresort shore-road running westwards for four kilometres to the head of Kinloch Glen, about halfway across the breadth of the island. From there its two rough branches go north to Kilmory and south-west over the Monadh Mhiltich pass to Harris. There is no public transport. An occasional Land-Rover lift might be found, but only one's own feet can be relied on. Distances however are undaunting. Bicycles probably would not help much.

ACCOMMODATION

The camping areas at Kinloch, below the shore road on the south side of Loch Scresort, are provided with toilets and fresh water. Limited stores can be bought at the Kinloch Post Office, but most supplies must be brought in from Mallaig. There are no litter disposal facilities on Rhum and campers are required to burn everything combustible and to remove with them from the island everything non-degradable. Fires of driftwood and forest deadwood are permitted. The daily charge for camping is small. Permission can be obtained for a limited amount of high camping in the hills, which is much to be recommended.

There are three bothies at Kinloch run by the Conservancy Council, accommodating groups of six to twelve; one at Dibidil restored by the Mountain Bothies Association, and one at Guirdil belonging to the Gatliff Trust. Permission for use of the bothies at Dibidil and Guirdil must be obtained at Kinloch from the Nature Conservancy Council warden; advanced bookings cannot be made. There is also a restored bothy-lodge at Harris for use by the Conservancy staff; not open for non-conservancy use except rarely and by special arrangement. There is no deadwood and seldom driftwood to be found at Dibidil (or Guirdil) and climbers should carry fuel with them if they visit. Excellent accommodation can also be had at Kinloch Castle: full board at the front, in Edwardian style; hostel accommodation, either self-service (meals provided) or self-catering, at the rear. Reservation in advance is absolutely necessary. Part of the Castle is a period-piece museum of the Edwardian era. The interior helps to dispel one's inevitable "red elephant" reaction (W H Murray) to the castle's exterior, but also emphasises the castle's Edwardian ostentation.

GENERAL DESCRIPTION

The extreme ruggedness of Rhum is striking both from afar and from its shores. The island is roughly diamond shaped with the sandy bay of Kilmory at the northern end and the rocky 180m headland, Rubha nam Meirleach, at its southern tip. Harris Bay divides the otherwise unbroken line of rugged cliffs that stretches from this southernmost point to the western corner of the island, forming the treacherous south-west shore. Kilmory is about the only part of Rhum where a few acres of relatively flat land can be found. Drainage from the centre of the island runs in four directions and even from the pass at the head of Kinloch Glen it runs in three. The walk from this pass down to Kilmory gives splendid vistas over the small low-lying island of Soay to the Cuillin of Skye.

Both Harris and Kilmory bays reward visits; each eight to nine kilometres from Kinloch. Harris provides a well-located camping or bivouac base for some of the finest rock in the Rhum Cuillin, which form the south-east third of the island. An incongruous Greek-style mausoleum at Harris was built by Lady Bullough, the widow from 1939 of Sir George Bullough, who inherited the island from his father at the turn of the century and then began construction of the castle at Kinloch with sandstone brought from Arran. Rhum was bought by the Nature Conservancy Council in 1957 when Lady Bullough died - at the age of 98.

Geological Structure

Much of Rhum consists of a gently sloping platform of Torridonian purple-red sandstone, hugely intruded in the south and west by a variety of igneous rocks. In the northern half of the island, as well as along its eastern shores and in the southern corner, the Torridonian rock is exposed in abundance. The Long Loch Fault line runs north to south from Kilmory bay through Long Loch to the gabbro cliffs of Inbhir Ghil.

The three northernmost peaks of the Cuillin (Hallival, Askival and Trallval) represent the remains of one of the many volcanoes that erupted along the eastern Atlantic seaboard in Tertiary times. They comprise a complex of basic and layered ultrabasic igneous rocks including gabbro, peridotite and allivalite; the latter being named after Hallival which was given as Allival on earlier maps. Barkeval at the northern end of the Rhum Cuillin is supposedly the largest mass of peridotite in Britain. The southernmost peaks, Ainshval and Sgurr nan Gillean, consist mainly of quartz-felsite on a base of Torridonian sandstone.

To the west of the track over the Monadh Mhiltich to Harris the predominant rock is granophyre, which gives good hill-walking. However, outcrops of basalt, which in places overlie the granophyre (and the Torridonian rocks further north), are badly fractured. For example, the dramatic Orval Pinnacle on the north-west flank of Orval is extremely loose and was until recently thought to be unclimbable.

Further basaltic outliers in the west include Bloodstone Hill, so-called for the beautifully coloured semi-precious stones (chalcedony, heliotrope, agate) formed in vapour cavities of the basaltic lava. Fragments of these stones can be found here and there in the steep and loose grassy screes that generally form the north-western flank of this hill and its neighbour Sgorr Mhor. (Not to be confused with the Sgorr Mor summit of the Torridonian rocky headland at Rhum's southern tip). The steep western cliffs are a conglomerate of granophyre and microgranite.

Plant and Wild Life

The northern part of Rhum, from glens Shellesder and Kinloch to the 15-kilometre wide sound dividing the island from Skye, is almost entirely moorland. Much of it is now used for red deer research and, in the east, for experimental forestation. A small area of natural woodland remains above the north shore of Loch Scresort, while the castle at Kinloch is pleasantly set in fine - if originally imported - woodland. Another small 'imported' area of attractive woodland is to be found on the north banks of the fresh-water loch at Papadil.

Flora almost everywhere is of the moorland and wet-heath varieties and include many imported species such as the Norwegian sandwort and *saxifraga nivalis*. Primroses, violets and sea pinks are abundant. Smallish shrubs grow here and there, even near the ridges, including least willow. The Nature Conservancy has catalogued more than 1800 kinds of plants overall and a vegetation map has been published.

Birdlife over the whole island abounds. The Conservancy list 196 species: from Manx shearwater to arctic skua and tree pipit to golden eagle. Little auks have been seen in recent years and the Conservancy has a well-established programme of re-introducing the sea eagle. The whole island is a bird-watcher's paradise.

THE HILLS

The main mountains of Rhum are in the south and west; by far the finest comprising the Rhum Cuillin which occupy the south-east third of the island. The traverse of the main ridges and summits of the Rhum Cuillin is rated one of the classic mountaineering tours of Scotland. It involves only occasional moderate scrambling and, on a good day, provides some of the most memorable views of mountain and sea to be found anywhere in Europe.

From a base at Kinloch the full traverse of the six principal peaks from Barkeval to Sgurr nan Gillean, returning by the Dibidil path, takes between eight and eleven hours. Any part of the ridge however is easily reached from Kinloch, Harris or Dibidil and shorter excursions can be planned, linking two or three or more summits, as time and weather allow. A feature of the Cuillin peaks of Rhum is their compactness. With the exception of Ruinsival and possibly Barkeval, none of the mountains forming the Cuillin can be regarded as isolated from the others.

For this reason, and because the climber making a first visit to Rhum will probably plan to cover at least a section of the main traverse, we depart from the normal pattern of first describing each of the principal mountains separately and give at the outset a description of the main Cuillin traverse - starting from a base at

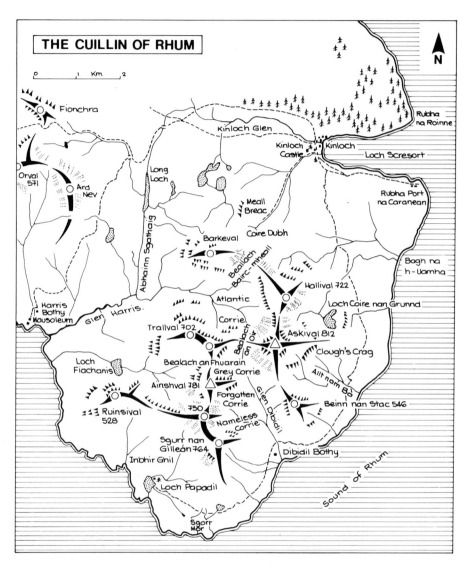

Kinloch. Subsequently, each of the Cuillin peaks is taken as a mountain by itself; giving there the description of alternative routes to the individual summits to assist a climber planning to traverse only a section of the main Cuillin, from Kinloch, Harris or Dibidil.

The Cuillin Traverse

The traverse of the main ridges and summits of the Rhum Cuillin is nowhere as difficult as the main ridge of the Skye Cuillin and involves no climbing beyond moderate scrambling provided that two or three short sections (the Askival Pinnacle, the south arête of Trallval and the upper north ridge of Ainshval) are avoided.

Barkeval (left), Hallival and Askival at the head of the Atlantic Corrie

These sections add interest; they are no more than moderately difficult on a dry day.

From Kinloch, a start can be made to include Barkeval, approached by the Allt Slugan path into Coire Dubh, or by following first the Harris road west from Kinloch to reach the western flank of Barkeval and thence its summit - taking in some interesting easy scrambles up the Torridonian terraces on this flank. For a shorter day, omit Barkeval and climb direct to Hallival after gaining the Bealach Bairc-mheall from Coire Dubh. If the Barkeval summit is gained from Coire Dubh it is the westernmost (second) cairn from the bealach. It gives a fine viewpoint of the main peaks of the Rhum Cuillin and its inclusion is recommended for this reason alone. A gracefully shaped, flattish rocky ridge leads from Barkeval to Hallival. From there the sound separating Rhum from Canna is hidden and, looking north-west, the island of Canna appears as an extension of Rhum. Views of the Cuillin of Skye to the north are unsurpassed anywhere.

The ridge from Hallival to Askival is grassy but 'airy'. On a clear day it gives magnificent views over Eigg and the Ardnamurchan peninsula, to Ben More on Mull and the Moidart region of the mainland. It is also peppered, as are all the steep grassy slopes between the rock tiers flanking the ridge on either side, with the nesting 'burrows' of the Manx shearwater, to which these birds return noisily in their thousands after dusk. The final section to the summit of Askival is of gabbro, and a pleasant scramble. The Askival Pinnacle, some 50m below the summit, is more of a slab than a gendarme. It is no more than moderately difficult and gives a fine

Looking south from Hallival across the Bealach an Oir to Ainshval

approach to the summit. On a wet or misty day it can be turned easily to the east.

Askival is Rhum's highest peak. It has a natural stone triangulation pillar and from there the views past Hallival to Skye in the north, and of the mainland to the east and south, are quite dramatic. On a day of good visibility the hills of Barra and South Uist can be seen across the Sea of The Hebrides, some 60 kilometres to the west.

To continue the main Cuillin traverse, descend Askival's west ridge to the Bealach an Oir (*pass of gold*) and gain the summit of Trallval by its east ridge, which gives easy scrambling. There are two summits to Trallval, some 50 metres apart. The eastern summit is slightly the lower and must be crossed, when approaching either from the Bealach an Oir or from the Bealach an Fhuarain, to reach the higher of the two along an airy ridge between them. Apart from this ridge, which requires care but gives no problems, any scrambling difficulties on the eastern or southern flanks of Trallval can be avoided. The southern flank or ridge down to the Bealach an Fhuarain (*pass of the springs*) is steep and finding the start requires care. Its descent gives an impressive view - especially in swirling mists - of the dark upper north ridge of Ainshval.

Trallval is also the last of the gabbro on the Cuillin ridge; Ainshval, and Sgurr nan Gillean to its south, being of felsite on Torridonian sandstone. If these two summits are being omitted, a return to Kinloch can be made from the Bealach an Fhuarain by skirting Trallval to the Bealach an Oir and traversing below Askival and

Ainshval from the summit of Trallval

Allival across the Atlantic Corrie of Glen Harris; or a similar traverse, rather longer but more scenic, can be made by contouring first south-eastwards at about the 500m level, then crossing the bealachs to south and east of Askival and descending Coire nan Grunnd to the Dibidil path (taking care not to overshoot the path which is sometimes indistinct). Either of these return routes shortens the day, from Kinloch and back, to around five to seven hours. To complete the full Cuillin traverse, over Ainshval and Sgurr nan Gillean plus the return to Kinloch, a further three to four hours should be allowed. Alternatively, a night in the Dibidil bothy or a bivouac at Harris can be planned.

The dark upper ridge of Ainshval is of Lewisian gneiss and, while only moderately difficult, its lower section can be awkward when wet - especially in descent. The view of this ridge on the descent from Trallval is deceptive; it looks difficult to turn but can be by-passed with a grassy track to the east, using then a short easy chimney to gain the broad rocky ridge at about one third its height to the summit. If descending this ridge from Ainshval, it is important to locate the top of this short chimney before dropping too low. Alternatively, the whole of the lower section of this ridge can be skirted well to the west; and likewise the upper section can be turned entirely to the east, by using an indistinct path high up in the screes of the Grey Corrie.

The summit of Ainshval is flat. Views down Glen Dibidil to the sea emphasise the remoteness of this glen - which cuts deeply into the Cuillin range of Rhum and

Trallval (left) and Ainshval from the Bullough Mausoleum at Harris

is the home of the eagle as well as of large herds of red deer. From Ainshval too, the small and beautifully shaped tower-like summit of Beinn nan Stac, flanking the eastern side of Glen Dibidil, is seen at its best.

The section of the traverse from Ainshval to Sgurr nan Gillean is a grassy walk. However, a subsidiary top, unnamed on the Ordnance Survey map, exists between the two peaks and can cause confusion in the mist (as it has for some unwary parties, judging by the log-book in the Dibidil bothy). The summit is clearly demarcated, at the junction of the ridge with the long whaleback, Leac a'Chaisteil, which extends out westwards towards Ruinsival. The top is grassy, with a small cairn, and it should be named. Suggestions for a name have included Sgurr nan Goibhrean (*peak of the goats*) and the more logical An Caisteal (Hamish Brown).

Added interest to this final leg of the Cuillin traverse, on a clear day, is provided by views of the huge slabby buttresses that sweep down from the ridge into Glen Dibidil. The summit of Sgurr nan Gillean has an exposed atmosphere, given to it by the 60m high crag that flanks it to the north-east. This same crag causes a descent from the summit by the east ridge to be steep and hazardous; thus a much better descent to Dibidil is by the south ridge for some 300m, followed by a descending traverse to the bothy. From there the quickest return to Kinloch is by the Dibidil path.

Barkeval (591m)

The summit of Barkeval is most easily reached from Kinloch. The mountain lies at the northern edge of the Rhum Cuillin, roughly at the centre of the island. To the north is low moorland, thus the peak of Barkeval gives splendid views of the Skye Cuillin. In addition, being lower than the remaining peaks of the Rhum Cuillin, it provides an excellent viewpoint for these.

Either of the two routes described for the Cuillin traverse can be taken for Barkeval. The track up the Allt Slugan burn commences from behind the castle, using a gate on the south side of the road to Harris, soon after this leaves Loch Scresort. The path peters out at a height around 250-300m in Coire Dubh, after passing an impressive rock chasm into which the burn funnels at about the 150m contour. The grassy slope here is an array of wild flowers. From the bealach, the summit of Barkeval (second cairn) is easily reached; about two hours from Kinloch.

The more interesting route, although longer (two to three hours) follows the Harris road from Kinloch until past the waterfalls where it turns south - leaving it there to follow the line of the Long Loch Fault. Either side of the river and the loch can then be taken to approximately the Allt Cul a'Mhill from where short scrambles on the peridotite outcrops on the west flank of Barkeval can be included in making for the summit.

This flank of Barkeval also makes a good approach to the summit from Harris. Alternatively, the south face of the mountain, where some of the longest moderate scrambling on Rhum is to be found (the Barkeval Southern Crags), makes a fine approach to the summit.

Hallival (722m)

Hallival from Loch Coire nan Grunnd

Apart from the route already described in the Cuillin traverse from the Bealach Bairc-mheall and over or by-passing the subsidiary Cnapan Breaca, Hallival can be approached from the Dibidil path to its north-east (see Paths and Walks for the approach to this path from Kinloch). Either of the north or north-east ridges to the summit can be gained from the Allt Mor na h-Uamha, where the going is steep but easy. The north-east ridge is also the quickest approach to Hallival from the small and delightful sandy bay, Bagh na h-Uamha, where good camping and a landing by boat in fine weather can be found. To its south-east, the summit of Hallival is flanked by three rock tiers that overlook Coire nan Grunnd. An ascent of the indefinite east ridge of the mountain can be made, but the north-east edge of the uppermost of these three rock tiers has to be climbed to gain the summit's grassy eastern shoulder, and it is of Very Difficult standard.

Askival (812m)

The most attractive approach to the summit of Askival from Kinloch is to gain the Bealach Bairc-mheall from the Allt Slugan path and traverse Hallival, taking in or by-passing the Askival Pinnacle on the north ridge of Askival. Alternatively, the Dibidil path approach to Hallival can be taken first. The summit of Askival has four distinct and symmetrically placed ridges giving the mountain, the highest on Rhum, its fine shape. The ridges to north and west are included in the Cuillin traverse. The south ridge gives moderately difficult climbing from the unnamed easy bealach (Bealach nan Stac perhaps) to its south. This flank of Askival is usually avoided in the Cuillin traverse by descending its west ridge to the Bealach an Oir; however it provides an interesting ascent of the mountain from Glen Dibidil (see Dibidil Horseshoe p267).

The east ridge of Askival, although steep - especially just below the summit where care is needed in mist - is easy. The top section, below the natural stone triangulation pillar, is not truly a ridge but forms the summit rocks of Askival; there are still buttresses here to be explored. Lower down, the east ridge is more defined and descends steadily to roughly the 550m contour from where it extends east-wards to a distinct Prow, unnamed on the Ordnance Survey map.

The Prow is formed by crags buttressing its north-east flank above Loch Coire nan Grunnd, and its south-east flank (Clough's Crag) facing Beinn nan Stac. Finding the nose of the Prow between these crags, if descending in mist, is straightforward with care, and gives an easy route down to the Dibidil path above Lochan Dubh or further to the north by traversing above or below Loch Coire nan Grunnd. The entire corrie is a desolate grey hollow of ice-hewn rock, with Hallival - appearing more massive from this side - towering above. It provides, though, the fastest ascent of Askival from Kinloch or from the Bagh na h-Uamha.

Trallval (700m)

In addition to the south and east ridges that form part of the Rhum Cuillin traverse, the summit of Trallval can be reached from Glen Harris or Glen Fiachanis by its long easy west ridge, with a final scramble to the west summit. The rock ridge from there to the slightly lower east summit is also easy, but exposed.

The twin summits, being central and lower than the remaining peaks, give fine views of the Rhum Cuillin in all directions; especially from north through east to south-west, with the mainland peaks of Kintail and Knoydart framed by Hallival and Askival and those of Moidart floating beyond the long saddle of Eigg.

Some 200m below the summit ridge, at the head of the south-west corrie, is Harris Buttress. About 300 metres further north-west, and slightly higher, is Triangular Buttress at the westernmost point of a series of broken peridotite outcrops on this south-west flank of Trallval. Both buttresses give fine rock climbing with scope for further exploration. From the east summit of Trallval a return to Kinloch, descending to the Bealach an Oir and traversing Atlantic Corrie below the west flank of Askival, takes two hours.

Ainshval from the east ridge of Trallval

Ainshval (781m)

The summit of Ainshval is the second highest on Rhum and provides a pleasant climb in itself from Glen Dibidil or Loch Fiachanis, gaining first the Bealach an Fhuarain. The rocky ascent from there to the cairned summit is easy, with care, as described in the main traverse of the Cuillin. This deceptive north to north-north-east ridge forms the northern flank of the Grey Corrie, south of the Bealach an Fhuarain. It offers scope for a winter climb when conditions are right. On the southern flank of Grey Corrie is the prominent east ridge of Ainshval which provides a choice of moderate scrambles to the summit just south of two grassy gullies that run down to Glen Dibidil. These gullies are steep and unpleasantly loose, but in the right condition would give good climbing in crampons to reach a possible winter climb above.

From the summit of Ainshval, after a short descent and climb to the unnamed top to its south, the grassy one-kilometre long ridge to Sgurr nan Gillean is almost level. This ridge builds fine cornices during the usually all-too-brief periods of snow on the island, making Ainshval plus Sgurr nan Gillean a good winter excursion from the Dibidil bothy when the right conditions prevail.

Sgurr nan Gillean (764m)

The grassy ascent of Sgurr nan Gillean from Dibidil is steep and tedious but commands magnificent views over Eigg and the mainland. It is best to follow the

Dibidil-Papadil path southwards for half a kilometre before climbing west and then north-west to reach the south ridge to the summit. This avoids the rocky and grassy spurs that fall steeply to the east from the summit into Glen Dibidil. In the winter especially, these east slopes should be avoided, particularly in descent, unless conditions are suitable for crampons. When they are, on the other hand, the steep rocks to the north-east below the summit of Sgurr nan Gillean offer the prospect of a winter route, approaching from Dibidil by the Nameless Corrie (see OS 1:10,000 map).

Ruinsival (528m)
The low-lying crags on the north and west flanks of Ruinsival form an outlier of the igneous intrusions, and variations of gabbro, that comprise the geological core of the northern section of the Rhum Cuillin. They give splendid scope for the rock climber based at Harris, especially when the higher peaks are shrouded in cloud. Similarly the traverse of Ruinsival and Sgurr nan Gillean will provide a satisfying short day (from Harris or Dibidil), which in the mist can be a challenging hillwalk. The summits are joined by nearly two kilometres of grassy ridge, Leac a' Chaisteil, with an airy exposure to the north where rocky screes run down into Glen Fiachanis (or Sandy Corrie) and, nearer the summit of Sgurr nan Gillean, into Nameless Corrie to the north-east.

The Dibidil Horseshoe
The remote wilderness of Glen Dibidil is dramatic and the bothy there forms a good base from which to explore climbs on Beinn nan Stac, on Askival's south ridge and on Trallval. It provides also an excellent point from which to traverse the horseshoe of peaks that flank the glen, from the 'gashed' summit of Beinn nan Stac to Sgurr nan Gillean, taking in Askival, Trallval and Ainshval.

The horseshoe is equally pleasant in either direction, although the lower altitude of Beinn nan Stac makes for an easier start. A line of crags protects the western flank of its grassy summit, and the easiest approach is therefore from the Dibidil path by the south-east ridge. Just below the top these crags give a short moderate scramble, which can be turned to the north-east, giving access to the broad col between Beinn nan Stac and Askival. From there, Clough's Crag extending out in two tiers north-eastwards to the Prow below the east ridge of Askival is prominent.

From the col the south ridge of Askival, taken direct, gives moderate to difficult climbing on good rock for a height of 200-300m over several hundred metres distance. The scrambling on this ridge is more difficult than any other on the Cuillin traverse of Rhum. It can be avoided if desired by traversing either to the south-west or the south-east of Askival and then taking the west or east ridges to the summit. The completion of the horseshoe from Askival to Sgurr nan Gillean is described in the main Cuillin traverse. The round tour from Dibidil takes five to six hours and gives as fine and as scenic a mountain day as any in the islands.

Ard Nev (556m)
Orval (571m)
The western hills of Rhum can be reached from Kinloch by taking the Harris track to the point where a path leaves it to cross the Monadh Mhiltich. The path climbs gently for two kilometres to the Bealach a'Braigh Bhig, from where the north-east ridge of Orval gives access to the Cairngorm-like summits of Orval and Ard Nev which give pleasant hillwalking with rare seascape views to north and west. The walk can be extended westwards by a grassy traverse along the rim of the corrie at the head of Glen Guirdil to take in Sron an t-Saighdeir.

From Harris, a pleasant traverse of these hills can be made over Ard Mheall. Alternatively, starting from Harris, the bealach (449m) between Orval and Ard Nev can be gained gently from Glen Duian, skirting below the west flank of Ard Mheall. The upper slopes here are strewn with basaltic dykes, while bouldery outcrops of Lewisian gneiss occur on the eastern slopes of these hills. The Orval summit lies due west from the bealach.

A descent from the summit of Orval to the north-east requires care and, especially in mist, it is probably best to descend eastwards a short way from the north-east shoulder - or even as far as the 449m bealach - before making for the Bealach a'Braigh Bhig.

Bloodstone Hill (388m)
From the Bealach a'Braigh Bhig the shortest route to Bloodstone Hill continues along the path from the Monadh Mhiltich, contouring below the north-face of Orval and up the grassy slopes just to east of the Bealach an Dubh-braigh. The Bloodstone Hill summit is grassy and lies at the edge of its north-west cliffs of grass and scree. Alternatively, from the Bealach a'Braigh Bhig the summits of the north-east ridge of Orval and Ard Nev can be gained and give access to the pleasant grassy walk described above, to Sron an t-Saighdeir. The steep northern ridge from the summit of Sron an t-Saighdeir can be descended to Bealach an Dubh-bhraigh, regaining the path to Bloodstone Hill. From there a walk south-westwards along the cliffs of Sgorr Mhor gives splendid views of Canna and beyond to the west coast of Skye, past the wide entrance of Loch Bracadale to Neist Point.

Fionchra (463m)
The broad grassy ridge of Fionchra forms a craggy hogback between Glen Guirdil and Glen Shellesder. The summit, at its south-eastern extremity, lies less than half a kilometre north of the Bealach a'Bhraigh Bhig from where it is easily climbed. Alternatively, if coming from Kinloch, it can be approached by a long moorland walk over Minishal (Black Hill).

PATHS AND WALKS
Apart from the Glen Slugan track up Coire Dubh, used by the hillwalker and climber to gain access to the Bealach Bairc-mheall from Kinloch (see Barkeval), the only paths on Rhum of any note are the well used Dibidil path, running south from Loch Scresort, and two in the west of the island; one through Glen Shellesder to Guirdil

and the other over the Monadh Mhiltich (see Orval) and the Bealach a'Bhraigh Bhig to Bloodstone Hill, which gives fine views across the Sound of Canna. The ruined shielings (and restored bothy) at Guirdil and the waterfalls at the foot of Glen Shellesder form points of interest that link these two paths into a round-trip walk from Kinloch taking four to six hours.

The start of the Dibidil path is not obvious. Just east of the jetty on the south shore of Loch Scresort is a small drinking-water burn (beside the first house on the shore road from jetty to the castle). Proceeding southwards up the burn some twenty metres and across the 'back' road leads almost directly to the start of the path. From there it rises steadily over a lower shoulder of Hallival to a height of 200m, giving magnificent views of the mainland peaks of Moidart and Knoydart to the east and north-east.

After crossing the burn below the Alt Mor na h-Uamha waterfalls, the path descends gently to the Allt na h-Uamha. It then undulates continuously over rough terrain, contouring for some eight kilometres well above the sea-cliffs. This section is both picturesque and dramatic. After rainfall, runs of water cascade down the ledges of dark rock to end foaming in the sea below, at all times accompanied by the deep booming of the swell as it builds up in the caverns and then musically ebbs from the walls and roofs formed in the tumble of rock from the cliffs.

Beyond the cliffs the path finally descends to the foot of Glen Dibidil, one of the most remote and rugged glens in all of the islands. The grandeur of this glen has been likened to Glen Coe, although it is only two kilometres long. The peak of Trallval stands boldly at its head. The ridge from Sgurr nan Gillean, tapering gracefully to Ainshval, flanks the western side of the glen, and the ridge from Beinn nan Stac to Askival flanks its eastern side. The glen itself looks south-east across the isles of Eigg and Muck to Moidart.

From just above and behind the restored bothy at Dibidil, the path climbs steeply again to 150m before falling gently for some three kilometres past the small Loch Dubh an Sgoir to the derelict lodge on the shore of Loch Papadil, a total distance of twelve kilometres from Kinloch. From Papadil, where the brown trout fishing is second to none in the Small Isles, the going is rough. There is no path or track but, by climbing from the shore at Inbhir Ghil and keeping well above the 200m contour around the south-west shoulder of Ruinsival, Harris Bay can be easily reached - six kilometres from Papadil. The route gives fine views of Rhum's western hills.

From Harris, a strong walker (or climber on a wet day) can complete the 26-kilometre circuit by taking the track over the Monadh Mhiltich back to Kinloch.

ROCK CLIMBING

Rock climbing as such on Rhum dates from around 1932 when climbers from the mountaineering clubs of Oxford and Cambridge universities explored routes on Hallival and later Askival. The first reported traverses of the Cuillin ridges, however, appear in Volume 1 of the SMC Journal (1891) by the ubiquitous Sir Hugh Munro himself. A resumé of rock climbing pre-war is to be found in the 1939 SMC Journal,

Wreck Bay on the south-west coast of Rhum

Jubilee issue. There remains much, by way of rock, yet to be explored on Rhum. For a concise and up-to-date guide to rock climbing, the reader is referred to the guidebook on Rhum by Hamish Brown (1988 edition) published by Cicerone Press (and to a forthcoming SMC Climber's Guide covering Skye, Rhum and Eigg). In the following pages a general picture is given, plus an outline description of one or two of the typical climbs.

Rock climbing on Rhum is almost all on sound variations of gabbro and is some of the best to be found in the islands outwith Skye. Its location can roughly be divided into three main areas: the crags and buttresses of Askival and its eastern corries, including the south-east face of Hallival; the cliffs on the south-west flank of Trallval including its summit crags; and the scattered rock tiers on the northern and western flanks of Ruinsival.

Askival and its adjoining corries form the largest area for extended explora-tion. Harris Buttress, on Trallval, provides the longest and steepest climbs. Ruinsival is the most compact area and the lowest, providing climbs that are easily accessible from Harris when cloud shrouds the higher peaks. Two additional craggy outcrops are not included in this general division. They are the cliffs to the south flank of Barkeval (the Southern Crags), which give the nearest rock climbing to Kinloch, and crags high up in Nameless Corrie to the north-east of Sgurr nan Gillean, just below its summit, which are easily the most remote and least explored on the island.

Trallval South-West Flank
The wall of gabbro on the south-west flank of Trallval, 120m high and 300 metres long, is at first sight repelling. It is misleadingly named Harris Buttress. While Harris Bay can be seen from the upper crags, below the east summit of Trallval, the buttress itself looks down into Sandy Corrie and commands a splendid view of Loch Fiachanis. It is reached most easily from Harris. The approach from Dibidil (or from Kinloch and the Bealach an Oir) is over the Bealach an Fhuarain, descending some 100m and traversing 300-400 metres north-west from the bealach.

Harris Buttress possesses some of the longest and finest routes on Rhum, although the loose rock on the higher sections requires care. An early recorded climb on Harris Buttress is *Archangel Route* (120m; Very Difficult); a classic and typical route with the distinct character of Rhum (M Ward and W H Murray 1948). The start is located from a prominent 'capstan' rock at the foot and roughly centre of the buttress.

The capstan is below an indistinct rock rib, easily seen from afar, but not well defined when close. Two shallow gullies run up either side of the rib. About fifteen metres to the east is an 80m vertical (black) roofed corner and a further twelve metres in the same direction there is a shallow, broken depression which runs up to a shattered block pinnacle.

Archangel Route starts at the rocks to the left of the depression. These give access to a platform at the left of the pinnacle, where - in the words of W H Murray - one must "Spread the wings of faith, and take a short bold flight across the gap", to cross the pinnacle. This leads to a prominent chimney, becoming a crack, to a broad ledge (right) leading to a shallow rock bay, and an "impressive" groove. Slanting leftwards, the route falls back into the face among broad steep slabs, and continues left to a corner giving a delightful climb on rough exposed gabbro.

From the top of the buttress a scree terrace leads to the upper crags, where a choice of short climbs (eg *Malindara*, Difficult, G E Little 1984; SMCJ Vol.33, p.186) leads to the summit ridge of Trallval. Archangel Route is one of the best recorded long climbs on Harris Buttress. The rib itself however, *Central Rib*, gives a sustained direct climb (D D Stewart and D J Bennet, 1950) - from just above the capstan - and is probably one of the finest routes on Rhum (90m; Hard Severe). A dark almost straight gully just to its right, awkward to start and slanting right, is *Right Central Gully* (90m; Very Difficult); and some twelve metres further east is *Guillotine* (123m; Very Severe) climbed in 1979 - R Barton and D Morris (SMCJ Vol.32, p.50).

Further north-west from Harris Buttress, and slightly higher, is the much smaller Triangular Buttress. It can be seen from the west summit of Trallval, although best from Ainshval. Climbs here are much shorter than on Harris Buttress, but often drier. Recorded routes range from *Ptarmigan Crack* (45m; Difficult - J Parish and party in 1947) which follows a chimney to right (east) of the triangle, to *Bloodstone Crack* (30m; Very Severe - M Ward and W H Murray 1948) to the left of the central gully; with *Botany Crack* (40m; Severe - D D Stewart and D J Bennet, 1950) to the right of this gully, in a recess guarded by a pinnacle at the foot of the steep slab. A twisting serpentine crack to right of Botany Crack is *Zigzag Route* (33m; Severe), leading to an overhung recess - where a difficult movement surmounts the overhang, or the wall to the left provides a Hard Severe variation (SMCJ Vol.32 p.356) which finishes in Botany Crack.

Both Harris and Triangular buttresses are easy of access from Harris or Dibidil, but can also be reached from Kinloch; either over the Bealach Bairc-mheall or by taking the Harris road from Kinloch and turning south to follow the Long Loch fault and the Abhainn Sgathaig river to skirt the west ridge of Trallval.

Askival North-West Buttress
Between the north ridge of Askival and its west ridge leading down to the Bealach an Oir, lies the North-West Face or Buttress of Askival which has some of the steepest gabbro on Rhum. The face is about 120m high and is seen well from Barkeval, Hallival or Trallval. The best approach from Kinloch is via the Bealach Bairc-mheall and the Bealach an Oir, traversing Atlantic Corrie below the buttress and climbing the west ridge of Askival to gain an easy rake leading north again below the crags; two hours from Kinloch.

The steeper section of these cliffs is to the left (north) where the *Askival Slab* and two main ridges are found; although a number of prominent ribs and ridges can be discerned. Askival Slab, first climbed by a party from the Oxford University Mountaineering Club in 1935, gives a Difficult 60m climb at its left-hand edge, or a Severe on its right-hand corner.

From Trallval the two main ridges stand out. The right hand of these, *Atlantic Ridge* gives an excellent Very Difficult, 110m climb; first ascended by W H Murray and M Ward in 1948. A start is made just to the right of the sharp left-hand edge of the main rib (cairn); not easy to find. A shallow 18m-high crack leads to a platform on this edge (a deep groove around the corner to the left identifies the platform). The climb proceeds to the right a few metres, and then up a steep 15m wall and continuously up good rock to end "suddenly at the summit" (W H Murray).

Another fine route, 100m - Severe with no escape, is *Edinburgh Climb* first ascended by an Edinburgh University Mountaineering Club party in 1947 (I Smart, H Nicol and C G M Slesser). It lies on the part of the buttress that can be seen from the north ridge, where the buttress (or face) looks nearly north. Its line takes a clearly discernable defect in the face; a cairn marks the start. The rock is easy for 5-6m, then follows a groove (the crux) and a traverse to a shelf with an obvious belay, before taking the easiest line to the summit rocks where the exposure soon reduces.

Hallival South-East Face

Good though short climbs on the three obvious rock tiers to the south-east of the massive pyramid of Hallival are easily reached in about two hours from Loch Scresort by rounding the foot of the north-east ridge and passing high into Coire nan Grunnd. The Middle Tier is formed by the main line of crags running from below the east summit ridge to the (unnamed) Hallival-Askival bealach. Anne Littlejohn and parties (SMCJ Vol.27, p.267; Vol.28, p.319) pioneered a few of the routes here in 1961-66; eg. *Right-Hand Buttress Direct* (24m; Very Severe); and I Clough and parties many more, on the Lower South-East Tier, in 1967 (SMCJ Vol.29, p.52).

The East Ridge of the Summit Tier, leading to the summit's grassy eastern shoulder, is a pleasant 60m of Very Difficult climbing. Below this is *Oxford Groove* (60m Severe; OUMC party 1933) which cleaves both tiers just south of the East Ridge. *Choochter Rib* (60m; Very Difficult; I Clough and K Ross, 1967; SMCJ Vol.29, p.52) gives a disjointed climb from the lowest rocks of the Bottom Tier just below Oxford Groove. The climb does, however, provide an interesting approach to the upper tiers. It starts close to the rib below Oxford Groove, takes in a short slab on the right, a shelf to the left, a mantleshelf onto the nose (a flake), and an awkward move to a recessed overhanging ledge. Finally, a chimney and a 15m crest or ridge leads to the steep grassy ledge between the Lower Tier and Middle Tier.

Barkeval South Crags

The extensive peridotite outcrops of unusual rock on the southern flank of Barkeval provide some excellent long moderate scrambles as well as recorded Difficult and Severe routes and scope for further exploration. The South Crags are easily reached in about two hours from Kinloch, over Barkeval, using the Coire Dubh path and descending from a marker cairn some 30 metres east of the summit cairn. This leads down to the top of the appropriately named, and easy, *Honeycomb Arête*. This indistinct 'arete', and the more distinctive *Narnia Arête* lying one gully to the west, provide useful descents to the grass and scree of *The Rectangle* at the foot of the crags. Many of the routes there were first climbed in 1967 (SMCJ Vol.29, p.51).

The Waterslide, a prominent wide-scooped gully some 40 metres further west, becomes eventually the grassy scree chute down to Glen Harris. To the west of the Waterslide is *Western Isles Buttress* (100m; Difficult) and just to the west again a conspicuous Green Patch. From the top of The Rectangle are splendid moderate routes: *Broad Buttress* (120m; Moderate) which can be climbed anywhere, and Narnia Arête (100m; Moderate) to its right. The start of the disjointed *Rose-Root Slab and Crack* route (70m; Severe) lies across a small bay to the west of Western Isles Buttress (and west and below the Green Patch). The wide gully to right (east) of Honeycomb Arete gives access to a subsidiary gully and to *Aficionado* (51m; Severe - SMCJ Vol.32 p.356). The peridotite rock everywhere on these crags is enjoyable and peculiar to climb.

Ruinsival

A proliferation of short, but interesting and demanding climbs can be found on the several rock tiers that form the north-west and northern flanks of Ruinsival. The routes have been poorly described on the whole but a helpful attempt to sort out the confusion has been made by Anne Littlejohn in 1962 (SMCJ Vol.27, pp.268 and 280) as well as in Hamish Brown's guide to climbing on Rhum. The crags are best explored from a base at Harris. The general lines of the routes are seen well in views from the north-west.

From north to south on the north-west flank the buttresses - not all clearly distinguishable from afar nor even from close to - have been named: *North Buttress, Woden's Wall, Thor's Buttress, Frigga's Buttress, South Buttress* and *Green Wall,* with Summit Buttress above. All have short 25-35m routes on sound rock, mostly of standard from Difficult to Very Difficult, with Severe to Very Severe routes on North Buttress and Green Wall.

On the northern flank, *Highlander Buttress*, which forms almost the north ridge to the summit shoulder, has slightly longer routes of 35-35m, Severe to Very Severe. Below it is North Buttress and Woden's Wall which together form a Lower Tier. Across the corrie to south-east of Highlander Buttress, on the north to north-north-east flank of Ruinsival and above the Lower Tier, is *Giant's Staircase* with no less than nine rock steps forming a north-east or north-north-east ridge to the summit shoulder (180m Very Difficult; J G Parish and H Nicol 1947). Its staircase profile is an impressive feature of Ruinsival when seen from the Kinloch-Harris track.

Just to the east of the Giant's Staircase is the *Fiachanis Face*, more correctly a two-tier corrie, with a "probably unclimbable" Bulging Wall. Serious rock exploration here and on various bulges and crags further east again should be worthwhile. Fork Slab, for example, 50 metres or so east of Bulging Wall, has a central crack, dividing into three smaller cracks - all climbed (20m Very Difficult; H Brown and J Matyssek 1966).

Askival Prow

Clough's Crag and the Coire nan Grunnd crags, which form respectively the south-east and north-east flanks of the eastern Prow of Askival, provide a variety of short and pleasant 30-60m climbs ranging in standard from Difficult to Severe. Almost all were pioneered by I Clough with various companions in 1967; although two routes (*Consolation Crack,* 20m Difficult, and *Right-Hand Buttress Direct,* 24m Very Severe)

were first climbed by A Littlejohn
and E Nisbet in 1961). Short new
routes are still to be found on
Clough's Crag (*Satisfaction*, 24m
Very Severe; SMCJ Vol.32 p.356).

Pinnacles and Stacks

Considerable climbing fun is to
be found on the many coastal
stacks and cliffs. Often much of
the interest is in making the
approach; low tide is usually to
be recommended. Papadil Pinnacle, at the seaward end of Loch
Papadil, is one of the most enjoyable if only for its setting. The
short 30m climb to the summit of
this stack (north-east face trending south-east to a deep crack in
the seaward edge) is at least
Difficult, belying both its appearance and recorded descriptions.

Stacs nam Faoileann I and
II are near Dibidil. The first is
encountered one kilometre or so
before Dibidil, below the path
from Kinloch, and is climbed by a
groove to the landward; the second, the more shapely, is a little
to the south and above the first.

The Orval Pinnacle

For its ascent the sea-cliffs must first be descended for about 30m. The Dibidil and
Papadil shores and cliffs offer plenty of scope for scrambles and even serious
exploration. For example, a handful of Very Severe routes have now been explored
on Covenanter's Point, just to south-west of the Stacs nam Faoileann. Fist and
Finger Stack, 500 metres to south-east of Rubha Sgorr an t-Snidhe, is a striking twin
stack joined to the shore by a neck of gravel that covers at high tide (*Pinkey Crack*
- Severe; SMCJ Vol.29, p.427).

Inland, and of importance to the serious rock enthusiast, is the notorious
Orval Pinnacle. Prominent on the north-west flank of Orval (grid reference 335 997),
its ascent is a serious E-grade 30m climb (G E Little, 1984) on metamorphosed
basalt. The route is desperately loose (SMCJ Vol.33, p.176).

EIGG

MAPS :   Ordnance Survey   1:50,000 Sheet 39
                                          1:25,000 Sheet 261 (NM 38/48)
              Bartholomew   1:100,000 Sheet 50

PRINCIPAL HILLS

An Sgurr	393m	463 847
Beinn Tighe	315m	448 868
An Cruachan	299m	486 878
Beinn Bhuidhe	336m	482 904

ACCESS

The Caledonian MacBrayne passenger ferry from Mallaig calls at Eigg three times a week in summer months; serving also Rhum, Muck and Canna. The steamer 'lies off' at Eilean Chathastail (*castle island*) at the south-east corner of the main island. Transfer is by the Eigg Estate launch to the small jetty in Galmisdale harbour, entered from the north or the south (depending on the state of the tide) through the narrow channel between Eilean Chathastail and Eigg. A day or two, or more, can be had on Eigg en route to or from Rhum at no extra fare. Charters and less regular sailings can also be obtained from Mallaig (Bruce Watt Cruises; telephone 0687 2283) and Arisaig (Arisaig Marine Ltd; telephone 0687 5678).

ACCOMMODATION

The Isle of Eigg Estate (telephone 0687 82413) owns several cottages and bothies near Galmisdale which are available for rent, plus an especially well-located fine bothy at Grulin (grid reference 456 842) - to which there is a well marked track from Galmisdale. Cottages can also be found to rent at Cleadale, overlooking the splendid sandy Bay of Laig, and full board at Laig Farm (telephone 0687 82437) where there are also caravans for rent. There are good camping places to be found in the south and north parts of the island, with permission from the Eigg Estate House at Galmisdale (permits at the Tea Room, from where general information on accommodation can also be obtained). There is a small post office and store near the schoolhouse midway between Cleadale and Galmisdale, and a resident doctor.

TRANSPORT

Bicycles are a help, and can be hired from the tea shop at Galmisdale. Car hire may also be arranged but the only surfaced road extends for six kilometres or so, from Galmisdale jetty to Cleadale.

GENERAL DESCRIPTION

The name Eigg derives either from the Norse *egg* for edge, clearly referring to the great An Sgurr that towers above Galmisdale with its long cockscomb of cliffs running east to west; or from the Gaelic *eag* for notch or hollow, alluding to the low saddle or neck between An Sgurr and the northern hills which also forms a distinctive feature of the island when seen from afar. The island is eight kilometres from north to south and five kilometres from west to east; kidney shaped, with the huge sheltered Bay of Laig cupped gently into the north-west shore - the gentlest shore of all the Small Isles. To the north of there, at Camas Sgiotaig, the visitor will find one of the best stretches of quartzite singing sands in the Hebrides. When dry, they 'squeal' musically if scuffed by foot or hand. The bay, and the extended lowland northwards from there to Blar Mor, is also the most fertile land of the Small Isles.

The 'Scuir of Eigg', as An Sgurr is famously known, is a wedge of pitchstone lava, forming a unique two-kilometre long ridge that culminates in an overhanging tower of columnar pitchstone at its sharp eastern extremity. It forms a notable landmark from the mainland. At one stage in its geological history An Sgurr nursed a small glacier and several huge blocks of pitchstone have been carried down to Eigg's rocky south-west coast. The ice appears to have flowed from a noticeable gap in the south-west escarpment; a terminal pitchstone moraine can be discerned streaming down from there to the coast.

Near Galmisdale, to the north side of Kildonnan Bay, are the interesting ruins (although only 500 years old) of Kildonnan Church. On its north wall is a stone inscribed with the arms of Clan Ranald, dated 1441, and in the graveyard a finely carved 15th century cross. More carved stones are preserved at Galmisdale House.

Plant and Wild Life

The low saddle between the north and south settlements, Galmisdale and Cleadale, is covered in moorland heather and bracken. A few trees survive in sheltered spots by the roadside, where harebells and irises also grow. A well wooded area surrounds the sheltered Galmisdale Bay, alive with wild garlic. Wild flowers in every part of the island are abundant, including campion, thyme, golden rod, wild strawberries, willow and a variety of giant heathers.

In the Cleadale amphitheatre, under the huge cirque of cliffs forming the western edge of Beinn Bhuidhe, fields of corn and yellow hay stretch to the sea. The crofted land there undulates and small gardens of fuchsia, veronica and honey-suckle line the road. Out to sea, on this sheltered side of Eigg especially, hundreds of Manx shearwater often float in rafts on the ocean. Curlews are common among the rocks in the hills, as are puffins on the sea-cliffs. Peregrine falcons will be seen circling An Sgurr and its ramparts.

The Nature Conservancy Council has designated seven Sites of Special Scientific Interest on Eigg. These cover almost half the island and include both the areas of high ground - An Sgurr in the south and Beinn Bhuidhe in the north. They are designated for their important flora, fauna and features of geological interest. Climbers and walkers should take care not to damage or disturb them. In particular, the geological features of the pitchstone tower of An Sgurr are of note, and are of special scientific interest. Needless to say, nesting birds should not be disturbed anywhere on the island, especially on the many crags and escarpments.

The Cuillin of Rhum from An Sgurr

THE HILLS

An Sgurr (393m)
Beinn Tighe (315m)

The summit of An Sgurr is easily accessible from its north-west flank, to where there is a good path from Galmisdale along its north side. The path is unmarked on the Ordnance Survey map. The start can be found (at approximately grid reference 473 841) on the track that runs south-west from Sandavore. To reach it from the Galmisdale pier road, take the track running westwards through the edge of the wooded area, from where a path crosses a field to a gate alongside (to north of) a cottage that backs onto the Sandavore track. The path to An Sgurr leaves the track about a hundred metres south-west of the cottage and passes close to the nose of the Sgurr, heading for Loch nam Ban Mora.

A branch of the path strikes southwards, some 400 metres before the loch, to pass through a rocky gully on the north side of the Sgurr. The path quickly gains a bealach at the western end of the summit ridge, where a portion of an old stone wall is probably the remains of a prehistoric fort. The ridge itself is formed from the crystalline 'tops' of pitchstone columns and is pleasantly rugged. The airy walk to the dramatically exposed final summit is a particularly enjoyable experience, and the view, as can be expected, is unsurpassed on Eigg.

A pleasant day's traverse can be made of the summits of An Sgurr and Beinn Tighe, skirting Loch nam Ban Mora and Loch Beinn Tighe, and thence returning

An Sgurr from Galmisdale

either north-east to Laig or by the coastal track and path to Galmisdale above the Grulin Iochdrach shore. Views to the north, of Rhum and parts of Skye beyond, are especially fine.

Beinn Bhudhe (336m)
An Cruachan (299m)
In the north of Eigg, the hill-mass of Beinn Bhuidhe forms a moorland plateau overlooking Cleadale, virtually surrounded to west, north and east by 30-150m cliffs. Mostly these are broken by grass terraces which make pleasant approaches to the plateau as well as offering cliff-faces for exploration. The quickest approach to the Beinn Bhuidhe summit, at the north-west corner of the plateau, is to strike eastwards from a path that leads to the Bealach Talm (Thuilm) above Tolain, north of Cleadale. The plateau can be easily reached from there, up grassy slopes and ledges just to south of Dunan Thalasgair. Alternatively, a heathery moorland traverse of An Cruachan and Beinn Bhuidhe can be made from the road to their south, although the summit of An Cruachan is featureless and the summit cairn can be difficult to find.

PATHS AND WALKS
Apart from the track to Grulin marked on the Ordnance Survey map and the unmarked but well-trodden path described for An Sgurr, and leading also to Loch nan Ban Mora, there are fine cliff-top and shoreline walks to be found on Eigg.

The cliffs along the south coast conceal many caves. The best-known of these is the Cave of Francis, or Massacre Cave, where the notorious MacLeods of Skye are reported to have suffocated nearly four hundred MacDonalds (the entire population of Eigg), when they went into hiding there in the winter of 1577 after avenging themselves of a pillage and raping visit to the Isle by the MacLeods. The cave is about a kilometre and a half from the harbour along the south shore. A track runs south-westwards from a stile (on the left of the track through the wood from Galmisdale) to a cottage, from where a sheep track leads to the cliff fence, above the Uamh Fhraing, and to a zig-zag track down to the shore beside the burn (grid reference 475 835). Just east from there, is Massacre Cave, which has a low entrance passage. One or two MacDonalds, it is said, were able to hold this entrance against the murderous MacLeods, who eventually gathered and set alight large piles of brushwood in order callously to asphyxiate every one of the 365 men, women and children who supposedly took refuge in the cave within. The cave is large but whether it could truly hold nearly 400 people at once is debatable.

Turning westwards along the shore, from the zig-zag track down to the burn, leads to the huge Cathedral Cave, open to the sea at high tide and even recently used for occasional Catholic services - a custom supposedly originating from the 1745 persecution. In some places along the shores here a black glassy volcanic selvage can be seen extruded through the layers of rock; an effect similar to that found on the Oigh-sgeir rocks 25 kilometres to the north-west. Fossilised coniferous trees are also to be found, one good specimen being located high up from the shore at the foot of the rampart of An Sgurr (at the foot of Botterill's Crack). To the west of Grulin is a huge fallen block, Clach Hosdeil.

ROCK CLIMBING

Most of the rock climbing of serious interest is in the south, on the southern rampart of An Sgurr. This almost continuous line of cliffs and buttresses, stretching west to east for over two kilometres, is truly impressive when viewed from the sea to the south of Eigg. Recorded climbing there dates from 1967 although *Collie's Cleft* (60m; Severe) is named after the alleged climb by Collie, in 1908, of this distinct groove in roughly the centre of the *Main Wall*.

Useful descriptions of climbs by I Clough and parties (1967; SMCJ Vol.29, p.54), of *Botterill's Crack* (50m; Severe), *Eagle Chimney* (75m; Hard Severe) and *The Flue* (80m; Very Severe) are given in Hamish Brown's Guide to Rhum (Cicerone Press, 1988). This includes *The Nose* (100m; Very Severe and A3; six bolts and two pegs) first climbed by C Boulton and K Jones in 1970 (SMCJ Vol.29, p.399), which follows a left-slanting groove to gain and climb the central overhanging section, and *Purphura* (120m; Severe) to the right of the gully used for descent at the west (left) end of the main wall (P Moores and S Shaley; SMCJ Vol.31, p.393).

More recently, G E Little and D Sadler (1987) have explored extensively the entire line of these pitchstone crags and their fine buttresses. Numerous challenging climbs are now recorded (SMCJ Vol.34, p38-43). They have identified several new buttresses westwards from the Main Wall: *Big Cave Buttress, Chimney*

The Southern rampart of An Sgurr

Buttress, Beehive Buttress, Ocean Wall, Village Wall. The reader is referred also to the forthcoming SMC Climber's Guide to Skye and the Hebrides.

In the north of Eigg the almost continuous line of cliffs on the east, north and west of the moorland plateau extend in total for nearly ten kilometres. The rock is poor but one or two bold routes are recorded on the Cleadale Face, overlooking Cleadale and the Bay of Laig. *Laig Buttress* (45m; Severe) and *The Pod* (50m; Very Severe) which provide climbing similar to gritstone. Also in the south of Eigg there is a small outcrop of crags, overlooking the Bay of Poll nam Partan just north of Galmisdale. They provide gritstone-like climbing, with routes of up to 20m or so.

OIGH-SGEIR

Some eight kilometres to the south-west of Canna and fourteen kilometres west of Rhum lies a tiny group of islands, with an important lighthouse on the largest (easternmost), Oigh-sgeir. The rocks are of pitchstone, similar geologically to An Sgurr on Eigg, with which it may have at one time been continuous. The lighthouse keepers on Oigh-sgeir have their own miniature golf course.

CANNA

MAPS *:*   Ordnance Survey   1:50,000 Sheet 39
                                     1:25,000 Sheet 232 (NG 20)
              Bartholomew   1:100,000 Sheet 50

PRINCIPAL HILLS
    Carn a'Ghaill   210m   264 065
    Compass Hill   137m   278 062

ACCESS

The Caledonian MacBrayne's steamer from Mallaig, which serves the other Small
Isles, calls at Canna. There is a good harbour in the south-east corner of the island,
between it and the isle of Sanday to which Canna is connected by a bridge. The
steamer ties up at the pier which is used also by local fishing boats.

ACCOMMODATION

The island is owned (since 1981) by the National Trust for Scotland. A holiday home
(ten beds), ten minutes walk from the pier and operated by the Trust through its
office in Edinburgh, is available for rent. There is little else in the way of accommodation on Canna, occasionally a cottage for rent, but plenty of good camping can be
found.

GENERAL DESCRIPTION

The high moorland plateau, culminating in Carn a'Ghaill (210m) gives pleasant
craggy and scenic walking but offers no real climbing. There is an isolated stack on
the shore, half a kilometre north of the harbour entrance. Its vertical conglomerate
walls give little prospect of a climb. A narrow grassy neck almost joins it to the shore
and its summit is crowned with the remains of a forbidding stone tower, An
Coroghon, where a Clanranald chief is said once to have imprisoned his unfaithful
wife. Sir Walter Scott wrote of its scary inaccessibility:

> "Seek not the giddy crag to climb
> To view the turret scathed by time;
> It is a task of doubt and fear
> To aught but goat or mountain deer."

    The grassy walk to Compass Hill - so named for making even a nearby
mariner's compass unreliable - is easy and scenic from An Coroghon. It gives
splendid views of the Skye Cuillin and Rhum.

    Antiquities on Canna include the remains of a cashel (or nunnery) on the south
shore four kilometres west of the harbour, set between the lower and upper cliffs
near to Rubha Sgorr nam Ban-naomha, to which it gives its name (*holy woman's
skerry*). The cliffs there are impressive as far as Dun Channa, at the westernmost tip
of the island, which has been fortified by a wall. The north-eastern sea cliffs, from
Blar Beinn Tighe to below Compass Hill are also fine, with two inaccessible sea-
stacks, Iorcail and An t-Each, but the rock is mostly conglomerate and not attractive
for climbing.

MUCK

MAPS :   Ordnance Survey   1:50,000 Sheet 39
                                            1:25,000 Sheet 274 (NM 47/57)
             Bartholomew   1:100,000 Sheet 50

PRINCIPAL HILL
   Beinn Airein   137m   403 792

ACCESS
Steamers do not call at Muck. Visitors are usually met off the Caledonian MacBrayne ferry at Eigg by motor launch. Occasional sailings from Arisaig can be negotiated (Arisaig Marine Ltd; telephone 0687 5678) or chartered from the Isle of Muck Farms (telephone 0687 2362). The shores of Muck are treacherously rocky and its poorly sheltered harbours, Bagh a'Ghallanaich to north-west and Port Mor in the south-east, are congested with skerries.

ACCOMODATION
Most of the island is occupied as a sheep and dairy farm, but there are cottages for rent and good camping to be had, with permission from the farm; also a barn can probably be arranged in bad weather. There is a small guest house at Port Mor (telephone 0687 2362) from where information can also be obtained about cottages for rent. Caravans are banned from the island.

GENERAL DESCRIPTION
Muck is structured from a sheet of basalt, giving it typical ledges and grassy terraces edged by dark columnar cliffs. Two kilometres of road link the farm in the north-western harbour, where the sands and views of Rhum are fine indeed, with Port Mor which has a small serviceable pier as well as a craft shop and tea room.

The island is a mass of flowers, with a variety of alpine plants and mosses: dwarf juniper, crowberry, root sedums, mountain catspaw and others, all growing 500m or more below their usual altitude. A few imported trees, planted in 1922, form a wood beside the road north of Port Mor.

WALKS
Walking on Muck is given interest by several dykes of dolerite. Beinn Airein in the south-west of the island is an easy grassy hill with steep cliffs to its south-west, as well as to its south-east where they fall straight to the sea in the deeply set and poorly sheltered bay, Camas Mor. A prominent rock pinnacle, The Spichean, to the west side of this bay is worth exploring. Many seabirds nest there as well as on the nearby cliffs, including guillemots, razorbills, kittiwakes and puffins, none of which nest elsewhere in the Small Isles.

On the rocky headland that forms the west side of Bagh a'Ghallanaich is a Bronze Age burial circle, now used as the island's family graveyard. From there, at low tide during springs, a scramble over seaweed covered rocks can be made to Eilean nan Each (*horse island*). To its south the headland, Lamb Island, becomes cut off from Muck at high water. Eilean nan Each especially is a sanctuary for seabirds.

CHAPTER 16

THE LONG ISLE: LEWIS AND NORTH HARRIS

The Western Isles, or Outer Hebrides, are frequently referred to as 'The Long Isle'. They comprise the largest single group of Scottish islands and form an archipelago-chain almost 200 kilometres long from the Butt of Lewis to Barra Head, running approximately north-north-east to south-south-west. The Long Isle lies to the west of Skye; 60 to 90 kilometres west of the Scottish mainland, from which it is separated by the Minch north of Skye and the Sea of The Hebrides south of Skye. Between Skye itself and the central section of the Long Isle, where North Uist and Benbecula arch westwards, is the Little Minch. The narrowest sea passage is 22 kilometres, from the east coast of North Uist to the westernmost headland of Skye, An Ceannac, north of Neist Point.

The Island of Lewis and Harris forms the northern half of the Long Isle and is by far its largest land mass. The disjointed tail stretching like an enormous backbone southwards from Harris, broken by transverse sounds of which the Sound of Harris and Sound of Barra are the largest and most navigable, gives the chain an appearance - from above - of the floating skeleton of a dinosaur. A useful overall view is given by Sheet 1 of the Ordnance Survey (1:250,000) Routemaster Series.

The total land area, although this includes a profusion everywhere of lochs and lochans which comprise almost one quarter of the map area, is nearly 3,000 square kilometres. The land supports a population of around 30,000; a surprising seventeen of the islands in the chain being inhabited, although four fifths of the population to-day live on Lewis and Harris. Some thirty or more of the islands in the chain were at one time inhabited.

Geologically, the Long Isle is built almost entirely of the oldest known rock to be found in Europe, grey Lewisian gneiss. Much of the land is close to sea-level and is covered everywhere with moorland wastes of dark peat, interlaced with an endless congestion of fresh water lochs and burns. Along the whole of the eastern seaboard of the chain barren outcrops of glaciated gneiss give the landscape an almost desolate appearance, contrasting dramatically with the the western shores where huge sandy beaches have been formed by the Atlantic rollers. These enchanting beaches stretch along almost all of the western seaboard, the whiteness of their sand dunes emphasised by the adjoining velvet-green fields of undulating machair. Between the western shores and the Lewisian gneiss to the east lies the inhospitable peat. Here the land is unable to support croft nor almost any kind of

St Clements Church at Rodel

plantlife except for moorland heathers.

 The name Hebrides derives from the Norse *Havbredey*, meaning islands on the edge of the sea. The proximity to water gives, when the weather permits, a special quality to the light. Reflection from the deep clear water, of the surrounding seas as well as from the myriad of inland lochs, produces a luminosity that heightens colouring in the hills and accentuates the rock edges of the outcrops. At other times the storm clouds come racing in from the west, or the sea and land mists envelop all. The climate mostly is mild, without extremes of cold and heat, or rainfall, but the wind blows almost always, and strongly - especially in the north - for two to three days in four.

 The Long Isle has a fascinating history and pre-history. Ancient monuments abound throughout the chain of islands: from the prehistoric standing-stone complex of Callanish in Lewis, which ranks next to Stonehenge as the most important in the British Isles, to Barra's impressive medieval Kiessimul Castle built as a fortress on a rock island in Castle Bay. Elsewhere are to be found pre-historic chambered cairns, stone-circles, standing stones, duns, brochs and beehive burial cairns; while more recent history is marked by the remains of many black (earth-roofed) houses on the one hand, and fine churches like those of St Moluag in the north of Lewis and St Clements at Rodel in the south of Harris on the other. St Clements, especially, has fine and unique examples of Celtic sculptured effigies, in green sandstone.

To the climber the most important island is that of Lewis and Harris. We therefore begin in the north. Indeed more than nine tenths of the Long Isle's significant mountains are in Lewis and North Harris. These together, lying north of the narrow isthmus between the Atlantic and the Minch at Tarbert, make almost a separate island in themselves. Moreover the mountain structure of the Long Isle is such that the two important sea-lochs, West Loch Tarbert and East Loch Tarbert, form a natural geographical division, as sharp as any of the sounds to the south between the islands. Thus we cover Lewis and North Harris in this chapter as Part I of the Long Isle.

LEWIS

MAPS :   Ordnance Survey   1:50,000 Sheets 8 and 13
            Bartholomew   1:100,000 Sheet 57

PRINCIPAL HILLS
NORTH LEWIS

Beinn Mholach	292m	356 387
Beinn Bragar	261m	266 435

WEST LEWIS (UIG)

Mealisval	574m	022 270
Cracaval	514m	030 253
Laival a' Tuath	505m	025 244
Laival a' Deas	501m	025 235
Griomaval	497m	012 220
Tahaval	515m	042 263
Teinnasval	497m	041 254
Tamanaisval	467m	043 237
Suainaval	429m	078 309

SOUTH-EAST LEWIS (PARK)

Beinn Mhor	572m	254 095
Muaithabhal	424m	258 115
Beinn na h-Uamha	389m	270 119
Mor Mhonadh	401m	271 139
Gormol	470m	302 069

ACCESS

A crossing of the Little Minch by Caledonian MacBrayne vehicle and passenger ferry, from Uig in Skye to Tarbert in Lewis (1 hour 45 minutes, two or three sailings daily), is the quickest approach to Lewis and Harris. MacBrayne's steamers also cross from Ullapool to Stornoway (three and a half hours - three sailings daily in summer, two in winter).

There is an airport at Stornoway, with air services (British Airways) twice daily except Sunday from Glasgow and twice daily Monday to Friday from Inverness. Daily flights between Stornoway, Benbecula and Barra are operated by Loganair Ltd (except Sundays).

TRANSPORT

Roads on the island are mostly single-track and winding, making map distances deceptive. That said, the roads are good and a car is worth taking, or hiring in Stornoway.

Bus services to the remoter hill areas of Lewis are either infrequent (Uig) or non-existent (Park). Only two days a week are there buses (Post Office Corporation - telephone 0851-2166) from Stornoway to Timsgarry in Uig; while for Eishken in Park it is necessary to hire a taxi from Stornoway. To other parts of Lewis, for example Carloway and Callanish, there are buses usually daily from Stornoway (always excepting Sundays).

Bicycles would help and can be hired in Stornoway, and sometimes in Tarbert, but distances to Uig (52 kilometres from Stornoway) are daunting and road surfaces, especially to Eishken from the A859 road (for the Park hills) not very suitable. If time is limited, therefore, a car is highly recommended.

A canoe (kayak) or collapsible dinghy would also be a valuable asset; for example, to cross Loch Seaforth from the western side of the loch to reach the hills immediately to its east. The Gatliff Trust hostel at the edge of the south-east Harris hills (grid reference 229 018), at Rhenigidale to which there is now a good road, would then become a base also for some of the Park hills to the east of Loch Seaforth.

ACCOMMODATION

Camping by the white sands of Uig or Mangersta can be recommended and there are several houses that offer bed and breakfast accommodation as well as full board at some lodges and converted farm houses - such as Baile-na-Cille (where the cuisine is exceptional) at Timsgarry, by the fine Uig Sands. Information on locally available accommodation can also be obtained from Baile-na-Cille (telephone 085-175-242).

For the Park hills accommodation is scarce. Apart from the excellent Gatliff Trust hostel at Rhenigidale on the Harris side of Loch Seaforth, there is only the secluded holiday lodge at Eishken. Recently developed fish-farming in Loch Shell has meant improvement of the road from Seaforth Head to Eishken and limited camping - with permission from the Lodge - is feasible in the Park hills.

GENERAL DESCRIPTION

Stornoway in Lewis is the only town with burgh status in the Hebrides. It is the administrative centre of the Western Isles and has a population of nearly 6000. It grew from a fine natural harbour and is the centre of the local fishing industry.

The northern part of Lewis has little of hillwalking or climbing interest. The only hills are those of the Barvas group - eight kilometres north-west of Stornoway - Beinn Mholach or *shaggy hill* (292m), Beinn Barvas (280m) and Beinn Bhearnach

(278m); and in the west near Carloway, Beinn Bragar (261m) and Beinn Rahacleit (248m). The Barvas hills, rounded and peaty, require an approach walk of five kilometres from either the A857 or the B8010. The western hill group is more rocky and can be approached from Shawbost by several surfaced peat roads. One of these, into Glen Mor Shawbost, leads almost to the base of some promising looking cliff-faces on the north side of Beinn Bragar. All the hills of Northern Lewis are surrounded by peat moorland and the approach walks are usually boggy, even in dry weather.

At the Butt of Lewis, where the rugged headland is well worth a visit, fine 200-300m sea-cliffs and a few stacks offer several prospects for exploration. Little has been recorded however, except near the lighthouse. About two kilometres south-west from the Butt of Lewis lies Pygmies' Isle (Luchruban on the map) so-called, supposedly, because of the small bones (probably animals') and other remains found there. A deep cleft almost separates it - and does so at high tide - from the mainland of Lewis. At its summit is a chambered cairn, to which the scramble is easy, though exposed.

Lewis is full of such antiquities. The magnificent standing stones of Callanish, now the property of the National Trust for Scotland, richly reward a visit, as do the Carloway Broch and the museum at Shawbost. Along the whole length of the west coast of Lewis good examples of standing stones, stone circles, brochs and duns can be found. In the dunes of the splendid Uig sands near Ardroil the magnificent walrus-ivory chessmen of Norse origin were found in 1831, hand-carved and dating from the 12th century.

Lewis is separated from Harris, to its south, by the deep incisions into the island made from west and south-east respectively by Loch Resort and Loch Seaforth. So deeply do these two sea lochs cut into the island, which is 35 kilometres broad at this point, that they approach to within barely 10 kilometres of each other; making this the length of the border between Harris and Lewis, running south-east from Kinloch-resort to Vigadale Bay opposite Seaforth Island.

Roughly central between the two sea-lochs, along this border and running northwards from it, is the largest inland loch in Lewis and Harris, Loch Langavat; one kilometre wide and 12 kilometres in length. The deepest inland loch is almost on the western seaboard of Lewis, Loch Suainaval. Like Loch Morar on Scotland's mainland, it runs out to sea (at the Uig Sands) by a river only a few hundred metres in length and has a fresh-water depth some 50 metres or more below sea level.

The B8011 road to Uig passes through some fine west-coast scenery, including - as it leaves West Loch Roag at Miavaig and enters Glen Valtos - an impressive narrow canyon extending for two kilometres with steep 70m rock faces to either side. At its narrowest the floor of this gorge is only 60 metres across. The head of Glen Valtos reaches a shallow pass above Timsgarry, overlooking the two-kilometre stretch of magnificent tidal sands, Uig Sands.

HILLWALKING IN LEWIS

Little Loch Roag, the sea-loch running from north to south to the east of Loch

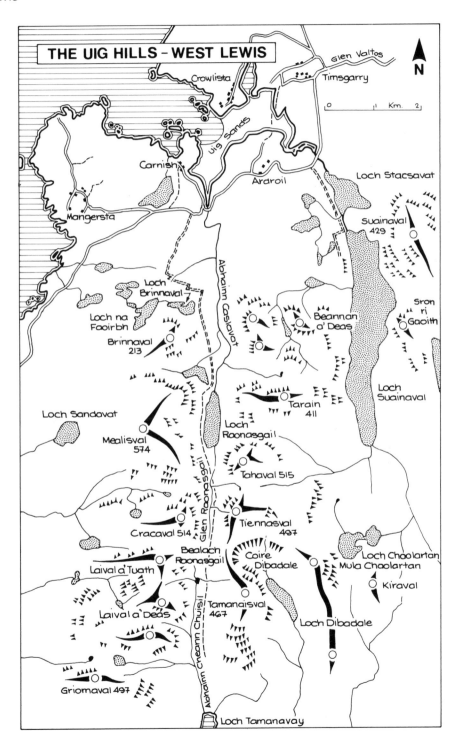

THE UIG HILLS – WEST LEWIS

N

0 | Km. 2

Glen Valtos
Timsgarry
Crowlista
Uig Sands
Carnish
Araroil
Loch Stacsavat
Mangersta
Suainaval 429
Sron ri Gaoith
Loch Brinnaval
Loch na Faoirbh
Brinnaval 213
Abhainn Caslavat
Beannan a' Deas
Loch Suainaval
Loch Sandavat
Tarain 411
Loch Roonasgail
Mealisval 574
Tahaval 515
Glen Roonasgail
Cracaval 514
Tiennasval 497
Bealach Roonasgail
Coire Dibadale
Loch Chaolartan
Mula Chaolartan
Kiraval
Laival a' Tuath
Laival a' Deas
Tamanaisval 467
Abhainn Cheann Chuisil
Loch Dibadale
Griomaval 497
Loch Tamanavay

The Uig hills from Timsgarry across the Uig sands

Suainaval, and Loch Resort running eastwards to within six kilometres of Morsgail Lodge at the head of Little Loch Roag, carve out from the island of Lewis the western hill-group known as Uig. Likewise in south-east Lewis, Loch Seaforth and Loch Shell (Sealg) almost surround the hills of Park (Pairc) by sea-water. These two groups, Uig and Park, provide the only extensive hillwalking on Lewis. The hills of each group are of quite different character. The Uig hills are rugged and, besides providing some spectacular hillwalking, they offer several prospects for rock exploration including some of the finest sea-cliffs in Scotland. The hills of Park, to the east of Loch Seaforth, are relatively featureless but give attractive walking in fine scenery. Those of Uig are drier. Both groups are formed chiefly of Lewisian gneiss.

THE HILLS OF UIG

The Uig mountains form a compact group split into two lines of hills by the deep and relatively straight glens of Raonasgail and Tamanisdale. These glens come head to head at the Bealach Raonasgail. The glen of that name runs north from the bealach to Loch Raonasgail and then north again, becoming the Abhainn Caslavat which flows to the sea at Uig Sands. Similarly, Glen Tamanisdale, running south from the bealach, becomes the Abhainn Cheann Chuisil which runs to the sea in Loch Tamanavay. A new road (unmarked on the Ordnance Survey map - see sketch map on page 289) runs from the B8011 to the south end of Loch Mor na Clibhe, and is being extended as far as Loch Tamanavay. Information concerning use of the road by visitors can be obtained from Baile-na-Cille (085-175-242).

The Standing Stones at Callanish

A traverse of the hills to either the west or the east of the line of the Raonasgail and Tamanisdale glens provides a pleasant day's hillwalking. The western group especially, from Mealisval to Griomaval, can be strenuous - depending, as anywhere, on the particular route and number of summits encompassed. From Loch Brinnaval and back along the path through Glen Raonasgail, takes five to seven hours. On a clear day the views from the tops include the Flannan Isles, some 30 kilometres across the sea to the north-west, and the St Kilda group, lying 90 kilometres to the south-west on the Atlantic horizon. North to south traverses are preferable, for the constant fine views obtained of the Harris hills.

The eastern set of hills makes for marginally the more scenic day, if only by reason of the western hills then providing a splendid foreground for views to seaward. A feature of both sets is the large amount of exposed grey rock, softened by a delightful number of tiny lochans tucked away in the hollows between the hills. Care in mist is essential, especially avoiding the steep rocky eastern flanks of Mealisval and Cracaval and western slopes of Tahaval and Teinnasval.

A traverse of all the main summits of the Uig hills makes a strenuous but rewarding day. It can be undertaken from a base at Ardroil or a camp at Loch Brinnaval, taking in either the western set or eastern set of summits first. Almost 1,900m of climbing is involved and at least seven to nine hours from Loch Brinnaval and back should be allowed, even omitting Griomaval. The new road into Glen Raonasgail can be used with permission from the estate. It starts on the peat road from the B8011 close to Uig Sands, some two kilometres south-west of Ardroil, and links with the path shown on the map at grid reference 034 278, providing easy access as far as Loch Tamanavay.

Traversing the eastern set of hills first is slightly the preferable, both for a gentler start to the day and scenically, taking the morning and evening sun into account. An easy ascent of Flodraskarve Mor, plus a traverse of Cleite Leathann and Cleite Adam, makes a good approach to Tarain and Tahaval. The steep descent from there to the bealach between Tahaval and Teinnasval is grassy and scenic, especially keeping to the south-west flank of Tahaval, and the climb to Teinnasval is without difficulty. The shallow drop and traverse then to the summit of Tamanaisval - nearly two kilometres to the south - is grassy and pleasant, skirting above the impressive cliffs that fall steeply into Coire Dibadale.

The descent into Glen Tamanisdale from Tamanaisval can be made almost anywhere on its west or south-west flank, heading either for the Allt Ruadh to the west of the glen if Griomaval is to be included in the day, or to the narrow steepish glen that climbs westwards between Laival a'Deas and Naidevala Muigh if both this hill and Griomaval are being omitted. Alternatively Naidevala Muigh is easily ascended to its south-east from the Allt Ruadh, and Laival a'Deas approached from there.

The walks over Laival a'Tuath, Cracaval and Mealisval are stony but straightforward; the slope ascending Mealisval from the rocky bealach to its south-east being particularly bouldery. A descent of the north-west shoulder of Mealisval can be made, carefully avoiding the precipitous north face, and then striking directly north-north-east, taking a line west of the low-lying Brinnaval and east of Loch na Faoirbh, to the prominent new road leading to the coast road close to Uig Sands.

Mealisval (*link-stead* or *farmstead fell*) (574m)

Being the highest of the Uig hills and the northernmost of its western group, Mealisval gives the most distant views seaward to the Flannan Isles and St Kilda. The easiest ascent to its summit is by the western flank, leaving the coast road near Islivig or Brenish and passing then south or north of Loch Sandavat. The quickest and driest, however, is to take the path to the west side of Loch Raonasgail from the end of the new road at the south end of Loch Mor na Clibhe and after half a kilometre climb the steep grassy and rocky gully westwards to the bealach just to north of the summit. Alternatively, the deep glen running westwards from Loch Mor na Clibhe can be followed skirting the north face of Mealisval and the north-west flank of the mountain taken to its summit.

The north-east shoulder of Mealisval, named Mula Mac Sgiathain, has an impressive north-facing precipice almost 300m high overlooking Loch Mor na Clibhe. The cliff is named (on the Ordnance Survey 1:10,000 map) Creagan Tealasdale. Its eastern section forms a narrow corrie above Loch Mor na Clibhe and the face there is cleft almost from the summit to the corrie floor by a large fissure called the Palla Glas. This cleft, on close inspection from below, comprises a main gully and - to its left - a discontinuous lesser gully which starts about one third the way up the main gully. The gully walls on both sides give disjointed rock pitches of varying standard, mostly wet and overgrown.

The shoulders, or buttresses, to either side of the corrie containing the Palla Glas are easily climbed; they afford some pleasant scrambling in places. The eastern side of the corrie gives cleaner rock and the buttress on this side, close to the gully, gives virtually continuous moderate and interesting scrambling with one Difficult short pitch about a third of the way up. The right (western) side of the corrie is the more vegetatious. Indeed some potentially good rockclimbing to the right of the Palla Glas is marred by the almost luxuriant vegetation.

Cracaval (*crow fell*) (514m)

The fine rocky bealach between Mealisval and Cracaval holds three small lochans, from where a broken bouldery ridge leads to the summit of Cracaval. This approach to the summit, starting either from the coast road or Loch Brinnaval and first climbing Mealisval, is probably the most pleasant. The south-east ridge of the mountain, from the Bealach Raonasgail is also easy and provides a route for ascent (or descent) using the road through Glen Raonasgail. Care, however, must be taken to avoid the east face of Cracaval overlooking this glen; the crags there are steep and loose, and the grassy slopes below them bouldery and unpleasant.

From Mealista, at the southern end of the coast road overlooking the Mol Forsgeo Sands, an interesting route to Cracaval, and drier than most, can easily be found. Height, and less boggy ground, is gained quickly by heading for the small hill Taireval and then skirting north of the hidden and picturesque Loch na Clibhe; or take in first the craggy west ridge of Laival a'Tuath and the summit of this hill, with an easy - steep but short - descent from there south-eastwards to the bealach south of Cracaval.

Laival a'Tuath (514m)
Laival a' Deas (501m)
Although separate summits, the two Laivals form virtually one mountain split by the east-facing narrow, deep and inhospitable corrie above Loch a'Chama, where waterfalls cascade from the shallow rocky bealach between the two summits. The entire east side of the mountain, overlooking Glen Tamanisdale, is uncomfortably precipitous and should be avoided. The Laivals (*Tuath* is the Gaelic for north and *Deas* the Gaelic for south) are best climbed from Mealista or included in a traverse of the western Uig summits. From the North Laival a descent can be made, taking the south-west flank of Cracaval, to the Bealach Raonasgail. The rock scenery on this flank of Cracaval is remarkable.

Griomaval (*Grim's fell*) (497m)
Griomaval, with its southern shoulder, Steinisval, is the southernmost of all the Uig hills. Its summit affords a fine view of the Harris hills as well as an impressive glimpse down the 250m steep cliff-face on its north side overlooking the hidden and appropriately named, Dubh Loch. This face is best approached from the west, along Glen Tealasdale, and forms a feature of the mountains there when seen from the coast road south from Islivig. The approach glen gives its name to the Tealasdale slabs on the face, where a range of good routes are recorded with more to be explored.

The most interesting, and probably the best, approach to the summit of Griomaval is to take Glen Tealasdale from the coast south of the point where the narrow surfaced road that runs through Mealista ends at a small fishing jetty. A rough path passes to north of Dubh Loch and ascends to the bealach beyond, west of Loch Braighe Griomaval, which can be skirted to its north. From there the east slope to the summit of Griomaval is easy. The western slope of the mountain is straightforward, but probably less tedious in descent.

Tahaval (515m)
The highest of the eastern group of Uig hills, Tahaval, appears on first sight the least interesting. The easiest approaches to the summit are from either the north-east, over Tarain and descending from there to west of the attractive Loch Mor Braigh an Tarain, or from the south, over Teinnasval. The north-west flank however is rocky and rises steeply from Loch Raonasgail. Inspection of its south-east ridge looks worthwhile. Good climbing is probably to be found there with lines to the summit (none recorded).

Teinnasval (497m)
The summit of Teinnasval can be approached from the glen of the Allt Bealach Raonasgail by taking the easy south-west flank of the hill from the Bealach Raonasgail. The route skirts the top of Coire Dibadale giving splendid views south-eastwards down to the loch at the foot of the steep north-east cliffs in this impressive corrie.

On the Far South Buttress of Sgorran Dubh Teinnasval

While similar to its neighbour Tahaval in some of its features, Teinnasval - the lower of the two - has a much more interesting west face, formed into three or four distinct buttresses. This face, some 150m in height, is named Sgorran Dubh Teinnasval. The rock is of granite and granite pegmatite.

A stone shoot, which forks halfway up the face, splits it roughly into two parts. The northern section is named *North Buttress*; between the branches of the fork is *Central Buttress*; and to the south, *South Buttress*. Further south again is *Far South Buttress*. The North Buttress is broken and gives good moderate scrambling in dry weather. The upper part of the Central Buttress, which can be reached from the stone shoot, also affords moderate scrambling to the summit plus harder lines of ascent. The lower part offers some serious rock exploration. South Buttress offers fine rock-climbing; routes from Very Difficult to Very Severe are now recorded. Far South Buttress is less extensive and its lower section can be turned to the south by a grassy shelf.

Tamanaisval (*harbour fell*) (467m)

The bealach south-west of Teinnasval, to north of Tamanaisval, is a fine position. It looks impressively down into Coire Dibadale and at the same time into the deep incision between the east and west groups of Uig hills formed by the Allt Bealach Raonasgail. The walk from the Bealach Raonasgail to the summit of Tamanaisval, although steep at first, becomes gentle and grassy.

On this approach to the mountain the finest feature of Tamanaisval - its north-east face above the head of Loch Dibadale - is hidden and a descent from the summit down the easy south-east ridge is worthwhile for the views of this face alone. Nearly one kilometre in length and rising over 120m from the head of the loch, Creag Dhubh Dibadale forms the highest and boldest inland rock face in Lewis. It was reported, by R G Folkard and M J Fox when they explored it in 1948, as ".... the most unrelenting wall of rock that we have seen anywhere." The rock is firm and steep. A few Very Severe routes are now recorded on the face, as well as several of Extreme grade.

Tarain (411m)

The lower-lying but rugged area of small hills between the shallow Abhainn Caslavat glen and the enormously deep Loch Suainaval, two kilometres to its east, is unusual. The highest point is the summit of Tarain, easily reached by pleasant walks over or between the smaller hills to its north and north-east, or from Loch Brinnaval. The amount of exposed rock on these small hills, to north and east of Tarain, is remarkable considering their altitude (their craggy tops average 240m). Their eastern flanks drop steeply into Loch Suainaval.

The rocky summit of Tarain can be reached directly from Loch Mor na Clibhe by an easy ascent of its north-west shoulder. This approach, followed by a traverse of the low rocky region north-eastwards to the weir at the mouth of Loch Suainaval, and following the partly surfaced track from there back to the B8011 road, makes a fine short day. The two most north-easterly of the small hills in this region, Beinnan a'Tuath (232m) and Beinnan a'Dheas (252m) - immediately west of Loch Suainaval - provide short but interesting rock-climbing of all grades. This climbing is chiefly on their slabby north faces, less than three kilometres from Ardroil and only one or two kilometres from the new road by Loch Brinnaval.

Suainaval (*Sweyn's fell*) (429m)

Across Loch Suainaval, and rising steeply from its north-eastern shore, is the last of the Uig hills, Suainaval - isolated from the main group. The only feature of interest on the mountain, apart from its steep west face overlooking Loch Suainaval, is the smaller outlier on its south flank - Sron ri Gaoith (253m) - whose western slope also drops steeply into the loch. Both these rocky slopes are heavily broken with grassy gullies and ledges. Sron ri Gaoith, however, has two of its west-facing buttresses now named: Flannan Buttress, the furthest north, and to its south, the more prominent Ardroil Buttress. Both have reported routes of Very Difficult grade. The summit of Suainaval is a short hillwalk either from Carishader to its north-east, or from the coast road between Ardroil and Timsgarry. The Carishader approach is the drier and more pleasant, starting on the track along the Uisaig River.

THE HILLS OF PARK

The Park group of hills, although slightly the nearer to Stornoway and considerably closer to Tarbert than those of Uig have a greater sense of remoteness, despite the hills themselves being far gentler. This is partly the result of their being virtually surrounded by water, but mostly because of the almost complete absence of roads and habitation.

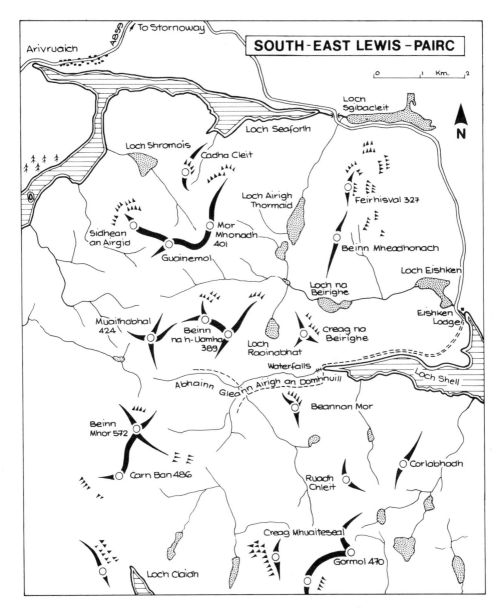

SOUTH-EAST LEWIS – PAIRC

To Stornoway

Arivruaich

Loch Sgibacleit

Loch Seaforth

Loch Shromois

Cadha Cleit

Loch Airigh Thormaid

Feirhisval 327

Sidhean an Airgid

Mor Mhonadh 401

Beinn Mheadhonach

Guainemol

Loch Eishken

Loch na Beirighe

Muaithabhal 424

Beinn na h-Uamha 389

Creag na Beirighe

Eishken Lodge

Loch Raoinabhat

Waterfalls

Abhainn Gleann Airigh an Domhnuill

Loch Shell

Beannan Mor

Beinn Mhor 572

Carn Ban 486

Corlabhadh

Ruadh Chleit

Creag Mhuaiteseal

Gormol 470

Loch Claidh

They give pleasant hillwalking and have a number of features that resemble the Paps of Jura, although being far less distinctive. The highest hill in the area, Beinn Mhor, with its southern shoulder, Carn Ban, forms a prominent feature seen from almost the full length of the Stornoway to Tarbet road running down the west side of Loch Seaforth.

Between Beinn Mhor and its adjacent hill Muaithabhal, to its north, is the most deeply cut bealach in the region, from which the Abhainn Sgaladal Mhoir runs west-north-west to Loch Seaforth and the Abhainn Gleann Airigh an Domhnuill east to Loch Shell. The ground to the west of this bealach is boggy; to the east it is drier and offers pleasant camping (but no fuel) by the tiny lochan just below the bealach (beware the midges).

The narrow track to Eishken has now been surfaced and a forestry road continues round the small headland, Rubha na Moine, from the Eishken Lodge for one to two kilometres westwards along the north shore of Loch Shell. A stalker's path leads from there to a fine timber bridge at the sharp head of the loch, below some splendid waterfalls. From the south side of the bridge a shepherd's path continues westwards, up the shallow glen to turn southwards after two kilometres to a tall pole planted by the local shepherds to form a landmark in the frequent mists that shroud these hills.

Beinn Mhor (572m)

Beinn Mhor is easily reached from the path leading westwards from the waterfalls at the head of Loch Shell, by following this for two and a half kilometres and then heading for the south-west shoulder of the hill above the rocky Sron Thorcasmol. From the pleasantly sharp, grassy summit, views across Seaforth Island and the North Harris hills are superb; to the east is the full length of Loch Shell and to south-east, beyond the Sound of Shiant, lie the Shiant Isles. There is a good anchorage at the head of Loch Shell (as well as in Tob Eishken on the northern side of the loch) and a landing by boat there, or using a moored yacht as base, provides a pleasant approach to these hills - as to many on the eastern seaboard of the Long Isle.

Muithabhal (424m)
Beinn na h-Uamha (*hill of the cave*) (389m)
Mor Mhonadh (*great moor*) (401m)

To the north of the Abhainn Gleann Airigh an Domhnuill, the rounded summit of Muaithabhal, the twin grassy summits of Beinn na h-Uamha, and those of Mor Mhonadh, Guainemol and Sidhean an Airgid, can all be traversed easily in a day. The hills are relatively featureless and the going easy if frequently wet and soft. The only possible scrambling there is on the north edge of Cadha Cleit, which would make a good approach to the region from the north if a landing by canoe was made at Tob Mhic Cholla in the north-east extremity of Loch Seaforth.

Gormol (*blue fell*) (470m)

In the continuously hilly south-east of Park, Gormol and its south-west shoulder, Crionaig (467m), look attractive from Beinn Mhor and Muaithabhal, with crags on their west and south-west flanks. However, they are even more remote and misty than the central and northern hills of the area. Likewise, Caiteshal and its tempting crags overlooking Loch Seaforth at the south-west extremity of the Park hills would be difficult to reach unless by boat or canoe from the Rhenigidale hostel across the mouth of the loch.

ROCK CLIMBING IN LEWIS

All rock climbing of any significance in Lewis is in the Uig district, either on its inland crags, or on its magnificent sea-cliffs at Ard More Mangersta. The inland crags generally are of dark grey gneiss, striated but firm. The finest inland rock-face, and probably the least climbed to date, is Creag Dhubh Dibadale on the north-east face of Tamanaisval above the head of Loch Dibadale. The first recorded examination of this face was by R G Folkard and M J Fox in 1948. They remarked on its potential for rock climbing, although were unable to force a route more than 50m of the way up the face.

The sea-cliffs of Uig are of fine-grained granite with many quartzite and pegmatite intrusions. The best known, named dramatically the *Painted Wall Zawn,* is two minutes scramble from the end of the road northwards out of Mangersta to the Gob Rubha Phail.

Lesser crags in Uig - though nonetheless important - include Sgorran Dubh Teinnasval, the western cliffs of Teinnasval overlooking Glen Tamanisdale, and Creagan Thealastail, on the north-east shoulder of Mealisval. The first reported exploration of both appears to have been in 1948, by R G Folkard and party.

Creag Dhubh Dibadale

This cliff-face can be reached from Glen Raonasgail over the bealach between Teinnasval and Tamanaisval, using the new road from the B8011 to Loch Mor na Clibhe.

Two routes there were recorded in 1970 (SMCJ Vol. 29, p. 398) - *Via Valtos* (150m; Very Severe), which follows an obvious crack-line to the left-hand (south) side of the face, by A Ewing and W Sproul, and *Solitude* (170m; Very Severe), a crack to right of the central wall of the crag, by J Ball and M Reeves; also one in 1974 (SMCJ Vol.30, p.383) by R Archbold and G Cohen - unnamed (230m: Very Severe) following a slight ramp to north of Via Valtos.

The pioneering of Extreme exploration on Creag Dhubh Dibadale began in 1980 when M Fowler and A Strapcans forced the *Panting Dog Climb* (180m; E2) which takes a direct line above the slabby tongue of red rock to the right (north) of Via Valtos. Exploration of the crag continued in 1981 with two Extreme routes - *Take Two* (120m; E1), starting on slabs at the foot of a slanting ramp to right of Solitude (C Watts and S Victoris), and *The Big Lick* (177m; E2) which starts to left of and gains the red tongue of rock (M Fowler and A Meyers). The rock is generally sound and firm though some cracks and ledges are discouragingly vegetatious. There is scope on Creag Dhubh Dibadale for further Extreme exploration.

Tealasdale Slabs

The next most important inland crag in Lewis is the Tealasdale Slabs on Griomaval - reported in an early edition of the Islands Guide to be "hopeless and manifestly unclimbable"! This cliff-face can be easily reached from the coast-road, south from Islivig, along Glen Tealasdale. Many good climbs are now reported on its overlapping slabs; ranging from Very Difficult to Extreme. The climbing appears to have been first explored in 1968 by R Sharp and W Sproul (SMCJ Vol.29, p.280). They

Creag Dhubh Dibadale

gave the ambiguous name *Golden Gully* (240m; Difficult) to the prominent grassy rake that separates the west buttress from the main slabs. They also pioneered - in the following year - the route *Islivig Direct* (240m: Severe) which takes a direct line, of crack and corner, from the tail of the lowest slabs to the summit of Griomaval.

     In 1970, C Forrest and party reported the rock as clean and sound, giving Mild Severe climbing for most of its height (SMCJ Vol.29, p.426). These climbers made the route *Lochlann* (240m; Very Severe) and the same year J Ball and M Reeves climbed *The Scroll* (300m; Severe). Several further routes, from Difficult to Very Severe, have since been found (SMCJ Vol.30 p.267).

Sgorran Dubh Teinnasval

The recorded rock climbing on Sgorran Dubh Teinnasval is chiefly on its South Buttress, to the south of the prominent forked stone shoot. Folkard's route (147m; Difficult) ascends this buttress from its lowest rocks, trending northwards to finish north (left of) the summit overhang. The buttress features four narrow gullies, or grooves; the main one forked, with a deep incision cut steeply into it from a short distance up. To the right (south) is a fine edge, and beyond are three parallel narrow rock gullies, with ribs between.

     In 1972, T Fletcher and party (SMCJ Vol.30, P.165) climbed the first (southernmost) rib - *Flannan* (120m; Very Severe) - and B Clarke and party (SMCJ Vol.30, p.166) made a route between this rib and Folkard's South Buttress route - named enigmatically *Nosferatu* (185m; Very Severe). There are routes here still to be pioneered, as well as on Far South Buttress where shorter climbs exist of similar grade.

Creagan Tealasdale

The nearest crag to Ardroil, Creagan Tealasdale, probably has the least remaining potential in Lewis for new routes. Folkard's route here took a line on its central buttress to the west of the Palla Glas. In 1970, M H Moar and G Lawson (SMCJ Vol.30, p.164) climbed *The Porker* on the same buttress (90m; Severe) - a more or less direct line, following overlapping slabs to the west of the waterslide.

Sea-Cliffs and Other Crags

Other inland crags are still being discovered in Lewis: the west-facing rocky slopes of Sron ri Gaoith, above Loch Suainaval offer routes Difficult to Very Difficult (SMCJ Vol.30, p.262). However some of the finest rock climbing to be found in Lewis is on the sea-cliffs. Those north of Islivig, mostly of gneiss, were the first to receive attention (SMCJ Vol.30, p.83) as well as those at Garry Bay in North Lewis beyond New Tolsta, where the pinnacle rock, known as the Grey Castle, offers prospects; but these are nothing to the superb and awe-inspiring cliffs to the north-west of Mangersta.

It is probable that early climbs were made on the sea-cliffs of Mangersta in the 1960's but the first extensive exploration began in the early 1980's when members of the Lochaber Mountaineering Club discovered and named the *Painted Wall Zawn* at Gob Rubha Phail, and the nearby *Flannan Zawns* at Ard More Mangersta. Extreme exploration began in 1985 when D Cuthbertson and G Latter and others, including J Moran and D Pearse, made many Extreme routes on the Painted Wall Zawn (21-27m) and Flannan Zawns (30-39m), and on *Red Walls* (33-78m) to their south. Some Severe and Very Severe routes have also been climbed on Ard More Mangersta. The classic route there is *North Atlantic Crossing* (Mild Very Severe and E5; 99m) which takes the rising girdle of rock from the headland (grid reference 000 326); another which is particularly pleasant is the attractively named *Sunset Ridge* (75m) which is no more than Difficult.

NORTH HARRIS

North Harris is separated from South Harris by the narrow neck of land, barely half a kilometre across when the tide is high, between East Loch Tarbert, which opens to the Minch, and West Loch Tarbert which opens to the Atlantic.

MAPS :   Ordnance Survey   1:50,000 Sheets 13 and 14
                Bartholomew   1:100,000 Sheet 57

PRINCIPAL HILLS
CENTRAL GROUP

Tomnaval	552m	165 079
Clisham	799m	155 073
Mulla-fo-dheas	743m	143 077
Mulla-fo-thuath	708m	140 085
Mullach an Langa	614m	143 095
Uisgnaval Mor	729m	121 086
Teilesval	697m	125 091
Sron Scourst	491m	106 098
Stulaval	579m	134 124

WESTERN GROUP

Cleiseval	511m	079 083
Oreval	662m	084 100
Ullaval	659m	086 114
Sron Ulladale	442m	080 133
Tirga Mor	679m	055 115
Ceartaval	556m	043 127
Husival Mor	489m	023 117

SOUTH-EAST GROUP

Sgaoth Iosal	531m	155 043
Sgaoth Aird	559m	166 040
Gillaval Glas	471m	149 022
Toddun	528m	210 030

ACCOMMODATION

The eastern and south-eastern hills of North Harris are all within walking distance from Tarbert where the Tarbert Hotel and one or two guest houses give full board or bed and breakfast. The excellent Gatliff Trust hostel at Rhenigidale (grid reference 229 018) is an eight kilometre walk from Tarbert, but can now be reached by road (unmarked on the Ordnance Survey map) from the A859 near Urgha. The hostel gives a splendid base for Toddun, the farthest south-east of the Harris hills, but is otherwise of little use to the climber unless equipped with a canoe or boat to reach the western Park hills of Lewis.

Occasional bed and breakfast accommodation can be found on the B887 road to Hushinish and camping is possible, with local permission, in the south-east corner of Hushinish Bay. Good camping places generally are scarce and, away from the sea machair, usually wet and midge-infested. However, camping places will be found in Glen Ulladale, accessible from Loch Chilostair by a good stalker's path, as well as in Glen Stuladale, accessible from Glen Meavaig.

TRANSPORT
As for Lewis, a car is recommended for access to the more remote hills, although a bicycle from Tarbert can be used and could even be an advantage. For example, the surfaced road from the weir at the mouth of Lochan Beag (one kilometre east of Amhuinnsuidhe) to the dam at the south end of Loch Chilostair, belonging to the North of Scotland Hydro Electric Board is closed to cars but accessible by cycle, as is the well made-up private track from the B887 into Glen Meavaig.

Buses run only infrequently from Tarbert to Hushinish, with no regular service. Taxis can be hired in Tarbert. Regular buses, two or three daily except Sundays, from Stornoway to Tarbert, are operated by Harris Garage Co Ltd (telephone 0859 2441). They call at Ardvourlie and Maaruig and can be of help for the Clisham hills and the south-east hill group of North Harris.

GENERAL DESCRIPTION
The region between West Loch Tarbert and the border between Harris and Lewis to the north-east and extending as far as East Loch Tarbert and Loch Seaforth, is the most mountainous part of the Long Isle. Together with its adjoining regions, it forms the largest area of hills in all of the Hebrides, including Skye. The land area covered is approximately 25 kilometres by 10 kilometres; possibly the largest continuously mountainous stretch of country in the British Isles outside of the mainland of Scotland. It includes the highest hill in the Western Isles, Clisham, as well as the finest rock feature in the Hebrides - the massive, bulging and overhanging headland of Sron Ulladale, which towers above Loch Ulladale.

The region is divided naturally into three groups of mountains by Glen Meavaig and by the line of lochs forming the pass taken by the A859 road from Ardhasaig to Maaruig. The western and central groups form a broad rampart of hills between Harris and Lewis, from the A859 westwards to Hushinish. They comprise the Forest of Harris - all treeless deer forest - peaty and nearly devoid of plant-life. Apart from its hills, the whole region has very much the character of Lewis. The true, gentler character of Harris begins south from Tarbert.

The hills of North Harris are almost entirely of Lewisian gneiss, with a tendency for the rock to be pink in the west and grey in the east. At the westernmost point of the Harris hills is the Hushinish peninsula, where machair abounds and the bays, especially on the south side, are formed from splendid sweeps of shell sand. The island of Scarp, now no longer supporting permanent inhabitants, dominates the mouth of Loch Resort. Holiday houses can be rented there. The island rises to 308m at Sron Romul, with crags for exploration where the summit drops north-

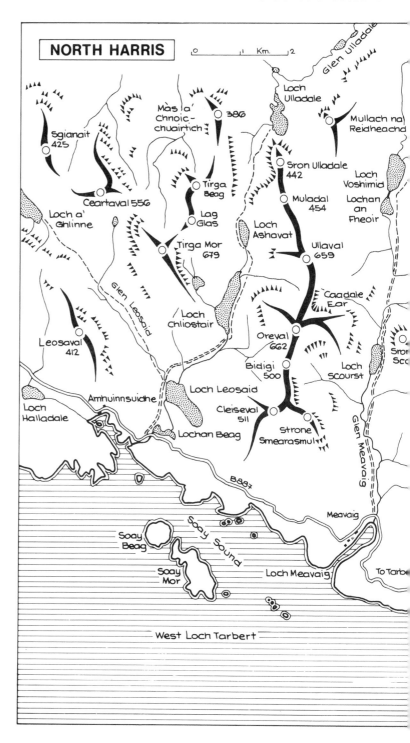

NORTH HARRIS

0   1   Km.   2

Glen Ulladale

Loch Ulladale

Sgianait 425

Màs la' Chnoic- chuairtich

386

Mullach na Reidheachd

Sron Ulladale 442

Loch Voshimid

Lochan an Fheoir

Tirga Beag

Ceartaval 556

Muladal 454

Lag Glas

Loch a' Ghlinne

Loch Ashavat

Tirga Mor 679

Ullaval 659

Caadale Ear

Glen Leosaid

Loch Chliostair

Leosaval 412

Oreval 662

Sron Sco

Bidigi 500

Loch Scourst

Amhuinnsuidhe

Loch Leosaid

Loch Halladale

Cleiseval 511

Lochan Beag

Strone Smearasmul

Glen Meavaig

B.887

Meavaig

Soay Sound

Soay Beag

Soay Mor

Loch Meavaig

To Tarbe

West Loch Tarbert

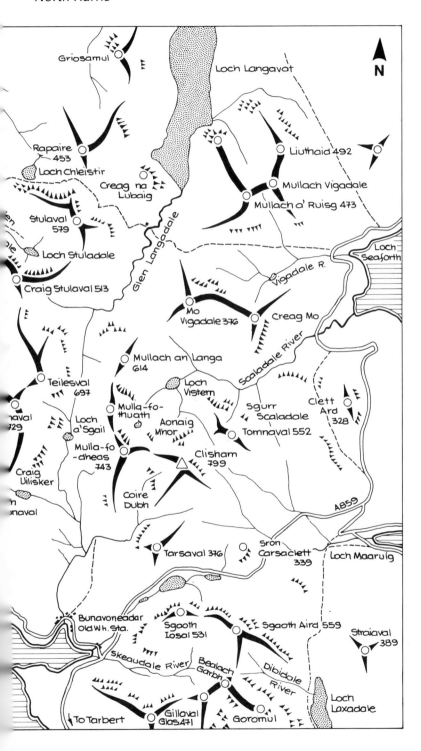

Griosamul

Loch Langavat

N

Rapaire
453

Loch Chleistir

Creag na
Lubaig

Liuthaid 492

Mullach Vigadale

Mullach a' Ruisg 473

Stulaval
579

Loch Stuladale

Loch
Seaforth

Glen Langadale

Vigadale R.

Craig Stulaval 513

Mo
Vigadale 376

Creag Mo

Scaladale River

Mullach an Langa
614

Loch
Vistem

Teilesval
697

Sgurr
Scaladale

Clett
Ard
328

Mulla-fo-
thuath

729

Loch
a'Sgail

Aonaig
Mhor

Tomnaval 552

Mulla-fo
-dheas
743

Clisham
799

Craig
Uilisker

Coire
Dubh

naval

A859

Tarsaval 376

Sron
Carsaclett
339

Loch Maaruig

Bunavoneadar
Old W.h. Sta.

Sgooth
Iosal 531

Sgaoth Aird 559

Straiaval
389

Skeaudale River

Bealach
Garbh

Dibidale
River

Loch
Laxadale

To Tarbert

Gillaval
Glas 471

Goromul

Uisgnaval Mor(left) and Mulla-fo-dheas from Ardhasig

Oreval (left) and Sron Scourst from Loch Meavaig

wards to the sea. A local fisherman's ferryboat serves the island from a pier at North Hushinish.

Bird-life in North Harris is at its best on the wind and spray swept peninsula south-west of Hushinish. Fulmars, shags, guillemots, rock doves and a variety of common coastal birds nest in the hollows of the hills and low cliffs of pink gneiss. North of the peninsula are familiar indications of old lazy beds, running in some places hundreds of metres up the hillsides.

HILLWALKING IN NORTH HARRIS

The hills of North Harris contain no less than nine summits of over 600m, but only one (Clisham) over 750m. They divide into three groups: the central or Clisham group, east of Glen Meavaig and north-west of the Stornoway to Tarbert road; a western group lying west of Glen Meavaig and south of Loch Resort, stretching westwards to the Atlantic seaboard; and a south-east group which lies north-east of Tarbert, between there and Loch Seaforth. The peaty nature of the ground in these hills makes the glens and lower slopes generally soft, at times boggy, but height is gained quickly in almost any direction and where the glens are long, good stalker's paths usually exist. The central group contains the highest hills, so we start there. It divides into the Clisham hills and the Uisgnaval hills, east and west of Abhainn Loch a'Sgail.

THE CLISHAM HILLS

The group of hills that includes Clisham, the highest peak of the Western Isles, forms a prominent horseshoe ridge of summits enclosing Loch Vistern at the head of the Scaladale River. Seen from the south-east, Clisham is a fine-shaped peak and the edge of the steep crag on its north flank, Aonaig Mhor, is well defined; while from the south-west, the inhospitable broken tiers of rock in Coire Dubh dominate the view, drawing the eye away from the shapely ridge above that connects Clisham with Mulla-fo-dheas, more than a kilometre to its west-north-west.

Clisham (799m)
Tomnaval (552m)
Mulla-fo-dheas (*south summit*) (743m)
Mulla-fo-thuath (*north summit*) (708m)
Mullach an Langa (*long summit*) (614m)

A climb to the summit of any of the Clisham hills is perfectly straightforward from a near point on the A859 Tarbert to Stornoway road to their south and east. The nearest approach for Clisham alone is from the bridge by which the A859 road crosses over the Maaruig River, where a car can readily be parked. There is no clear path but by following the river for half a kilometre, skirting Sron Carsaclett, the south flank of Clisham and then its south-east ridge are easily ascended. For Mulla-fo-dheas followed by Clisham, a good route is provided by the western flank of Coire Dubh, Mo Buidhe, approached by the path leading from the derelict whaling station at Bunavoneadar.

The complete traverse of the group can be made starting and finishing near the bridge over the Scaladale River, just to south of Ardvourlie. The driest and most pleasing start is to take the old drove track that leaves the Tarbert to Stornoway road half a kilometre before the bridge as it descends from the south to Ardvourlie, to the north side of Caisteal Ard (grid reference 186 095). Skirting Caisteal Ard and Clett Ard, head for the south-east shoulder of Tomnaval. This easy peak can be by-passed to its south or - more enjoyably -included in the approach to Clisham. From the grassy bealach between the two mountains, the slope to the summit of Clisham is stony and the final ridge narrower than would appear from afar; its width almost fully taken up by the large Ordnance Survey cairn surrounding the triangulation pillar there.

The short summit ridge of Clisham is aligned south-east to north-west. A grassy and rocky north ridge runs out from its north-west extremity to Aonaig Mhor. Care is needed here in mist. From the north-west end of Clisham's summit ridge a rounded stony slope, running almost due west, drops steeply to a long grassy bealach. This leads, with an easy short ascent, to the small grassy eastern summit of Mulla-fo-dheas (named An t-Isean on the Ordnance Survey 1:25,000 map). Beyond this subsidiary peak the ridge narrows again, dipping to a small green and bouldery bealach, and then rising steeply to the rocky main summit of Mulla-fo-dheas.

From the summit of Mulla-fo-dheas a descent can be made by its south to south-west shoulder, Mo Buidhe, picking up the path below the Abhainn Horabray, west of Creag Ghreine-brigh and leading down to the long-derelict whaling station at Bunavoneadar near the head of Loch Bun Abhainn-eadar. It is much more pleasant however, if time and weather permit, to continue the interesting horse-shoe of summits, from Mulla-fo-dheas over Mulla-fo-thuath to its north and then over Mullach an Langa and Mo Vigadale, descending by Creag Mo to Ardvourlie or Vigadale Bay.

The north-west ridge that descends from Mulla-fo-dheas is narrow and bouldery - with fine crags dropping away to its east. The ascent then to the northern peak is grassy, with good views of the steep but broken crags of Aonaig Mhor to the north side of Clisham. Mulla-fo-thuath has an attractive summit, with fine crags to its west and south-west (short but worth inspection) and broken crags, dropping away into a grassy corrie, at the extremity of its north-east shoulder. The crags are avoided by descending the stony slope due north. A long grassy bealach and then easy slopes lead to the rounded summit of Mullach an Langa (614m). Views from there include a long stretch northwards of the huge Loch Langavat, and a striking profile to the south-east of Sgurr Scaladale. The latter is a fine line of cliffs to the north-west of Tomnaval overlooking the head of Glen Scaladale, nearly a full kilometre in length and over 240m high.

From Mullach an Langa the grassy descent to north-east skirts the eastern extremity of the Cnoc a'Chaisteil crags on its north-facing slope. At this point the crags are steep and broken; at their farther (western) end they are moderately easily climbed by a rib of regular shaped blocks, for 80m or so, to a sloping platform and a 'loose' block at the top.

The next and last small hill in the horseshoe, Mo Vigadale, has minor crags to its north, which enhance the walk from there down its north-east shoulder to the bays of Ardvourlie or Vigadale; alternatively a descent can be made into Glen Scaladale. These easy descents skirt to north or south of the east-facing Creag Mo crags, which lie barely a kilometre from the road.

The full Clisham horseshoe, from Caisteal Ard to Ardvourlie, or to the bridge (on the A859) over the Scaladale river, takes from four to five hours. A pleasant extension is to descend from Mo Vigadale northwards to the Bealach na h-Uamha (200m), below the attractive lochan at the foot of Tom Ruisg, and to take the easy shoulder of Mullach a'Ruisg to its grassy summit (473m). From there a walk over Mullach Vigadale and Liuthaid (492m) can be taken before descending to the Abhainn a'Mhuil path to Aline Lodge on the A589. Even more pleasant, is to descend north-westwards from Liuthaid to Loch Langavat and then skirt below the craggy headland, Creag na Clibhe, past the lochan and old shielings to reach the Abhainn a'Mhuill path. This adds two hours or so to the Clisham horseshoe.

Uisgnaval Mor (729m)
Teilesval (697m)
Sron Scourst (491m)
Stulaval (*Stuli's fell*) (579m)

To the west of the Clisham horseshoe and the Abhainn Loch a'Sgail, in the central group of North Harris hills, is a small group of which Uisgnaval Mor is the highest. It forms a twin summit with Teilesval, its close neighbour to the north-east. The pair show up well as one mountain from the south, lying directly west of the deep bealach formed by the Abhainn Loch a'Sgail and the Allt a'Sgail, the latter becoming the Langadale River which flows into Loch Langavat.

The long south-west ridge of Uisgnaval Mor gives a very pleasant way of ascending this group of hills from the head of Loch Meavaig, heading for the shoulder above Creag na Speireig and keeping above the small line of bouldery crags to the north-east of little Loch Brunaval. Views of the Clisham group and the south-east Harris hills are excellent. The summits are stony, but pleasant grassy ridges run out north-westwards from Uisgnaval Mor to the sharp headland of Sron Scourst, and northwards from Teilesval to skirt the top of Coire Sgurra-breac. An easy descent can be made south-westwards to Loch Scourst in Glen Meavaig from the col half a kilometre south-east of Sron Scourst.

From the summit of Teilesval the grassy ridge above Coire Sgurra-breac leads to Craig Stulaval and Sron Ard, from where a pleasant descent can be made south-westwards to Glen Meavaig or, with care, from between Sron Ard and Craig Stulaval (near to the Sron Ard end of these cliffs) dropping northwards to pick up the path down Glen Stuladale. Preferable to the latter descent, however, is to retrace to the summit of Creag Stulaval (513m) and take the rounded grassy east ridge of this hill, above its north-facing crags, to the fine bealach above Loch Stuladale. The descent from there down Glen Stuladale is straightforward. If time permits it is rewarding first to make the easy ascent of Stulaval which gives fine views of Loch

Langavat. The best descent from there is probably to retrace to the bealach and take the path down Glen Stuladale.

WESTERN HILLS OF NORTH HARRIS

The hills to the west of Glen Meavaig form a distinct western group. They stretch unrelentingly to the sea, maintaining an average summit height approaching 500m for a distance of some 11 kilometres from east to west. Steep-sided summits of 300m and over extend to within a kilometre of the coasts to north and west. Although not especially commanding in height, these hills become more and more remote and rugged as one goes west to Hushinish, or north-west to Loch Resort. The highest (and roughly central) of the western group is also the most isolated — Tirga Mor, which lies to the west of the group's most important glen, Gleann Chliostair.

Oreval (662m)
Ullaval (*wolf fell*, or *Ulli's fell*) (659m)
Cleiseval (511m)
Sron Ulladale (*wolf hill* or *wolf head*) (442m)
The highest in the small group of hills immediately to the west of Glen Meavaig is Oreval. With its neighbour Ullaval, one kilometre to the north, it forms a shapely twin-summit mountain when viewed from the foot of Glen Stuladale, at the mouth of Loch Voshimid. From here too the striking narrow and craggy corrie, Caadale Ear, below the north-east shoulder of Oreval is seen at its best.

The bouldery summit of Oreval is easily reached from the southern end of Loch Scourst in Glen Meavaig, or from the dam at the southern end of the man-enlarged but picturesque Loch Chliostair to its west. A more interesting approach, however, is first to climb Cleiseval from the B887 road near to the small hamlet of Cliasmol, overlooking Soay Sound and the small islets Soay Mor and Soay Beag in West Loch Tarbert. From there, the south-west shoulder of Cleiseval, just to west of the short low-lying crags of Mulla Cleiseval, gives a pleasant grassy line of ascent to the stony summit.

As might be expected, from the selection of Cleiseval by the Ordnance Survey for a triangulation pillar, the summit is a fine viewpoint. Crags fall away steeply to its north, as well as eastwards from the north-east shoulder and from the small bouldery bealach which is gained by a stony descent to north-east. From there the stony and grassy ridge veers northwards and leads to the grassy intermediary summit of Bidigi (500m).

Apart from this short stony north-east descent ridge from Cleiseval, the rounded ridges and shallow bealachs of the group, stretching northwards across Oreval, Ullaval and Muladal (454m) to the summit of Sron Ulladale are all straight-forward grassy walks. The route described, starting from Mulla Cleiseval and extending to Loch Ulladale - which is reached from Sron Ulladale by descending first eastwards from its summit - takes only two to three hours and is one of the most pleasant hillwalking expeditions in the region. It ranks an extremely good second to the Clisham horseshoe; with the added feature, after descending the east flank

Tirga Mor from the south-east

of Sron Ulladale, of viewing one of the most awe-inspiring rock towers in the whole of the British Isles - the strone above Loch Ulladale.

The huge bulging overhang that forms the northern extremity of Sron Ulladale is seen at its best from the western slopes of Mullach na Reiheachd to its north-east, or from Tirga Mor to its south-west. Splendid boulders at the foot of the strone provide ample camping and bivouac sites, though for both camping and climbing here, midge cream is as mandatory as glacier cream is on Mont Blanc.

A return to the B887 road can be made by the splendid path up Glen Ulladale, below the magnificent West Wall of Sron Ulladale, and thence to the North of Scotland Hydro Electric Board dam at the southern end of Loch Chliostair. An alternative return route, from Loch Ulladale, is to take the glen running south-east from the loch, over the bealach to the north-west of the Gormul Mor crag and descend from the small lochan there to Loch Voshimid and the Glen Meavaig private road. This road makes a good approach to Sron Ulladale if permission (rarely given) to use it with a vehicle can be obtained. It runs to within three kilometres of the strone.

Tirga Mor (679m)
Ceartaval (556m)

The highest summit in the western group of North Harris is that of Tirga Mor. While easy, it is also the most rugged when taking all directions of approach into account. The hill towers above Loch Chliostair, but is awkward to ascend from there except by its relatively steep and slabby south-east ridge approached from the dam at the south end of Loch Chliostair. Grassy gullies between the slabs make this ridge straightforward. It forms the south-west edge of Tirga Mor's south-eastern corrie, which contains the hidden Loch Maolaig, and provides a short ascent from the dam with fine views.

Starting from the B887 road, the quickest ascent of Tirga Mor is to take the private road leading to the dam, and branch westwards onto the path up Glen Leosaid from the bridge over the River Leosaid. After one kilometre, strike due north up the steep but straightforward south flank of Tirga Mor. In many ways, however, the most pleasant route is to continue along the Glen Leosaid path for a further kilometre, as far as Gill Avay, and climb the shallow glen there to a grassy bealach between Tirga Mor and Ceartaval beyond and above the attractive Loch Braigh Bheagarais which nestles there.

From this bealach, both the summit of Ceartaval and the steep east flank of Glen Modale to the north of Tirga Mor, can be easily reached. The hilly shoulder of Tirga Beag and Lag Glas are readily gained also from this glen, to give a north-east approach to the summit of Tirga Mor; or its summit ridge can be more directly gained from the grassy bealach between Tirga Mor and Lag Glas. The summit of Tirga Mor has a prominent stone-circle cairn surrounding its Ordnance Survey triangulation pillar. The views from there are fine, as might be expected. A descent can be made by the north-east flank to Glen Ulladale, giving splendid views of the overhanging nose of Sron Ulladale, or southwards to regain the Glen Leosaid path, making a pleasant traverse of the mountain.

SOUTH-EAST HILLS OF NORTH HARRIS
The compact group of hills, south-east of the A859 road where it cuts through the North Harris hills from West Loch Tarbert to Loch Maaruig, is all within easy reach of Tarbert. The group is divided roughly in two by Glen Laxadale, through which a good path runs south to north.

Sgaoth Iosal (*low wing*) (531m)
Sgaoth Aird (*high wing*) (559m)
Gillaval Glas (*Gilli's fell*) (471m)
The hills to the west of Glen Laxadale form a fine west-opening horseshoe set around the deep glen formed by the Skeaudale River. The ridge running from Sgaoth Iosal over the highest, Sgaoth Aird to Gillaval Glas and its western extension Cnoc Eadar Da Bheinn, can be easily reached from the A859 road to its north.

From Tarbert, a direct ascent of the southern slopes of Gillaval Glas is awkward. These slopes are formed of highly glaciated and polished rock, broken by grassy gullies and by a profusion of perched blocks. A better start for a traverse of the horseshoe ridge is from the west, almost anywhere on the A859 road between Caolas na Sgeir, and Ardhasaig. The stony summits of the two subsidiary peaks to the west of Gillaval Glas are easily accessible from there and provide a good approach to the summit of Gillaval Glas. The ridge above the precipitous north-facing cliffs of Geoan Dubh, overlooking the Skeaudale River, gives impressive views of Loch Seaforth.

The northern face of Gillaval Glas itself is also precipitous, especially just to the west of the summit, but the descent to the fine bealach between it and Beinn na Teanga is easy; as is the pleasant climb to the shapely summit of Beinn na Teanga followed by a grassy descent to the magnificent narrow Bealach Garbh at the heads of both the Skeaudale River and the Dibidale River. From here the two Sgaoths on the northern side are straightforward and give fine views of the Clisham group to their north.

A smaller horseshoe, set around the Dibidale River provides an alternative approach to the Bealach Garbh from the Glen Laxadale path. The easiest ascent is the south-east ridge of Sgaoth Aird, Sron an Toister, with fine crags to either side, especially to the north above Coire Scrien. From the Bealach Garbh a variety of routes and traverses can be selected. The Dibidale River glen is susceptible to mist rolling in from the sea to the south-east and care at the bealach is then necessary. Both limbs of this small horseshoe have steep crags on their north facing sides; Sron an Toister, on the northern limb, and Creag na h-Iolaire on the southern, below Goromul. These faces, particularly on Sgaoth Ard, have recorded routes of Severe to Very Severe standard.

Toddun (528m)
To the east of Glen Laxadale the hills continue to Loch Seaforth in the east, and to East Loch Tarbert in the south. The only notable hill in this area is Toddun. For climbers based at the Gatliff Trust hostel at Rhenigidale, the south-east ridge of Toddun makes a pleasant ascent. Its summit can be reached easily from anywhere on the new road to Rhenigidale from Maaruig. A fine - even strenuous - day, is to include Toddun plus its smaller neighbour to the west, Straiaval (389m), in a traverse of Sgaoth Iosal, Sgaoth Aird and Gillaval Glas. This round of peaks is also a fine objective from the Gatliff Trust hostel.

PATHS AND WALKS
One of the finest walks in Harris is to Loch Ulladale which is easily reached by the excellent stalker's path along Gleann Chliostair from the dam at the southern end of Loch Chliostair, to which there is a private (North of Scotland Hydro Electric Board) road from the weir joining Lochan Beag to Loch Leosavay. The bus from Tarbert to Hushinish, along the B887, will stop at the foot of this private road if requested. The path northwards from the dam, after climbing some 100m from Loch Chliostair, skirts attractively to the west side of Loch Ashavat and then rises over a slight bealach to descend magnificently into Glen Ulladale. This path forms the easiest and quickest route for return to the B887 from Loch Ulladale following the traverse of Ullaval and Oreval from Cleiseval.

Excellent low-level walks can also be made along the track through Glen Meavaig to Sron Scourst and to Loch Stuladale, as well as from Vigadale Bay to Loch Stuladale. These paths can be rewardingly linked if transport can be arranged. The extensive north-facing crags of Craig Stulaval, which form with Stulaval a fine horse-shoe ridge from Sron Ard to Creag Chleistir, give Loch Stuladale an impressive setting. Sron Ard and Sron Scourst also are rewarding of inspection from below.

Sron Ulladale

A low-level link between Loch Morsgail in Lewis and Loch Leosaid in North Harris provides an interesting (if sometimes boggy) walk, with prominent views almost constantly of Sron Ulladale. A start is made from Morsgail Lodge, reached by track from the B8011 road that skirts the south end of Little Loch Roag. The full walk to Lochan Beag, starting by stalker's path to Morsgail Forest and thence down the Gil Roisgil Cham to Kinloch-resort, using the shallow five kilometre-long glen formed by the River Housay and the Ulladale River to reach Loch Ulladale is 18-19 kilometres. For transport, at both end-points, either bus time-tables have to be studied carefully or a lift from passing vehicles must be relied on (not unreasonable optimism on Harris).

ROCK CLIMBING IN NORTH HARRIS
Almost all of the serious rock climbing in Harris centres around Sron Ulladale and its dramatic west and north-east faces. Two lesser crags, but important, for their accessibility as well as some fine routes, are in the central or Clisham group, both in Glen Scaladale. They are Sgurr Scaladale, at the head of the glen to the north-east of Clisham, and Creag Mo, the east-facing cliffs on the north side of the glen, only one kilometre from the road bridge over the Scaladale River. In the south-east group the cliffs on the north side of Sgaoth Aird, (extending eastwards to Sron an Toister) and those to the north-east of Goromul, overlooking Glen Dibidale (Creag na h-Iolaire), are of note as also are those on the north side of Gillaval Glas and the south-west flank of Sgaoth Iosal. While, also in the central group, west of Uisgnaval Mor and overlooking the bealach at the head of Glen Meavaig, Sron Scourst and Sron Ard have potential.

Sron Ulladale
Sron Ulladale terminates the northern summit ridge of Ullaval above Loch Ulladale, and is best approached by the stalker's path from Loch Chliostair. A huge bulk of the cliff overhangs by several metres - making it one of the finest rock features in the British Isles and possibly the finest inland cliff. It towers 270m above the head of the loch and its West Wall is 250m high for over a kilometre from the Nose above the loch to the South Buttress in Glen Ulladale.

The remarkable overhanging nose of the strone is seen at its best from the north-east. The whole cliff here is split, from its summit to the bouldery slopes at its foot, some 300m below, by a deep slanting gully (Great Gully); with an even deeper cleft to its north, forming a recess from the summit down to an amphitheatre platform, about halfway up from the base of the crag. From this rush-covered platform (Rush Shelf) H J Irens and F Solari, in 1938, pioneered the first recorded route (180m Very Difficult) to south (left) of the massive overhang. The climb is ill-defined but slants leftwards across the Great Gully to finish by a less steep buttress to the left. Irens and Solari described the climb as "a good mountaineering route"

The west face of the strone is equally awesome. This massive wall (West Wall) towers above Glen Ulladale, running southwards from Loch Ulladale for a full kilometre to its southern buttress, which is split from left to right by a prominent diagonal gangway. The whole of the rock-face is of firm grey gneiss and maintains a height of some 250m over its full length. It is striated vertically with shallow grooves, nearly all of which are roofed by an overhanging seam of rock near the top, and broken by horizontal seams at lower intervals. The only unaided (Very Difficult to Very Severe) routes here, first pioneered as recently as 1961 by R B Evans and party, start on or close to the South Buttress and The Gangway.

In 1967, by which time surprisingly few climbs had been recorded, J Grieve described the West Wall as a "Tiger's Paradise"...and the rock-face as, "seamed with dozens of grooves, topped with overhangs, up which the eye of faith can trace lines of intricate beauty". Despite many climbs (mostly Very Severe and Extreme) now recorded on the West Wall between South Buttress and the bulging Nose of the strone, much remains for rock exploration.

There is good - if midgey- camping to be found under Sron Ulladale, a little above the loch to its east. There are also splendid bivouac sites among the boulders at the foot of the strone.

Sron Ulladale - North-east Face

The Great Gully, splitting the north-east face and forking awkwardly in its upper half, gave R B Evans and party in 1961 (SMCJ Vol.27, p.265) a disappointingly grassy and disjointed climb, with only two significant pitches (12m and 27m; Very Severe) both in the square amphitheatre about one third of the way up. This point was also reached, traversing in from the right (north), by R G Folkard and party in 1948 (*Amphitheatre Approach* - 30m; Difficult). The climbing above mostly follows the Irens and Solari route.

On the buttress to the east (left) of Great Gully, Evans and party also pioneered *Tyke* (190m; Severe) which they reported as having a vegetated start but becoming a good line, on superb rock, to the pleasant easier slabs above the prominent terrace. *Iron Butterfly*, climbed in 1969 (SMCJ Vol.29, p.280), follows a similar — if not identical — route to Tyke. Further west (right), on this north-east wall, M A Reeves and J Ball in 1965 (SMCJ Vol.28, p.211) climbed *Inversion* (175m; Very Severe), a tortuous route of "great character" which starts from the grass and shrub covered ledge (Rush Platform) to right of the recess and takes a line up the centre (cairn) of the steep, clean face above, to left of the bulging overhang.

Sron Ulladale - West Wall

Almost all remaining unaided climbing has been on the slightly misnamed West Wall of the strone; perhaps more correctly the east wall of Glen Ulladale. Three climbs were made on this west face by R B Evans and party in 1961 (SMCJ Vol.27, p.266): *The Gangway* (60m; Difficult) on the *South Buttress*, which takes a steep corner and then pleasant slabs, above the prominent rake splitting the buttress from left to right; *South Buttress* (100m; Severe), which reaches The Gangway from the steep wall below, traversing beneath the overhangs and taking a smaller broken gangway through to the upper wall; and *Midgard* (180m; Very Difficult) a fine exposed route starting near South Buttress, to the left (north) of The Gangway, and slanting continuously leftwards and upwards beneath the many rock-overlaps to

D Scott on the first ascent of The Scoop, Sron Ulladale

break through to the summit in an "easy gangway" (R B Evans) to the right of the huge bulging overhang.

In 1967, J Grieve and parties, who described the rock as drying very quickly after rain, pioneered several direct routes on the West Wall: *Eureka* (130m; Very Severe) taking a direct line up the front of the South Buttress on "superb rock"; *Prelude* (180m; Mild Severe) to left (north), near to the start of Midgard, crossing this route and keeping central of a clean ribbon of slabs; *Aurora* (200m; Very Severe) 40 metres further north, starting at a "vague weakness of grooves" and using pegs to reach good holds over the bulge of a small triangular overhang.

Sron Ulladale - The Nose
In 1969, J Porteous and K Spence made the first direct ascent of the strone's nose: *Stone* (210m; Very Severe A2), starting at the lowest point on the main north-west face, to the right of the nose, and making for the prominent quartz ramp and "twin-crack corner" (later parties called this a groove) splitting the upper part of the face. In the same year extreme aided climbs of the nose direct were made: *The Scoop* (170m; Very Severe A4) by D Scott and party taking several days (30hrs total climbing); and a similar climb up a central groove to the right of The Scoop, by K Spence and J Porteous.

Subsequent parties (M Fowler and A Meyers in 1981) found alternatives on Stone, and 'freed' the climb. In the same year S Victoris and C Watts (SMCJ Vol.32 p.356) climbed *Flakeway to the Stairs* (125m; Hard Very Severe, 5a) which takes a line of flakes well to the right (west) of Stone, and left of an obvious inverted staircase. Exploration of the nose continued in 1985: between Stone and Flakeway to the Stairs, closer to the latter, D Cuthbertson and P Moores climbed *Beyond the Ranges* (110m; E4) which follows a line of right-facing corners and flakes just to right (west) of a pink quartz intrusion.

In 1987 J Dawes and P Pritchard climbed most of The Scoop free (200m; E7) with fixed ropes in nine pitches. They returned to the strone in 1988 and pioneered probably the hardest free climb yet: *Knuckle Sandwich* (E7) taking, in six pitches, the lower half of Knucklehead and the top half of The Nose. J Dawes took two days to lead the crux pitch. The route includes a linking traverse (5A) between the two earlier climbs.

Creagan Leathan
This further crag in Glen Ulladale is slowly becoming important. It is opposite the West Wall of Sron Ulladale. R B Evans and party (SMCJ Vol.27, p.266) first explored the cliffs in 1961 and recorded a route which they named ominously *Windwhistle* (95m; Very Difficult) on its central, attractively continuous, rock-rib. In 1981 M Fowler and A Meyers made two more routes, both Hard Very Severe 5a: *Little Red Rooster* (66m) taking the obvious red streak of rock to the left (south) of the steep buttress; and *Grey Rib* (75m), which they reported as the better route, to its right.

Sgurr Scaladale
The remaining rockclimbing crags in Harris pale by comparison with Sron Ulladale. The two in Glen Scaladale compete for importance. Sgurr Scaladale gives the longer routes. In 1930, Botterill and party climbed the *Central Gully* (160m; Difficult) traversing onto the western buttress at the finish. The central rib was climbed in 1954 by N S Tennent and M K Tennent.

In 1961 R B Evans and party (SMCJ Vol.27, p.266) made a fine steep route on Sgurr Scaladale's main buttress, *Miolnir* (130m; Very Severe), starting in a cleft in a dark wall to left (east) of Central Gully, and breaking out to a deep groove still further east. To the right of Miolnir is the steepest section of the cliff, where a black wall with a prominent line of overhangs, slanting upwards left to right, fell to an Extreme climb by M Fowler and A Meyers in 1981 - *Panorama* (177m; E2).

The *West Buttress* (225m; Very Severe) was climbed by A Powling and D Yates, in 1969, taking more or less a direct line from the lowest rocks just to left of its prominent gully. Generally, the gullies on Sgurr Scaladale tend to be vegetatious, while the ribs and walls are cleaner and firm.

Creag Mo

R B Evans and party were also the first to record, in 1961 (SMCJ Vol.27, p.266), a route on Creag Mo - *Miny* (105m; Severe), which starts on slabs below the prominent right-hand (northerly) grass terrace and finishes in steep grooves above the terrace. The same finish to this route is shared by *Gollum* (100m; Severe), climbed by M A Reeves and B Reeves in 1965 (SMCJ Vol.28, p.210), but starting further to the right on the lower slabs. In that year, too, M A Reeves and J Ball made the 100m Hard Severe route *Smeagol*, which takes a line a few metres to south of Gollum and also finishes in the same groove above the grassy terrace. A route named *Footpad* (100m; Very Severe) from the steep lower rocks, a little to the north of Gollum, was climbed by B Clarke and J Macdougall in 1972 (SMCJ Vol.30, p.165); it appears to take a groove different from Gollum's, above the terrace.

Meanwhile, in 1969, the slabs further south (left) on Creag Mo were climbed by P T Newall and C G Winfield (SMCJ Vol.29, p.28) who also forced a disjointed (heathery) route above the slabs, making an overall 100m climb - *Herbivore* (Very Severe). In 1980 four new routes were climbed on Creag Mo, Hard Very Severe and Extreme: three by M Fowler and A Strapcans (*Macbeth, Little Bo Peep* and *King Lear*) and one by C Victoris and C Watts (*Wee Gommy*). The decade intervals between these recorded explorations, on a crag as accessible as Creag Mo, speaks volumes for the infrequency of visits to the Harris and Lewis crags.

Glen Meavaig

Surprisingly few other crags in the North Harris hills have been explored for their rockclimbing potential. In Glen Meavaig, which runs between the western and Clisham groups, and sharply separates them, Sron Ard remains without recorded climbs, while Sron Scourst (on whose north flank Irens and Solari scrambled in 1938) appears to have surrendered only its far western edge to a "direct line" (90m; Mild Severe) climbed by C G M Slesser and D J Bennet in 1967 (SMCJ Vol.29, p.49). The Glen Meavaig crags probably offer less prospects than crags in the south-east.

Glen Laxadale

Of the Harris hills in the south-east group, Sgaoth Ard has most potential, more than may be surmised from the few climbs recorded. In 1954 G S Johnstone gave a useful description of all the crags in the area (SMCJ Vol.25, p.226).

Those of Sgaoth Ard are on its north face, 150m high and broken into several buttresses of which only three, at the western end, offer serious climbing. The eastern buttresses which peter into the smaller crags of Sron an Toister, are grassy but give good scrambling.

Sgaoth Ard is easily reached from Glen Laxadale or by a shorter approach from the A859 road to its north. *Slab Wall* is the furthest west (right) buttress on its north face; next, eastwards, is *No.1 Buttress*, and then *No.2 Buttress*, separated from No.1 by a scree gully. No.2 Buttress, gives 75m of good scrambling followed by 75m of Hard Difficult climbing on granitic gneiss and hornblendite.

No.1 Buttress has a prominent nose, forming the east wall of a deep cleft. The nose was first climbed in 1966 by H Small and J W Graham (SMCJ Vol.29, p.48); it gave a 70m Very Severe route, *Hauds*, which takes a steep line of a narrow gully and grooves, finishing to the right, up 35m of easier rocks above a pinnacle. A variation Severe finish to this route was recorded by I G Rowe and P MacDonald in 1969 (SMCJ Vol.29, p.280), traversing right from the pinnacle for six metres to take the edge of the buttress to the top.

Glen Skeaudale

The north-facing cliffs of Gillaval Glas overlook the Skeaudale River. The main crag, Cnoc Eadar Da Bheinn (known locally as Gillaval Dubh), is easily accessible from the Ardhasaig Bridge over the Skeaudale River but offers serious climbs only high up on its eastern buttress - to which the ascent is tedious.

East of the summit of Gillaval Glas, below the two small lochans on its north-east shoulder is a 75m high crag which slightly overhangs a grassy ledge. The only reported climb on this crag was by G S Johnstone in 1954, *Lochan Crag* (60m; Very Difficult) on steep, slabby and "beautifully clean" rock. There are several potential short routes on this crag.

The Sron a'Sgaoth crags, on the south-west shoulder of Sgaoth Iosal, also overlook the Skeaudale River. Several steep slabs here offer promise of good climbs, while the northern extremity of these crags - overlooking the A859 and easily accessible from there - have three or four buttresses that give 60m or more of moderate to difficult scrambling. Further to north, on the north-west flank of Sgaoth Iosal, good scrambling (60-90m) can be found, but little more.

Loch Resort Crags

Crags in the western group of Harris hills have had little attention. In 1969, R Sharp and W Sproul explored the Loch Resort coast. They reported (SMCJ Vol.29, p.281) a climb to north side of Taran Mor (303m), naming their route, descriptively, *Sundowner* (135m; Severe). It follows the line of an almost hidden gully that splits the mountain. The northern crags of all the lower hills overlooking Loch Resort would be worth inspection. They can be reached by a challenging coastal walk from Glen Cravadale to the west; starting from either the path through Glen Leosaid or the path from Hushinish to Cravadale.

CHAPTER 17

THE LONG ISLE: SOUTH HARRIS, THE UISTS AND THE BARRA ISLES

The character of The Long Isle changes notably to south of the tiny neck of land formed by West Loch Tarbert and East Loch Tarbert in Harris. To the north, the hills of Lewis and North Harris are rugged, with mountain outcrops of Lewisian gneiss interspersed by uninhabited moorland of deep peat. Immediately to the south, the land is fertile by comparison: machair in abundance in the west, and studded with crofts, lazybeds and fishing activity in the rocky maze of bays and lochs in the east.

The contrasting characters of west and east in Harris continue southwards throughout the remaining islands in the chain. The strip of machair in the west becoming always broader, and the mountain spine of grey gneiss in the east ever narrower. The area of fertile land increases with the machair, as does the population. Fishing predominates in the east, agriculture in the west.

The hills in the Long Isle from Tarbert southwards are generally lower and less rugged than those in the north. South Uist possesses the most important of these hills, as well as the only remaining rock climbing in the Long Isle of any note. The islands at the southern end of the chain - the Barra Isles - have a character similar in some respects to Coll and Tiree, but much more isolated. Although affected by the Clearances, the inhabitants of the Barra Isles clung to their faith and the people there today are mostly Catholic, contrasting with those further north.

North-west from North Uist is the tiny island group of Haskeir, and off its west coast, the Monach Isles. Descriptions of these groups are included with other outliers in Chapter 20, while islands in the Sound of Harris, between South Harris and North Uist, are covered here as part of the Long Isle. The largest and hilliest in the sound, Berneray and Pabbay, mark its western entrance together with the hilly Toe Head peninsula which is joined to the westernmost tip of South Harris by a marshy strip of land and tidal sands, making it almost an island in itself.

Offshore to north-east of Toe Head is the shapely island of Taransay, whose description is included with offshore islands in Chapter 19. Taransay almost closes the wide mouth of West Loch Tarbert at the northern boundary of South Harris. The distance from there to Barra Head in the far south is fully 150 kilometres; while from

321

the Sound of Harris to the Sound of Barra is 80 kilometres. A single-track road (the A865) runs between the latter two sounds, connecting North Uist, Benbecula and South Uist. Sheet 1 of the Ordnance Survey Routemaster Series is recommended for an overall view.

SOUTH HARRIS

MAPS :   Ordnance Survey   1:50,000 Sheets 14 and 18
            Bartholomew   1:100,000 Sheet 57

PRINCIPAL HILLS

Beinn Dhubh	506m	089 007
Ceann Reamhar	467m	118 991
Bleaval	398m	031 915
Roineabhal	460m	043 861
Chaipaval	365m	973 924

ACCESS

The Caledonian MacBrayne passenger and vehicle ferry service to South Harris, a two-hour crossing from Skye, sails twice-daily from Uig to Tarbert, as for North Harris. In summer months, this ferry serves Tarbert direct from Lochmaddy in North Uist; during winter months it calls first at Uig on Skye. A small passenger and car ferry also operates in summer between Newtonferry (or more correctly from the jetty in Loch nam Ban), at the northern tip of North Uist, and Leverburgh across the Sound of Harris.

The nearest point of Skye to South Harris is the Waternish peninsula. A distance of only 24 kilometres (13 nautical miles) across the Little Minch separates Waternish Point from Renish Point, which forms the southern tip of Harris and marks the eastern entrance to the northern passage through the Sound of Harris. Thus the crossing is a short one for sailing boats (although any crossing of the Minch in a small boat should be treated with respect) and South Harris, as well as the Uists, is popular for visiting yachts in the summer. There is a splendidly sheltered harbour in Loch Rodel north of Renish Point, and several sheltered anchorages in the Sound of Harris.

TRANSPORT

The bus service in South Harris is operated by Harris Garage Company Ltd in Tarbert (telephone 0859 2441). From Tarbert two buses per day (except Sundays) run to Rodel and back along the coast road through Luskentyre. For exploring any other part of the island a car is strongly recommended.

ACCOMMODATION

Good hotels are available at Tarbert and at Rodel in the south, to where buses run from Tarbert. Bed and breakfast accommodation is usually easy to find in South

*Looking north from Traigh Scarasta to the hills of North Harris, with Ben
Luskentyre just to the left of cloud capped Clisham*

Harris, along the coast road in the west, and in the south at Leverburgh and at
Northton. Plenty of good (if sometimes windy) camping places can be found
especially along the broad strip of machair in the west. There is also a lodge at
Scarasta - run as a luxury 'period' hotel - and a hostel belonging to the Scottish Youth
Hostels Association on Loch Stockinish in the east (grid reference 136 910).

GENERAL DESCRIPTION

South Harris is virtually an island; measuring roughly 12 kilometres west to east,
and 18 kilometres south to north from the Sound of Harris to where the Minch and
the Atlantic are separated by no more than half a kilometre across the tiny neck of
land at Tarbert. The eastern seaboard region, south from Tarbert, is named the
'Bays': Scadabay, Grosebay and Cluer (Chluar bay), north of Stockinish, where the
head of this loch is Bayhead; then Geocrab, Flodabay, Finsbay and Lingarabay (and
another Bayhead) to the south-east of Loch Stockinish. The countless tiny inlets
along this coast form excellent harbours for small fishing vessels with plentiful
sheltered sites for tiny villages. The small sheltered inlet on Stockinish Island is used
as a lobster pond.

Compared with the north, there is an air of prosperity. Most of this is derived
from fishing, crofting and weaving; it is a prosperity that owes much to the
exceptional toil and resourcefulness of the crofters who settled in this rock and
water desert when the fertile land to the west was 'cleared' for sheep. They collected
seaweed and peat and formed the lazybeds (raised beds of man-made weathered

soil, laid in the hollows of the striated rock) that now run for hundreds of metres up the hillsides in some areas. Without soil enough to bury their dead, they carried these to the fertile west - a long haul of which the evidence remains to this day, in the large number of funeral cairns at the resting places by the road to Luskentyre.

Threading its way through the Bays district is the Golden Road, so-called because of the cost per mile when it was built in the 1930's. It snakes around the tortuous coastline, weaving through the jigsaw of inlets, bays and fresh-water lochans which in some places are separated by no more than the road itself. Everywhere is grey glaciated gneiss, blue iridescent water and occasionally a green crofting oasis. The whole district is one of those small interesting freaks of nature in which the Hebrides abound.

The Luskentyre sands in the west (Traigh Luskentyre) is a feature of South Harris as unusual and interesting as the Bays district in the east. The tongue of sand there, when the tide is out, is three kilometres long and over a kilometre wide. The rocks at its head are ablaze with sea pinks in May and June and the marrum sands and machair that fringe the bay teem with rabbits. Sand pipits and starlings provide a strange contrast in the birdlife of this coast.

To the west of the southern half of the Bays district is the Loch Langavat of South Harris; four kilometres in length, north to south, and almost a kilometre across at its widest. To west again, beyond a five-kilometre stretch of featureless hills, is a further sweep of coastal sands, at Scarasta, joining mainland Harris to the peninsula of Toe Head. A fine short walk can be made along the south coast of this peninsula to a ruined chapel, which gives the name Rubh' an Teampuill to the small headland there, or more challenging excursions made to the natural arches on its north coast.

At Rodel, in the south, is the magnificent St Clements Church (key available at the hotel) which has a square central tower, making it unique in the Outer Hebrides. The church was built originally around 1500, by the 8th MacLeod of Dunvegan in Skye, Alasdair Crotach. His effigy, sculpted in green sandstone in 1528, lies entombed in a fine arched recess. The church has twice been restored, the last time in 1873. To the west of Rodel is Leverburgh (formerly Obbe) and the remains of Lord Leverhulme's industrial fishing activity, a relic of his attempt to bring prosperity to Harris in the 1930's.

THE HILLS OF SOUTH HARRIS
The only two hills of note in South Harris are Ben Luskentyre (Beinn Dhubh -506m), in the north-west corner, and Roneval (Roineabhal - 460m), at the southern tip of Harris. Both are straightforward and without special features, apart from the fine views from their summits plus the steep north-east corrie of Roneval and the Uamasclett rock-face to the north-east of Ceann Reamhar (467m), the eastern summit of Ben Luskentyre.

Ben Luskentyre (506m)
The Luskentyre group comprises a shallow six-kilometre crescent of hills stretching from Beinn Dhubh, the highest and far western summit, to Ceann Reamhar and the

unexpectedly rugged Uaval More (358m) in the south-east corner. This hill is tucked between the Lochanan Mora and River Horsaclett to its north-east, and a profusion of lochans, Loch Laxdale, Loch na h-Aibhne Gairbhe and Loch Bearasta Mor to its south-west. The line of Luskentyre hills makes pleasant walking from south-east to north-west, culminating on Beinn Dhubh, where the summit has unsurpassed views of the North Harris hills (western group) to north, and the extraordinary Luskentyre sands on which it looks directly down to its south. The easiest ascent of Beinn Dhubh is its gentle south-west flank from Luskentyre.

A rough path leads westwards from Tarbert along the south coast-line of West Loch Tarbert, 100m or so above the shore, below Cnoc na Clioche and then the Uamasclett crags, as far as the steep and impressive north-facing corrie of Beesdale. The shoreline has some difficult steps in places which give it added interest and place it in the class of a mountain walk for an 'off day'.

Roineabhal (*rough-ground fell*) (460m)

The conspicuous summit of Roineabhal (Roneval) at the southern extremity of Harris is as much a landmark from sea, guiding vessels from the Little Minch to the sheltered harbour of Loch Rodel at the mouth of the treacherous Sound of Harris, as it is from land. The summit, which is easily reached from the bealach at the heads of Glen Rodel and Gleann Shranndabhal (Srondeval), commands a magnificent view over the congestion of rocks and islets in the sound.

On the north face of Roineabhal is a prominent corrie, down which water-falls feed the Abhainn a'Choire in the all-too-frequent wet weather that this headland of Harris attracts from the Atlantic to the west and the Minch to the east. The corrie appears to dry quickly after rain, but the rock is loose and offers little in the way of climbs.

Bleaval (*butter fell*) (398m)

North-west of Roineabhal and west of Loch Langavat is an extensive group of lower hills rising to a stony summit (and triangulation pillar) on the highest, Bleaval. The region is roughly circular, five kilometres in diameter. The hills are quite rocky but without any rock exposures of climbing interest.

To ascend Bleaval requires a long moorland and boggy approach walk from the A859 to its north-east or, more pleasantly, the use of a canoe or dinghy on Loch Langavat from the narrow but well made-up road from Leverburgh to Ardvey. The hill is perfectly easy to climb.

Chaipaval (*bowl-shaped fell*) (365m)

Beyond the wide stretch of Scarasta sands, to the west of the Bleaval hills, is the remarkably hilly Toe Head peninsula which contains several natural rock arches on the north shore. The summit hill of the peninsula is Chaipaval; a worthwhile objective for its views - St Kilda 65 kilometres due west, the Skye Cuillin 75 kilometres south-east and, five kilometres to north-east, the shapely and now uninhabited island of Taransay (see Chapter 19).

ISLANDS IN THE SOUND OF HARRIS

The Sound of Harris is studded with islands and rocky islets. Visits, especially to the larger islands, are invariably interesting. At the western (Atlantic) entrance to the sound Berneray and Pabbay are the largest, and are not to be confused with their namesakes of similar size south of Barra. They are also the most shapely and - together with the hilly Toe Head peninsula - form useful landmarks for boats seeking to enter the sound from the west.

MAPS :   Ordnance Survey   1:50,000 Sheet 18
              Bartholomew   1:100,000 Sheets 53 and 57

ACCESS
Loch Borve in Berneray is served by regular passenger and vehicle ferry from Loch nam Ban in North Uist (five to six crossings daily except Sundays), but access to any other island in the sound is only possible by locally arranged boat-hire. Private local charter from Berneray is usually easily arranged to Pabbay and Boreray.

ACCOMMODATION
On Berneray there is an excellent, newly renovated hostel at Baile (grid reference 932 814) owned by the Gatliff Trust. Otherwise there is little by way of accommodation on any of the islands; though sometimes a deserted house for shelter can result from local enquiry.

GENERAL DESCRIPTION
Berneray is interesting not so much for its shapely hills Beinn Shleibhe (93m) and Borve Hill (85m) - albeit that these are conspicuous from the west - but for the remarkable huge dunes running the full four kilometres of its sandy west shore and for a two-kilometre length of its north shore. The dunes are 15 metres high in places - which is the height that the breakers can reach there in the fury of an Atlantic storm. The island has no peat. It is fertile, with a permanent population of 300; mostly lobster fishermen and sheep farmers. The inhabitants are nestled around Bays Loch and Loch Borve. Although close to North Uist, the island is part of the Parish of Harris.

The splendid sands of Loch Borve dry completely at low tide. Both Borve Hill and Beinn Shleibhe are perfectly easy walks. They give fine views of the sound and North Uist. It is said that until about the 16th century, the island was almost connected to Pabbay, but strong winds and tides slowly scoured and swept away the sands. An interesting and prominent standing stone lies between the thriving village of Borve and Loch Borve.

Pabbay, to the north-east of Berneray across the three-kilometre Sound of Pabbay, is now uninhabited. Its south-east coast has fine dunes, though less magnificent than those of Berneray. The island's one hill, Beinn a'Charnain (196m), is the highest in the group. It has a shapely, rocky summit with triangulation pillar - and fine views of the sound and its surrounding hills as might be expected. Pabbay has a history of illegal whisky distilling. On its southern shore is an old burial ground.

Landscape of North Uist, looking towards Eaval

NORTH UIST

MAPS : Ordnance Survey 1:50,000 Sheets 18 and 22
Bartholomew 1:100,000 Sheet 53

PRINCIPAL HILLS

Eaval	347m	899 605
North Lee	262m	927 660
South Lee	281m	918 654
Marrival	230m	808 700

ACCESS

Caledonian MacBrayne's steamer (car-ferry daily, except winter months) from Uig in Skye, or from Tarbert in Harris, to Lochmaddy on Loch nam Madadh in North Uist. There is a road bridge from Benbecula, to where there is an air service from Glasgow. From Lochmaddy the A865 coast road almost encircles the island; the circular link being completed by the extraordinary moorland 'continuous causeway' road (the A867) from Strunmore, one kilometre north-west of Lochmaddy to Clachan-a-Luib in the south-west. This road is a series of causeways - called sconsors - for a distance of 12 kilometres or more.

TRANSPORT

Post buses, operated by the Post Office Corporation (telephone 0876-3330), run once a day Mondays to Fridays from Lochmaddy to Benbecula airport and back, and encircle the island from Lochmaddy through Baleshore and Locheport twice a day Mondays to Saturdays. Taxis are also available in Lochmaddy.

ACCOMMODATION

Lochmaddy has, in addition to its tiny cottage hospital, a bank, a garage and the only hotel in North Uist - apart from a Lodge at Langass on Loch Eport on the track from the A867 to Loch Langass. There are guest houses also at Lochmaddy (bed and breakfast) as well as the island's youth hostel (grid reference 918 687) belonging to the SYHA. The Gatliff Trust also now owns a fine hostel (grid reference 809 625) at Claddach Baleshore, opened in 1982 and recently renovated.

GENERAL DESCRIPTION

Much of North Uist is sunken peat moorland, an incredibly wet bogland of which Lochmaddy is the proud capital. The hotel there caters mostly for fishermen, for whom the island is a paradise of fine brown trout. Of the fresh-water lochs, Loch Scadavay is the finest (as well as the shallowest). The complexity of its shores is such that they measure 75 kilometres in length for a loch area of only four square kilometres. It is claimed that there are over 300 islands in the loch; though only 175 can be counted in the 1:10,000 Ordnance Survey map.

There are many ancient remains on North Uist; among them the fine chambered cairns and stone circle of Croinebhal (Craonaval) south-west from Locheport, and the remarkable neolithic cairn of Barpa Langass on the north-west flank of Ben Langass. The latter is a burial chamber some five metres high and 22 metres across which to this day can be entered through a well-constructed tunnel, though this is slowly deteriorating. More recent history is marked by several ruins, such as those of the 16th century medieval monastery Teampull na Trionaid (*Chapel of the Trinity*), supposedly rebuilt in the 16th century, near the shore to the west of Carinish (grid reference 816 603). Natural phenomena include the fine rock arch ten metres high at Griminish Point in the north-west corner of the island.

Loch nam Madadh is a frequent haunt of visiting yachts and small boats from Skye and the Scottish mainland. These, as well as the youth hostel at Lochmaddy, form excellent bases for exploring the shores of Loch Scadavay and - especially if a dinghy or canoe is to hand - the three eastern hills of North Uist.

THE HILLS OF NORTH UIST

Eaval (347m)

The highest hill, Eaval is almost completely surrounded by water. A boat is about the only way of reaching it, short of a tedious and boggy walk threading between the maze of lochans from the west, for which map and compass are paramount. The hill is perfectly easy to climb. It has fine crags on the north side and a triangulation pillar on its stony and grassy summit.

North Lee (262m)
South Lee (281m)
These two hills are more easily reached by foot than is Eaval; although for their ascent, too, a boat makes the approach far more pleasant - especially from Loch Eport where a landing in Aird Bheag gives an attractive ascent of both hills. Like Eaval they are perfectly easy to climb. Overland from Lochmaddy involves a walk of two kilometres north-west from the pier on the A865 road, followed by two and a half kilometres south-west on the A867 'causeway' and then four kilometres east-south-east over wet peaty moorland. The summit cairn of North Lee is half a kilometre due south-west of its triangulation pillar. All three peaks provide fine views to the west of the most unusual terrain in which they are set; a checker-board of peaty land and water. To their east is the Little Minch and a fine aspect of Skye, with a particularly splendid skyline of the Red and Black Cuillin.

Marrival (230m)
Almost central in North Uist is the small hill group of Marrival which gives a remarkable view of Loch Scadavay and the amazing water-dominated land spreading south-eastwards for ten kilometres to end abruptly at the steep west flank, Guala Mhor, of North and South Lees. The three grassy summits, Ben Aulasary (217m), Marrival and its eastern outlier Marrogh (170m), make a pleasant walk, easily accessible from the partly surfaced track directly to their west along the Abhainn Ceann a'Bhaigh from the A865 road. Below the south-east flank of Marrogh are crags and an interesting chambered cairn.

BENBECULA

MAPS :   Ordnance Survey   1:50,000 Sheet 18
            Bartholomew   1:100,000 Sheet 57

PRINCIPAL HILL
   Rueval   124m   826 534

ACCESS and TRANSPORT
There are no steamer ferries to Benbecula. Access is by road from North Uist or South Uist, or by air to the small airfield built in the north-west corner by the Royal Air Force during World War II. An army base was established on the island in 1958 and expanded in 1971, along with the construction of a missile range in South Uist. Buses on the island are operated by the Post Office Corporation and Co- Chomunn an lochdair Ltd.

GENERAL DESCRIPTION
The name Benbecula derives from the Gaelic, Beinn a'bh-faodhla, *mountain of the fords*, referring to its one hill Rueval and to the days when a crossing to the island from either North Uist or South Uist meant literally to ford the straits separating the Uists from Benbecula. Traffic was possible for about two hours only at low tide.

There are now road bridges or causeways across both straits. The bridge in the south was built between this century's two world wars and finished in 1943; while the crossing between North Uist and Benbecula - also more a causeway than a bridge - was completed only since mid-century. Before then the North Ford - its route marked by beacons and cairns and ever shifting with the sands - was open to traffic for only an hour or so before and after low water.

Benbecula is low-lying and windswept; machair in the west and endless wet, peaty moorland in the east. The west coastal road passes through the tidy crofts and farms of its 1300 population (not counting 500 military personnel now stationed on the island). So flat and low-lying is the land here that from only a short distance out to sea, especially in the west, the houses appear to grow from the sea. The indigenous settlers form a harmonious mixture of Catholic and Protestant; bridging between the Long Isle's northern Protestant following and the Catholicism of its south. In more ways than one Benbecula has always been a 'stepping stone' between the Uists. Thus it was here that Prince Charles Edward Stewart remained in hiding for weeks until - disguised as Flora MacDonald's maid with the help of Lady Clanranald - he escaped to Skye.

Rueval (124m)

This solitary hill on Benbecula is a prominent landmark across the fords from north or south. The A865 road now runs across Benbecula from south to north, by-passing the coastal road, and Rueval can be easily climbed from this road using a track and path from Market Stance (whose name has obvious origins). A shorter and more attractive approach, although just as boggy, is from Kyles of Flodda to the north, passing between the fine Loch Olavat and the aptly named Dubh Loch. Either walk to the summit of Rueval is worth-while for its views - as always in this strange land dominated by water. A return by the well-trudged path, to the road at Market Stance, gives an eight to nine kilometre circuit. To the south-east of Rueval, this path passes close to the cave where it is said that the Prince hid for two days in June 1746 waiting while Flora MacDonald organized his escape.

WIAY ISLAND

In the totally different, rocky south-east corner of Benbecula is the island of Wiay, with one or two small rocky hills. The highest, Beinn a'Tuath, is no more than 102m, but it stands out from the flatness of the surrounding land and sea. A well-made pier at Peter's Port (built in 1896 but unused to the point of becoming a planner's folly) would serve the island of Wiay, but even approaching it by sea can be dangerous. Today it is used by the Army for training divers.

SOUTH UIST

MAPS :   Ordnance Survey   1:50,000 Sheets 22 and 31
             Bartholomew   1:100,000 Sheet 53

PRINCIPAL HILLS

Ben Tarbert	168m	807 396
Hecla	606m	826 345
Ben Corodale	527m	820 329
Beinn Mhor	620m	809 311
Ben na Hoe	257m	816 285
Sheaval	223m	767 271
Arnaval	252m	780 256
Stulaval	374m	807 242
Triuirebheinn	357m	813 213

ACCESS

Caledonian MacBrayne's car ferries from Oban (6-hour passage; daily in summer, except Sundays) call at the principal place in South Uist, Lochboisdale (on Loch Baghasdail). On alternate days the ferry calls first at Castlebay on Barra. Access is also available by road from North Uist to where the MacBrayne's steamer from Uig on Skye and from Tarbert on Harris can be used; or by air to Benbecula and then by road. A Caledonian MacBrayne 'island hopscotch' ferry ticket is excellent value for South Uist, North Uist and Harris.

TRANSPORT

A minibus service, operated by Co-Chomunn an Iochdair Ltd (telephone Benbecula 08704 205) runs Mondays, Thursdays and Saturdays from Stilligarry to Creagorry via West Gerinish, and Tuesdays and Fridays from Talla an Iochdair to Creagorry via Ardivachar. Private hire of the minibus can also be arranged with the operator.

ACCOMMODATION

There is a high-class hotel at Lochboisdale, convenient for the southern hills, and roadside guest houses in the north-west and south-west corners of the island - on the A865 and on the B888 - neither of which is near enough to the main hills to be useful without a car. An excellent ten-bed hostel at Howmore (grid reference 757 365), owned by the Gatliff Trust, makes a good base for the whole of the northern group of hills. However, if a boat to Corodale Bay on the east coast can be arranged, a camp in Glen Hellisdale forms the finest base for these mountains.

GENERAL DESCRIPTION

South Uist is scenically the Long Isle at its finest. It is also the second largest island, to Harris and Lewis, with a population approaching 2,500. The unbroken 30-kilometre stretch of machair in the west produces, throughout the spring and summer, a wonderful variety of colours and scented tiny blossoms. The island is predominantly Roman Catholic, of which small roadside shrines are visible evidence, as well as a modern church, with an Irish flavour, at Garrynamonie (Gearraidh na Monadh) in the south-west.

For the full length of the west coast there are long sweeps of glistening white shell-sand, broken every few kilometres by flat rocky headlands. Inland from the broad strip of machair, and running also for the island's full length, is a host of lochs and lochans, fringed with waterlillies and filled with brown trout and salmon. Birdlife, on these inland shores, ranges from swans to swallows and is unsurpassed in the Outer Hebrides, as is the fishing. The bogland beyond, to the east, is barely inhabited and is backed by the fine, west-facing scarps of the island's imposing spine of hills along its eastern seaboard.

The largest of the inland lochs in the west, Loch Druidibeg, is a huge Nature Reserve. It spreads from the sandy, limy machair of the west, to the peaty, acidic moorland of the east. Its innumerable islands, islets and shore-line peninsulas make ideal habitats for all kinds of waterfowl, including the rare grey-lag geese. Similarly, its shallow calcerous shores are sometimes the only known location in the British Isles for certain species of flora; one example being the rare American pondweed - unique to the Uists.

The east coast of South Uist is deeply penetrated by three important lochs. Taken in order from north to south, as well as by increasing size, these are Loch Skipport, Loch Eynort and Loch Boisdale. Both of the latter, lochs Eynort and Boisdale, seem practically to cut through to the west coast. For example, at the western end of Loch Eynort, over seven kilometres from the east coast, there are two tiny village settlements, South Locheynort and North Locheynort, which are well to the west of the island's north-east to south-west mountain belt. The tidal tip of Loch Eynort comes to within three kilometres (and only one or two inland lochans) of the machair at Ormiclate on the west coast. There is also a man-made channel linking Loch Skipport with Loch Bee in the west, which in turn opens almost directly into the Atlantic at the western end of the South Ford separating South Uist from Benbecula.

Loch Boisdale is the largest of the eastern sea-lochs and the most important. Around the sheltered harbour of its northern arm has grown Lochboisdale, the only village of any size on the east coast of South Uist. The village now struggles westwards through North Lochboisdale to Daliburgh (Dalabrog) on the west coast road - the A865 that runs north from there to Lochmaddy in North Uist. The centre of Lochboisdale has shops, a bank, a comfortable hotel (catering especially for fishermen, stalkers and the many visiting yachts), a school, police station and Tourist Information office. At Daliburgh there is a small hospital.

THE HILLS OF SOUTH UIST

The two large sea lochs, Eynort and Boisdale, divide the belt of hills running the length of the eastern seaboard into three groups. The northernmost group is the largest and highest, containing Hecla and Beinn Mhor. It is bounded in the north by Loch Skipport and in the south by Loch Eynort. The central group, between lochs

Eynort and Boisdale, is smaller and lower; its highest hill is Stulaval. Finally, to south of Loch Boisdale, the lowest and least interesting group comprises the hills from Easaval to Roneval lying west to east in the south-east corner of the island, overlooking the Sound of Eriskay. A lower hill, but significant, is the slightly isolated Ben Tarbert at the north end of the island.

By far the most important hills in South Uist, indeed in the Long Isle chain outside of Harris and Lewis, are Hecla, Ben Corodale and Beinn Mhor. They are shapely mountains from almost anywhere on the island, especially so from the north-west where the steep west-facing flank of Beinn Mhor forms a prominent landmark at the south-east end of the continuous ridge profile formed by their summits. The round of these three hills, in either direction, makes a fine excursion with 1200m of climbing. The best approach, if the start and finish are to be at the same point, is from Loch Dobhrain on the A865, from where a peat road or track runs for nearly a kilometre south-eastwards (as far as grid reference 776 340). The round of Beinn Mhor, Ben Corodale and Hecla from there takes five to seven hours.

Hecla (*hooded shroud*, or *shrouded hill*) (606m)
The most pleasing ascent of Hecla is by its long north-east shoulder; especially if a landing by boat can be arranged on the Ornish headland from one of the exquisite rocky bays - Caolas Mor or Caolas Beg - on the south shore of Loch Skipport.

Otherwise an approach to this shoulder of Hecla can be made from the ruined shielings (grid reference 833 382) to which there is a path from the B890 road, starting near to the derelict pier on Loch Skipport. There are almost no paths or tracks in the area south from these shielings and the going is rough, although relatively dry; a mixture of craggy bluffs and heathery peat. The best line is south-eastwards, passing south of Loch Bein, to gain Maol Martaig or the bealach just to its south. The climb from there takes in the north-east and lower of Hecla's two summits and the sharp grassy ridge that joins them. The northern side of Hecla shows a mass of fractured rock (gneiss) but the summit is grassy. A compass there is unreliable.

The mountain can also be climbed by its north-west shoulder, Maoil Daimh, but the approach across moorland from Lochskipport to north is peaty and boggy. A better approach to Maoil Daimh is from Howmore to its west; though if an approach to Hecla from the west is to be made, then this is driest from Loch Dobhrain, taking first the peat road running south-eastwards for nearly a kilometre from the northern end of Loch Dobhrain. The best line then is to skirt the north-west shoulder of Beinn Mhor - Maola Breac - and head for Maoladh Creag nam Fitheach, thence to the bealach south-west of Hecla (the north bealach of Ben Corodale). From there the grassy and stony ascent to the summit of Hecla is steep but straightforward.

Ben Corodale (527m)
Ben Corodale, known also locally as Feith-bhealach (although more strictly this is the stony bealach, plus subsidiary top, just to its south), has a bouldery summit (cairned) and a steep, though short, rocky north-west ridge. This ridge, above the

Hecla and Ben Corodale from the north-west peak of Beinn Mhor

broad north bealach, at the heads of glens Usinish and Dorchay, has a deep cleft dividing it into two buttresses. Either of these gives pleasant, moderately difficult scrambling to the summit when the rock is dry.

Alternatively the buttresses and ridge can be turned to the east by a sloping grassy traverse leading by a small scree gully to Ben Corodale's short summit ridge. Similarly, a descent of the north-west ridge from the summit to the north bealach, which requires care in mist or if the rock is wet, can be avoided by taking this short scree gully, which runs north-eastwards from the ridge some 50 metres east of the summit cairn.

Both the north bealach and the Bealach Hellisdale are conspicuously ice-worn, in contrast to the summits on either side (Hecla, Ben Corodale and Beinn Mhor) which are 300m to 400m higher, showing that the huge ice-field which streamed out to the Atlantic, from what is now mainland Scotland, was not deep enough here to cover these peaks. The ice-polished gneiss on Spin (356m), the western flank of Beinn Mhor, gives additional evidence of this.

Beinn Mhor (620m)

The quickest but least rewarding ascent of Beinn Mhor is from Arinambane, on the shores of Loch Eynort to its south-west. A good path (unmarked on the Ordnance Survey map) passes south and then east of Loch nam Faoileann for more than a kilometre, to the north-east corner of the loch. From there the going north-

The summit of Beinn Mhor

eastwards is boggy until the heathery slopes to the Bealach Crosgard are reached, from where the ridge to the summit is mostly grassy. This route gives an easy descent from Beinn Mhor, following a traverse of the summit from Hecla or Ben Corodale. Indeed, if transport can be arranged, the traverse of these three summits from Loch Skipport to Loch Eynort makes an excellent and memorable excursion requiring six to eight hours.

The approach to Beinn Mhor direct from Loch Dobhrain, as for Hecla, is surprisingly dry, taking the peat road or track south-eastwards from the north end of the loch. Then head for the north-west shoulder of Beinn Mhor, Maola Breac, which leads first to a small subsidiary grassy peak (608m) marked by a stone-circle cairn, from where a narrow though easy grassy and rocky ridge leads to the summit's triangulation pillar. This final section of the ridge has several bouldery pinnacles which in mist produce a few false summits. In clear weather the view eastwards from the ridge down Glen Hellisdale and seawards to the Small Isles and the Cuillin of both Rhum and Skye is spectacular.

Beinn Mhor is also pleasantly approached over Ben Corodale. Its north-east shoulder above the Bealach Hellisdale is broken and rocky; indeed some good scrambling can be found there. The ascent of the shoulder from the bealach to the summit ridge of Beinn Mhor is easy, but care is needed if descending this flank from the summit in mist, especially on the section directly above the Bealach Hellisdale which has several short but vertical rock steps.

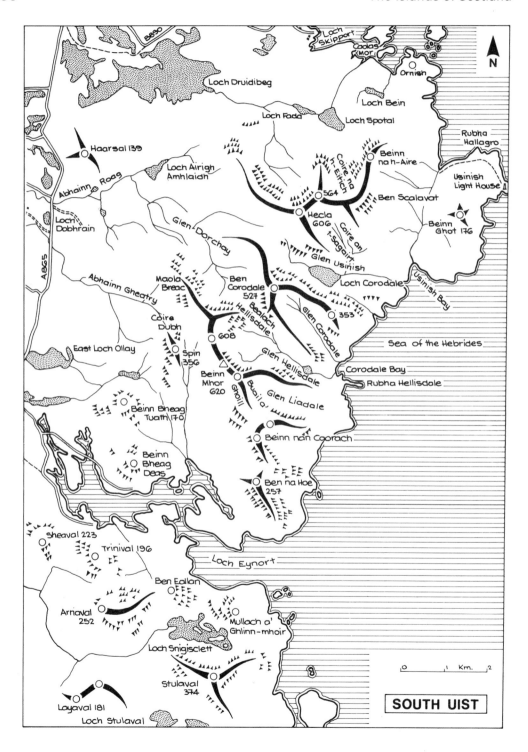

SOUTH UIST

Attractive approaches to Beinn Mhor can also be found from the east and south-east, using a boat to land either in Corodale Bay at the foot of Glen Hellisdale (when weather in the Hebridean Sea permits), or in the tiny bay, Sloc Dubh na Hafn, on the north shore of Loch Eynort. From this small bay the ascent of Beinn Mhor, over Ben na Hoe (257m) and Beinn nan Caorach, gaining the south-west grassy and rocky ridge of the mountain, makes a pleasant excursion. From Glen Hellisdale the finest feature of these mountains, the east-facing corrie of Beinn Mhor, at the head of the glen, is seen at its best.

Beinn Mhor and the south-east ridge of Ben Corodale form a tight horse-shoe around Glen Hellisdale. From the foot of the glen the rocky ridge above the precipitous north-facing south wall of the corrie can be gained easily, climbing first to the small bealach to the west of Maoladh nam Feannag. The ridge west-north-westwards from there leads to a prominent cairn on a small grassy subsidiary top on the summit ridge of Beinn Mhor, some 300 metres south-east of the summit and its triangulation pillar. Likewise, an ascent by the ridge flanking the north sides of Glen Hellisdale, traversing into the Bealach Hellisdale, makes a fine approach. The cliff-face that forms the south wall of Coire Hellisdale, the North Cliffs of Beinn Mhor, is divided by narrow gullies and chimneys into the Hellisdale Buttresses.

Stulaval (374m)
Triuirebheinn (357m)

The central group of hills, south of Loch Eynort, contains some ten distinct summits, only two of which exceed 300m. These are Stulaval, whose north face towers steeply above Loch Snigisclett for more than one kilometre west to east, and Triuirebheinn three kilometres to its south-south-east. In the long grassy Bealach a'Chaolais between these two hills are the remains of several chambered cairns, as well as an earth house still in a reasonable state of preservation.

The hills of this central group are mostly covered with grass and heather, with little rock exposed, except on Stulaval whose north-west ridge makes a pleasing excursion, especially if approached from the north, over first Sheaval (223m) and then Trinaval and Arnaval (*eagle fell*) (252m), leaving the road-end at Unasary on the south shore of inner Loch Eynort. The round of hills to the east and north of Loch Snigisclett, with magical views of Loch Eynort, can be used for a return to Unasary; or, if transport can be arranged, the most pleasant excursion is to continue down from the rocky summit of Stulaval, to Bealach a' Chaolais above Loch Stulaval, and from there traverse Triuirebheinn, the Bealach an Easain and Beinn Ruigh Choinnich (271m). Lochboisdale and the A865 road can be reached from the last summit by descending north-westwards to stepping stones (if the tide is low) at the mouth of Loch a'Bharp, or to a prominent water storage enclosure and thence a footbridge across the river north-west of Auratote.

The full traverse of this small group of hills is equally fine in either direction; to the north are good views of Beinn Mhor and Hecla, and to the east, when the weather is clear, the Small Isles and the Cuillin of Skye. In good visibility the Stacs of St Kilda can be seen 80 kilometres to north west, and the Cairns of Col — if the sea is calm to the south-east

The Hellisdale Buttresses of Beinn Mhor

ROCK CLIMBING ON SOUTH UIST

The north-facing Hellisdale Buttresses on Beinn Mhor, which can be reached in two hours from Loch Dobhrain over the Bealach Hellisdale, are divided by six gullies - forming seven distinct buttresses. These give excellent 100-150m climbs, on firm grey gneiss with good holds and pitches of varying difficulty from Moderate to Very Severe. There are harder routes and variations to be explored.

The first recorded ascents were in 1932 by M Botterill and party, who climbed *Gullies Nos. 4* and *5* (numbered from the east). In 1936 all the buttresses were climbed by C Ludwig, D Dawson and J MacLennan, who recorded useful descriptions of the routes but without detailed grading. *Buttress No. 1* and *Buttress No. 2* are the steepest, with awkward overhangs. *Buttresses Nos. 6 and 7* are the longest but the easiest. The gullies tend to be slimy and vegetatious.

ERISKAY

The island of Eriskay, off the southern tip of South Uist, belongs more to the Uists than to the Barra Isles.

ACCESS

The only harbour, and a fine one, is Acairseid Mhor in the east. However, a jetty in the north serves for a locally operated car-ferry from Ludag in South Uist. There is also access from Barra, by private fishing-boat charter.

GENERAL DESCRIPTION

Eriskay is a small island, four kilometres long by two and a half kilometres wide, but it is the largest in the Sound of Barra and the most important, south of the Uists, next to Barra. Its name comes from the Gaelic, Eiriosgaigh, *Eric's Isle*. The island was made famous during the Second World War by the shipwreck (on Calvay island to its north-east) of the SS Politician with a cargo of 24,000 cases of whisky. The event inspired Sir Compton Mackenzie's book *Whisky Galore!* The north-west coast of Eriskay was also the first landfall made by Prince Charles Edward Stewart on his way from France to the Scottish mainland. This coast has several shell-sand beaches and the most southerly is still known as Coileag a'Phrionnsa (*the Prince's beach*).

The island is remarkably prosperous. The community of 200 is almost entirely Roman Catholic. There is a shop, school, post office and a church in the main settlement of Balla in the north-west.

THE HILLS

Eriskay's two prominent hills are Ben Scrien (185m) in the north, overlooking the Sound of Eriskay, and Ben Stack (122m) in the south, overlooking the Sound of Barra. Either of their grassy tops can be reached in half an hour from the road, which runs between them from Acairseid Mhor to Balla. The views from both tops are fine. The sounds surrounding the island, especially the Sound of Eriskay and the Sound of Stack between Eriskay and Eilean Leatham (*the Stack*) immediately to south, are shallow, with sandy sea-beds that give the water all around a luminous emerald colour from above.

There is a large amount of blown sand in the west and north-west, and in the marrum grass the rare sea-convolvulus (*calustega soldanella*) can be found; the only known locations elsewhere in the Isles where it grows are South Uist, Vatersay, the Barra Isles, and the Monach Isles (to the west of North Uist - see Chapter 20).

THE BARRA ISLES

The Barra Isles comprise the southern termination of the Long Isle and consist of a scattered chain, 36 kilometres in length, of fifteen or more islands. Barra is by far the largest, and only Barra and Vatersay are permanently inhabited.

MAPS :   Ordnance Survey   1:50,000 Sheet 31
             Bartholomew   1:100,000 Sheet 53

PRINCIPAL HILLS

BARRA

Ben Erival	200m	690 044
Ben Verrisey	197m	683 026
Heaval	383m	678 994
Ben Tangaval	333m	638 991

VATERSAY and MULDOANICH

Heishival Mor	190m	626 964
Ben Rulibreck	83m	623 941
Meall Domhaich	153m	688 940

SANDRAY

Cairn Galtar	207m	640 915

PABBAY

The Hoe	171m	594 873

MINGULAY

Macphee's Hill	224m	566 841
Carnan	273m	553 828

ACCESS

Castlebay on Barra is served regularly (three days a week) by the Caledonian MacBrayne's steamer from Oban (car ferry). The service calls also at Lochboisdale in South Uist, alternating with Castlebay for the day's first call.

Barra has also a small airport, Cockle Strand, on Traigh Mhor - the huge expanse of sands in the north-east of the island. The airport has a daily service from Glasgow. A local ferry-boat runs three days a week with the mail from Castlebay to Vatersay and can occasionally be hired, by private arrangement, for visits to the remainder of the Barra Isles.

The only other access to these islands, for those fortunate or lucky enough, is by private launch or sailing boat. Yachts from the mainland are frequent visitors in calm weather - or in sudden storms when the excellent shelter of Castle Bay or Cornaig Bay in the Sound of Vatersay, makes these popular havens.

TRANSPORT

From Castlebay there is a bus service to Eoligarry in the north and a passenger ferry from the jetty there to Ludag in South Uist. Probably a passage to Berneray could be negotiated from Castlebay on the tender that serves the Barra lighthouse at Skate Point on Berneray.

ACCOMMODATION
The only accommodation is the hotel in Castlebay, plus bed and breakfast in a few places elsewhere in Barra.

BARRA
The island is named after Saint Barra of the 6th century for whom no particulars appear to survive. The splendid Kiessimul Castle, in Castle Bay, was the fortress and ancestral home of the Macneills. It was abandoned in 1747 for Eoligarry in the north, but has now been restored and is permanently occupied. It can only be approached by water, even at low tide; regular visits for the public are available.

Barra has a population of approximately 2000 in its 70 square kilometres land area. The basis of the island's economy is crofting (both sheep and cattle) and fishing. The islanders are almost all Catholic. Despite the religious persecution of the 17th century, the people steadfastly clung to their faith. They are hardworking, bilingual - although Gaelic is predominantly spoken - and have an air of relaxation and joyfulness that contrasts noticeably with Lewis in the north. Barra's highest hill, Heaval, has a white statue of the Virgin Mary and Child (erected in 1954) on its south-eastern flank overlooking Castle Bay.

The island is unexpectedly hilly, as one observes from the grassy and toothy summit (glaciated gneiss) of **Heaval** (383m), when looking north. The full round of Barra's hills north of Castle Bay - Heaval, Hartaval, Grianan, Ben Verrisey, and Beinn Mhartainn - involves almost 1000m of climbing. From Castlebay this round, taking in the fine chambered cairn of Dun Bharpa west of Cora-bheinn, covers a distance of some 15 kilometres and makes a pleasant grassy hillwalk, with constantly fine views in clear weather. The grassy hill **Ben Erival** (200m) in the north, overlooking Barra's unique Traigh Mhor airfield, is easily climbed from the road to its south; this hill can also make a three-kilometre extension to the round of Barra's southern hills.

Similarly **Beinn Tangaval** (333m), in the south-west, can make a pleasant excursion on its own or be included as a three-kilometre extension of the main excursion of hills. A descent westwards from Ben Tangaval leads to the sea cliffs and a fine natural arch at Doirlinn Head. On this west coast, southwards from Doirlinn Head, are several interesting arches and coves sculpted by the wind and waves; while two kilometres north from Doirlinn Head are the (probably pre-Viking) remains of Dun Ban. At Borve point, further north again, are Barra's finest standing stones. Over 400 species of plant have been recorded on the island and 150 different birds.

VATERSAY, SANDRAY and PABBAY
The island of Vatersay together with its off-lier Muldaonich helps to shelter Castle Bay. Both are hilly. The two hills of Vatersay, **Heishival More** (180m) and **Ben Rulibreck** (83m) are joined by a narrow neck of sand-hills and machair. But for these, the north and south halves of Vatersay would form separate islands. The island's population is over 100; its main settlement in the south has a school and a post office.

To the east of Vatersay is a three-kilometre chain of islets and stacks, culminating in the dark hump of Muldoanich which rises 152m from the sea. This island once had a chapel, known by its Gaelic name Maol Domhnaich. It was also, at one time, kept as a deer forest. Sea eagles used to nest there and are, today, occasional visitors of its cliffs.

To the south of Vatersay, across the one kilometre-wide Sound of Vatersay, lies Sandray - a roughly circular island some two and a half kilometres in diameter. It has a huge sweep of white sand on its eastern shores that forms a well-known landmark from the Sea of the Hebrides. **Cairn Galtar**, the island's one hill, is grassy. Two hilly and rocky islets, Lingay and Greanamul, lie in the Sound of Pabbay to the south-west of Sandray.

Pabbay's one hill, **The Hoe,** has a name of nautical origin; its summit lies above the conspicuous cliff headland in the south-west. The meaning of the name Pabbay, however, is *hermit's island* or *priest's isle*. Like its namesake in the Sound of Harris, the island was presumably chosen for religious retreat because of its isolation. From its heathery hill-summit the land slopes grassily to a steep dune of sand in the east, Bagh Ban, above which there are still the remains of a chapel and burial ground. The island's population of a dozen or so was removed, according to Compton Mackenzie, for illegal distilling. In the north-east corner are the remains of Dunan Ruadh, *the red fort*.

MINGULAY and BERNERAY

Mingulay is the third largest of the Barra Isles, next to Barra and Vatersay. Its name comes from the Norse for *big isle* or possibly *bird island*. On its western side, only a few metres offshore, the precipitous stack of Lianamul is said to be clustered with thousands of birds, and is certainly snow-white with guano. It was once connected to Mingulay by a rope bridge.

Now deserted, Mingulay had a population of around 150 in the 1880's. The sea-cliffs on the west side are magnificent; Biulacraig being sheer for a height of some 210m, competing in grandeur with some of the finest on St Kilda. Here too, on Mingulay, the islanders once climbed these crags to harvest the sea-birds' eggs. A large puffin colony nests on the ledges among the stacks and caves.

The highest point of the island is the grassy summit of **Carnan** (273m) in the south-west. To the north is **Macphee's Hill** (224m); named after the rent collector for Macneill of Barra. He was once put ashore - it is said - and found the inhabitants all dead or dying of the plague; his companions rowed away from him in fear, on hearing this news, leaving the unfortunate Macphee on his own for a year!

Across the narrow Sound of Berneray from Mingulay is the island of Berneray. Its name comes from the Norse, *Bjorn's isle*. The huge 180m cliffs of Berneray at Barra Head form the southernmost tip of the Long Isle. The fine Barra Head lighthouse is in the western corner of the island, above equally fine cliffs at Skate Point. There is no shallow water offshore and these cliffs take the full fury of the Atlantic in its frequent storms.

CHAPTER 18

ORKNEY AND SHETLAND

The islands in the north, spreading north-eastwards for almost 300 kilometres from the northern tip of Scotland, are regarded collectively as the Northern Isles. From a glance at a chart, or a map such as the one on page x, it will be seen that together they extend over an area of sea as large as that covered by the Outer Hebrides, plus Skye, the Small Isles, and at least Mull, Coll and Tiree. They fall, geographically and geologically, into the two well-known and distinct groups of Orkney and Shetland. In both, however, the islands are more widely scattered than in any of the Hebridean groups.

Even the extent of land in the Northern Isles is seldom appreciated. The area of land in Orkney and Shetland, taken together, is six sevenths of that in the Western Isles. The islands of Shetland cover more than half the Long Isle's land area and those of Orkney over one third. By comparison Skye covers an area equal to three fifths the land area of the Long Isle. The combined population of Orkney and Shetland is 40,000, a third larger than the number living in the Western Isles. The land is almost wholly agricultural, with a well-developed network of roads on all the larger islands. Both groups are included on Sheet 1 of the Ordnance Survey Routemaster Series.

It will also be noted - geographically at least - that the isolated but inhabited islands of Foula and Fair Isle appear to fall respectively to Shetland and Orkney. Administratively, however, Fair Isle as well as Foula is treated as part of Shetland. Likewise, the outlying Sule Skerry and Sule Stack (or Stack Skerry), lying 60 and 65 kilometres west of Mainland Orkney, but only 45-50 kilometres off the north coast of mainland Scotland, are regarded administratively as part of Orkney. Indeed, Orkney's only gannet colony nests on the more westerly, Sule Stack. As outliers, both are covered in Chapter 20.

ORKNEY

MAPS :   Ordnance Survey   1:50,000 Sheets 5, 6 and 7
            Bartholomew   1:100,000 Sheet 61

PRINCIPAL HILLS
MAINLAND

	Ward Hill	269m	335 080
	Wideford Hill	225m	412 116
	Milldoe	221m	358 207

HOY

	Ward Hill	479m	228 023
	Cuilags	433m	210 034
	St John's Head	370m	188 035
	Knap of Trowieglen	399m	240 985

ROUSAY

	Blotchnie Fiold	250m	417 289
	Kierfea Hill	235m	423 322

ACCESS AND TRANSPORT

Comprehensive up-to-date information on travel to Orkney, by sea and by air, can be obtained from a brochure published by the Orkney Tourist Board which has an office in Kirkwall. The only seaports of any size are Kirkwall and Stromness on Mainland Orkney.

Stromness is tucked into the south-west corner of Mainland, sheltered by a 50m-high headland that runs for four kilometres south-eastwards from Breck Ness. The harbour of Stromness lies on the Mainland side of the inner (eastern) end of the narrow Hoy Sound, which separates Mainland from Hoy. A car and passenger service to Stromness (P & O Ferries) operates, normally Mondays to Saturdays (plus Sundays in July and August), from Scrabster, near Thurso on the Caithness north coast; a two hour crossing. Sailings are daily, but this frequency is stepped up in the months of May to October. The service is roll-on roll-off but advanced booking is recommended. A new roll-on roll-off vehicle ferry service, between Gills Bay, Caithness, and South Ronaldsay, to be operated by Orkney Ferries Ltd, is to commence in 1989 with sailings planned several times a day.

From John O'Groats, the Thomas and Bews ferry company runs a passenger (or passenger and bicycle) service between Duncansby Head, Caithness, and the southernmost point of Orkney - Burwick, at Brough Ness on South Ronaldsay. This service is seasonal - usually April to September - and often subject to weather. The crossing is just 40 minutes, with normally two to three sailings daily; more in July and August, less in September. A roll-on, roll-off ferry service is planned for this route.

A weekly service is also operated by P & O Ferries between Aberdeen, Stromness and Lerwick in Shetland. The passage from Aberdeen to Stromness in

Mainland Orkney takes eight hours (Saturdays); the return (Fridays) takes the same time. All the P & O ferries have roll-on, roll-off vehicle loading. The company also runs a freight vessel, serving Leith, Aberdeen and Stromness (plus Shetland), which can accommodate twelve passengers and has a roll-on, roll-off facility for cars.

The Orkney Tourist Board brochure also gives flight information. Kirkwall has a medium-sized airport, to which there are services (Loganair and British Airways) daily from Glasgow, Edinburgh, Aberdeen, Inverness and Wick. Loganair also operate scheduled services between several of the islands in Orkney; including Mainland, Stronsay, Eday, Sanday, Westray, Papa Westray and North Ronaldsay. These islands have small airstrips, often on grass. The world's shortest known scheduled flight (two minutes) is from Westray to Papa Westray. Loganair advise that the flight time can be shorter if winds are favourable.

Travel between the islands by boat is also relatively easily arranged. The Orkney Islands Shipping Company, Kirkwall, operates regular ferries and cruises; while less formal motor launches, used largely as school buses, will take visitors on their 'school runs' when room and weather permit. They can usually be privately chartered for ferry service during school holidays. Rousay, Egilsay and Wyre are served by frequent roll-on, roll-off ferries from Tingwall on Mainland; and Hoy, South Walls and Flotta from Houton (south-west Mainland).

All of the islands have good networks of well-surfaced roads. Bicycles can thus be a pleasure in Orkney, and the inter-island ferry launches will always take bicycles when they have space. Cars can be hired on Mainland, where distances can make car, or coach (several tour services operate) a sensible choice. Vehicle ferries operate lift-on-off services between Kirkwall and a few of the islands - Rousay, Eday, North Ronaldsay - and between Stromness and Lyness on Hoy.

ACCOMMODATION

A wide range of accommodation is available, especially on Mainland; from four crown hotels (Scottish Tourist Board rating) to self-catering static caravans for rent. A wealth of information can be obtained from the Orkney Tourist Board offices at either Broad Street, Kirkwall, or Ferry Terminal, Stromness. Plenty of bed and breakfast accommodation can be found on Mainland Orkney, but little on its other islands. There are hostels operated by the Scottish Youth Hostel Association in Kirkwall and Stromness on Mainland, also two on Hoy, at Rackwick (grid reference 199 998) and Orgill (grid reference 233 037), operated by the Orkney Islands Education Department. There is also a hostel on Eday, near the Bay of London (grid reference 562 333), operated by Eday Community Enterprises, and one open all year on Papa Westray (grid reference 493 515) owned and operated by the Papay Community Co-operative.

There are two official campsites on Mainland; one at Stromness and one at Kirkwall. Much of the island is agricultural and crofting land, thus for camping anywhere else local permission should be sought. On Hoy, where cliff-climbing as well as hillwalking (and cycling perhaps) are at their best for Orkney, superb headland and inland camping is feasible almost anywhere - provided one is equipped to withstand the frequent strong winds and sudden squalls. Camping is discouraged, however, in the area of the Nature Reserve.

Outwith Lyness, on Hoy, there is little by way of accommodation, although bed and breakfast can be found at Quoyness (Whaness on earlier Ordnance Survey Landranger Series maps) on the north-east coast of the island. A well-placed cottage or two, as well as a caravan, are available for rent at Rackwick on the coast between Moor Fea and Mel Fea - near to Rora Head and the Old Man of Hoy.

GENERAL DESCRIPTION

The name Orkney is from the Norse and, since the suffix *ey* is old Norse for islands, it is incorrect to speak of the Orkneys, and even Orkney Islands is not strictly correct. There is ample evidence of the Norse settlement, which dates from the 9th century when the islands were colonised by the Viking marauders and used as a launching pad for their murderous assaults on the monasteries of Ireland.

Orkney has more than 70 islands, of which eighteen are inhabited today. The total population is over 19,000, in a land area overall of 975 square kilometres. Nearly 7,000 live in Kirkwall, while Stromness accounts for another 2,000. The total extent of the islands is some 85 kilometres south to north and 33 kilometres west to east.

The nearest point of Orkney to the Scottish mainland is Brough Ness at the southernmost tip of South Ronaldsay, only nine kilometres from Duncansby Head. These two headlands are separated, however, by the most turbulent stretch of sea in the British Isles - the Pentland Firth. This dangerous strait protects the main entrance to Orkney's famous Scapa Flow, the Churchillian stronghold of the British Naval Fleet in World War II and the place where many ships of the German fleet were scuttled after World War I. The sunken wrecks attract many divers.

Geologically, the Orkney archipelago is formed almost entirely of Devonian Old Red Sandstone with just a few basaltic dykes. The strata are inclined at only a slight angle, which results in superb sea cliffs, especially in the west. Apart from these, the island profiles are generally flat, with rounded tops even when hilly.

The soil is fertile and, though bare and treeless, the moors are a carpet of tiny wild flowers in spring and summer; wild lupin, rare primula and sea-pinks abound. Prosperous farmland is to be found everywhere. Fish-farming is also now a rapidly expanding occupation. The climate, due largely to the Gulf Stream, is temperate; although this description, while technically correct, ignores (for the hillwalker or climber) the wind-chill feature of the weather. Nonetheless, the average minimum temperature in Orkney in winter is higher than in London and the average rainfall lower than at Torquay in Devon. The winds, or rather their reliability, made South Ronaldsay in Orkney the site of the first wind-generated electric power station (although only 22 kilowatts) to be connected to the national grid. A crucial difference between winter and summer in Orkney latitudes is the number of daylight hours; in midsummer the sun is above the horizon for more than eighteen hours of the day.

Prehistoric relics are widespread. Orkney has the finest archaeological discoveries, especially of neolithic man, in Britain. At the Bay of Skaill, in Sandwick

The perfectly preserved interior of a Stone Age dwelling at Skara Brae

on the west coast of Mainland, is the best preserved Stone Age village in Europe, Skara Brae; while the Ring of Brodgar standing stones in Stenness, south-west Mainland, compete in importance with those of Callanish in Lewis. Also to be found in Stenness is probably the finest chambered tomb in western Europe, Maes Howe, dating from around 3000 BC. Another chambered cairn of the same period, named the Tomb of the Eagles after the many eagles' claws excavated among the burials there, is to be found on South Ronaldsay. Orkney also has fine examples of later eras: Bronze Age barrows, Pictish brochs, Viking settlements, Papae churches and Stewart castles. Medieval farmers unknowingly dismantled many of the prehistoric monuments but ample remain, and often in excellent states of preservation.

The islands are also a paradise for maritime birds : red-throated and great northern divers, Slavonian grebes, whooper swans and widgeons, pintail and long-tailed duck, red-breasted mergansers, hen harriers, golden plovers and purple sandpipers, great skuas, kittiwakes and fulmars, arctic terns, guillemots, puffins, short-eared owls and twite. Many of these may be found in the Nature Reserve, administered by the Royal Society for the Protection of Birds, at Mid Hill (grid reference 336 249) in north Mainland. There are nine such Nature Reserves in Orkney; four on Mainland and one each on Westray, Papa Westray, Rousay, Hoy and Copinsay. In contrast to the abundance of birdlife, there is little animal life; no foxes or deer (except for deer-farming on Westray), although the Orkney blue hare breed in many of the islands. Reptiles too are absent, no snakes or frogs are found.

HILLWALKING IN ORKNEY
The principal hillwalking in Orkney is on Hoy and Rousay, while splendid coastal and cliff-top walks can be found on almost all the islands.

MAINLAND
Wideford Hill (225m)
Ward Hill (269m)
Wideford Hill above Kirkwall, and Ward Hill above Orphir, provide fine views of the archipelago of islands and the waters of Scapa Flow and the Pentland Firth. The views give ample reward for the climbing of these hills, out of proportion to their height, although the road to the summit of Wideford Hill makes it common now to drive there by car. The south slopes of Ward Hill are a rifle range and are noted as a 'danger area' - signalled by the flying of a red flag. Underground chambered cairns on the northern slopes of Wideford Hill are worth visiting; they probably date from between 2000 and 3000 BC.

Milldoe (221m)
The gentle slopes of Milldoe in the north-east of West Mainland give fine views to east and north-east. The plateau there, from Ernie Tooin over the summit of Mid Tooin (distinguishable as a summit only by its triangulation pillar), gives dry gentle walking to Hammars Hill above Gairsay Sound. Near this north-eastern tip of West Mainland, on Burgar Hill, is the site of an experimental three megawatt wind-turbine electricity generator.

Above Stromness, Brinkies Brae (Brinkles Bray on the later Ordnance Survey Landranger map, Sheet 6) is of Dalradian granite. This summit is geologically the oldest known outcrop of rock in Orkney, it was once an island in a huge freshwater loch.

The finest coastal walk on Mainland is from Stromness above Breck Ness and the cliffs of Black Craig, past the caves at Neban Point and Yesnaby and the interesting Borwick Broch, to the spectacular neolithic village of Skara Brae at the Bay of Skaill. The full distance is some fourteen kilometres in one direction. Return transport by road can be arranged locally, if desired. Alternatively, this cliff walk can be done from north to south, giving - on a clear day - spectacular views to south and south-west, as far as Cape Wrath.

A feature of the rugged west coast of Mainland are the many sea-stacks, most of which are reported to have been climbed at one time or another, but not all recorded. There are endless prospects here for rock climbing. Prominent among these stacks are North Gaulton Castle, to the north of Neban Point, and Yesnaby Castle which is located just south of Brough of Bigging.

HOY
MAP : Ordnance Survey 1:25,000 Sheet 33 (HY 10/20 and part of HY 30)
Hillwalking on Hoy is the best to be found in Orkney. The island is the second in size to Mainland, but is the highest and by far the wildest of the group. Its name comes from the Norse, *high*. Hoy contrasts dramatically with other islands in Orkney; four

fifths of the island is covered with moorland heather and rough grassland. In the past the inhabitants supported themselves almost entirely by fishing. Rackwick, at the northern end of the south-west coast, once supported a thriving fishing community; now, but for two or three crofting families, there is little more than a fish farm. All the hills on Hoy are in its northern half and can be easily approached from Rackwick or from Linksness which is reached by privately operated boat services from Stromness.

The Burra Sound separating Hoy from the small sparsely populated but green island of Graemsay off its north-east corner has a scattering of wrecks. A large part of the island's population of about 400 live in South Walls, an almost detached peninsula in the south-east, joined by a narrow isthmus hardly wider than the road (the B9047) that connects it to Hoy. The narrow channel between South Walls and Hoy is Long Hope, which gives its name to the famous lifeboat stationed at Upper Salwick in Aith Hope, south of The Ayre isthmus. The length of Hoy stretches a distance of sixteen kilometres from Long Hope north-westwards to St John's Head, the spectacular sea-cliffs in the north-west.

Ward Hill (479m)

The highest summit, Ward Hill, is easily climbed by its north-west shoulder from Sandy Loch two kilometres south-east of the pier at Linksness. The Norse meaning of *glen* is slightly different from the Scottish and the narrow stony bluff on this shoulder of Ward Hill is named Glen of Greor; while sections of the north-eastern braes on Ward Hill, overlooking the Bay of Quoys, are named Glen of the Horn and White Glen. The summit of Ward Hill is almost flat; there are two cairns, with a fresh-water spring at the westernmost, and a triangulation pillar. The views from there are fine.

Cuilags (433m)
St John's Head (370m)

Cuilags is a fine shaped hill and the second highest on Hoy, two kilometres to the north-west of Ward Hill. It also is an easy climb from Sandy Loch, or by its southern shoulder if the traverse from the main (north-east) summit of Ward Hill, round the top of the Redglen burn to its south-western summit (356m) is first made. From the grassy top of Cuilags, the two-kilometre walk to St John's Head is almost level, and from there a breathtaking walk leads south-south-westwards along the top of this spectacular six-kilometre line of unbroken cliffs to Rora Head. The walk gives also an impressive view of the Old Man of Hoy, from Scarsa and the Tuaks of the Boy. The many species of seabirds nesting in these cliffs, and some rare alpine flowers to be found in the grassy moorland above, have led to Hoy being designated as a Site of Special Scientific Interest.

Knap of Trowieglen (399m)

The remaining hill on Hoy is the Knap of Trowieglen. About the only interesting approach to its summit is from the north, ascending between the Trowie Glen itself and the Dwarfie Hamars. The unusual Dwarfie Stane, below the Hamars, rewards a visit. It is the only tomb in Britain cut from the solid rock, and dates from 1900 BC.

The Old Man of Hoy

Measuring externally some eight metres in length by five metres wide and two metres high, it has an inside passage and two separated cells hewn, it is said, by a legendary giant for himself and his wife.

ROCK CLIMBING ON HOY

The 'Television Age' of climbing, at least in the UK, commenced in 1966 with the dramatized (second) ascent of *Original Route*, on the east face of the Old Man of Hoy, first climbed earlier that year by R Baillie, T W Patey and C J S Bonington. The climb, partly aided (138m; E1), was enacted for the BBC. The late Tom Patey wrote (SMCJ Vol.28, p.322) "This well-known landmark in the Pentland Firth provided a six-hour climb on the 18th July, two days having been previously spent in reconnaissance and roping the climb as far as the top of the second pitch. The route followed the landward face of the pinnacle, which was denuded nearly a century ago by the collapse of the gigantic second leg which spanned an archway and is shown on prints of the early 19th century. This may account for the very unreliable nature of the rock as far as the 300ft contour, although we have no first-hand information regarding the south and seaward faces, both of which should provide equally spectacular lines."

"The long second pitch of 100ft overhangs a total of 15ft throughout its length and was climbed entirely by artificial methods, although much of the pitch might have gone free had the rock been in any way trustworthy. The remaining 350ft was entirely free climbing and very spectacular. Most of the pitches overhang and the route spirals slightly, so that doubled ropes should be fixed in position during the ascent, to avoid bottomless abseils!"

The following year, J Brown and I MacNaught-Davis climbed the *South Face Route* (150m; E2), and D Haston and P Crew the *South East Arête* (145m; aided). Two more routes were established in 1975 and 1982, and then in 1984 another television attack on the Old Man produced *A Fistful of Dollars* (141m; E5), a free and direct version of the South-East Arete and *A Few Dollars More* (E3; 135m), taking a prominent crackline in the centre of the north face gained by first traversing the West Face and regarded as the best route on the Old Man of Hoy; both climbs were made by M Hamilton and P Whillance (with P Braithwaite).

Meanwhile in 1969, St John's Head was climbed for television and then, in 1970, by E W Drummond and O Hill for the Sunday Telegraph. These climbers first took two days to descend the cliff-face, from the top, and then five days making the first ascent of *Longhope Route* back to its summit. St John's Head itself is split from the mainland of Hoy by a wide notch, which gives no more than a moderate scramble. From its summit to the beach is a vertical drop of 342m - the third highest sea-cliff in the British Isles (next to The Kame on Foula in Shetland, and Conachair on Hirta in the St Kilda group). Descent is by abseil; virtually free, which the wind, by causing rope-twisting, can make into a 'spinning epic'.

A new extreme route on St John's Head, *Big John* (429m), was climbed in 1988 taking the "Soaring" arête to the left (north) of Longhope Route.

ROUSAY
Blotchnie Fiold (250m)
Kierfea Hill (235m)

From Mainland Orkney, a mail-boat service operates daily to Rousay, across the Eynhallow Sound, and to the smaller island of Egilsay across Rousay Sound. Cars can be hired on Rousay; or, the roll-on, roll-off car ferry from Tingwall serves Rousay and other islands regularly.

Next to Hoy, Rousay has some of the best hillwalking in Orkney. Blotchnie Fiold and Kierfea Hill are easy walks with plenty of interesting antiquities everywhere on the island; the Midhowe Chambered Cairn (grid reference 373 304) is outstanding. On neighbouring Egilsay, is the famous Round Tower and Church of St Magnus, standing a hundred metres from where one of the Orkney earls, Magnus, was murdered.

The small island of Eynhallow, which gives the sound its name, is a bird sanctuary. Over 30 species of birds nest there regularly. The waters surrounding the island, known also as the *'vanishing island'*, are turbulent. Eynhallow, which has an early monastery, was the Holy Island of the Norse settlers. Nowadays, large numbers of seals gather there.

SHETLAND

MAPS : Ordnance Survey   1:50,000 Sheets 1, 3 and 4
           Bartholomew   1:100,000 Sheet 62

PRINCIPAL HILLS

MAINLAND

Ronas Hill	450m	305 835
Royl Field	293m	396 285

BRESSAY

Ward of Bressay	223m	503 387

NOSS

Noup of Noss	181m	553 399

PAPA STOUR

Virda Field	87m	152 619

FOULA

The Sneug	418m	947 397
The Kame	376m	940 401
Hamnafield	344m	958 392

FAIR ISLE

Ward Hill	217m	208 734

UNST

Hermaness Hill	200m	606 176
Saxa Vord	280m	632 167

ACCESS AND TRANSPORT

P & O Ferries serve Lerwick on Mainland from Aberdeen; three to four sailings per week and almost daily in summer months. The crossing is usually overnight. Once a week, in both directions, the boat calls at Kirkwall in Orkney.

Shetland's main airport is Sumburgh, at the southern tip of Mainland. With the development of off-shore oil, the frequency of flights to Sumburgh increased dramatically. As many as four per day (British Airways) now operate from Aberdeen, and two per day from London, Birmingham and Glasgow. Tingwall airport near Lerwick is smaller. Flights to there are operated by Loganair; two per day from Aberdeen, one per day from Edinburgh. Loganair also operate a daily schedule, except Sundays (and subject always to change) from Tingwall airport, to Whalsay, Fetlar and Unst, using an eight-seater Islander aircraft; plus twice-weekly flights to Fair Isle, and weekly to Foula and Out Skerries.

There is a public bus service throughout Mainland, Yell and Unst. However, while this may be perfectly adequate for the islanders, it is impossible to see even Mainland Shetland without some form of personal transport - unless one has several weeks in which to accomplish it. A car can be hired at Lerwick, also bicycles.

Between the islands there are frequent passenger and drive-on-off vehicle ferries. These link most of Shetland with Mainland; the islands of Unst, Yell,

Whalsay and Bressay being served by as many as twenty or more crossings daily in both directions. Passengers are also carried, for nominal fares, on cargo vessels that serve Foula from Walls in west Mainland, Fair Isle from Grutness in south Mainland, Papa Stour from West Burrafirth on Mainland, and Out Skerries from Lerwick.

ACCOMMODATION

There is a wide range of accommodation available on Shetland, from luxury hotels to official campsites. An information brochure is published by the Shetland Tourist Organisation in Lerwick. Guest houses are plentiful and even tiny Foula has three, although Fetlar only one. Camping almost anywhere is permitted although local permission should always be sought; a friendly reception to camping enquiry can be virtually relied on. Camping on Fair Isle is not permitted, however, and use of the official campsite on Fetlar is encouraged. Practically everywhere is grassy, though the ground is often peaty and shelter from the almost constant winds can also be difficult to find. The Scottish Youth Hostels Association operates a hostel at Lerwick, owned by the Shetland Islands Council.

GENERAL DESCRIPTION

Shetland (or Zetland) is the most northerly part of the British Isles and once a part of the Viking kingdom. It numbers over a hundred islands in all; only fourteen of which are inhabited. The total population of Shetland is 21,000, of which more than 16,000 live on Mainland, with nearly half this number (over a third of Shetland's total population) living in Lerwick. The other important centres on Mainland are Scalloway and Stenness in the north-west, Sandness and Walls in the west; while the off-shore oil industry has brought more recent prosperity also to Sullom Voe. Outside of Sullom Voe the principal industries are crofting and fishing, and to a lesser extent knitting - for which Shetland is justifiably famous.

Geologically, Shetland was a mountainous region of the Scottish and Scandinavian pre-Ice Age continent. In the course of millions of years the vast area was slowly eroded by rivers and by the sea, and the weight of ice accumulated during several ice ages caused the land to sink until all that was left was Shetland.

The most common sedimentary rock is old red sandstone, but a huge variety of different minerals and rocks can be found. Although two parallel bands of limestone occur across the middle of Mainland, the spine of Shetland is of hard metamorphic rocks - mostly schists and gneiss - stretching from Unst in the north to the southern tip of Mainland. Peat extends over a large part of the land as a result of the poor drainage by these rocks, which contain large deposits of copper and iron ores, plus chromite, serpentine, talc and limestone - though little by way of commercially useful minerals.

Apart from one small experimental forestry plantation on Mainland, there are no trees in Shetland. The windy climate and closeness to the sea account for this, although remains of tree-stumps have been found in the peaty bogs in places, pointing to a climatic change in geologically recent times bringing stronger winds and colder temperatures.

Present-day variations of temperature and rainfall with the seasons are small. Winters are mild, average temperature not falling below 5°C; which is exceptionally warm for such northern latitudes - Lerwick being 260 kilometres north of Aberdeen and further north than the southernmost tip of Greenland. On the other hand, summer temperatures rarely exceed 16°C.

Shetland has excellent examples of prehistoric habitation, dating from well before 2000 BC. More than 60 Neolithic dwelling places have been found on the islands. The most impressive, because of their size (some are over twelve metres high), are the brochs; the huge ones on Mousa and at Loch of Clickimin near Lerwick on Mainland being the best preserved anywhere in Europe. The most important finds, however, are the Stanydale Temples on Whalsay, the Bronze Age and Iron Age remains at Jarlshof at the southern toe of Mainland, and a priceless collection of Celtic silver (now in the Edinburgh Museum although a local industry, Shetland Silvercraft, make replicas) found on St Ninian's Isle off the west coast of South Mainland. This small island also revealed (in the 1950's) a pre-Norse church and a Bronze Age burial ground.

Shetland is unique in the British Isles for its birdlife. Breeding birds of the islands include divers, dunlins, merlins, mallard, shelduck, glaucous gulls and whimbrels. Snowy owls nest on Fetlar and on Ronas Hill, west Mainland, with king eiders and surf scoter also to be found in Ronas Voe. Kittiwakes and artic skuas (known locally as bonxies) nest in almost all the islands, while Slavonian grebes and velvet scoters will often be seen at Sullom Voe. Other species include red-throated divers, tufted ducks, red-breasted mergansers, fulmars, herons, whooper swans, shags and black guillemots. The moorlands support lapwing, wheatear, curlew, jackdaws, woodpigeons, fieldfares and redwings, to name only a few; while winter visitors to the islands include barnacle geese, hen harriers, jack snipe and little auks.

Mammals in Shetland are not so numerous, most having been brought by man. Rabbits, blue hare and even hedgehogs have been introduced. Even the Shetland pony, found widely especially on Unst, was probably not originally native. Shetland long-tailed field-mice are indigenous, and otters are widespread (their local name is *dratsie*). The islands are also well-known for both freshwater and sea angling.

HILLWALKING IN SHETLAND
The finest hillwalking in Shetland is on the isolated island of Foula. Next comes Mainland, which has the highest of Shetland's hills, and then Bressay and Noss. The sandstone nature of the islands makes generally for grassy and meadowy hillwalks; while the general flatness of the land surrounding the hills makes for fine views from their summits.

MAINLAND
Ronas Hill (450m)
Royl Field (293m)
Although Ronas Hill in north-west Mainland is the highest in Shetland, the hills on Mainland are mostly low and covered with rough grass and heather. The ascent of

Ronas Hill is an easy walk from Collafirth Hill, to where there is a track from North Collafirth on the A970. The view from the summit is remarkable. All around, in almost every direction, are interesting crags, stacks, caves and natural arches, like those of Muckel Ossa and Little Ossa out to sea, to north-west.

To the south, across Ronas Voe (*Voe* is Norse for *inlet*), is the Ura Firth, which opens southwards on the east side of a large promontory named the Ness of Hillswick. The vertical sea-cliffs on the western shores of this Ness, or peninsula, are sharpened by the huge 30m-high rock pillar, The Drongs, standing out to sea beyond Houlma Sound and the shapely Isle of Westerhouse. Across the small bay of Sand Wick, to the north-west of Hillswick, can be seen the fine red Heads of Grocken.

To the south-west is another huge promontory, Esha Ness, whose precipitous sea-cliffs give a brilliant display of colours in the sun; while far to the south, some 70 kilometres from Ronas Hill, at the southern extremity of Mainland, the west-facing 280m cliffs of Fitful Head show up sharply in clear weather. These sea-cliffs have some fine rock climbing potential, of "considerable height and exposure and not many birds", in the words of Tom Weir. On the Esha Ness cliffs are the famous Holes of Scraada (grid reference 213 793). In heavy seas and at high (night) tide, a wall of water crashes from the seaward side of a cave there into the Holes which form a sunken bay.

Hillwalking above Fitful Head can also be recommended for its views northwards of Mainland, and southwards to the islands of Orkney when the weather is clear. Likewise the Clift Hills of south Mainland, overlooking Clift Sound, provide a grassy walk with fine views to the north; commencing with Royl Field or with Scroo (248m), approached from the road westwards from Clapphoull on the A970 road, and then keeping to the western edge of the hills over Holm Field and Muskna Field to descend finally to the road below Troubleton overlooking West Voe of Quarff (10-12 kilometres). Throughout Shetland there are many similar superb coastal walks.

BRESSAY and NOSS
Ward of Bressay (223m)
Noup of Noss (181m)
The Cave of Bard, below the western sea-cliffs of the Bard peninsula of Bressay, is probably the most spectacular feature of this island. A boat (and a flashlight, or torch) are needed for a visit; its wide entrance is only accessible from the sea. The deep water at the entrance is very clear and produces a brilliance of colours on the walls and roof. Beyond the narrows inside the entrance, is a spacious 'hall' with fine stalactites reaching down from its roof. The Ward of Bressay, highest point on the island, is an easy walk from any direction.

The Giant's Leg at Bard Head also rewards inspection; the rock there, sculpted by the seas, is impressive. Likewise on the Isle of Noss, off the east coast of Bressay, the sea-cliffs are huge and the rock-forms spectacular - as are the enormous numbers of birds that nest in these cliffs.

The Noup of Noss is a fine promontory with vertical drops of 150m into the sea on all sides. Seabirds there also are prolific. The sea stack, Holm of Noss, stands 48m high across a gap of 20 metres or so from the cliffs and the caves of Feadda Ness. An engineer who roped his way to the summit of this stack in a box cradle is said to have fallen and drowned on the return. The island of Noss is a Nature Reserve.

PAPA STOUR

A complete circuit of Papa Stour (*priest's large island*), which can be combined with a climb to its highest point, **Virda Field** (86m), takes several hours of strenuous going. The shores of the island possess some of the finest sea-caves in the British Isles, as well as a congestion of stacks, skerries and inlets; not to mention birds.

UNST

Hermaness Hill (200m)
Saxa Vord (280m)
The hills of Unst are in the north of the island. The two highest, Hermaness Hill and Saxa Vord, are at the northernmost extremity - to either side (west and east) of Burra Firth. They both have paths to their summits. Saxa Vord has a large RAF station, with 'golf-ball' (radar) scanner and tracking installation, manned by 800 men and providing employment for many islanders. Herma Ness is a bird sanctuary and Hermaness a National Nature Reserve.

A kilometre to north of the Herma Ness shores are the spectacular skerries and stack of Muckle Flugga; its summit crowned with a lighthouse, the most northerly inhabited point of the British Isles. Further north again, by half a kilometre, is Britain's most northerly uninhabited island, Out Stack.

FAIR ISLE

Ward Hill (217m)
Some 36 kilometres south-south-west of Sumburgh Head lies Fair Isle, whose name belies its almost completely precipitous and inaccessible shores. The ferry from Gruteness, north of Sumburgh on Mainland, serves the pier in North Haven behind Bu Ness on the east coast of Fair Isle. The island is a Nature Reserve and is owned by the National Trust for Scotland, whose hostel, in the South Haven west of Bu Ness peninsula, is available for accommodation by arrangement. It is also the site of a small wind-generated electric power station.

There are natural sandstone arches and stacks around the whole island; many to be seen from the highest point, Ward Hill, which is an easy walk. Some of the finest arches are on Sheep Rock, a steep promontory on the south-east coast; a landing there is tricky, as is the climb to its summit (132m). The cliffs are of sandstone and on its summit were once grazed the sheep that gave - because of their natural colours - Fair Isle its fame for all-over patterned jerseys (nowhere, in a true Fair Isle pattern, should the motif repeat).

Fair Isle's isolation (the name probably derives from the Old Norse meaning *far isle*) makes it a sanctuary for migrant birds in spring and autumn. The bird observatory at North Haven, rebuilt in 1969, has a permanent staff monitoring and

The wild coastline of Papa Stour

recording the constantly changing bird population. Besides claiming 320 recorded species, the island also has its own - the Fair Isle wren. Because of the island's isolation this bird has developed a different song and behavioural pattern from the mainland variety.

FOULA
The Sneug (418m)
The Kame (376m)
Hamnafield (344m)
A landing by boat can be made on Foula in a small inlet, Ham Voe, in the island's eastern coast. The hills of Foula, all in the west, are steep and conical. Settlement of Foula is confined to the low-lying plain curving for five kilometres from north to south and occupying the eastern third of the island.

A fine hillwalk starting at the so-named Landing Strip in the south-east, takes in Hamnafield and Brustins to the summit of The Sneug three kilometres north-westwards from the Heddlicliff below Landing Strip, and thence to the headland in the north-west above The Kame; returning by North Bank and Soberlie Hill to the track at Mucklegrind. The total circuit is eight to nine kilometres and takes three to four hours.

Of these hills, taken in the opposite direction, Tom Weir writes : "Soberlie Hill is the most dramatic climb you can do on Foula, because the edge of Soberlie is a cliff, rising with every foot of ascent until you land on North Bank leading to the celebrated Kame, greatest precipice of Foula. It presents itself dramatically. You climb up a steep ridge linked to the backbone of the island, then suddenly you find yourself overlooking nothing, just a vertical plunge of 375m, more frightening than anything on St. Kilda in my opinion".

The Kame is in fact not only the 'greatest precipice of Foula', it is almost the highest vertical cliff in the British Isles coming second only to Conachair (430m) on St Kilda. Moreover, the whole of the west coast of the island is buttressed by enormous walls, with great scope for routes, though very difficult of access. Thus Foula has considerable potential for rock climbing.

The weather, though, can be hostile: Tom Weir continued, "Although it was July, we wore gloves, such was the cold on top of The Sneug, at 418m the second highest hill in the Shetlands. In another mile we were blown across the Brustins and down the ridge of Hamnafield, exhilarated at such a fast and effortless descent".

From The Sneug, the highest summit of Foula, there is a magnificent view of the whole west coast of Shetland and of much of Orkney.

CHAPTER 19

OFFSHORE ISLANDS

The foregoing chapters of this guide cover the larger islands and island groups around Scotland's coast. There remain innumerable small islands, of which this chapter describes the more important ones lying close offshore, while the next and last chapter covers those that are classed as outliers.

The majority of offshore islands are in the west and the north-west. They include islands in the Inner Sound between Skye and the mainland, and those close to the shores of the Long Isle. The only islands of note in the east, off the North Sea coast, are the Bass Rock and the Isle of May - both close inshore in the Firth of Forth. These too are described in this chapter, which covers a large spread of islands, taken clockwise around the coast from Ardnamurchan northwards.

Almost all the offshore islands have at one time been inhabited or used for grazing sheep or goats. Many lie in sheltered sounds or within the mouths of large sea lochs and are virtually inshore islands. Some, like the Summer Isles in Loch Broom and Rona in the Inner Sound of Skye, give fine walking but are only of marginal interest to climbers. Others, like the Shiant and Ascrib islands are so small that they have little scope for either walking or climbing, and their chief interest may be for bird watchers or skin-divers. Islands such as Handa and Raasay are different again. The former is a cliff-girt bird sanctuary, whose Great Stac of Handa lying off its northern cliffs can only be scaled by a Very Severe climb; while Raasay, in Skye's Inner Sound, has climbs on its summit crags ranging from Mild Very Severe to Extreme.

EILEAN SHONA

MAPS : Ordnance Survey   1:50,000 Sheet 40
                                         1:25,000 Sheet 275 (NM 67/77)

PRINCIPAL HILL
        Beinn a' Bhaillidh   265m   649 742

ACCESS
Permission to land on the island must be obtained from Eilean Shona Management Ltd (telephone 0967 85249). A private track to the adjoining Shona Beag fords the North Channel at low tide from the A861 road, three kilometres south of Glenuig. Shona Beag and Eilean Shona are separately and privately owned.

ACCOMMODATION

Cottages can be rented from Eilean Shona Management Ltd, near to the estate house in the south-east of the island and at South Shore. No camping is permitted on Eilean Shona or Shona Beag.

GENERAL DESCRIPTION

Eilean Shona, as its Gaelic name implies (although the derivation *old ford* is also probable), is a scenically beautiful island. For the most part it is steep and rocky but with gentle grassy meadows, bordering some superb shell-sand beaches at the south-west extremity and attractive mature woodland in the east. Three kilometres in length, west to east, by two kilometres north to south, the island splits the entrance to Loch Moidart. The North Channel dries and the ford from the mainland across this channel to Shona Beag, to which Eilean Shona is joined by a narrow neck of land, is passable for two to three hours at each low tide. There are few roads or tracks, and from Shona Beag to Eilean Shona the going is rough.

The hillwalking on Eilean Shona, while never strenuous, can be rugged. The island is composed of rough igneous rock, with several small outcrops which also provide a few 10-12m climbs, ranging from Moderate to Very Severe. No routes are recorded. The highest point, Beinn a' Bhaillidh, is ill-defined but carries a triangulation pillar. The terrain is split into western and eastern hilly regions by two streams, the Baramore Burn and the Allt a' Chlachair, which flow respectively north and south from a shallow bealach forming a watershed roughly in the centre of the island.

The western region gives a fine hillwalk, from Cruach a' Choire (157m) over Cruach Bhuidhe (199m) and Sgurr an Teintein (176m), with outstanding views of the Small Isles. A descent can be made eastwards from the northernmost summit to Baramore and thence by path to the old schoolhouse some 500 metres further east. From there an easy and pleasant ascent of Beinn a' Bhaillidh can be made, or the path continues along the steep north shore to the delightfully forested eastern end of the island. Alternatively the rough path up the Baramore Burn leads to the well-defined path from Bailetonach eastwards to the neck of land adjoining Shona Beag. Both islands are rich in birdlife and Eilean Shona has a fine herd of red deer.

To the south of Shona Beag is the densely wooded Riska Island and to its south the drying rocky islet holding Castle Tioram (*dry castle*), which was built by the MacDonalds of Clanranald in the 13th century. The castle and its surroundings were involved in both the Jacobite risings of 1715 and 1745, and the castle was almost destroyed on the orders of Clanranald after the failure of '45, although part remained habitable. The ruins of the castle are under the protection of the Department of the Environment.

SOAY

MAPS :   Ordnance Survey   1:50,000 Sheet 32
                                       1:25,000 Sheet 217 (NG 31/41)
              Bartholomew   1:100,000 Sheet 54
HIGHEST POINT
     Beinn Bhreac   141m   462 155

ACCESS
A boat from Arisaig calls approximately once a month; otherwise special arrangements need to be made with Arisaig Marine Ltd (telephone 0687 5678) for a landing
during one of its daily summer runs to the Small Isles. Boat hire can also be arranged
from Mallaig (Bruce Watt Cruises Ltd; telephone 0687 2283).

GENERAL DESCRIPTION
Soay, in the words of Malcolm Slesser, is a jewel. It lies off the southern tip of
Minginish in Skye, four kilometres due west of Elgol on the Strathaird peninsula.
Dwarfed by the Skye Cuillin, which tower over it only a kilometre or two across the
Sound of Soay to its north, the island appears low and almost flat from the sea as
from the land.
       Some fifteen kilometres to its south-west the Cuillin hills of Rhum form a
bold skyline, making the views from Soay's high ground - where good walking is to
be found - especially fine in almost any direction. Five kilometres in length, west to
east, the island has two deeply penetrating harbours in the north-west and south-
east, pinching it into the shape of an hourglass with a narrow waist measuring little
more than 300 metres across. The northern harbour, entered over a shallow bar
from the Sound of Soay, is the more sheltered and was used to develop a basking-
shark fishery by Gavin Maxwell who bought the island in 1946. A jetty and small
processing factory were built, but fell into disuse a few years later due to the lack of
demand for shark oil. The project was briefly revived in the 1950's by Tex Geddes,
who had been harpooner to the earlier shark fishery, but by the mid-50's all but
Geddes and his family of the remaining crofters had been evacuated to Mull.
       The island is composed of Torridonian sandstone and is not specially fertile,
but in the low saddle near its centre there grows a profusion of bushes and
deciduous trees. This saddle and the south-east harbour shelter the islanders'
cottages. Today Soay has a small but apparently stable population of about sixteen,
working two large crofts.

CROWLIN ISLANDS
Close to the Applecross shore, the Crowlin Islands comprise an interesting close-
packed group of three islands; Eilean Mor, the largest, Eilean Meadhonach and
Eilean Beag. The easternmost is Eilean Mor; two kilometres long (north to south),
a kilometre and a half wide, and little more than one kilometre from the mainland.
It is also the highest, rising to 114m at Meall a'Chois. A fine, extremely narrow
harbour is formed between Eilean Mor and Eilean Meadhonach.

SCALPAY (SKYE)

MAPS : Ordnance Survey   1:50,000 Sheet 32
                                   1:25,000 Outdoor Leisure Map (Sheet 8)
        Bartholomew   1:100,000 Sheet 54

PRINCIPAL HILLS

Mullach na Carn	389m	606 293
Beinn Loch a'Mhuilinn	291m	627 297
Beinn Reireag Bheag	225m	588 225

ACCESS

There is no public access to Scalpay; private charter can be arranged from Broadford, six kilometres to the south-east.

GENERAL DESCRIPTION

The island of Scalpay (*cave island*) is surprisingly hilly. It measures six kilometres by five and is separated from the Strathaird region of Skye by the Caolas Scalpay (pronounced *kyles*, meaning *narrows*), no more than 200 metres wide at low tide. A stretch of the island's shore along these narrows is cultivated and wooded, as well as areas at the eastern extremity, around a small tidal harbour and near to Scalpay House. For the most part, however, the island is rough heathery hillside with the going pleasantly dry - a result of its being well sheltered by Skye.

From the bouldery summit of Mullach na Carn (392m), Scalpay's highest point to which the going is rough from almost any direction, the views of the Red Hills and Bla Bheinn on Skye are especially fine. Two kilometres north-east of this hill is the gentler summit of Beinn Loch a'Mhuillinn (291m) which can be reached by path from Scalpay House; while three kilometres to its north-west lies Beinn Reireag Bheag (225m), to which a track leads along the island's south-west shore. The latter hill has steep western slopes that descend to a rocky coast peppered with caves.

Scalpay has several fine lochs and streams. The camping and fishing are good. A large area of conifers has been planted in the north-west where deer farming is being developed with the support of the Highlands and Islands Development Board. In the south-east, near to Scalpay House, are the remains of a chapel, Teampuill Fraing, built on the site of a previous Celtic cell.

LONGAY and PABAY

One and a half kilometres to the east of Scalpay lies the triangular-shaped rocky island of Longay, at the south-eastern end of a reef that runs parallel to Scalpay's north-east shore. Longay rises to a grassy top of 69m.

Three kilometres to the south-east of Longay is Pabay (*hermit's isle*) two kilometres off the Skye coast near Broadford. This island, like others of the same name throughout the Hebrides, is relatively flat and fertile. It is run as a farm and has some holiday cottages to let.

RAASAY

MAPS :   Ordnance Survey   1:50,000 Sheet 24
                                                   1:25,000 Sheets 171 (NG 44/54) and
                                                                187 (NG 43/53)
                   Bartholomew   1:100,000 Sheet 54

PRINCIPAL HILLS
         Dun Caan   443m   578 395
         Beinn na Leac   319m   592 373
         Beinn na h-Iolaire   254m   600 503

ACCESS
A vehicle and passenger ferry, operated by Caledonian MacBrayne, serves East
Suisnish on Raasay from Sconser on Skye. The ferry makes four or five crossings
daily, Mondays to Saturdays (crossing time 15 minutes).

TRANSPORT
There is a narrow road running the length of the island, but no petrol nor public
transport is available

ACCOMMODATION
Full board or bed and breakfast can be found at the Isle of Raasay Hotel (telephone
047862-222) and Churchton House (telephone 047862-226). Self- catering accommodation is available, details of which can be obtained from the Tourist Information
office, Portree; (telephone 0478-2137). Raasay has a fine youth hostel, the Allan
Evans Memorial Hostel, near Oskaig. Excellent camping can be found, the island
being well sheltered from the west by Skye. There is a good general store at
Inverarish.

GENERAL DESCRIPTION
Raasay is part of Scotland's Highland Region. The island lies in the Inner Sound, to
the east of Portree and the Trotternish peninsula of Skye, across the three kilometre
wide Sound of Raasay. This sound narrows to less than a kilometre opposite
Inverarish, near the southern tip of the island, but widens as it runs northwards so
that the northern part of Raasay, plus the whole of the island of Rona to its north,
lie closer to the Applecross region of the mainland than to Skye.
        The island measures twenty kilometres in length north to south, and
averages four to five kilometres in width; similar in size and roughly in shape to Coll,
but very much more hilly. Its crofting inhabitants once numbered several hundred.
Raasay now has a stable population of about 150, settled chiefly in the south-west
around Inverarish and Churchton Bay. The main occupation is crofting and the
language is Gaelic. An iron ore mine was opened before the First World War in the
hillside above Inverarish, and German prisoners of war were made to work there.
It stayed open only until 1919. The remains of the ore trans-shipment station are still
to be seen near the restored cottages at East Suisnish. The ferry service to East

Suisnish from Skye was established in 1976 after a long campaign by the islanders, and has helped to stem the island's decline.

Churchton Bay is named after the 13th century chapel dedicated to St Molnag. Its ruins stand on an ancient burial ground, together with two other buildings dating from the 11th century. Nearby is a Pictish stone, engraved with 7th century Ogam (cf p27), which stands near the signpost for Temptation Hill, so-named by one of the lairds who was tempted by the view there to become the island's owner. Raasay House, on the north side of Churchton Bay, has been a fine building in its day but is now dilapidated and boarded up; it is a stark illustration of the disgraceful neglect to which the island and islanders have been subjected, mostly by absentee landlords, since the 1840's. The house, backed by mature mixed woodland with fine oaks, stands on the site of the ancestral home of the MacLeods of Raasay. The previous lodge, along with almost all the cottages on the island, was burnt down in the reprisals following the 1745 uprising. The present house was visited by Johnson and Boswell in 1773 during their famous tour of the Hebrides. They were impressed by Raasay's civilised prosperity and its apparent recovery from the merciless treatment the islanders received after Culloden.

Subsequently, during the potato famines of the 1830's, MacLeod of Raasay - unlike most of the lairds of his day - exhausted his fortune in trying to help the islanders. He was eventually forced to sell his home and emigrate, leaving the way open for the neglect that followed, as well as for Raasay to become an important centre of a breakaway section of the Free Church - formed in 1893 by MacFarlane. This Kirk had an exceptionally uncompromising doctrine and, to this day, the Sabbath on Raasay is observed as strictly as anywhere in the Hebrides. Raasay has also been famous in the past for its pipers. The finest was John MacKay, who was discovered as a child and sent to study pipe music on Skye. He and his son Angus were reportedly two of the most talented pipers of all time.

THE HILLS

The southern part of Raasay is composed of Torridonian sandstone penetrated by two areas of granophyre. In some of the Torridonian shales are to be found the oldest fossilised plant remains yet discovered. The north of the island is of Archaean gneiss. In the central hills, near Glame where the narrow island road crosses the Glam Burn, large areas of loam soil occur between 200m and 300m. This feature, almost unique in the Highlands, suggests that the greater part of Raasay escaped glaciation, thus accounting also for the extensive ancient and rare flora to be found in the steep grassy slopes of the east coast, below the long rocky escarpment of Druim an Aonaich.

Dun Caan (443m) and Beinn na Leac (319m)

Dun Caan and the more rugged Beinn na Leac, separated by two kilometres of bogland, are formed probably from a dolerite sill similar to those in Trotternish on Skye. A good path starting up the Inverarish Burn, turning northwards one kilometre after emerging from the pleasant woodland, and then passing between Loch na Mna and Loch na Meilich, leads to Dun Caan. The summit is flat, its truncated appearance forming a landmark from many points in the Cuillin hills of Skye. The views from Dun Caan, of the Skye Cuillin to south-west and south, and the Applecross hills to the east, are enchanting; made the more so by the immediate environment. Boswell is reported to have danced a reel of pleasure on its flat summit.

From Dun Caan's summit (triangulation pillar) another, rather wetter, path descends to Loch Eadar da Bhaile on the island road. A longer excursion can be made northwards for seven kilometres along the Druim an Aonaich, to the wooded coastal settlement of South Screapadal where a path leads through the Raasay Forest to Brochel and the remains of Brochel Castle. Alternatively, from the summit of Dun Caan, bouldery slopes can be descended south-eastwards passing south of the attractive and secluded Loch a'Chadha-charnaich, to the small area of woodland at Hallaig lying below the rugged but easily ascended north-east shoulder of Beinn na Leac. The summit of this hill is disappointingly boggy and it is best to descend either westwards to the path leading to Glen Lodge and Inverarish, or eastwards to the much drier path through North Fearns. The latter is recommended also for an approach from the south to Beinn na Leac along the delightfully wooded path through South Fearns from East Suisnish.

Beinn na h-Iolaire (254m)
The bare grey gneiss of this hill in the north of Raasay, and the superb views northwards of Caol Rona and the island of Rona, make its ascent a worthwhile excursion. A path leads close to the hill from Torran and Arnish, starting where the road ends at Brochel. The ascent to Beinn na h-Iolaire's triangulation pillar is easy and provides a fine objective along with the walk to the northern tip of Raasay. The shielings there today are the remains of a once thriving fishing community.

ROCK CLIMBING
On Dun Caan's summit crags there are recorded rock climbs ranging from *Flying Flakes* (22m; Mild Very Severe) to *Fear of Flying* (23m; E1, 5b) which are reached by roping down from the summit triangulation pillar. Fear of Flying takes an arête to left (north) of the main buttress and then a finger crack to the top. Flying Flakes takes a cleaved crack to the right of the former. A buttress further to the right gives *Wardern's Slab* (22m; Hard Severe 4a) which follows a slabby ramp and corner past an obvious overhang. There are more short routes here to be explored.

RONA

The island of Rona in Skye's Inner Sound is sometimes called South Rona to distinguish it from the outlying island of Rona, north-east of Lewis. It lies nearly mid-way between the northern tip of Applecross and the Trotternish peninsula of Skye.

MAPS *:*   Ordnance Survey   1:50,000 Sheet 24

                                      1:25,000 Sheet 155 (NG 65/75)

           Bartholomew   1:100,000 Sheet 54

PRINCIPAL HILL

        Meall Acairseid   125m   623 576

ACCESS

There is no regular access to Rona. Local charter is available from Portree by private arrangement. The island's main harbour, Acairseid Mhor in the south-west, is frequented by yachts from Portree.

GENERAL DESCRIPTION

The island of Rona is composed of glaciated Archaean gneiss. It measures eight kilometres in length from south to north, and averages just less than two kilometres in width. The island forms an extension northwards of Raasay, from which it is separated by Caol Rona whose one kilometre width is broken by two rocky islets composed of almost bare gneiss.

      Rona is uninhabited but for Royal Navy personnel and the lighthouse keepers, who man the Nato signal station and lighthouse at the northern tip of the island. At one time there were three fishing settlements, two schools and a church. Services were also held in Church Cave, a huge cavern on the east coast, in which the pews and a fine altar can be seen today - carved from natural rock.

      The largest settlement was around the fine sheltered south-western harbour Acairseid Mhor (*big harbour*). In the 16th century this deep inlet was known as Port nan Robaireann (*the port of robbers*) and the island - then thickly wooded - was the retreat of pirates who raided merchant ships in the Minch and the Inner Sound. Rona is now the home of seals and seabirds. A century ago cattle from Raasay were kept on the island, but now only sheep are grazed there, tended from Skye.

      From the 17th century until the Clearances, Rona belonged to the MacLeods of Raasay. The crofters evicted from Raasay - when the MacLeod chief was forced by economic ruin to emigrate - settled around Acairseid Mhor and Acairseid Thioram (*dry harbour*). At the end of the First World War the island, like Raasay, was in a further state of decline and a group of its islanders (the Rona Raiders) seized areas of fertile land and cottages on Raasay after crossing Caol Rona with their sheep and cattle by rowing boat.

Meall Acairseid (125m)

Rona's highest point, which carries a triangulation pillar, is formed partly from a feldspar dyke, of which there are two or three to be found in the centre of the island. Pink feldspar cliffs are also in evidence below the lush woodland on the north side of Acairseid Mhor. A good path leads from a derelict cottage there to Meall Acairseid, and beyond (not marked on the Ordnance Survey map) between Sgath a'Bhannaich (110m) and the long eastern rib of gneiss - passing Loch Braig - to the lighthouse at the northern end of the island.

The path from Meall Acairseid also runs southwards to the remains of Rona's southern settlement, Doire na Guaile. This path also leads, at the southern tip of the island to the ruins of an old monastery, An Teampull.

EILEAN TRODDAY and FLADDA-CHUAIN ISLES

MAPS :   Ordnance Survey   1:50,000 Sheet 23
                                         1:25,000 Sheet 127 (NG 37/47)

The island of Trodday (*troll's isle*) lies two kilometres off the northern tip of Skye. Roughly circular, nearly a kilometre in diameter, it is distinctive - as is Trotternish - for its basaltic columnar cliffs. The island's cap is of fertile grassland, rising gently to a height of 45m and offering good camping for the climber or canoeist who may wish to land and to explore the 20m to 30m climbs on its sea-cliffs (no routes so far recorded). Trodday once supported a herd of dairy cattle. It has an important navigation light; the flow of the tides between it and Skye can be deceptively fast.

The picturesque Fladda-chuain Isles comprise a distinctively shaped small archipelago of stacks and islands set in an arc to the north-west of Trodday, some five kilometres from this island and from Rubha Hunish at the north-west tip of Trotternish. Composed chiefly of basalt, the islands have plenty of scope - in calm weather - for short routes (30-40m) on sound rock. The prospects for camping on their flat meadowy tops are good, though in dry weather a shortage of drinking water could easily occur. On the largest of the group, Fladda-chuain, which measures over a kilometre in length, are the remains of St Columba's Chapel. The smallest, Gearran Island, which has a splendid natural arch, is also known as Lord MacDonald's Table (he is said to have hidden title-deeds there before setting out to take part in the 1745 uprising). Between these two islands is the highest of the group, Gaelivore Island, its two halves joined by a narrow rocky neck, with the western half rising to 56m.

ASCRIB ISLANDS

MAPS :   Ordnance Survey   1:50,000 Sheet 23
                                         1:25,000 Sheet 137 (NG 26/36)

In the mouth of Loch Snizort in north-west Skye, where the loch opens wide into the Little Minch, lies a scattered group of islands and stacks named the Ascrib Islands. The origin of their name is unknown. Spread over an area of sea measuring some five kilometres by four, they are uninhabited but for a large colony of puffins which burrow into weathered ledges on the basalt sea-cliffs. The stone for the ancient Casteal Uisdein, near Stein on Skye, is said to have been quarried there.

The Shiant Islands: Garbh Eilean from Eilean Mhuire

SHIANT ISLANDS

MAPS :   Ordnance Survey   1:50,000 Sheet 14
                                      1:25,000 Sheet 108 (NG 19/29)

PRINCIPAL HILL
Mullach Buidhe   160m   415 987

The Shiants are a small group of enchanting islands (their name derives from the Gaelic of this meaning, *Na h-eileanan seunta*) lying in the Minch six kilometres from the east coast of Lewis, and 20 kilometres due north of Trotternish in Skye.

ACCESS

A visit to the Shiants requires calm weather. Private charters for a landing can be arranged from Tarbert in Harris, and from Lochmaddy in North Uist. The two largest of the islands, Eilean an Tighe and Garbh Eilean, are joined by a tiny neck of land - a natural causeway - and the bays to either side provide temporary harbours in fine weather. Landing elsewhere by boat is made hazardous by many sunken rocks, especially on the western shores. The islands are set in the Minch and there are nearly always large seas running. These can be at their worst in the Sound of Shiant, between the Shiant Islands and the Park coast of Lewis.

GENERAL DESCRIPTION

The Shiants have captured the imagination of many writers and were indeed at one time owned by the author Sir Compton MacKenzie who renovated a cottage on Eilean an Tighe (*island of the house*) to spend summers writing there. The group was last inhabited permanently by about 10 people in 1901. Sheep now graze there, tended from Scalpay (North Harris), and several families of brown rats live in the scree and at the foot of the cliffs.

The highest hill in the group is Mullach Buidhe on Garbh Eilean (*rough island*). The views from there are spectacular, as they are also from the grassy high ground of Eilean an Tighe to its south. The north and east shores of the group are impressively sculpted from columnar basalt rising 120m from the sea. The rock, however, is not good for climbing.

Eilean Mhuire (*Mary's island*), lying to the east of Garbh Eilean across a one kilometre wide strait, has particularly fine natural arches on its south-west shore, where a boat landing is especially hazardous in the swell. Its summit plateau is huge, with vast areas of old lazy-beds, and the remains of St Mary's Chapel. A smaller natural arch is also to be found at the northern tip of Garbh Eilean; the slabs above it are said to be climbable. Like so many of the more isolated Hebridean islands, the Shiants have an astounding bird population; fulmars, puffins, kittiwakes, guillemots, shags, barnacle geese in winter and many others that breed there in thousands.

TARANSAY (SOUTH HARRIS)

MAPS :   Ordnance Survey   1:50,000 Sheet 18
                                           1:25,000 Sheets 98 (NA 90/NB 00) and
                                                     107 (NF 99/NG 09)

PRINCIPAL HILL
      Ben Raah   267m   034 019

ACCESS

There is no public access to Taransay. Private arrangements can be made from Borve or Seilebost on the A859 road between Luskentyre and Leverburgh.

GENERAL DESCRIPTION

Lying across the two kilometre wide Sound of Taransay from Luskentyre in South Harris, the island of Taransay appears as two shapely hills joined by a narrow sandy isthmus of dunes. There is no accommodation to be found there despite its past population, which numbered 75 or more. Cattle and sheep are now grazed on the island, which measures nearly five kilometres north to south and some six kilometres west to east.

Ben Raah on the larger, eastern section of Taransay is an almost conical hill of grey gneiss with grassy gullies. The climb to its triangulation pillar is rough and heathery. From the west the route is attractively interspersed with lochans, where the fishing and camping are good. The views of mainland Harris from Ben Raah are magnificent. There are two interesting duns, but little is known of their history.

SCALPAY (NORTH HARRIS)

MAPS *:*   Ordnance Survey   1:50,000 Sheet 14
                                     1:25,000 Sheet 108 (NG 19/29)

PRINCIPAL HILL
Ben Scoravick   104m   237 957

ACCESS
A regular car-ferry service operates across the Sound of Scalpay to mainland Harris.

GENERAL DESCRIPTION
The island of Scalpay, lying sixteen kilometres south by west from the Shiant Isles, in the mouth of East Loch Tarbert in Harris, has - for its size - an unexpected prosperity. With a narrow sound (the Sound of Scalpay) to its north and a deep passage (Braigh Mor) to its south-west, it virtually blocks the entrance to the loch and provides Tarbert harbour with crucial shelter from the Minch. Scalpay, however, has its own harbour - to its landward side - even more sheltered than Tarbert. This accounts for the island's prosperous fishing industry, which supports a population of 500.

  The only hill of note is **Ben Scoravick** (104m) in the east of the island, where there is also an important lighthouse. There are innumerable inland lochs and lochans dispersed over its eight square kilometres of land area. An interesting walk, perhaps when the Harris hills are shrouded, is to thread north-eastwards between the lochans from Kennavay - at the end of the only road - over Ben Scoravick and descend to the east coast. A coastal walk from there southwards to visit to the lighthouse is worthwhile (it has also a restaurant), with a return walk by a path (unmarked on the map) along the south coast of the island. Scalpay, it is said, was an important refuge of Prince Charles Edward Stewart during his wanderings after Culloden.

OFFSHORE ISLANDS IN THE NORTH-WEST

Several small islands and stacks of interest to climbers lie close to Scotland's north-west coast, in the sea-lochs of Wester Ross and Sutherland. For the hillwalker, probably the only ones of importance are the Summer Isles; for the rock climber, on the other hand, the stacks on the north side of Handa and close to Cape Wrath (eg Am Buachaille - see *North-Western Highlands* SMC district guide) are of more interest.

THE SUMMER ISLES

MAPS :   Ordnance Survey   1:50,000 Sheet 15
                                          1:25,000 Sheets 101 (NB 90)
                                                                   102 (NC 00/10) - for
                                                                   Horse Island

PRINCIPAL HILL
         Meall Mor   122m   989 071

ACCESS

The largest island in the group and most accessible is Tanera Mor in the north-east, near to the north shore of Loch Broom. Access to Tanera Mor is by boat from a pier two kilometres north-west of Achiltibuie or by charter from Ullapool. Private charter, or a friendly fisherman, is needed to reach any of the remaining islands or islets in the group.

GENERAL DESCRIPTION

The Summer Isles comprise a group of small islands and skerries that extend ten kilometres north to south, and for more than six kilometres west to east, spreading right across the entrance to Loch Broom. The name derives from their use by the mainlanders for summer grazing. All but Tanera Mor are now uninhabited and birdlife everywhere on the islands is rich.

TANERA MOR

Some four square kilometres in area and lying one kilometre or so from the Achiltibuie shore, Tanera Mor rises to the heathery summit of Meall Mor in the south. A century ago herring-curing stations on the island supported over a hundred inhabitants. They lived mainly in the settlements of Ardnagoine and Garadheancal, to the north and south respectively of a large bay in the east named The Anchorage - one of the best natural harbours to be found in north-west Scotland. By the 1930's the population had declined to zero. Sir Frank Fraser Darling farmed the island during most of the Second World War, and wrote about this in his book *Island Farm*. However, following that period, the islands remained uninhabited until the 1960's when the Summer Isles Estate restored the schoolhouse and several cottages as holiday accommodation.

         There is now a permanent population of around nine on Tanera Mor, with the Summer Isles official Post Office at Ardnagoine still issuing its own stamps, accepted by H M Post Office, for conveying mail to mainland destinations.

The islands are formed of Torridonian sandstone mostly covered with peat, pasture and heather. On Tanera Mor and its neighbour, Tanera Beg, merganser ducks breed along the sandy shores; while on the shores of Tanera Beg, and those of Eilean Fada Mor, lying between Tanera Mor and Tanera Beg, unusual displays of pink coral can be observed at low tide. Near to An Lochanach on Tanera Mor, flag irises, honeysuckle and willow can be found as well as aspen poplars, which grow to three or four metres in height.

PRIEST ISLAND

The second largest and most isolated of the Summer Isles, Priest Island (Eilean a'Chleirich), is at the south-west extremity of the group; lying seven kilometres from Tanera Mor, in line with the entrance to Little Loch Broom.

The red sandstone of the Summer Isles is prominent on Priest Island. The shores are rugged, with steep cliffs in the north-west and south-west. The island is formed of two large masses of sloping sandstone, covered with heather in the south and pasture in the north, separated by a shallow glen which holds two fine lochans - said to be frequented by otters. To north of the glen the growth is rich: crowberry, buckthorn, bell heather and ling, bog asphodel and bog cotton are abundant. According to Fraser Darling, pigmy shrews can also be found on Priest Island, near caves in the south. From there the climb to the island's highest point (76m), which is formed from a ridge of sandstone, is steep. The northern slopes of this sandstone ridge are even steeper, with rugged cliffs in places consisting of fluted columns that make a fine display in the summer evening light.

There are fully eight lochans on Priest Island, all reputed to have excellent fishing. During the 19th century, when Tanera Mor was a centre for illicit distilling, the southern caves of Priest Island were used for storing smuggled whisky.

HANDA

MAPS *:*   Ordnance Survey   1:50,000 Sheet 9
                                     1:25,000 Sheet 61 (NC 14)

HIGHEST POINT
        Sithean Mor   121m   131 484

ACCESS

A local fisherman operates a frequent ferry service to the island from Tarbet, or a boat can be hired from Scourie.

GENERAL DESCRIPTION

Lying off the Sutherland coast, just north of Scourie Bay and some five kilometres south of the entrance to Loch Laxford, Handa rises to 123m at Sithean Mor close to its western sea-cliffs. The island is of Torridonian sandstone, mostly cliff-bound. It forms a Torridonian outcrop separated by half a kilometre of sea, the Sound of Handa, from the mainland foreshore of Lewisian gneiss. The island is a bird sanctuary and permission to visit it must be obtained from the Royal Society for the

Protection of Birds.

Handa is three kilometres in diameter, and mostly covered with heather, peat-bog and rough pasture. The island was inhabited once by as many as seven families, said to have had a 'queen'. As on St Kilda, the menfolk held daily parliament to decide the day's work. The potato famine caused their emigration to America in 1848 and Handa became a burial place for the mainlanders.

The red sandstone cliffs, forming Handa's north and west coast, rise fully 120m from the sea. An impressive 115m stack, the Great Stac of Handa, lies in an inlet off the northern sea-cliffs, supported on three pillars of sandstone. Its flat summit is separated by a 15-metre gap from the island's cliff-top. The Great Stac was the scene of a remarkable 19th century exploit, recorded in *Fauna of the North-West Highlands* (1904) by Harvie Brown, when the inhabitants of Handa made a roped traverse to the stack's summit.

A dramatic re-enactment of the traverse, using 20th century equipment and Tyrolean techniques, was made in 1967 by T W Patey and party, who recorded: "....We stretched 600 ft of linked nylon ropes from side to side of the inlet so that the centre of our rope lay across the top of the Stac. To use the best anchorage points we had to cross the gap obliquely, so lengthening the Tyrolean traverse to 120 ft. Without the aid of jumars it would have been difficult to overcome the considerable sag in the rope. Additional excitement was provided by numerous seabirds cannoning into the taut nylon and by two guillemots on the Stac who started pecking the rope which had invaded their territory. The appalling 350 ft chasm [be]neath made this a most impressive occasion". Their experience makes the exploit of over a century ago even more thought-provoking than the renowned feats of the St Kildans.

The Great Stac was ascended in 1963 by G Hunter, D Lang and H MacInnes. The route (115m; Very Severe), which they named *Great Arch*, is on the north face or seaward side of the stack, starting at a steep green wall. The climber must step almost directly from his or her boat, needed to reach that side of the Great Stac, onto the wall where a piton has been placed in a corner. The route, on excellent rock, takes the wall to the right of the corner, and gains another ledge and a steep groove which is traversed leftwards above the overhangs of the Great Arch. From there it surmounts a wall and another overhang above a hidden corner, leading to an easier 45m or so of broken rock to the summit. The climb is reported to be surprisingly bird-free.

Another stack, or more correctly a huge flake which has been cleaved from the north cliffs of Handa, Stachan Geodh Bhrisidh, lies some 300 metres east of the Great Stac and can be reached by descending steep grass from the cliff-top. It was climbed in 1969 by G Hunter and D Lang, taking a route (60m; Very Severe) on the landward side from a stance in a corner, marked with an arrow.

The Great Stac of Handa

OFFSHORE ISLANDS IN THE EAST

Surprisingly few islands are to be found off Scotland's east coast. The only two of prominence are the Bass Rock and the Isle of May, close inshore in the Firth of Forth.

ISLE OF MAY

MAPS :   Ordnance Survey   1:50,000 Sheet 59
                                        1:25,000 Sheet 364 (NO 60/61)

ACCESS

Ferry hire is available from Anstruther. A post boat also sails from Crail, and can be used provided an overnight stay is intended.

GENERAL DESCRIPTION

The Isle of May is a surprisingly green island. It lies nine kilometres off the Fife coast, well out in the mouth of the Firth of Forth. The island is narrow, with a total length, including the small islet of Rona at its northern end, of just under two kilometres. Most of its coast is fringed by sea-cliffs rising to a height of 45m in the south-west, with many caves. The South Ness caves are associated with 17th century smuggling. There is scope for rock-climbing; the rock being relatively sound and clean with some fine small sea-stacks.

The island is now owned by the Nature Conservancy Council and managed as a National Nature Reserve. A small hostel is available to scientists monitoring the large colonies of resident and migratory seabirds. Guillemots, puffins, cormorants, fulmars, terns and eiders are common, but no gannets. The island became a celebrated pilgrimage after St Adrian was murdered there in the 9th century by the Danes. The remains of a chapel can be found in the south. A track runs along the spine of the island. A lighthouse, built in 1814, stands near the highest point (grid reference 654 993). To its south, a steep-walled gorge cuts into the west coast and has been dammed to form the island's water supply.

INCHKEITH

MAP :   Ordnance Survey   1:25,000 Sheet 395 (NT 28)
Midway across the Firth of Forth at the point where it narrows to about eight kilometres between Edinburgh and Kinghorn, lies the island of Inchkeith. Roughly triangular in shape, a kilometre in length and half a kilometre wide, the island is generally rocky and rises to 54m at its northern end. Geologically it consists of sheet of igneous rock in a stair-like formation, with thin bands of shale, coal and limestone. A late Pictish ruler made the island his home in the 9th century. With its attendant stacks, Seal Carr, Iron Craig and Long Craig, Inchkeith is a huge bird sanctuary owned by the Royal Society for the Protection of Birds.

THE BASS ROCK

MAPS : Ordnance Survey   1:10,560 NT 58 NE and part NT 68 NW (one sheet)
                                     1:25,000 Sheet 396 (NT 48/58/68)

ACCESS

Although in summer months regular boat trips from North Berwick will circle the Bass Rock for passengers to view the enormous bird population, there is no ferry service and access is by arrangement. Permission to land, normally given readily with the reasonable restriction of employing a given boatman (F Marr, North Berwick - telephone 0620-2833), should be obtained from Sir Hugh Dalrymple of North Berwick (telephone 0620-2903) although informal permission can also be given by the boatman.

GENERAL DESCRIPTION

The Bass Rock lies at the southern entrance to the Firth of Forth, two kilometres due north of Tantallon Castle near North Berwick. The island rises from the sea to a height of 108m (grid reference 602 874) and is over half a kilometre in diameter, making it a prominent landmark from the sea and from the coast.

      The island is formed from the remains of a volcanic plug and is composed almost entirely of an igneous rock called phenolite. The shores everywhere are cliff-bound and peppered with deep caves, of which one forms a remarkable tunnel right through the island from west to east. Its entrances, in West Cove and East Cove, are exposed fully only at low water but it has a ceiling height of at least six metres for its entire length of 150 metres. At low water springs it is possible, if a landing is made by boat or canoe, to walk right through the tunnel, which has a deep sea pool at its centre.

      The landing place is in the south-east, below the lighthouse built on the remains of a fortress which incorporated the earlier and ancient cell of St Baldred. Sea-cliffs virtually ring the Bass Rock, attaining a maximum height of around 90m in the east where they plunge vertically into the sea. The friable rock makes the island less attractive to climbers, but the cliffs are a sanctuary for seabirds. From the lighthouse there is a concreted path running north-eastwards to the top of steps that descend to a disused foghorn. Other paths along the cliff-tops are now impossible to use because of the enormous and protected gannet population. The light has recently been automated and apart from the seabirds the island is uninhabited.

      From the steps leading down to the foghorn, a shallow gully gives access to a large terrace cutting across the cliffs at half height. The gannets make even this terrace impossible to explore and the rock is, anyway, uncomfortably loose in places.

      Over 20,000 gannet nesting sites cover the cliffs from west through north to east, as well as large areas of the shallow slopes above. The cliff-tops are an unusual habitat for gannets, the result of there being too little space on the cliffs themselves for the increased population. Gannets were once regarded as a delicacy and Queen Victoria is said to have received an annual dish of young gannets from the Bass

The Bass Rock

Rock. Kittiwakes are also prominent on the western cliffs. The huge number of birds cause a snowstorm effect when disturbed. Puffins were once reported to tunnel burrows into the island's cap of turf, but have long since been displaced by the gannets. A colony of shags now nests among the rock stacks in the south-west corner of the island. Vast amounts of guano fertilise the Bass Rock which supports many species of flowering plant, including the rare Bass mallow (or tree mallow) also found on Ailsa Craig.

CRAIGLEITH

Four kilometres to the west of the Bass Rock is the round island of Craigleith, rising 50m from the sea with vertical cliffs on its southern side. Little is known of the island's history; it is rocky and barren, but a paradise for gulls, seals, shags, cormorants and now puffins. The rock of this island is also phenolite, but at an easier angle than the Bass Rock. Together with Lamb and Fidra, two small steep-sided islets with ecclesiastical histories lying further west along the East Lothian coast, Craigleith is owned by the Royal Society for the Protection of Birds, from whom permission to land must be obtained.

CHAPTER 20

OUTLYING ISLANDS

Scotland has many important outlying islands, chiefly in the west and the north well out to sea, some Hebridean and some northern in character. Those with important mountain peaks are wholly in the west, largely the result of extensive glacial activity. In sharp contrast to the west, no major islands lie out to sea off the east coast, though a few lie close inshore in the Firth of Forth, and are described under Offshore Islands in the foregoing chapter.

In the north, the isolated Sule Skerry and Sule Stack are administratively part of Orkney, although lying nearly 65 kilometres west of its main archipelago. Further west, but still in the north, the outlying islands of Rona (sometimes North Rona to distinguish it from the Rona in the Inner Sound of Skye) and Sula Sgeir are regarded as Hebridean outliers. They lie some 60 kilometres north-east of Lewis and, like the Flannan Isles and the historic St Kilda group (lying 70 kilometres, respectively north-west and due west of the Sound of Harris), may be included geographically with the Long Isle as Hebridean.

The outliers in the north are taken first, then those lying outside the Long Isle to its west, including the Monach Isles, and finally the major outlying group of St Kilda.

RONA and SULA SGEIR

MAPS :   Ordnance Survey   1:50,000 Sheet 8
1:25,000 Sheet 39 (NC 27/37; inset planned)

ACCESS
These islands have no regular ferry access. However, sheep are grazed on Rona and are gathered annually during July or August by the crofters from Lewis. Usually a visit then is not difficult to negotiate if discreet enquiry is made at the right time on Lewis. Otherwise private boat charter needs be arranged. Permission to visit Rona or Sula Sgeir, must be obtained from the Barvas Estates Ltd, North Lewis, and from the Nature Conservancy Council (Regional office in Inverness; telephone 0463 239431).

RONA
North Rona, as the island of Rona is sometimes called to distinguish it from the other Rona east of the Trotternish peninsula of Skye, lies 70 kilometres north-north-east

Toa Rona, the summit of Rona

of the Butt of Lewis. Its name is from the Gaelic *ron-y*, meaning *island of seals*. All of its shores are bounded by steep cliffs, which make landing on the island difficult.

Rona is now a National Nature Reserve, some two square kilometres in area. Shaped like a giant bird's foot, it has two massive promontories to the east and south-west, and a long lower one to the north. The eastern promontory is the highest and finest, rising to 180m - Toa Rona. All of the land is grassy and fertile but there are now no permanent inhabitants; the last known ones left in 1844.

On the gentle pasture slopes between the east and south-west promontories lie the remains of a small village that housed several families, probably originally Norse settlers from the 8th century. The ruins of St Ronan's Cell (or Church), a drystone construction now partly overgrown, are also to be found there.

Sula Sgeir

Some 20 kilometres west of Rona, and 65 kilometres due north of the Butt of Lewis, lies the tiny isolated island of Sula Sgeir. Its narrow goose-neck shape gives the island its name; from the Gaelic *solan*, meaning *goose*. The island is little more than half a kilometre long and 200 metres wide, with an interesting sea-cave running right through it from west to east. The rock is hornblende gneiss. There are bothies in the grassy centre, used by the men of Ness who are authorised legally by The Nature Conservancy Council - which owns Sula Sgeir - to harvest the young gannets (*gugas*) from the island. This arrangement ensures the stability of the gannet population.

FLANNAN ISLES

MAPS :   Ordnance Survey   1:50,000 Sheet 13
1:25,000 Sheet 59 (NB 14/24)

The Flannan Isles lie 31 kilometres north-west of Gallan Head in Lewis. They comprise a scattered group of seven or more entirely cliff-bound (hornblende gneiss) islands, also known as The Seven Hunters. Their total land area - almost all grassy - is less than a square kilometre. Brona Cleit is the westernmost and tiny Gealtaire Mor the easternmost; some six kilometres apart. From north to south the group covers two kilometres.

All of the shores are treacherous and a landing is possible only in moderate weather; the best landing being on the south-western shore of the largest, Eilean Mor, on which there is a lighthouse - standing 99m above high water. It was built before the turn of the century and was the scene of a Marie Celeste type mystery in December 1900, when - in foul weather - its three lighthouse keepers went missing without trace, leaving oilskins still hanging and a meal half-eaten. The log-book talked of damage to the island's west landing pier, but a cliff suicide attempt by one of the keepers was also propagated as an explanation, the other two dying in trying to save him. Theory was soon difficult to disentangle from fact; especially with the publication in the early 1900's of Winifred Gibson's poem *Flannan Isle*. The light is now automatic, so the islands have no permanent inhabitants.

The remains of the 8th century Chapel of St Flannan are also to be found on Eilean Mor. During the 16th century the McLeods of Lewis used to visit the islands to hunt wild sheep and collect seabirds' eggs. A few sheep only are grazed there today by the crofters from Lewis.

HASKEIR

MAPS :   Ordnance Survey   1:50,000 Sheet 18
1:25,000 Sheet 88 (NA 91/NB 00)

ACCESS

A landing anywhere by boat is difficult. There is no regular access but private charter from Griminish in North Uist can usually be arranged with local fishermen.

GENERAL DESCRIPTION

Some 12 kilometres west-north-west of Griminish Point, the north-west headland of North Uist, is a small group of sea stacks and arches. These comprise Haskeir Island and Haskeir Eagach. They are the haunts of grey seals and puffins. The book *Island of Disaster* by Lewis Spence was based on Haskeir Eagach. This is the most south-westerly of the group, and it alone consists of five distinct islets (or stacks) with narrow deep-water channels between them.

Haskeir Mhor reaches a rocky summit in its north - where there is also a splendid rocky bay - and the lowest land on the island is at its centre. Sea pinks and campion, unusually large, give the scene a mass of colour when they are in blossom. A sea-cliff in the north is known as The Castle; nearby there is a natural arch over which one can walk without difficulty.

THE MONACH ISLES

MAPS :   Ordnance Survey   1:50,000 Sheet 22
                                             1:25,000 Sheet 135 (NF 66/76)

ACCESS

Private charter can be arranged with local fishermen from Baleshare on North Uist.
The islands are uninhabited and there is no public access.

GENERAL DESCRIPTION

The Monachs are also known as Heisker. They form a small group of islands lying
12 kilometres west of Baleshare on the west coast of North Uist, from which the
group is separated by the Sound of Monach. The channel between the two main
islands Ceann Iar and Ceann Ear dries at low tide. The length of the one island thus
formed is five kilometres west to east.

The small island of Shillay to the north-west, separated from Ceann Iar by the
Sound of Shillay, is only a few hundred metres across at its widest, while Stockay,
to the north-east of Ceann Ear, is even smaller. A lighthouse on Shillay, which can
be seen on a clear day from North Uist and Benbecula, is now abandoned. All four
islands are chiefly of machair protected by a congestion of sand-swamped reefs
around all of their shores. A small once-inhabited village on Ceann Ear, deserted
only in the 1940's, is now in a state of disrepair but its old schoolhouse is still
weatherfast. It is used from time to time by visiting lobster fishermen. The homes
of this village were unusual in having grain-drying kilns built within them.

The group of islands is now a Nature Reserve. Permission to visit must be
obtained from the North Uist Estate, Lochmaddy, or from the warden at Loch
Druidibeg. White-fronted and barnacle geese winter in the islands, while terns (the
arctic, common and little varieties) as well as fulmars and herons, nest in the
remains of drystone walls and on the vertical faces of sand dunes - an unusual habit
caused by the absence of sea-cliffs. The tiny island of Stockay is a grey seal nursery.

SULE SKERRY and SULE STACK

MAPS :   Ordnance Survey 1:50,000 Sheet 6

Sule Stack and Sule Skerry, lying 40 kilometres and 45 kilometres north-east of Cape
Wrath, are true outliers with no public access, colonised by puffins and storm
petrels. The island of Sule Skerry is the larger, measuring half a kilometre north to
south and some 400 metres west to east. It is the site of an important lighthouse. The
smaller, Sule Stack (or Stack Skerry), is a granite outcrop rising 37m above the sea
and the home of a large colony of gannets.

THE ISLANDS OF ST KILDA

It is fitting, from the perspective of the climber, to finish this guide to the Islands of Scotland with the furthest outlying group, St Kilda. The islands and stacks of this historic group are not only spectacular in every sense, including mountainous and maritime remoteness, but have the distinction of being the scene of a native tradition of climbing.

Rock climbing was practised by the native St Kildans primarily for the purpose of fowling, on which the people relied almost entirely for their livelihood. However, it was also - as a natural consequence - a pastime of pride and manhood. The art of climbing among the men of Hirta, and their courage and skill as cliff-fowlers, were matters of personal emulation and of testing a man's fitness to support a family.

MAPS :   Ordnance Survey   1:50,000 Sheet 17
                                        1:25,000 Sheet 1373 (NA 00/10 and NF 09/19)

PRINCIPAL HILLS AND STACKS

HIRTA

Conachair	430m	010 003
Mullach Mor	361m	093 002
Mullach Bi	360m	080 994
Oiseval	293m	109 993

DUN

Bioda Mor	175m	105 974

SOAY

Cnoc Glas	378m	063 016

SOAY STAC	60m	074 013
STAC BIORACH	72m	072 013
STAC LEVENISH	56m	133 966

BORERAY

Mullach an Eilein	384m	155 054
STAC AN ARMIN	196m	152 064
STAC LEE	172m	142 049

ACCESS

There is no regular access to the St Kilda group of islands, which lie 70 kilometres out to sea due west of Pabbay at the western extremity of the Sound of Harris. They are owned by the National Trust for Scotland and managed by the Nature Conservancy Council as a Nature Reserve. The National Trust runs frequent cruises and organizes working parties for repair and restoration of the historic cottages and other buildings on the island of Hirta. The entire group has been designated as both an Ancient Monument and a National Scenic Area by the Secretary of State for

St Kilda. Stac an Armin and Boreray

Scotland. The islands are also recognised as a Reserve by UNESCO, and listed as a World Heritage Site by the International Union for the Conservation of Nature.

The group comprises three main islands, Hirta (or St Kilda) the largest, Soay close by to the north-west, and Boreray lying seven kilometres to the north-east. Off Boreray are two huge stacks, Stac an Armin and Stac Lee; while close to Hirta, and almost connected to it, is the island of Dun plus Stac Levenish two and a half kilometres to its east-south-east.

A reliable landing by boat can only be made in Village Bay on the south-east of Hirta, and then only in settled weather. The island of Dun protects the bay from the south-west but in easterly or south-easterly winds the heavy seas make Village Bay impossible to approach.

A small bay on the north-west shore of Hirta, Glen Bay, affords some shelter from southerlies and a safe landing can also be made there in calm weather. In strong winds the squalls of wind everywhere, and particularly in Glen Bay, can be extremely violent and unpredictable. The unrelenting Atlantic swell can also set into Village Bay during and after storm winds from any direction, making an anchorage there untenable for days. The St Kildans had always to beach their boats out of reach of the stormy seas in Village Bay. It is quite possible to be marooned on St Kilda for weeks.

HISTORY

More has been written about St Kilda, including over a hundred books, than about any other comparable island or land mass in the world. The islands and their inhabitants caught the attention of visiting journalists and then public imagination more than a century ago. The Victorians visited the island in droves to witness this spectacular example of primitive living. Until that time the St Kildan community had lived in virtual isolation for probably more than a thousand years. Indeed the precise origin of Hirta's inhabitants is not known.

The community developed its own finely adapted economy, making full use of the huge gannetries on Stac Lee and Stac an Armin and other colonies of seabirds which nest on all of St Kilda's awesome cliff-faces. A good account of their remarkable way of life, which included a St Kildan parliament of menfolk that met each morning to discuss the day's work, can be found

The Lover's Stone

in Thomas Steel's book, *The Life and Death of St Kilda,* Fontana Books (published by Collins), 1975. Although the menfolk were masters of the cliff-face, the St Kildans had a matriarchal society as in all of Celtic Britain; the womenfolk were the masters of the economy. Feathers of the seabirds were sold to the mainland to help pay the rent to the landlords of Harris. Fulmars supplied oil for lighting and preserving.

The Victorian visitors brought disease and unrest to the people. Hirta's population numbered 180 in a census of 1697. It had declined to 73 by 1921 and, totalled only 36 when the people of St Kilda were evacuated at their own request to the mainland and to Skye (with Government assistance) in 1930, by which time the art of climbing too had declined considerably. It is clear, though, from the innumerable reports - indeed also from early photographs taken by the many sightseeing visitors - that cliff-climbing and fowling was a community affair, undertaken by the menfolk working as a team.

The jagged outline of Dun across Village Bay

Ropes were used, made of plaited horsehair; and the climbing was done bare-foot or in coarse socks. The party would move together on the easier crags, but one man at a time on the steeper cliffs. The techniques that evolved were interestingly similar to those developed, just as naturally, in early Alpine climbing. On St Kilda, the most able man led, and would then also be held on the rope from above while reaching for eggs or snaring fowl. Gannets and puffins formed an important part of the St Kildan's diet.

The art of climbing was almost exclusively utilitarian and, not surprisingly, the ability to climb became a mark of manhood. Norman Heathcote, in an article on *Climbing in St Kilda* (SMCJ Vol.6, p146) and in his book (*St Kilda, 1900*), tells of the *Lover's Stone*, in the south-west corner of Hirta overlooking the island of Soay, on the south-west flank of Mulach Bi and some 300m north-west of Cleigeann Mor.

The crag, it is said, had to be climbed by any aspirant to marriage with a St Kildan girl. On reaching the summit stone, the young man was supposed to balance on one foot (some say on the heel only, with the sole of the foot unsupported) and to grasp the other foot firmly with both hands for a finite time; this by way of courtship display plus proof of sufficient courage and ability to harvest the birds and eggs from the many such crags and cliffs of St Kilda. Perhaps to be preferred - in the words of Norman Tennent - is remaining single; but then, one senses from the consistency of the reports on this initiation, also a social failure. Fantasy may have played a part in the reporting of such climbing exploits, but there is little doubt of the authenticity of the St Kildans' climbing teamwork.

HIRTA

The largest of the group, St Kilda itself, or Hirta, measures three kilometres west to east and barely two kilometres north to south; yet it possesses three rocky and grassy summits of over 360m, as well as the highest cliff-face in the British Isles, the north-facing sea-cliffs of Conachair, (430m). The rock consists of granitic grano-phyre in the north-east, with gabbro in the south-west of the island; similar to the Red Cuillin and Black Cuillin of Skye, but with extraordinarily steep and exposed grassy gullies. A compass is unreliable on Hirta.

The Army conspicuously occupy the foreshore of Village Bay, manning an early-warning missile tracking station erected near an Ordnance Survey triangula-tion pillar on Conachair, to where there is now a road. Fortunately the summit of Conachair is at a higher triangulation pillar and the views from there down the sheer north cliffs to the sea and out to Boreray and its majestic 'sentries', Stac Lee and Stac an Armin, are unforgettable.

Although less continuously vertical than The Kame on Foula in Shetland, the Conachair cliffs are higher and made even more awesome by several sections of huge overhang. These northern sea-cliffs of Hirta have only recently (in 1987) been climbed from their base, though the St Kildan fowlers extensively harvested there from top-ropes. As well as seabirds, which nest everywhere on the cliff-faces, the Soay sheep that inhabit the island can be found feeding in the impossibly steep grass gullies.

In the west of the island is the second highest summit, Mullach Bi (360m), with a complex grassy and rocky ridge running from north to south and dropping precipitously to the sea. It overlooks The Cambir, whose name defies origin, at the north-western extremity of Hirta, as well as the dramatic island of Soay and its attendant stacks, Soay Stac and Stac Biorach. Mullach Bi also looks down on the remains of the earlier northern settlement, which lies in Gleann Mor above Glen Bay (or Loch a'Ghlinne).

An amphitheatre of hills around Village Bay is formed by Oiseval, Conachair, Mullach Mor, Mullach Sgar and Ruaival. To walk these tops is a memorable experience, with the persistent atmosphere of a visit to a past age. The views down to the neat row of cottages that once formed the village Main Street, and to the deep blue water of the bay itself in fine weather, has a picturesque quality belying the ruggedness of the terrain. The lower slopes are littered with well-constructed beehive shaped stone cleits, used by the St Kildan community for drying its crops of rye grass and barley which had to be cut green. They were used also to store fulmars' eggs and feathers, as well as those of gannets after the annual harvest of these birds from Stac an Armin and Stac Lee.

The horseshoe around Village Bay, from Oiseval to Ruaival, is completed almost without perceptible break by A'Bhi and Bioda Mor, on Dun; the island of Dun being separated from the south-east tip of Hirta by only a few metres of sea at low water. An attempt to complete the horseshoe gives a sharp reminder of the terrain. Dun, so close, is inaccessible without boat or a resort to swimming and a landing from either is a matter for contemplation if not - in practice - of considerable risk. In calm weather a landing by boat can be achieved on a steeply sloping granite shelf close to a cave at the north-western end of the island.

DUN

The island of Dun - which averages only 200 metres in width - is deceptively long; with a narrow rocky crest running south-eastwards for a kilometre and a half to the small promontory of Gob an Duin, which terminates in a final rock arch named Gob na Muce. The crest of the island is pinnacled, giving it the appearance of a miniature Cuillin ridge. The Admiralty Pilot states that the crumbling and inconspicuous ruins of a castle exist on Gob an Duin, but the absence of any sign of these ruins suggests that the report derives from the shape of the ridge.

SOAY

The island of Soay is formed by a single mountain rising precipitously from the sea-bed, producing towering sea-cliffs with a flattish inclined grassy summit. The land area is one square kilometre. Like Hirta, its north-facing cliffs are spectacular, with overhangs in the north-east at Geo Ruadh. The sound between Soay and Hirta, some 400 metres wide, is navigable with care; it contains three impressive stacks, Soay Stac, Stac Biorach and Stac Dona.

The first recorded climb of Stac Biorach, apart from those by the native St Kildans, was by C Barrington in 1883 (Alpine Jnl. Vol. 27, p195; see also Heathcote's *St Kilda*). However R Moray's account of St Kildan climbing there in 1698 is surely the first description of rock climbing in Scotland: ".... after they landed, a man having room for but one of his feet, he must climb up 12 or 16 fathoms high. Then he comes to a place where having but room for his left foot and left hand, he must leap from thence to another place before him, which if he hit right the rest of the ascent is easy, and with a small cord which he carries with him he hales up a rope whereby all the rest come up. But if he misseth that footstep (as often times they do) he falls into the sea and the [boat's] company takes him in and he sits still until he is a little refreshed and then he tries it again, for everyone there is not able for that sport".

BORERAY

Boreray and its close neighbours, Stac Lee and Stac an Armin, are separated by some seven to eight kilometres of sea from Hirta. Viewed close-hand, from a boat encircling the group, the ever changing juxtaposition of the three islands can only be described as staggering. Boreray itself is spectacular, a mountain of rock and scree rising precipitously from the sea with one main summit, Mullach an Eilein (384m), in its north to south length of one and a half kilometres. The summit has a fine south-east ridge as well as two steeper ones running south-westwards and northwards to the sea. Even in calm weather the sea surges around the base of the cliffs, which extend virtually all round the island, although steep screes run to the summit in places as H Balharry and M Boyd recorded in 1969.

Traces of lazybeds near the summit ridge indicate a bygone settlement of

Boreray, but by the 1890's the St Kildans were visiting the group only three or four times a year to harvest the seafowl. The weather and seas there can change with dramatic suddenness; Heathcote, when he visited Boreray, reports his party having to shelter its boat in a cave all night.

Stac an Armin (196m)
Stac an Arm in is the highest sea-stack in the British Isles. It lies 300m from the north-west point of Boreray. Landing is difficult, but its ascent is reportedly easy. R Balharry and party climbed it in 1969.

Stac Lee (172m)
Stac Lee is the most impressive of all the stacks. It towers from the sea with vertical cliffs all round, except for its slightly more gently angled south-east corner, usually seen only from the southern tip of Boreray. Its massive crown of guano, brilliant white in the summer sun, set in a deep blue sea, gives it the appearance of a massive iceberg about to topple.

      R Balharry and M Boyd climbed Stac Lee in 1969 and reported afterwards: "According to the books, the St Kildans lassoed an iron peg, then a man was hauled up from the boat. The tradition is of a difficult landing, and we had on our life-jackets. When the moment came that the boat was on the highest swell we stepped out, found slippery hand and footholds and began climbing. We didn't waste time. It was near vertical, but there were plenty of holds, and in twenty feet we were on a ledge".

      "The first hundred feet was easy enough, but the bit beyond was a different story. You looked straight down to the sea, and the only way above was up a blank wall".......... "The birds were screaming like an excited crowd at a football match. Straight below was the sea, the orange life-jackets, and the boats like tiny slugs. The next bit was actually overhanging, then in another twenty feet a ledge with a good belay"........ "'There was a small bothy on top, beautifully dry inside, and capable of holding two men, but two fulmars had taken over."

ROCK CLIMBING
To reach almost any rock climb on St Kilda requires either a boat or a traverse of short-cropped grass at a daunting angle. Seabirds in their thousands provide the rock routes with further protection. During the nesting months the cliffs and stacks can become ankle-deep in excrement; while in winter, when the rock is washed clean by Atlantic storms, the seas are almost invariably too rough to permit a landing at any cliff-base. This protection by a combination of bird and sea does not end there: thick sea mists are frequent and can be a menace to navigation as well as to route-finding, while even when conditions are at their best the rock ledges are defended by densely packed and fiercely screaming birds. The skuas, in particular, have an unnerving practice of dive-bombing the intruder.

      In September 1987 the National Trust for Scotland permitted an experimental visit by climbers to St Kilda, to assess their impact on this closely guarded Nature Reserve. A party of ten, led by Chris Bonington and sponsored by Independent Television News, successfully explored the northern cliffs of Hirta and pioneered

Boreray seen from Hirta at sunrise

routes on the Conachair cliff-face. They made first ascents of this impressive face reaching the foot of the cliffs in inflatable dinghies from Village Bay. The first moves, from bobbing inflatable to rock-face, were frequently the least predictable. First ascents of nineteen routes were made in all, on firm granite, varying from E5 (*Edge of The World*) to E6b.

POSTSCRIPT

The St Kilda group holds a fascination for both climber and mariner. In any description of the Scottish islands it is difficult to separate the mountain and marine aspects in their appreciation and adventure. Indeed with more and more climbers claiming also to be sailors, or yachtsmen, the combination of mountain and sea has increasing appeal.

This author and the previous author of the Islands Guide (Norman Tennent), had the good fortune in 1982 to visit St Kilda together under sail. A few extracts from the log-book on that occasion illustrate the appeal well. "Tues. 4 July 03.30h: Struggled awake to Norman's call from the helm, matter-of-factly but with thinly veiled excitement, 'Land on the starboard bow, Skipper'. I could hear the seas from my bunk as they roared along the eight-metre length of the wooden hull. *Malin* had been cruising throughout the night at five to six knots. Norman had taken over the watch at 02.00h, and now *Malin* too was dancing to the rhythm of the large waves, enjoying her triumph".

"Visibility was poor. Hirta, as we assumed this land to be, was only three cables [50 metres] off. We had half circumnavigated the island before we were convinced this was Boreray. Then it was necessary to allow our landfall to disappear into thick fog as we headed by compass once more, on a bearing for Hirta. How easily it would have been to sail right through the St Kilda group without sighting any of the islands. Only from our log-reading could we gauge that we were close".

"Excitement rose again, as we sighted Hirta and finally, in thick mist, the distinctive island of Dun at the south-east extremity of Village Bay. With the dawn light rapidly sweeping the stacks and hillsides, the grey ocean became a silvery green; the mist was lifting from summits in a glorious show of technicolour. We sailed into Village Bay and, sheltered now from the constant north-easterly, dropped anchor alongside a solitary fishing boat. It was 05.00h. We lay peacefully at anchor as the day came to life. Birds in unimaginable numbers and varieties were circling the stacks and peaks, whose summits remained hidden in majestic layer of mist, ..."

And two days later - "Thur. 15 July 1500h: .... reluctantly, with a feeling that one day we must return, we streamed the log and headed *Malin* eastwards. The sun was now burning the mist from the peaks and the views of Boreray and her neighbouring stacks were framed in deep blue sky and sea; the massive Stac Lee especially fine at close hand, with its brilliantly white (guano) crown. We watched for a long while as the now familiar skyline of towering pillars sank slowly below the horizon. Late evening found us seeking out the poorly charted south harbour of the Monach Isles whose flat sea-washed sandy marsh-land character contrasted strangely with the spectacle of St Kilda......"

SELECTED BIBLIOGRAPHY

Climbing

Skye: Walking, Scrambling and Exploring, Ralph Storer, David & Charles, London, (1989)

Rock and Ice Climbs in Skye, James R Mackenzie, Scottish Mountaineering Trust, Edinburgh, (1989)

The Cuillin of Skye, B H Humble, The Ernest Press, Facsimile edn (1986)

Black Cuillin Ridge Scrambler's Guide, S P Bull, Scottish Mountaineering Trust, Edinburgh, (1986)

Scrambles in Skye, J Wilson Parker, Cicerone Press (1983)

Climbers Guide to Arran, W M M Wallace, Scottish Mountaineering Trust, Revised edn (1979)

Arran This Summer (SMC Journal), W Skidmore, Scottish Mountaineering Club, Volume XXX1, (1978)

The Islands of Scotland, Norman Tennent, Scottish Mountaineering Trust, Edinburgh, (1971)

Mountaineering in Scotland, and Undiscovered Scotland, W H Murray, Diadem Books, (1951)

The Islands of Scotland (Excluding Skye), W W Naismith, Scottish Mountaineering Club, Edinburgh, (1934)

Rock Climbing in Skye, Ashley P Abraham, (1908)

General, Natural and Social History

Skye, The Island, James Hunter and Cailean MacLean, Mainstream Publishing Co, Edinburgh, (1986)

St Kilda and Other Hebridean Outliers, Francis Thompson, David & Charles, London, 2nd edn (1988)

The Shetland Story, Liv Kjorsvik Schei and Gunnie Moberg, BT Batsford, London, (1988)

The Western Isles, Francis Thompson, B T Batsford, London, (1988)

Islay, Norman S Newton, David & Charles, London, (1988)

Scotland Underground (limestone caves of Skye), Alan L Jeffreys Anne Oldham, Rhychydwr, Crymych, Dyfed (1984)

Iona, John L Paterson, John Murray Ltd, London, (1987)

Mull and Iona, Peter H Macnab, David & Charles, London, revised edn (1987)

Harris and Lewis, Francis Thompson, David & Charles, London, 3rd edn (1987)

The Discovery of the Hebrides, Elizabeth Bray, Collins, London and Glasgow (1986)

Birds in Scotland, Valerie M Thom, T & A D Poyser Ltd, (Stafford), (for Scottish Ornothologist Club), (1986)

Orkney, Patrick Bailey, David & Charles, London, 2nd edn (1985)

Canna, J L Campbell, Oxford University Press, for National Trust for Scotland (1984)

Shetland, James R Nicolson, David & Charles, London, 4th edn (1984)

Birds of the Outer Hebrides, Peter Cunningham, Melven Press, Perth, (1983)

Island on the Edge of the World, Charles MacLean, Cannongate Publishing, Edinburgh, revised edn (1983)

Shell Book of The Islands of Britain, David Booth and David Perrott, Guideway Windward (1981).

Highland Man (Highland Life Series), Ian Grimble, Highlands and Islands

Development Board, Inverness, (1980)

Highland Flora (Highland Life Series), Derek Ratcliffe, Highland and Islands Development Board, Inverness, (1978)

Highland Birds (Highland Life Series), Desmond Nethersole-Thomson, Highlands and Islands Development Board, Inverness, (1978)

Birds of the Coast (Books 1 & 2), Reg Jones, Jarrod Colour Publications (1977)

Six Inner Hebrides (Eigg, Rhum, Canna, Muck, Coll and Tiree), Noel Banks, David & Charles, London, (1977)

Highland Landforms (Highland Life Series), Robert J Price, Highland and Islands Development Board, Inverness (1976)

The Island of Skye, Malcolm Slesser, Scottish Mountaineering Trust, Edinburgh, (1975)

Staffa, Donald B MacCulloch, David & Charles, London, (1975)

Highland Animals (Highland Life Series), David Stephen, Highlands and Islands Development Board, Inverness (1974)

Uists and Barra, Francis Thompson, David & Charles, London, (1974)

Hebridean Islands: Colonsay, Gigha and Jura, John Mercer, Blackie, Glasgow and London, (1974)

The Islands of Western Scotland, W H Murray, Eyre Methuen (1973)

Skye, F C Sillar and Ruth Meyler, David & Charles, London, (1973)

The Isle of Arran, Robert McLellan, David & Charles, London, 3rd edn (1970)

The Highlands and Islands (New Naturalist Series), F F Darling and J M Boyd, Collins (1969)

The Hebrides, W H Murray, Heinemann, London, (1966)

The Highlands and Islands, F Fraser Darling and J Morton Boyd, Collins (Fontana), London and Glasgow, 3rd impression (1964)

The Magic of Skye, W A Poucher, Chapman and Hall, London, (1949)

All About Arran, R Angus Downie, Blackie, Glasgow and London, (1933)

The Book of Arran, Volume I - Edited by J A Balfour, Volume II - Edited by W M Mackenzie, The Arran Society of Glasgow (1914)

Geology

British Regional Geology, The Tertiary Volcanic Districts of Scotland, J E Richey (Revised A G MacGregor and F W Anderson), H M Stationery Office, London, (1987)

An Excursion Guide to the Geology of Skye, B R Bell and J W Harris, The Geological Society of Glasgow (1986)

Geology of Scotland, Edited by G Y Craig, Scottish Academic Press (1983)

Geology and Scenery in Scotland, J B Whittow, Penguin Books (1977)

Travel

As an Fhearann (From the Land), Ed Malcolm MacLean and Christopher Carrell Mainstream Publishing, An Lanntair, Edinburgh, (1986)

Exploring Scotland's Heritage - Argyll and the Western Isles, Graham Ritchie and Mary Harman, H M Stationery Office, London, (1985)

Skye, Derek Cooper, Routledge & Kegan Paul, London, Paperback edn (1983)

Scottish Island Hopping, Jemima Tindall, Sphere, London, (1981)

The Misty Isle of Skye, J A MacCulloch, Eneas Mackay (first published 1905)

Journey to the Western Islands of Scotland, Samuel Johnson, Oxford University Press (first published 1775)

GLOSSARY OF SOME GAELIC AND NORDIC WORDS

GAELIC	ENGLISH
abhainn	river
acarseid	anchorage
achadh	field, meadow
ailean, aline	green field
a(i)rd	high promontory
aiseag	ferry
aisir	path
ault	steeply cut stream
aoine	steep rocky brae
aonach	plain by the shore
aros	house
ath	ford
bac	bank
bad	group, clump
b(h)aigh	bay
b(h)aile	town
b(h)an	white, fair
barr	top, summit
b(h)e(a)g	little
bealach	pass, col
bearn	gap
beinne	ben, hill
beithe	birch
b(h)reac	speckled
b(h)uidhe	yellow
binnean	small hill
bo, ba	cow
bo, bogha	sunken rock
bodach	old man
bradan	salmon
breac	trout
bruach, bru	steep hillside, bank
bun	foot of hill/stream
buachaille	shepherd
cailleach	old woman
caileag	girl
caladh	harbour
caisteal	castle
caora	sheep
camas, camus	channel, creek
carraig	rock
caol, caolas	kyle, firth

clach	stone
ceann, c(h)inn	head, point
cladagh	shore, beach
clachan	village
cnap, knap	knobby (hills)
cleit	reef
coig	five
cnok, knock	small hillock
coire	corry, cauldron
coille	wood, forest
corran	tapering point
coll	hazel
creag	crag, cliff
craobh	tree
crois	cross
da	two
cruach	heap stack
darroch	oa
dail	plain, dale
deas	south
dearg	red
diorlinn	isthmus
dobhran	otter
domhain	deep
donn	brown
drochaid	bridge
druim	back
dubh	black, dark
dun	mound, fort
each, eich	horse
ear	east
eas	waterfall
eilach	watercourse
eilean	island
fada	long
fadhail	tidal current
faich	meadow
fank	sheep-pen
fasgadh	shelter
fearn	alder-tree
feith	bot
fiacal	tooth
fireach	moor
fir, fear	man

fliuch	wet	port	port
fraoch	heather	rath	fortress
fuar	cold	rathad	road
fuaran	well	righ	king
		rinn	promontory
garbh	rough, harsh	ron	seal
geal	bright, white	ruadh	red, reddish
geodga, geo	narrow cove	rubha, rudha, rhu	long headland
gil	narrow glen		
glas	grey green	sal	salt water
gleann	glen, valley	sean	old, ancient
gobhar	goat	sga(i)t	skate
goirid	short	sgarbh	cormorant
gorm	blue	sgeir	rock, skerry
gualainn	shoulder of hill	sgurr	rock peak
		sron	high promontory
iar	west	sruth	tidal current
iasgair	fisherman	stac	stack, conical hill
inbhir (inver)	rivermouth bay	strath	river valley
innis	island		
iolaire	eagle	tarbh	bull
		tigh	house
lag, lagan	hollow in the land	tioram	dry island
leac	flat stone, slab	tob	bay
learg	hillside	tobar	well
leathen	broad	torr	heap, mound
leth	half, next to	traigh	beach, sand
liath	grey	tri	three
linne	sound, channel	tuath	north
lo(i)n	marshy pond or stream	tulach	hillock
long, luinge	large ship	uaine	green, wan
		uaimh	cave
machair	low grassy land	uig	bay
maol (mull)	high headland		
mointeach	moorland	**NORSE**	**ENGLISH**
mol, mal	shingly beach	brough	cliff peninsula
m(h)or	large, tall, great	castle	isolated stack
muir, mara (pl)	sea, loch	hope, wick, voe	sea inlet
mullach	summit	geos	breaks in coast (eroded by sea)
ob	haven	gloup	sea-tunnel (termin-
odhar	dun coloured		ating in air or
oitir	sand-bar, shoal		water hole)
or, oir	boundary, gold	hamar	rocky terrace (in a
ord, uird	round		a grassy hill)
os	rivermouth	loch	inland water
		ward hill	watch hill (with
plod	pool of water		fire beacon)
poll, puill	pond		

INDEX OF PLACE NAMES